THE LETTERS OF
Richard Brinsley Sheridan

RICHARD BRINSLEY SHERIDAN
by George Romney
Property of the Sir James Dunn Foundation, Beaverbrook Art Gallery, Fredericton, N.B.

THE LETTERS OF
Richard Brinsley Sheridan

EDITED BY

CECIL PRICE

VOLUME III

OXFORD
AT THE CLARENDON PRESS
1966

Oxford University Press, Ely House, London W. 1

GLASGOW NEW YORK TORONTO MELBOURNE WELLINGTON
CAPE TOWN SALISBURY IBADAN NAIROBI LUSAKA ADDIS ABABA
BOMBAY CALCUTTA MADRAS KARACHI LAHORE DACCA
KUALA LUMPUF HONG KONG

PRINTED IN GREAT BRITAIN

CONTENTS

VOLUME III

632. To George Lamb

Osborn MS. *Address*: Honble. | George Lamb. *Fr.*: R B Sheridan

[*6 Jan. 1807*]
Somerset Place
Tuesday Evening

O ye of little Faith—!
I send you the Correspondence[1] but remember you are
to return it to me—Honor bright. You will not understand
my scratches but were I to run over the Papers with you
your entire conviction would go with me (and of course
Lady Melbourne's) without our at all coming to Whitbreads conclusion or adopting the Propriety of his motion.[2]
There are some pencil marks and doublings down made
in my chaise of course even more unintelligible than the
rest— | yours truly | R B Sheridan

633. To Earl Spencer[3]

Earl Spencer MS. Copy.[3] Text from Lord Spencer's transcription.

Somerset Place
Jany. 13 1807

My Lord
In addition to the evidence of the Lord Lieutenants disposition in favour of Major Plunkett[4] contained in the
accompanying Letter, I beg leave to add that his case has
been so strongly recommended to me and from such
authority as I can entirely rely on that I do not hesitate to

---

[1] Probably 'Papers relative to the
Negociation with France, Presented . . .
to both Houses of Parliament, 22 Dec.
1806' (Hansard, 1st Ser., viii. 92–213).

[2] French ambitions were not solely
to blame for the failure of negotiations.
Whitbread's amendment on 5 Jan. wel-
comed 'any just arrangement by which
the blessings of peace may be restored
to his loyal subjects' (Hansard, 1st Ser.,

viii. 373).

[3] In a secretary's hand. It was sent
on 21 Jan. by Earl Spencer, as Home
Secretary, to the Lord-Lieutenant of
Ireland, the Duke of Bedford.

[4] Possibly Edward Plunkett, later 14th
Lord Dunsany (1773–1848), or a Major
J. Plunkett, who is noted in *Boyle's Court
and Country Guide* (Jan. 1807), p. 344,
as living at 9 Little Madox Street.

state how warmly I am interested in his behalf, as well as my conviction that your Lordship will never have reason to regret any protection which you may be pleased to afford him. | I have the honor to be | etc. | R B Sheridan[1]

Earl Spencer

634. To Richard Peake

Add. MS. 35118, ff. 101–3. *Address*: Mr. Peake

Somerset Place
Jany. 22 1807

Sir
  Of course you will not alter the Pay-List as sign'd by me in the pursuance of the Lord Chancellors order[2] at the irregular instigation of any Person whatever. I have heard of such an attempt having been made and even to set aside the written engagements of the Proprietors as in the case of Mr. Burgess with the utmost astonishment. I shall be returned to Town on monday when I will endeavour to understand this strange Proceeding | yrs | R B Sheridan

635. To G. Eves[3]

Harvard MS. *Address*: G. Eves Esq. *Dock*.: 24 Mar. 1807 | Mr. Sheridan | Gowing

24 Mar. 1807

Dear Sir,
  I shall be much obliged if you will meet me at the House of Commons at ½ past 4. I must rely on your not permitting so unnecessary an insult to be offer'd to me till I have had the Pleasure to see you. Should it not be inconvenient to you to come to Westminster I will see you punctually at eleven tomorrow | Yours | R B S.

[1] S.'s signature.
[2] Of 7 Sept. 1802. See Add. MS. 42720, ff. 1–34.
[3] As far back as 28 June 1798, William Laver, the Sheriffs' bailiff, had been ordered to distrain goods of S. to

value of £39. 7s. od., awarded to George Gowing. In the same period (May 1797 to Apr. 1798) Eves had collected £1,046. 2s. 11d. from D.L.Th. 'for Ladler on Evan's Bills': see D.L.Th. Ledger, 1795 to 1799 (Folger MS.).

636. To Thomas Creevey

J. R. Blackett-Ord MS. *Pub.*: *Creevey Papers*, i. 38.

[*1807?*]
Richmond-Hill
Monday in the
third day of Peace
and Tranquillity.

My Dear Creevey
You must make my excuse to the Lord Mayor. Pray vouch that you were to have brought me but my cold is really so bad that I should infallibly lay myself up if I attempted to go.

Here are pure air quiet and innocence and everything that suits me.

Pray let me caution you not to expose yourself to the *air* after Dinner—as I find malicious People disposed to attribute to wine what was clearly the mere effect of the atmosphere. My last hour to your Ladies as I am certainly going to die. 'Till when, however, | Yours truly | R B S.

637. To Eleanor Creevey

J. R. Blackett-Ord MS. *Address*: Mrs. Creevey | Park-Place | St. James's *Fr.*: R B Sheridan

[*9 Apr. 1807?*]
House of
Commons
near 7

I can't resist the Pleasure I have in telling you that William[1] has just sat down after making[?] as neat and as

---

[1] William Ord (1781–1855) was M.P. for Morpeth, 1802–32 (Judd). Ord spoke on 9 Apr. 1807, praising the late ministry for refusing to give the King a pledge that they would not advise him on the Catholic question. 'Such a pledge would have made the King absolute, and removed the responsibility of his ministers' (Hansard, 1st Ser., ix. 300). Ord spoke on 21 Mar. 1808 and 17 Feb. 1812.

spirited a short speech as ever I heard—and with very great effect and general applause | Yours ever | R B S.

tell my nieces all

638. To Viscount Howick

Grey MS. *Dock.*: Mr. Sheridan | May ye 1s[t]. 1807 | and my answer

1 May 1807
Friday

Dear Grey
    You have completely driven Tom out of Stafford,[1] which if you had seen his Letter to me to day after the Loss of his Place you would not think a light thing—I protest to God I would not have acted so towards the greatest stranger in the world or even towards a Political Enemy. Stafford has long by agreement been one and one. Monckton secured Pitts neutrality in my favor and has always acted quite fairly. As for *procuring me* Sir W Jerningham's[2] interest I never but had it most warmly in my favour and on my first application his steward was order'd now down . . . [?][3] by his Brother[4] and he proposed that young Jerningham Sir W's Son should go with me for which purpose I wrote to him yesterday.[5] Mon[c]kton has also had Sir W interest. Nor can I conceive He will withdraw it from him. This was the same to Tom as if He had it *singly* for Monckton is absolutely sure. Three new comers[6] have broke into the Borough all equally opposers of Tom and any of them getting Jerning-

[1] By supporting Sir Oswald Mosley as a candidate. See p. 5, n. 3.
    [2] Sir William Jerningham, 6th baronet (1736–1809). A great landlord in Staffordshire and Shropshire, he was a Roman Catholic and had been a friend of Richard Tickell's. See the *Annual Register . . . 1809*, p. 694.
    [3] Possibly 'none down' or, less likely, 'nunc demum'. Both words are difficult to read. The three dots appear in the original.
    [4] Edward Jerningham (1727–1812), poet and dramatist.
    [5] See p. 135. This suggests that the

son was not the eldest (George William) who succeeded his father in 1809, but either the second (William Charles Jerningham, 1772–1820) or, more probably, the third (Edward Jerningham, 1774–1822).
    [6] Sir Oswald Mosley, 2nd baronet (1785–1871), was bottom of the Stafford poll, but became M.P. for Winchelsea. Ralph Benson (1773–1845) retired before the poll because of a ruptured blood-vessel. Joseph Hanson, who had intended to stand, withdrew early in favour of Benson and Tom S. See the *Staff. Adv.*, 2 May 1807.

ham's interest must beat him—for Phillips is out of the question[1] yet without condescending to ask me a single question, and contrary I believe to the decorum usually observed both by ministers and heads of opposition where an understanding prevails in a Borough the arrangement is broken thro' and an intruder in a Place I might call mine for six and twenty years is arm'd by *you* with Power to throw out *my Son*.[2]

could I have been capable of acting so towards you judge how you would have felt and express'd yourself.

I was setting off to assist him tomorrow but now I see no use in it | Yours | R B S.

639. To Viscount Howick

Grey MS. *Dock.*: Mr. Sheridan | 2d. May 1807.

2 May 1807
Carlton-House
Saturday morning

Dear Grey

If I wrote warmly last night I hope you will not think it proceeded from any doubt of your good will or desire to serve Tom, but I was excessively vex'd at the mortification and defeat He was likely to experience from what I cannot think was any Fault of mine. You complain of want of communication on my Part.[3] I never knew with whom I could be call'd on to communicate on the subject of Stafford, I had heard that Freemantle Tierney[4] and Calcraft (who had

---

[1] He was elected now. At the Surrey Quarter Sessions of 1809 he was found guilty of obtaining money by false pretences. See Hansard, 1st Ser., xxiii. 327–8.

[2] *The Times*, 29 Apr. 1807, announced that Tom S. 'stands for Stafford, with every probability of success'. Its issue of 6 May noted that he had abandoned his canvass there.

[3] Grey had replied on 'Friday Night': '. . . You never communicated to us your intention of putting up Tom for Stafford. In this ignorance of your intention Sir O. Moseley was

encouraged by Freemantle to go down, and had actually set out a day or two before Tom left London. . . . This morning Mr. Jerningham, Sir William's Son, came to me to say that he was commissioned by his Father to offer me his support for any Candidates whom I would recommend. My answer was that Mr. Sheridan was my first object, and Sir Oswald Moseley the second; and that I would thank him to manage his interest accordingly. . . .' (Grey MS.)

[4] Tierney was in charge of seat distribution and found himself in some difficulty for 'the new Ministers have

exactly lost me Stafford before by allowing Sir C. Hawkins to evade his engagement with the Prince) were occupied in the distribution of Boroughs, but I could have no conception that when they came to Stafford Mr. Freemantle could have decided to send a Person there without saying one word to me. Freemantle must have known how perfectly safe Monkton was, and therefore it was really providing a direct opposition against me in case I follow'd the advice to decline standing for Westminster.—

However fortunately it is not too late in my humble opinion to set it all right, and in that case Mr. Jerningham is willing to set out with me directly and the Election will be safe. He will tell you that Sir O. M. is directly opposed to Tom—that Monkton is perfectly safe and that Nothing will go so much against the Grain with Sir W's Interest as the withdrawing it from him, who has had it these seven and twenty years—and indeed in that case so unpleasant is it to Mr. Jerningham himself that he will not go to Stafford at at all. Sir O.M. has *never made application to Sir W.* nor has he at this moment an idea that his interest has been ask'd in his favour. He might be frankly told your intention in his behalf, and if I find he has a better chance than Tom I will give up every interest to him—but surely He ought not to turn out Tom. The Prince is very desirous we should meet with Mr. J. for five minutes.—While you are reading this Mr. Jerningham will by his desire be here with me. The unsavage thing will be for you to walk down here for five minutes or shall we come to you at nine—? | yours truly | R B S

Burgess will give a Reason.

640. To His Son Tom

Osborn MS.

[*2 May 1807*]
Saturday

My Dear Tom
    It is very idle of you to miss a Days writing—and leaves

bought up all the seats that were to be disposed of, and at any prices' (S.   Romilly, *Memoirs* (2nd ed., 1840), ii. 206–7).

me in the Dark. I have had a violent altercation with Grey and Freemantle it—now comes out that Sir O. M. was recommended to go to Stafford by Freemantle and be d——d to him without saying one word to me and Grey yesterday told young Jerningham that after you He wish'd Sir O. M. to have Sir Williams second votes. I have however set all this right—and they will be disposed of entirely to your advantage—an excuse has been sent to Monckton for their being withdrawn from him but that remains to be considered. I am entirely for your arranging with Monckton. I set out tomorrow evening and Jerningham with me if you find my standing better[1] I have settled Ilchester[2] for you—for which I shall be return'd on tuesday—J Villiers[3] has written to Hester to say the King says you are not to be turn'd out[4]—but of this hereafter. Mind Sir O. M. has never applied to Sir W. J. nor has he the least idea that anyone has for him—so mum.

Mr. Jerningham puts his numbers at 60—with the peremptory exertion which now for the first time will be made—

an odd bit of news for you. Burdett and Paul have been fighting[5]—both wounded—Paul in the Leg—and Burdett thro' the thigh—both out of Danger—how I could have walk'd over the course | Yours ever | R B S.

If B. stands most of my Troups will support him. And with

[1] *The Times*, 29 Apr. 1807, reported that S. declined standing for Westminster, but an advertisement in its columns of 6 May requested his friends 'not to pledge themselves to any other Candidate, as a Deputation will this day see Mr. Sheridan with the most perfect confidence that he will withdraw his declaration of resigning'. His acceptance was advertised next day. Clearly, once Tom S. had abandoned the canvass at Stafford, S. stood for Westminster so that, if he were returned, he would vacate Ilchester in his son's favour.

[2] This seat had been purchased by Sir William Manners (*c.* 1766–1833) in 1802; and was now made over to the Prince's nominee in return for money and perhaps certain promises. See p. 230.

[3] John Charles Villiers (1757–1838), who was Comptroller of the Household 1789–90, and later 3rd Earl of Clarendon.

[4] S. claimed that if he (S.) 'would have consented to a little forbearance towards the present ministry', Tom S. could have retained his situation, but S. spurned the idea. See the *Europ. Mag.* li (1807), 403.

[5] The duel was fought at Coome Wood at 10.20 on 2 May. For its causes and course, see M. W. Patterson, *Sir F. Burdett and his Times, 1770–1844* (1930), i. 195–202.

all my heart for I will have nothing to do with the Popery Lord[1] nor the ministerial Brewer[2]

641. 'To the Worthy and Independent Electors of Westminster'

Pub.: *The Times*, 9 May 1807.

Hudson's Hotel, Friday evening, May 8, 1807.

Gentlemen,
Under the pressure of a Canvass so long delayed, it is not in my power at the moment to command the time necessary to explain to you the causes of that delay—that explanation you are entitled to, and you shall receive it from me on Monday next. In the interval, I request the favour of your Votes and support; and I feel it no presumption to rest my title to make that claim, on a reference to the whole of my public life and political conduct. I have the honour to be | With every sentiment of gratitude and respect. | Your obliged and devoted servant | Richard Brinsley Sheridan.

642. To W. A. Downs

Pub.: *Morrison Cat.* vi. 127.[3] *Address*: Major Downs.

[*17 May 1807*]
Sunday

Most recreant Major,
To quit the Field of Battle and fly to Cattamaran Wales[4] Tower at such a moment is a proceeding as unsoldierlike as unpatriotic. A court martial will be immediately held on your conduct, and I fear you will certainly be cashier'd if not

---

[1] Thomas Cochrane (1775–1860), afterwards 10th Earl of Dundonald. He was elected with Burdett as M.P. for Westminster.

[2] John Elliot.

[3] The manuscript is owned by Mr. Laurence Harvey, who has, unfortunately, mislaid it. Messrs. Maggs Bros.

printed a transcript of the first three paragraphs in their catalogue No. 819 (1953), item 993.

[4] *Ibid.*, 'Water'. If the following word was meant to be 'tour', the phrase would then mean 'to go for a river picnic'.

shot, for[1] carrying off the military chest[2] with you containing funds almost inexhaustible[3] of which Billy Brown has made oath is considered by the Pots,[4] Guy-Fox, and the Watermen as a great aggravation of your crime.

But most seriously there must be some fund either by your assisting us with the enclosed or by some other supply to be applied to-night or before nine to-morrow morning,[5] or we shall not one of us be allowed to show[6] our faces. I have seen all the leaders of our crew myself, and have satisfied them to wait till nine in the morning, when they will be content with a very little for the present, and then I have made an engagement for them all with Byng[7] for Brentford. This settled I do not fear having a very triumphant day tomorrow, altho' it should end in a final retreat.[8] We have order'd a dinner for a select party at the Albany, to which we shall proceed in a body from Hudson's.[9]

I need not urge to you how great this momentary emergency is.

Should General Ironmonger[10] be with you, beg him to send me another order for the car,[11] which when I call'd to-day at the Golden Cross the principal person told me

[1] Ibid., 'Your'.

[2] Downs was 'Receiver and Treasurer of the Subscription Fund for carrying on the Scrutiny' (*The Times*, 15 June 1807). It was revealed that in Nov. 1806, he had opened an account at the bankers, Hodsoll, Stirling & Co. 'Sums were advanced to his cheques, in order to defray part of the expences of the election. On stating for what purposes these sums were advanced, much laughter was excited. Guy Faux had been rewarded with £26; the Drury-lane Society, marrow-bones and cleavers, and a number of dumb performers, had also been paid liberally.' (*The Times*, 20 Apr. 1807.)

[3] Maggs's transcript, 'inexaustable'.

[4] Ibid., 'Poets'.

[5] Ibid. omits 'morning'.

[6] Ibid., 'shew'.

[7] George Byng (1764–1847), M.P. for Middlesex, 1790–1847 (Judd). The Middlesex election began at Brentford on 18 May.

[8] The state of the poll on 18 May was: Burdett, 2,728; Cochrane, 2,158; Elliot, 1,734; S., 630. Elliot, however, withdrew from the election next day.

[9] 'The Committee conducting Mr. *Sheridan's Election* will this day dine at the Albany Tavern, Piccadilly, to which they will proceed with Mr. Sheridan, from Hudson's Hotel, after the close of the poll. Tickets, 10s. 6d. each. . . .' (*The Times*, 18 May 1807.)

[10] Richard Ironmonger (*c.* 1772–1826). He was coachmaster at the Golden Cross, London; and later became a Brighton magistrate and M.P. for Stafford (1826).

[11] The Westminster election accounts for Nov. 1806 (in the archives of Westminster Public Libraries) contain a bill of expenses for 'attending canvassing with the Carr' for ten days. See also Rhodes, pp. 215–16.

had been countermanded. I have also sent an express to Barnet.

I send Richardson[1] with this, and was very near to coming to Staines myself. I am glad you have good weather for your party, to all of whom remember me.

643. To the Earl of Moira

Pub.: H.M.C., *MSS. of the late R. R. Hastings, Esq.* (1934), iii. 266.

[*19 May 1807?*]
Tuesday.

A thousand thanks for your attention in communicating the intelligence just received.—Elliot has done right, and I feel and know I have done right in maintaining the contest I have hitherto struggled with.[2] I have put down the cry of 'no Popery'—I have supported the honour of the last administration—I have opposed an attempt to create a mutiny in the Navy and I have vindicated the principles and memory of Fox. I am determined to go on, and if I am supported as I think I ought to be, I shall succeed.[3]

644. To Richard Taylor and Peter Adshead[4]

Pub.: The Times, 3 July 1807.

Richmond, June 20, 1807.

Gentlemen,
I request you will inform the respectable Body, whose

[1] A dresser at D.L.Th.
[2] The sequence of ideas here leads me to suppose that this was written on the day after Elliot withdrew from the Westminster election.
[3] He did not. The result was Burdett, 5,135; Cochrane, 3,708; S. 2,645.
[4] Agents for the journeymen calico printers of the counties of Lancaster, Derby, Chester, and Stafford; Lanark, Renfrew, Dumbarton, Stirling, and Perth. At their meeting at Manchester on 10 June, the printers had prepared

an address eulogizing S.'s 'high character' and adding, 'It must, Sir, afford you pleasure to hear, that you have been the great means of relieving several thousands of industrious men from that injustice and oppression which originally provoked our application to Parliament.' (*The Times*, 3 July 1807.) S. had helped them to prevent 'that extraordinary multiplication of apprentices which, before your interference, was so prevalent in our trade, you secured to us employment, and to our families bread'.

Agents you are that their approbations of my humble endeavours to serve them, though greatly overrated by their partial kindness, is as gratifying to my mind, as any thing the course of my parliamentary conduct can lead to.

An hasty prejudice on the subject of the grievance of which you principally complain, and a groundless apprehension that the relief you pray would interfere with the universal call that prevails for removing all restraints from matters of trade and manufacture, and which, though commendable as a general principle, it is the fashion of the time to push to a mischievous extreme, have, in my judgment, prevented Parliament from giving hitherto a dispassionate consideration to your case, notwithstanding the unanswerable report made in your favour by the Committee to whom your petitions were referred in the year 1806. I trust, however, that the liberality of your employers, and their regard to justice, as well as to their own ultimate interest, may render unnecessary, on your part, any farther application to the Legislature. Should, however, our reasonable expectations be disappointed, I have only to reassure you that when their claims are urged with temper and propriety, the weak will ever find in me an advocate against the powerful, and a firm opposer of the encroachments of avarice and oppression, however supported by wealth, or abetted by Parliamentary interest. | I have the honour to be, Gentlemen, with the sincerest good | wishes for your comfort and tranquillity, | R. B. Sheridan.

645. To Aaron Graham

Mentioned in Add. MS. 4270, f. 69.

[*24–25 June 1807*]

[Proposing meeting tomorrow and intimating that their—the Trustees'—letter of 23 June[1] is to him totally unintelligible.]

[1] The Trustees complained that they had written to Burgess on 19 Dec. 1806 about the fruit offices (i.e. concession for the sale of fruit at D.L.Th.) but had had no reply from S., and that they were going to call a meeting of the renters to discuss this. See Add. MS. 42720, f. 66.

646. To Viscount Howick

Grey MS. *Address*: Viscount Howick *Fr.*: R. B. Sheridan *Dock.*: Mr. Sheridan | June ye 26 1807

26 June 1807
Richmond
Friday morning

My dear Grey.
I am very unfortunate but thro the skill of my coachman I was jumbled under the wheel of my Barouche, which has gone over my knee[1]—and stir I cannot. I am most particularly mortified not to be in the house to Day but it is out of the Question. I shall be most anxious to hear of you.[2] | Yours ever | R B S.

647. To Aaron Graham

Add. MS. 42720, f. 71. Copy in Mrs. S.'s hand.

[27 June 1807]

My dear Sir,
I enclose a letter to the Trustees, of which I mean to send two more copies that each may have one. I wish to do justice to their good intentions,[3] but I mustn't be surprized at their attributing Burgess's negligence which you know how to account for and excuse, to me.—The threat of calling the

[1] A newspaper cutting of 29 June 1807 (Egerton MS. 1975, f. 163) reads: 'Mr. Sheridan . . . had nearly met with a serious accident on Thursday, by the overturning of his barouche; his leg became entangled between the spokes of the wheel which has confined him to a sofa ever since.'

[2] S.'s wife added a postscript: 'It is out of the question for S. to move from his Couch and he has had a great escape from both his legs being broken. He desires you will speak famously and so do I.'

[3] The Trustees had written to S. on 26 June to ask if he would put them

in possession of the fruit offices and of the rents of the houses owned by D.L.Th. On 18 July 1806 Burgess had written to Graham to say that he had authority from S. to pay them the rents, but that the fruit offices were so far pledged that it would take four years to get them free. The Trustees had interviewed Burgess on the subject in Dec. 1806, and on 18 Dec. Burgess had said that he would pay to Peake the money received from the rents and from the sale of refreshments, when the present charges were satisfied. See Add. MS. 42720, f. 68; and cf. f. 66.

Renters together while I have been giving up and doing every thing for them, and after such a Season in which I have had nothing to do, is indeed extraordinary! I shall address another letter to them and you tomorrow or next day. I am at last determin'd to look a little to myself—I am sure you will not misconstrue any thing I say in this or my other letter as applying unkindly to you—| Yrs ever | R B S

Richmond Hill
Monday

648. To Aaron Graham, John Hosier, and Randle Jackson

Harrow MS.: Rae, iv. 10. A copy ('To Trustees') is Add. MS. 42720, ff. 73–75. *Dock*.: 28 June 1807 | The Rt. Hon. R. B. Sheridan

Richmond
June 28th. 1807

Gentlemen

I am extremely sorry to perceive on the Part of the Trustees a continued disposition to avoid a clear manly and amicable communication on the subject of the Theatre altho' on my Part I have without reserve thrown every thing fairly open to them, without regarding in the least the limitation of their Powers and Duties, hoping to derive from their friendly Professions and exertions a degree of assistance and relief which I might be enabled to contrast with the enormous injuries done to me my Property and character by the misconduct of former Trustees acting under the alledged influence of legal advice—and I shall still be equally surprised and sorry to find myself disappointed in this expectation.

On the subject of the Rents and Fruit Offices which I now find to be the object of the Trustees application I can only say that I never 'till now knew that *the Trustees*[1] were not in the Receipt of them, I am confident that *I* have not been since I first proposed to make them over to them—and

---

[1] Add. MS. 42720, f. 72: '*they*'.

I am now ready to do it in any the most formal way for the benefit of the Trust which they can point out. As my object is to make every sacrifice for the Payment of the Renters I claim no merit in doing this—Only I must remind the Trustees that on a former occasion when a written agreement was enter'd into between me and the Trustees for this Purpose in the Life time of Mr. Hanson, the condition on the Part of the Trustees was immediately violated by a majority of them and the agreement of course cancell'd.[1]

It will I am sure afford you satisfaction to be informed that in the necessary intercourse which must subsist in the settlement of the affairs of the Theatre between the Proprietors and the Trustees my engagements or other avocations cannot in future be pretende[d] to occasion any irregularity, as I have made over the whole of my Property and interest not only in the Theatre but of every kind and description in Possession or reversion to three Trustees with the fullest Powers to act and conclude on my behalf in all matters and things wherein I am concerned until a final settlement of my affairs shall be accomplish'd, and every just claim upon me discharged. In them I place the most implicit confidence and I have no doubt but that their assiduous exertions in the task which however laborious and intricate they have undertaken with such friendly zeal will speedily put a stop to the many impositions which have oppress'd me and ultimately, after duly discharging all my just debts, rescue[2] for the benefit of my Family, a considerable Property from the confusion and Peril in which my inattention and imprudence may have placed it. The Gentlemen I refer to are Sir Robt. Barclay, Mr. Peter More and Mr. Thos. Bell—and from them I am confident you will experience the most cordial co-operation in your endeavours to retrieve the affairs of the Theatre, and that their first act will be to give you every assistance and satisfaction upon the subject of your present application to me—

I need not state the regret (I will not say dismay, for that the occasion does not call for) with which I learn that the

[1] Thomas Shaw (a hostile witness) declared in 1815 that he had heard the income of the fruit office was still S.'s personal property. (Harvard MS.) Cf. p. 128, n. 1.

[2] Add. MS. 42720, f. 73: 'reserve'.

total receipt of last year has fallen short more than eleven thousand Pounds of the receipt of the preceding season. I am naturally anxious to see an investigation of the causes of this, only observing without imputing the slightest blame to anyone, that to *me* it can in no respect be attributed as I never in the smallest degree interfered in the Theatre concerns or management in any one single instance whatever. But I cannot forbear to observe, that the experiment of such another season would wear a very serious aspect indeed!

I cannot conclude without requesting you to be assured that I am not insensible to nor unthankful for the Pains time and attention which you have gratuitously devoted, and I am confident with the best intentions, to the interests of the Property for which you are Trustees. At the same time I must repeat my conviction that a fair explicit and honourable co-operation between you as Trustees and the Proprietors of the Theatre or their representatives is absolutely indispensible to the common object which both Parties ought to have in view. I assert and can prove that all the embarrassments and difficulties that have oppress'd the Theatre and me from the first planning of the Building have been owing to former Trustees having pursued a different course. But they were instigated and deluded by the mercenary counsel of Those who had an interest and a Profit in promoting unceasing and wanton litigation; You cannot have review'd the *whole* of this subject without being convinced of the Truth of this, and I trust that in all your transactions with me or those who act for me you will pursue a very different line and adopt very different advice,[1] so that the Day may not be distant when I shall owe you gratitude for essential service render'd to myself as your constituents certainly will for the faithful discharge of your Duty towards them. | I have the honor to be, | Gentlemen, | with esteem and regard, | your obedient Servant | R B Sheridan

To Messrs Graham
  Hosier and Jackson.

[1] Tom S. wrote to the Lord Chamberlain on 30 May, asking him to grant few licences to other theatres; and on 22 June, inquiring if the theatre Greville intended to open would be licensed. See Salt MS. D. 1778/I.i |1705–6.

649. To Samuel Whitbread

Whitbread MS. 4125. *Wm.*: 1806

[1807?]
Tuesday two o'clock

My Dear Whitbread,

Something of the deepest importance has occurr'd to which £150 must absolutely be applied within two hours if I am to ensure my seat. The obstinate indiscretion and unauthorized Zeal of some friends is intolerable to think of. Observe I would not take the money as a Payment at present but as a Loan for a week and I must solemnly assure you that the enclosed Draft will punctually replace it on tuesday next, if after the Petition[1] is over any fund remains and the transaction is explain'd and consider'd as a fair election expence I may be reimbursed—I am very unwell or I would have sought you out myself— | yours ever | R B Sheridan

650. To Richard Peake

Add. MS. 35118, f. 143. *Wm.*: 1807.

[1807?]
D.L. Theatre
monday

My Dear P.

I have follow'd you to this Place and unfortunately you were gone just as I arrived. I have had a Letter from Baker apologizing for his not reserving the £20 for Parsons to Day but finding that Parsons *had* paid the rent and withdrawn himself and being dunn'd to Death by the small bills He thought it best that Parsons should wait a few days—the enclosed will explain. However I wish to keep my word with Parsons, and if you could send him a draft for his money at a week it will do. And by G—d in that interval, we will by hook

---

[1] 'May 23 1807, Westminster election finally terminated. . . . Mr. Sheridan expects to displace Lord Cochrane upon the Treating Act. . . .' (*Europ. Mag.*, 1807, li. 403.) S.'s petition came up for consideration in the Commons on 22 Mar. 1808, but since no counsel appeared to support it, the petition was discharged. See Hansard, 1st Ser., x. 1243.

or by crook cash James's bill on which you will then have advanced £72 including the Lottery Ticket[1] which I trust is gone. | Yours ever | R B S.

651. To William Huskisson[2]

Osborn MS. *Pub.*: Maggs Catalogue 306 (1913), item 1399.

July 25th. 1807

My Dear Sir

The Bearer is Mr. Wm: Henry Cole The Person whom I take the Liberty of recommending to your Protection. I beg leave to thank you for the kind manner in which you entertain'd my request as I have it very much at heart to remedy this poor man's disappointment, and allow me to assure you that if ever the time should come (at present we should agree I believe at a comfortable distance) when I might have it in my Power to be of service to any one recommended by you I should be most happy to shew my recollection of your kindness on the present occasion. | I have the Honor to be | with sincere esteem— | yours truly | R B Sheridan.

Right Honorable
G Huskisson.

652. To Michael Kelly[3]

Pub.: Moore, ii. 354–5.

August 30. 1807

... a plan by which the property may be leased to those

[1] See the draft (Salt MS.) in S.'s hand and reading:

Sir

Mr. Sheridan having but this Day apprized me of your applications to him for an account respecting the Lottery-Tickets I had the honour of transmitting to her Royal Highness the Duchess of York I take the Liberty of informing you that the price of the second Ticket was seven Pounds beyond the value of the £15 Prize belonging to the first, so the whole I paid for the second ticket being £22, I have only to trouble you to transmit to me the first Ticket without which the Prize cannot be obtain'd and £3. 10

I have

[2] 1770–1830. Secretary to the Treasury.

[3] Kelly was in Ireland and acted as intermediary in S.'s negotiations with the proprietor of the Dublin Theatre,

who have the skill and the industry to manage it as it should be for their own advantage, upon terms which would render any risk to them almost impossible;—the profit to them would probably be beyond what I could now venture to state, and yet upon terms which would be much better for the real proprietors than any thing that can arise from the careless and ignorant manner in which the undertaking is now misconducted by those who, my son excepted, have no interest in its success, and who can lose nothing by its failure.

653. To Thomas Holloway

Yale MS. *Address*: Thos. Holloway Esq | Chancery-Lane | *Fr.*:
R B Sheridan *Dock.*: Sheridan | to | Mr. Holloway | Novr. 14 | 1807

14 Nov. 1807
Friday
Novr.

Dear Holloway,
    If you will only get a Fortnights respite from Heath[1] I am positive the Trustees will extricate Shaw and pay the Demand on him as they ought to do. In the mean time pray manage so that it may not be necessary for him to stay away from his business.[2]—I know well that you will do everything in your Power to accommodate us and anything friendly to me.
    I wish much to see Shaw | your's sincerely | R B Sheridan.

Frederick Jones, for the purchase of a quarter share in D.L.Th. S. intended that Jones should buy the share and take over the management with Tom S. The negotiation dragged on into the summer of 1808 but then fell through. See Moore, ii. 354–6; *The Cabinet*, iv (1808), 62.
    [1] Holloway has drafted a reply to S. on the cover: 'I have so repeatedly assured Heath and his Son that the matter would be settled by you that I have lost all Credit with them . . . I will send your Note to Shaw immediately but I very much fear that if he goes to the Theatre he will immediately be taken in Execution. Do therefore Let me beg of you to exert yourself to relieve him from this unpleasant situation. If you could procure for the Moment about £150 he could I think obtain a respite but certainly not without.'
    [2] Leader of the orchestra at D.L.Th. S. agreed in Oct. 1803 (Harvard MS.) to secure to him part of D.L.Th. patent

654. To Richard Peake

McAdam MS. *Address*: Welwyn[1] November twenty two 1807 |
Mr. Peake | Charlotte-St. | Rathbone-Place | London *Fr.*: R B
Sheridan

22 Nov. 1807
Sunday

My Dear Peake

Pray let Frost[2] have a little money on Fairbrothers[3]
account on monday morning when He will be liberated—
as bail was provided before I left Town yesterday you can
stop it gradually from his salary but I would not for the
world have him continue in Prison another Day— | Yours
ever | R B S

655. To Aaron Graham, John Hosier and Randle Jackson

Harrow MS.: Rae, vi. 274b. *Dock.*: 10 December 1807 | The Rt.
Hon. R. B. Sheridan

Thursday 10th Decr:
1807

Gentlemen

It is impossible that any one can be more disposed than
I am to make every exertion to do justice to our renters.[4] The
Fact of my having got together between 5 and 6 thousand
Pounds for their use last year, without the assistance of a

[1] S. left London on 20 Nov. for a
visit to the Melbournes at Brocket Hall,
near Welwyn. See *The Star*, 20 Nov. 1807.

[2] John Frost (1750–1842), solicitor,
had been imprisoned for sedition in
1793. He strongly favoured parliamentary reform and took a leading part in
the Westminster elections, 1782–1807.
In that of 1807 he was S.'s agent. See
Cochrane's brief (Birmingham Pub. Lib.
MS.) and P.R.O. 30/8/137, ff. 99–103.

[3] Robert Fairbrother was S.'s confidential servant. See C. Dibdin the
Younger, *Professional and Literary*

Memoirs (1956), p. 142. Fairbrother
mentions (Add. MS. 35118, f. 121)
a complicated account that existed
between S. and Homan, through Frost
and Henson.

[4] Their dissatisfaction was expressed
at a meeting on 27 Jan. 1808, when
they set up a committee to ensure 'the
future regular payment of their Annuities, and the recovery of the Arrears now
due to them, as the fulfilment of the engagements on the part of the Proprietors
by the Trust Deed of 1793' (Add. MS.
42720, f. 86).

shilling from the Treasury, requires no comment, indeed it is ascertain'd that *the whole sum* paid to the Renters since the opening of the new Theatre has been rais'd by me in the same manner, and that they have never yet received a sixpence from the surplus Profits of the Theatre. As to the Rents of the Fruit offices and extra Houses my readiness to give them up to this object cannot be doubted, when a glance only is taken at what I have already done in this respect. I attribute the perilous state of the Theatre to the want of a fair and honourable Co-operation for the general interest between the Proprietors and the Trustees, and to this cause *alone* I attribute a loss to myself and family by Law[1] and otherwise of not less than fifty thousand Pounds, but the remedy cannot be accomplish'd by the interchange of official Notes. The fault shall not be mine if the proper mode is not pursued for which purpose I will come to the Theatre in the expectation of the Pleasure of meeting you tomorrow.

The Property is every way threaten'd, and its very existence is so by the inroads made on our legal rights and Patents[2] | I have the honor | to be | with great esteem | Yours truly | R B Sheridan

Messrs Graham Hosier and Jackson

656. To Richard Peake

Harvard MS. *Address*: Mr. Peake | Charlotte-St | Rathbone- | Place
Fr.: R B S

Tuesday
Decr: 20th: [*1807*]

My Dear Peake, be with me at one tomorrow in Gt. George St:[3] with the best account you have of the £3000 shares and where they are— | yours truly | R B S

[1] In his speech to the Lord Chancellor, S. asked for protection against lawsuits: 'One has cost me £1000, another £900, another 1100; and I am told the present will have already cost me 800gs.' (*Morn. Chron.*, 24 Dec. 1801.)

[2] See p. 26, n. 4.

[3] Farington, v. 45, mentions under 28 Mar. 1808 that S. had no house and his goods would be seized if he took one; so he lived at Peter Moore's, 7 Great George Street.

657. To the Prince of Wales

Windsor MSS. 41013–6. *Dock.*: Mr. Sheridan | 30th Decr. 1807.

December 30th: 1807

Sir

So often have I experienced your gracious allowance of some degree of *seeming* negligence on my Part in the discharge of the Duty I owe to you and still more of the ardent and affectionate Devotion I feel and ever have felt towards you that I will not at present trespass on your Patience by explanations or apologies for my not having lately intruded on your time while a measure which I have long had in contemplation remain'd yet unaccomplish'd. I am confident your Royal Highness will do me the justice to be assured that my late absence and my even foregoing apparently opportunities of waiting on your Royal Highness could never have proceeded from want of respect and humble attention.—But in truth situated as I was I deem'd it a matter of delicacy on my part and of due deference to your Royal Highness to avoid any personal communication on the subject of my intended resignation of the Receivership of the Duchy of Cornwall[1] until I had entirely removed some impediments which for a short time delay'd the actual execution of my Purpose.—I may have err'd in judgement but sure I am that the motive which influenced me was right and worthy to be approved of by your Royal Highness.

The Time and the manner in which you were graciously pleased to appoint me to that office will, come what events may, be to the end of my Days the proudest recollection of my heart—The return of his Majesty's unfortunate malady had placed your Royal Highness in a situation of the utmost delicacy and difficulty and you embraced that opportunity of publicly avowing your esteem for a man who had long been honor'd with your private confidence and whose highest ambition was to merit it. In doing this however I doubt not it is in your Royal Highness's recollection that you did not proceed a step until the decided and unanimous opinion of

[1] Lake had become Receiver General by Letters Patent dated 12 March 1807. See Rhodes, p. 259. The grant was made on Lake's return home and was for life.

the highest legal authorities had absolutely determined that it was wholly out of your Power to complete your original gracious pledge to Lord Lake, and that if I had presumed to decline the Office some other Person must of necessity have been appointed to it. Under these circumstances and truly and justly proud at such a crisis to have been so selected and appointed to your council I most gratefully enter'd on the situation. But the return of Lord Lake affording to your Royal Highness the Power of fulfilling your original gracious intention I should have considered myself unworthy of your favour or regard could I have hesitated one moment as to the Part it became me to take or omitted to give the earliest facility in my Power to the honourable ambition of so early and so long establish'd a connexion as Lord Lake's with your Royal Highness. In acting so I only recurr'd to a reserve not merely kept in my own mind but distinctly communicated by me long since to the noble Lords Brother Mr Warwick Lake as I am sure he will testify. And most sincerely do I wish the noble Lord health and Life long to serve you.

With regard to my feelings towards your Royal Highness allow me to say that I shall be most unhappy did I think that anything approaching to Professions could be necessary— my unalterable attachment and grateful devotion to you can cease only with my Life.

Before I conclude permit me to say that there is a circumstance which I mention'd to Colonel McMahon, tho' I do not give it much importance and which I think it right to submit to your Royal Highness when I shall have the honour of attending your commands, as it endeavours to implicate Lord Lake and myself in a very unjust and injurious report which perhaps your Royal Highness's judgement may consider as proper to be contradicted. But I will not trouble your Royal Highness on the subject in this Letter. | I have now only to entreat your Royal Highness to believe me | with every sentiment of the | sincerest and warmest attachment | your Royal Highness's | most faithful | and devoted Servant | R B Sheridan.

His Royal Highness
The Prince of Wales

658. To John Grubb

Harvard MS. *Address*: John Grubb Esqre. | Norton St. *Fr.*: R B S

[*c. 1807*][1]
Thursday
Evening

My Dear Sir
I have been very unfortunately prevented keeping two appointments with you lately—I shall be at home all tomorrow morning being prevented by indisposition from attending the Prince at Brighton. I should be happy to see you if you would favour me with a call between 2 and 4 | Yours truly | R B Sheridan

659. [To Richard Peake]

Osborn MS. *Dock.*: Mr. Sheridan | about | £35

[*1807–8?*]

My Dear Dick—I have bought so many useful things and been unexpectedly obliged to pay for some that I am quite aground—I send you the enclosed to assist to relieve—Fairbrother must have a little and some to send to me. I hate to anticipate but I cant help it this once.—I'll write you on our account for you shall not be in advance[2]—I think you are wrong about one of the five Pounds—was it not deducted from the last 35?—but I know you are correct and the mistake must be mine if there is one—give me a Line by to Days post.—What receipt last night? and what is the number of the Duchess' Ticket and IS IT UNDRAWN?[3]

[1] The Grubbe MSS. include a letter by R. Nowell of 22 Dec. 1807, addressed to Grubb at 58 Upper Norton Street.

[2] Five guineas a night for seventeen nights in May 1807 and for twenty-five nights in Sept. and Oct. were deducted by Chancery sequestration from S.'s salary.

[3] D.L.Th. Salaries, 1808–9 (Folger MS.) notes on 31 Dec. 1808 a payment of £16. 9s. 0d. for the 'remainder of last Lottery Ticket'. S.'s handling of the Duchess of York's lottery tickets is mentioned in another letter of this period: see p. 17, n. 1.

660. [To the Duke of York?][1]

Harrow MS.: Rae, v. 256.

[*Jan. 1808?*]
Mr. Whitbreads
Southill[2]
Biggleswade

Sir

It has not been possible for me to resist the very earnest importunity of Mrs. Sheridan that I should venture to trespass on your Royal Highness's time for a few minutes in behalf of the object of the enclosed memorandum.[3] She presumes so much on your Royal Highness's good-nature and clemency that she threaten'd to write herself if I declined it by preventing which I probably save your Royal Highness from receiving a much longer statement than I shall judge

[1] The Harrow cataloguer lists the letter as having been addressed to the Prince Regent, but it is possible that it is a fair copy or draft of the following: 'A.L.S., 8 pp., 4to., Biggleswade, Jan. 4. 1808, to the Duke of York.' This is noted in *American Book Prices Current*, xx (New York, 1914), 793, as sold by the Merwin Sales Company, on 17 Mar. 1914, lot 413.

[2] S. spent a week at Southill just before 9 Jan. 1808: see *Dropmore Papers*, ix. 170.

[3] This is in S.'s hand and is entitled 'Case of William Cook'. It reads: 'William Cook a young man who had lived with General Delancy and had always born[e] an excellent character was lately Shepherd to Mr. Daniel Hooker of West Horsley. Some sheep in Hooker's flock were claim'd by another Farmer in the neighbourhood of the name of Hillier, and ignorantly and hastily given up to him by Hooker whose testimony on the trial of Cook charged with having stolen these caused his condemnation tho Hooker is since convinced of his error. Cook was capitally convicted but in three Days after sent on board the Hulks for transportation. The affair occasion'd considerable

Talk in the neighbourhood and a general opinion of his innocence. Accordingly a Petition in his favour was sign'd by the Neighbourhood and sign'd also by Lord Onslow Dr. Weller Mr. Fullerton Clergyman of East Horsley where Cook lived, Hooker his Master and by a number of Gentlemen besides. The Petition was presented to his R.H. the Duke of York in August, who was graciously pleased to give immediate attention to its contents and Cook received his Pardon on condition of serving his Majesty. This he gratefully accepted and was sent to the Isle of Wight where on examination he was found to be afflicted with a disorder which made him unfit for the service. Instead of being discharged however He was sent on board the Prison ship and is now drafted with a diseased arm daily growing wors[e] into an african regiment consisting of the worst sort of Characters, and by the last accounts which his mother received of him very unlikely to live. He is now on board the Dido Frigate in Colne's harbour. All which is most humbly submitted to the humane consideration of his R.H. the Duke of York Commander in Chief.'

24

necessary, as Brevity is not a Lady's virtue where their feelings are interested.

I have extracted this poor man's case as concisely as I can, his afflicted relations, his mother and sisters in particular who are most respectable Persons represent to Mrs. Sheridan in excuse for their sanguine hope of the result of an application to your Royal Highness that a Petition presented to your Royal Highness in behalf of this unfortunate young man and sign'd by Lord Onslow[1] [and] Dr. Weller[2] was very graciously received by your Royal Highness and I can venture to assure your Royal Highness that there prevails in the neighbourhood an entire conviction of his innocence and of the error in the testimony upon which He was convicted, nor would any of them scruple to take him into their service should He thro' your Royal Highness['s] benign interference be restored to his occupation and the Protection of his Parents and afflicted [relations], whose misery and distress on this occasion has as I before took the Freedom of stating created a strong interest and Feeling throughout the Neighbourhood.

I have again to entreat your Royal Highness's pardon for this intrusion, and I shall only add that knowing your Royal Highness is always gratified by relieving the unfortunate where justice admits of it I do not presume to lay the least stress on the great obligation you will confer both on Mrs Sheridan and myself by your gracious decision on the present occasion | I have the Honor to be with | the utmost truth and respect | your Royal Highness's dutiful Servant | R B Sheridan

661. To Dennis O'Bryen

Add. MS. 12099, ff. 16–17. *Address*: D. O'Brien Esq. | Essex-St. *Wm.*: 1806.

[*19 Jan. 1808?*]
Tuesday

My Dear O Brien
It will be your fault if I am as mute[3] as a fish—to hear

---

[1] George, 1st Earl of Onslow (1731–1814), Lord-Lieutenant of Surrey.

[2] Rev. James Weller, D.D. (1743?–1832), Rector of Clandon-East, and of

Guildford St Mary. See *The Clerical Guide* (1817), p. 273.

[3] S. had announced that he would bring in a motion on Ireland as soon

from you now before 3 tomorrow would decide me a long talk with Lord Hutchinson[1] has much converted me—and so he has the Prince all advances to negotiation are finally rejected here. Staremberg[2] goes to Day | Yours ever | R B S

662. To Richard Peake

Salt MS. *Address*: Mr. Peake

[*Feb.–Mar. 1808?*]
Dinner on table
at 5 to a minute

Dear P.

It will be very convenient for me if you will eat your chops with me at the Wrekin[3] what I am doing is of immense consequence. I am now drawing up a notice to be serv'd on all these Place[s] and a caveat to Grevill. All to be sign'd by Brown[4] on the Part of the Duke of Bedford and both Theatres—I leave Town tomorrow—bring Dunn with you | yrs | R B S

663. To Colonel John McMahon

Windsor MSS. 41050–1. *Dock*.: Mr. Sheridan | March 7 1808

Private and confidential

March 7th. 1808

My Dear Mac—

I enclose you the Letter so long delay'd to the Prince, I

as Parliament met: see Add. MS. 41857, f. 75.

[1] John Hely-Hutchinson, 1st Lord Hutchinson (1757–1832).

[2] The Austrian envoy extraordinary, Louis, Prince de Starhemberg, repeated on 1 Jan. 1808 his government's wish to mediate between France and England. When Canning refused to negotiate (8 Jan.), Starhemberg quitted England (20 Jan.). See S.'s speech in Hansard, 1st Ser., x. 79.

[3] The Salopian coffee-house, Charing Cross ?

[4] Samuel Brown wrote to Tom S. on 2 Mar. 1808 about the deed he had procured from Harris. He believed it did 'not go that length that your Father conceives, for it is nowhere said that there shall be no other Places of Entertainment licensed by The Lord Chamberlain than The Opera at the Haymarket . . .' (Add. MS. 42720, f. 117). Once again S. appears to have been trying to frighten off competition by non-patent houses, with allusions to the 'final arrangement'. See also Folger MS. Y. d. 25 (4).

frankly leave it open that you may read it, and then I will trouble you to seal and deliver it. I have lost four Days in waiting for P. Moores answer to your's which I thought necessary to complete the assurance to the Prince that it is absolutely impossible for me to misapply the income of the Duchy[1] contrary to the Princes intention. You will see I have not touch'd in my Letter to the Prince on the scandalous misrepresentation which was made to him, on the silly ground of the Chancery sequestration, I am sure Lord Lake was merely misled, and knowing the Prince's regard for him, I have not urged a word of complaint, tho I have felt very sore, and really I cannot describe to you the mischievous extent to which this calumny has been propagated. I am very anxious to see his Royal Highness before wednesday's Debate[2] and will therefore be at Carlton-House to wait his Commands in the morning. I assure you my Letter does not contain half the sentiments of affection and respect I feel for him, and above all it does not half express my genuine motive for wishing to pursue my independent Line in Parliament—but upon my soul and faith that motive is that I may qualify myself to give in time to come a more powerful support to our Master. | your's my Dear Friend | sincerely | R B S.

I forgot to say that P Moore has been confined to his bed these five Days past.

664. To the Prince of Wales

Windsor MSS. 41052–4. *Dock.*: Rt. Honble R. B. Sheridan | Mar. 7. 1808

March 7th. 1808

Sir

If I have delay'd to express my thankful acknowledge-

[1] Lake had died on 21 Feb. 1808, but S. was not reappointed Receiver-General until 20 Apr. Richard Gray, Clerk to the Prince's Council, had held the office from 1 Apr., 'pro tempore'. See Rhodes, p. 259. It seems likely that Richard Gray had alleged that S. made over the Duchy income as security for debts of his own, but it is not certain, for both Richard and Robert Gray were Deputy Auditors and Deputies to the Surveyor-General of the Duchy of Cornwall. In addition, Robert Gray was the Prince's Vice-Treasurer and Commissioner of Accounts. For S.'s letters patent, see A.P.C. iv (1919), 191.

[2] Concerning Lord Wellesley's conduct in Oude. S. did not speak.

ments to your Royal Highness for the prompt and flattering manner with which you authorized Colonel McMahon, upon the lamented death of Lord Lake, to announce your gracious reappointment of me to the office I had so lately resign'd, from I trust the most proper Motives it is my humble hope that you will attribute that Delay to anything but a failure in the gratitude which I owe to your Royal Highness on this and so many other occasions.

Allow me Sir to say that I have deferr'd this dutiful expression of what I have felt because I thought it essential to my own character and even necessary to justify your Royal Highness's partiality and protection of me, that I should accompany my acknowledgements to your Royal Highness with a distinct and authenticated contradiction, of the false and calumnious report, however unintentionally propagated, that I had pledged and made over the income bestow'd on me as Receiver General of the Duchy of Cornwall as a security for Debts of my own.—On this subject Mr. Gray has acknowledged his error and fairly and handsomely appologized to me for any mistake which Lord Lake might have been led into by his, Mr. Gray's, misapprehension of the Fact.

With regard to the future I give *your Royal Highness the Pledge of my most solemn Promise that I never will allow the slightest incumbrance or anticipation to attach upon that income*, which derived from your Royal Highness's favour, will, in addition to the settlement now made of my affairs enable me to live with my family with comfort and without Debt or difficulty.

Sir, in addressing these few Lines to you, with the sincerity of a grateful heart I have yet something more upon a much greater scale to thank you for.—I mean the high and generous feeling which has prevented your influencing my political conduct in Parliament in this most unprecedented state of public affairs. I hold my seat in the House of Commons from *you*, Sir, and *you alone*. But yourg racious allowance to me to follow the course which the Habits Principles and Connexions of my past political Life exhort me not to abandon would be unsatisfactory and ungratifying to my mind if I did not blend with my grateful acceptance of that allowance a sanguine hope that whatever influence or weight in public estimation I may derive from persevering in that course can only ultimately tend to my becoming a more useful and efficient Servant to your Royal Highness, affording me I trust, should such a crisis arise, as I cannot but apprehend, better means and opportunities of proving the unalterable attachment and Devotion with which to the end of my Life I shall remain | Your Royal Highness's | most dutiful | and faithful Servant | R B Sheridan

665. To Aaron Graham, John Hosier, and Randle Jackson

Osborn MS. and Price MS.

Denbies[1]—
April 25th: 1808

Gentlemen,

Your Letter of the 22d inst. has follow'd me into the country.—I can only assure you that if you have not received from me the certificates, you have more than once, I admit, required, respecting the engagements of the Performers and the free admissions,[2] the omission has not proceeded from any disrespect towards you, or any disposition on my Part to dispute your title to call for such certificates—it has arisen simply from my conceiving that you had received the information you require from Quarters which you must know are much better able to give it to you than I can possibly be. Ever since I accorded to the Proposition deliberately made and earnestly urged by Mr Hosier at a special Meeting of the Renters that I should withdraw from all interference in the management and commit the whole to Mr Graham under the inspection of the Trustees I have considered the

[1] 'Denbighs, near Darking, . . . now in the possession of Joseph Denison Esq.' (*Ambulator* (1796), p. 82). S. was on friendly terms with William Joseph Denison (1770–1849), the banker and former member of parliament.

[2] The Trustees had sent (in 1807) the proprietors a long representation on the excessive number of free admissions:

see Add. MS. 42720, ff. 76–87. In a letter to Tom S. of 28 Apr. 1808, Randle Jackson complained that 'Mr. Harris sends in frequently towards 30 of a night . . . Mrs. Jordan *did not know* that 40 orders of a night could be injurious to the Theatre' (Add MS. 42720, f. 120). On 3 Feb. 1807, 547 people went in free.

Direction of the Undertaking as entirely in their hands, and carefully abstaining from any interference of any sort I was entitled to look to them as responsible for the success of the experiment. What alone rested with me I performed by directing that the Trustees should have full and free access to all the Treasurers accounts, Pay List proceedings of the board of management etc etc. And accordingly they establish'd themselves in the Theatre with a secretary paid by the Property etc. etc. If the experiment has totally fail'd the Fault has not been mine, unless it was an Error to have given way to the earnest wishes of the Trustees and the apparent concurrence of the meeting of the Renters. But it would be unpardonable indeed were I after the experience of the past to suffer this state of Things to continue. The sacrifices I have made in behalf of the Renters make any Professions on my Part in respect to them unnecessary, and the immense losses inflicted on me and my Property by the misconduct of former Trustees ought to make others cautious not to tread in their Steps. As to the Pay-List I have no doubt there have been enormous abuses in it, altho' I give full credit to the zeal and disinterested goodwill of Mr Graham to whom I consider myself and the Theatre as greatly obliged, to what this has been owing I have not hitherto had the opportunity of ascertaining altho I have little difficulty in[1] the remedy, but I have understood from Mr. Graham that the communication to the Trustees in this respect prescribed by the Lord Chancellors order[2] has been properly made by him. With regard to the second head the free admissions I have uniformly been of opinion that there could be but one mode of proceeding namely to cut them all off. And towards the effecting this the interference of the Trustees will be highly beneficial, and they have my most unqualified consent to and approbation of any mode they may propose for the accomplishment of this essential reform, tho' it may perhap[s] be doubted whether the measure be an object during the short remainder of the present season. I am always disposed to co-operate with the Trustees when their conduct and views have allow'd me, and during the recess I have employ'd myself in making a just statement of the Past and preparing

[1] Osborn MS. ends here.   [2] Of Sept. 1802.

a definitive Plan for the future, which will be communicated to them by my Friend and Trustee Mr. Peter Mo[o]re thro' whose agency the arrangements may be punctually and amicably communicated, assuming all Parties equally desirous as myself to protect the interests of the Renters and in one word to save the Property from irretrievable ruin.

I cannot conclude this without remarking that the late communications and propositions made to me are sign'd only by *two* of the Trustees, Mr. Graham's name not being to them—I remark this *at present* only to shew the uniform unfair treatment I experience. Two of the Trustees it seems are sufficient for every act of a hostile appearance, but when relief is to [be] given to the Demands on me under the Trust of Messrs Drewe and Hugh Hammersley, my Property is allow'd to be forcibly detain'd in their hands under the pretence that the consent of all *three* of the trustees is necessary to their Performance of the duties of their Trust. I shall write especially to Mr. Jackson, on this subject and my own Trustees have very properly directed a bill to be filed against Messrs Drewe and H. Hammersley—for in truth it is usage too gross and oppressive for any one to continue to submit to. | I will detain you Gentlemen no longer at present than to add that | I have the Honor to be | your obedient humble Servant | R B Sheridan.

Messrs Graham
Hosier and Jackson

666. To Richard Wilson

Pierpont Morgan Library MS. *Address*: Richard Wilson Esqr: | Lincoln's-Inn-Fields. *Fr.*: R B Sheridan

Holland-House
Monday May 2d 1808

My Dear Friend

I am greatly gratified by the interest you take in my affairs, knowing the sincerity of your Friendship for me, and confident that from your zeal and ability the most essential service may be derived in the settlement of my affairs.— I am now exerting myself thoroughly to accomplish this object, and I see every prospect of being at last freed from those difficulties and embarrassments in which my own imprudence, the negligence of Those whom I have employ'd and the monstrous impositions that have been practic'd on me have so long involved me, and which have so detrimentally interfered with my Time my spirits and my exertions.

I have profited by your kind Permission to appoint you one of my Trustees. The Deed I have executed is with Peter Moore, pray look it over, and direct a copy to be made for you. In my communications I will have no reserve of any sort, nor shall anything relating to past Proceedings or my present circumstances be held back. On the review of the whole tho' much may justly be imputed to my own negligence and procrast[inat]ion I am confident you will find that I have uniformly aim'd at what was just and honourable in my Dealings with all People and that there never was a human being who has been more the Prey of the Fraud and roguery of Others, and especially of Those whose Peculiar Duty it was to have assisted in protecting me and my Property—at the same time I feel assured that it will give you great satisfaction to see that, notwithstanding the past there yet remain adequate means of attaining and securing future comfort and independence to myself and my Family. Towards effecting this I want no pecuniary assistance, nor from private Friends will I accept any. A portion of the Time and trouble of such Friends and well wishers to me as you and Peter Moore will in a short compass of Time accomplish everything, and leave with me the most grateful sense of the obligations I shall owe you. | believe me | My dear Wilson | your's most sincerely | R B Sheridan

Richd. Wilson, Esq:

667. To Thomas Metcalfe[1]

Whitbread MS. 4094. Copy supplied by Metcalfe.

May 2nd 1808

Dear Sir

I have been lately at Polesden. I had heard a rumour of

[1] Hannrott and Metcalfe were the solicitors responsible for drawing up

my Timber there having been fell'd and sold which I totally
discredited not having heard a word on the subject even
from George Edwards! to my astonishment I find that this
has been the case and that £1400 in money has been carried
off by some body! if Hammersley and Nowell[1] have done
this I know not how to proceed for it seems to me to be
absolutely a felonious proceeding and not a subject for civil
redress. I am most impatient to see you and shall endeavour
to be in Lincolns Inn tomorrow. Mr. Phillips[2] also will meet
me there on Thursday at two—| Yours truly | R B Sheridan
Thomas Metcalfe Esq.

668. To Thomas Metcalfe

Whitbread MS. 4094. Copy supplied by Metcalfe.

Friday Night May 5 1808

Dear Sir,
   Having been much hurried I had not read your letter[3] over
when I saw you today. I have since perused it and there are
matters in it respecting which I must come to you for
explanation. I don't comprehend what is meant by the
Trustees having taken possession of the two Farms. They
can have no possession but as in Trust for me—and subject
to my right to manage my own estate under the Marriage
Settlements, securing to them Mrs. S.'s Pinmoney. Nor can
there exist any pretence for a Chancery Receiver—the idea

the marriage settlement of S. and Mrs.
S. in 1795; and Thomas Metcalfe of
Lincoln's Inn acted as attorney to the
Polesden property, and its trustees,
Grey and Whitbread.
   [1] Richard Nowell of Essex Street
was solicitor to Hammersley.
   [2] S. persuaded William Phillips of
Grosvenor Square to buy Yew Trees
Farm for him in 1805, and afterwards
filed a bill against Phillips to compel
him to convey the estate to the trustees,
Grey and Whitbread. Conveyance was
decreed to be made in payment into
court of £3,250. See the 'Disposition of

the Trust Funds' (Salt MS.).
   [3] Metcalfe had replied on 4 May
(Whitbread MS. 4094) saying, '. . . In
consequence of no regular Receiver
being appointed of the Property
the Trustees having possessed themselves of that part which was purchased by them have endeavoured to
prevent its being unproductive.' The
timber from Chapel and Phenice farms
had produced, when charges had been
paid, £1,203. 3s. 9d. A full account
of rents and dividends of the land man-
aged for the trustees by Metcalfe had
been sent to Whitbread.

is to me absolutely unaccountable—and I must desire that no step may be taken without my previous knowledge and concurrence. I shall see Mr. Whitbread on the subject immediately—by the error of your Predecessors[1] and the *misconstruction of the trustees* in consequence remember I am at least *six thousand pounds* out of pocket. I must decidedly look to these Matters myself. As to Chapel Farm,[2] I absolutely declare that Williter's Rent is by Agreement with me £200 per Annum clear, and that he shall positively pay for the past, and should not have it for double for the future. He is the worst Tenant possible and has long been warn'd to quit and shall not remain[3]—The water meadow by the Mole belonging to Phenice I have long engaged that Mr. Coombe should have paying its value to the Trustees.[4] This would greatly assist the Settlement with both Cocker[5] and Phillips which ought to be the main object with the Trustees together with the accomplishment of the inclosure[6] or half the value of Polesden will be lost. I was greatly surprized at your saying yesterday that *under the Trust* the whole estate *must be sold* at my death. I have taken care by my Will that not an acre of it shall be parted with, nor even a shilling again returned to the Funds—and it must be most clumsy management indeed if after the additional Purchases I have made it will not amply provide for my wife's jointure and that upon real security, and a real property to go to my son Charles. With the Funds they shall have nothing to do. All this we must deliberately talk over, and discuss with my

---

[1] See p. 82 for 'the Blunder or worse of Dunn'.

[2] Metcalfe mentioned in his letter of 4 May that he had let this 'to the then tenant at an increase of rent from £150 to £225'.

[3] Metcalfe replied dryly, 'A Tenant seldom proves a good one who is under an annual notice to quit as Williter was until the purchase was completed by the Trustees' (8 May).

[4] The Trustees had bought Venice in Great Bookham from Elizabeth Whitall and Mary Martyr in May 1806 (Polsden deeds). Mr. John H. Harvey informs me that the Polesden estate contained an isolated plot, called Hale Mead or Rouses Meadow, on the east bank of the River Mole and some three miles north of Polesden House. He identifies 'Mr. Coombe' as Harvey Christian Combe (c. 1752–1818) who was M.P. for London, 1796–1817, and had bought Downe Place, Cobham, in 1807.

[5] On 11 Dec. 1800 Sir William Geary had granted to J. R. Cocker the fields in Great Bookham, occupied by William Willeter, and excepted from the sale of Polesden in 1797. They amounted to 21 acres.

[6] See ii. 228.

friend and trustee Mr. Peter Moore. I will write to or see Mr. Phillips tomorrow after I have seen Mr. Hammersley | Yours truly | R B Sheridan

Thomas Metcalfe Esq.

669. [To Richard Wilson?]

Pub.: Myers Catalogue 343 (1945), item 406.

[*1808*]
My Dear Friend
   Can you dine with me at Richmond . . . and you will meet Jones from Dublin¹ who I think is born to preserve and establish my Property in D. L. Theatre. . . .

670. To Mrs. Atkins²

Osborn MS.

Saturday July 16th: [*1808?*]
Dear Madam
   I am confident that your good nature and Liberality will induce you to forgive the Liberty which a very old and sincere Friend takes in requesting you to allow an interview to my Friend Mr. Parsons the Bearer of this Letter. The motives and object of his application to you He will himself explain when He has the Honor of seeing you. I comply with all he desires from me by giving him these few Lines of introduction I cannot however omit to add my testimony to his being a very worthy and deserving man and also to assure you that any service you can render him will be most gratefully regarded by me | I have the honor to be | Dear Mr[s] Atkins | yours faithfully | R B Sheridan
To
   Mrs. Atkins

---

¹ On 1 Feb. 1808 (Osborn MS.), he bet S. a hogshead of claret that D.L.Th. would be 'indebted on this day two years Ten thousand pounds more, than it is at present.'

² A singer at Bath and C.G.Th.?

671. To John Hosier

Osborn MS. *Dock.*: 1808

Saturday July 23 [*1808*]

My Dear Sir

Finding Graham cannot be with us on monday and wishing much for a little country air not being at all well it will be a great accommodation to adjourn our meeting to the old Day Friday. I assure you I am hard at work for the Hive[1] and I am not discouraged but the contrary the more I look into the Details | Yours sincerely | R B Sheridan

J. Hosier Esq.

I have written to Mr. Jackson[2]

672. To the Prince of Wales

Windsor MSS. 41094–7. *Pub.*: Moore, ii. 362–5.[3] *Dock.*: R. B. Sheridan | July 23 | 1808

Saturday
July 23d. 1808

Sir

It is matter of surprise to myself as well as of deep regret that I should have incurr'd the appearance of ungrateful neglect and disrespect towards the Person to whom I am most obliged on earth, to whom I feel the most ardent dutiful and affectionate attachment and in whose service I would readily sacrifice my Life—yet so it is—and to nothing but a perverse combination of circumstances, which would form but a feeble excuse were I to detail them, can I attribute a conduct so strange seemingly on my Part and from nothing

[1] On 19 July S. had pledged himself to 'prevent improper Engagements—and Improvident expenditure of stores and frauds at the Doors . . . immediately abolish the free list . . . immediately make over to the Trustees for the time being the Rents of the Houses comprised in the Trust Deed of 1793. . . .' All these promises and others not fulfilled are detailed in Hosier's letter to S. on 21 Oct. 1808 (Add. MS. 42720, f. 145).

[2] On 20 July Jackson wrote to Graham and Hosier resigning his trust, 'Mr. Sheridan having now so decidedly agreed to the proposals of the Trustees' (Add. MS. 42720, f. 141).

[3] The versions in W.T. and Moore are both from drafts.

but your Royal Highness's kindness and benignity can I expect an indulgent allowance and oblivion of that conduct. Nor could I even[1] hope for this were I not conscious of the unabated and unalterable devotion to your Royal Highness which lives in my heart and will ever continue to be its Pride and boast.

But I should ill deserve the indulgence I request did I not frankly state what has passed in my mind, and which tho' it may not justify must in some degree extenuate apparent neglect.

Previous to your Royal Highness having actually restored me to the office I had resign'd I was mortified and hurt in the keenest manner by having repeated to me from an authority *which I then trusted* some expressions of your Royal Highness's respecting me which it was impossible I could have deserved. Tho' I was most solemnly pledg'd never to reveal the source from which the communication came I did for some time intend to unburthen my mind to my most honourable and sincere Friend and your Royal Highness's most attach'd and excellent Servant, McMahon—but I suddenly discover'd beyond a doubt that I had been grossly deceived and that there had not existed the slightest foundation for the tale that had been imposed on me, and, Sir, I do humbly ask your Pardon for having for a moment credited a fiction suggested by mischief and malice.

Yet extraordinary as it may seem I had so long under that false impression neglected the course which Duty and gratitude required from me that I felt an unaccountable shyness and reserve in acknowledging and repairing my error. To this Procrastination other circumstances unluckily contributed. One day when I had the honor of accidentally meeting your Royal Highness on Horseback in Oxford St. tho' your manner was as usual gracious and kind to me, yet you said that I appear'd to have deserted you privately and POLITICALLY. I had long before been assured, tho' falsely I am convinced, that your Royal Highness had promised to make a point that I should neither speak nor vote upon Lord Wellesleys case[2]—my view of this subject and my know-

[1] Possibly 'ever'. Moore prints 'even'.

[2] Wellesley-Pole (afterwards Lord Maryborough) stated in the Commons on 1 June 1808, that 'in full confidence

ledge of the delicate situation in which your Royal Highness stood in respect to the Catholic Question tho' perhaps inadequate motives yet encouraged the continuance of that reserve which my original error had commenced. These Topics being once pass'd (and sure I am that your Royal Highness would never deliberately have ask'd me to abase myself and forfeit all that is the worth of my public character, and all that can ever create a chance to render me useful to your Royal Highness—I mean the unpurchaseable consistency and sincerity of my political Principles) it was my hope fully and frankly to have taken that opportunity of explaining myself when I was informed that a circumstance which occurr'd at Burlington-House and which must have been heinously misrepresented had greatly offended you, and soon after it was stated to me by an authority which I have no objection to disclose that your Royal Highness had quoted with mark'd disapprobation words supposed to have been spoken by me on the Spanish Question,[1] but of which words I solemnly protest I never utter'd one syllable, at the same time reserving to myself the right to say that I should not be ashamed of the sentiment if I had utter'd it, nor could your Royal Highness I am convinced have condemn'd it.

Most justly may your Royal Highness answer to all I have stated by a single question—namely why have I not sooner explain'd myself and confided in that uniform Friendship and Protection which I have so long experienced at your hands. To this I have nothing to plead but a nervous pro-

not only of the innocence but of the highly meritorious conduct of Lord Wellesley he was ready to meet any thing [S.] had to urge however awful it may be to contend with the great talents and eloquence of [S.] matured and methodized on this question by six years' preparation'. In reply S. denied any slurs upon Wellesley's private moral character but declared he had always thought 'that noble lord betrayed too often a mischievous ambition that might be ultimately ruinous to the British interests in the East' (Hansard, 1st Ser., xi. 767–9). S. spoke at length on the Carnatic Question in the Commons on 17 June 1808. See *Speeches*, v. 371–6.

[1] S.'s speech on Spanish affairs is summarized in *Speeches*, v. 368–71; but is given at greater length and in the first person in Hansard, 1st Ser., xi. 886–9. In a letter with the postmark of 16 June, Whitbread stated to Grey: 'Sheridan in concert with Canning and against the wish and advice of all his Friends has been making a bother about Spain. He did all he could to create a Cry for himself as distinguished from all of us, but He was so exceedingly drunk he could hardly articulate. . . .' (Grey MS.) But see, also, G. Davies, 'The Whigs and the Peninsular War', *Trans. of the Royal Hist. Soc.*, 4th Ser., ii (1919), 114–18.

crastinating nature, urged and disturbed by great and op-
pressive private embarrassments and a feeling of I trust no
false Pride which however I will blame myself impells me
involuntarily to fly from the risk of even a cold look from the
quarter to which I owe so much, and by whom to be esteem'd
is the glory and consolation of my private and Public Life.

One Point only remains for me to intrude on your consideration but it is of a nature fit only for personal communication and I know you will grant me that opportunity.[1]
As to my office in the Duchy it would be insincerity and disguise in me not to see that your Royal Highness wishes
some different disposition of it—tho' my Patent is for Life
the surrender shall be at your Feet tomorrow, only Sir let
me implore you to respect me enough to give me credit for
the scorn with which I should reject any remuneration for
the sacrifice.—

You have the Truth and my Heart before you—you cannot be on half Terms with me. If I have seriously offended
you, I have lost what I never will attempt to repair or recover
the favour of a Prince and future Sovereign and you Sir will
have lost what I trust and hope to God you may repair the
next hour the service and honest devotion of a man not
a professing Sycophant to your Station and Power, but
a sincere and affectionate servant and Friend to your Hap-
piness and Glory. | I have the Honor to be with | every
Sentiment of gratitude and devotion | your Royal High-
ness's dutiful Servant | R B Sheridan

673. To ——

Harvard MS. *Dock.*: Sheridan

Queen-S[t.]
Tuesday
August 9th [*1808*]

Fidissima,

Will you come with me and dine at Randall's[2] on Thurs-

---

[1] From this point, the text differs
considerably from, and is longer than,
that printed by Moore.

[2] Mr. John H. Harvey has established

that Randall Farm, Leatherhead, was
owned by S.'s friend, Richard Ironmonger, in 1808. S. appears to have
rented it for at least fifteen months.

day? I go the next morning on to Brighton and if you have a mind to see the review[1] I'll take you and bring you back on sunday—

What say you? and we can discuss all the way— | Yours ever | R B S

Mrs. S. arrived here with Charles last night all well—too late tho' for Mrs. Scott who produced a fine Boy at two on Monday morn.[2]

674. To the Marquis of Tavistock

Yale MS. *Address*: To | The Marquis of Tavistock | etc etc etc. *Fr.*: R B Sheridan

Friday
August 19th 1808

My Dear Lord

Mr. Staunton[3] a very particular Friend of mine, and a Person of eminence in his Profession is very ambitious of the honor of being appointed Surgeon to the Regiment of local militia which I understand your Lordship is to command. I believe the emolument to be little or nothing but He conc[e]ives it to be a creditable distinction which he is anxious to procure. I have only to request you to excuse the Liberty I take in making this application and to add that should it be successful I shall feel myself particularly obliged. I beg my respects to Lady Tavistock.[4] I need not say how sincerely I wish you both joy. | I have the Honor to be, my Dear Lord | yours faithfully | R B Sheridan

[1] The Prince of Wales's birthday review (12 Aug.) at Brighton.

[2] When seeking Grey's patronage in a letter of 2 July 1818 (Grey MS.) Harry Scott stated that his son, Thomas Brand Graham Scott, was born in Hertford Street on 8 Aug. 1808.

[3] Possibly Robert Stanton, who was commissioned in the Third Dragoons in 1797. See W. Johnston, *Roll of*

Commissioned Officers in the Medical Service of the British Army (Aberdeen, 1917), p. 105. I owe the reference to Mr. W. R. LeFanu.

[4] Francis Russell, Marquess of Tavistock (1788–1861), later 7th Duke of Bedford, had married Anna Maria, daughter of Charles Stanhope, 3rd Earl of Harrington, on 8 Aug.

675. [To John Graham]

Osborn MS. *Dock.*: R B Sheridan | Curious Summons | to Randalls Surry

16 *Sept. 1808*
London
Friday

Laying aside all other engagements you are hereby charged and required to be personally present at Randalls Near Leatherhead in the County of Surry at eleven of the clock on monday morning next, in order that you may be present at a fishing Festival given on the Banks of our river Mole and that you be aiding and assisting in hauling the Nets and tackle to be used on the occasion | whereof on your allegiance fail not | done, in the Queen's Street | Sept. 16 1808 | R B S.

676. To the Proprietors of £3,000 Shares

Winston MS., 1808–9. Draft. *Dock.*: S's Letter | to the Proprietors | of the £3000 | Shares

Theatre Royal Drury Lane
September
16th. 1808.

Sir

The Trustees The Proprietors and the Board of management of this Theatre have directed me to apprize you that the abuse of the Privilege belonging to the Holders of the three thousand Pound shares can be no longer allow'd. The Proprietors and Trustees fully admit the right of the Proprietor of a three thousand Share to write an order for the nightly free admission of two Persons *subject to the general rule which regulates the right of giving orders in the Theatre* and which is equally binding on the Proprietors and the Performers. Under this Rule any Performer or even a Proprietor attempting to turn his Privilege into Profit and to sell his orders would be guilty of a Fraud. Precisely under the same restriction is the Privilege granted to the Purchasers of a three thousand Pound Share. You therefore are hereby apprized that the SALE of this Privilege is contrary to the intention and Letter of the Trust-Deed and that according to you the undoubted Privilege of writing free admissions for two, for each night of Performance in the same manner as the Proprietors themselves are empower'd to write, you must yet conform as the Proprietors themselves are to the prescribed mode of giving these free admissions, which is that the whole of such written order shall be *in your hand-writing with the names of the Play and the Date of the month and Day of the week.* To this rule the Proprietors and every actor conform—and I am directed distinctly to inform that no orders written by you unless written as prescribed above will be received.—I take the Liberty of adding from myself, knowing it however to be the opinion of the Proprietors and Trustees—that this regulation is intended to be and certainly will be ultimately for the Benefit of your Property which now is hourly depreciated by the injury done to the Theatre Receipt in consequence of the shameful Public sale of your orders at reduced Price even at the Doors of the Theatre

677. To Richard Peake

Harvard MS. *Wm.*: 1808

[*1808?*]
The Hoo[1]
Tuesday

My Dear Dick
Very few Things in Life would I assure you give me more pleasure than to contribute towards making *you* easy and happy for the rest of your Days and it shall go hard but I will do it.

Pray get your List of Renter[s] ready to compare with mine distinguishing the original subscribers. I may say to you in *confidence* that Hosier is attempting every rascality to carry his own iniquitous ends. But I'll crush him. I am as we say of our Troops in high health and Spirits | Yrs |
R B S

[1] *The Times*, 8 Sept. 1807, reported that S. was on a visit to 'the Hon. Mr. Brand at the Hoo, on a shooting party'. Possibly the visit was repeated in the following year at the same season.

678. To Richard Peake

Add. MS. 35118, f. 104. *Address*: Leatherhead October thirty |
Mr Peake | Charlotte-St | Rathbone Place | London *Dock.*: Mr
Sheridan about £35 *Fr.*: R B Sheridan

30 Oct. 1808
Sunday

I am undone for want of £35—I trust I shall have it by to-
morrows coach that I may get to Town, tuesday| Yours| R B S

679. [To Aaron Graham, John Hosier, and William Houlston]

Winston MS., 1808–9. *Dock.*: Proprietors | Letter for | assisting the |
Sufferers by | the fire

[*1808*]
Theatre Royal Drury-Lane
Board of Management

Sir
The Disposition of the Proprietors of Drury-Lane-
Theatre to assist the suffering Parties by the late Destruction of Convent Garden Theatre[1] is most sincere and earnest
but feeling that the sanction of the Trustees is necessary to
justify the measures they wish to adopt I am directed to
request if not particularly inconvenient to you your presence
at the board of management as *speedily* as possible.

680. To Richard Peake

Add. MS. 35118, ff. 149–150. *Address*: To Peake *Dock.*: Mr.
Sheridan about raising him supplies

[*Oct.–Nov. 1808?*]
Cock at Sutton[2]
Tuesday

My Dear Peake
I determined to remain here yesterday to work uninter-
rupted at various matters. Ward is now returning to Town
and I to Randalls, He will bring to you the Proposed Letter

---

[1] 20 Sept. 1808. D.L.Th. offered the
use of its wardrobe in performances by
C.G.Th. company at the King's Theatre: see *Morn. Post*, 23 Sept. 1808.

[2] Twelve miles from London, and
the first stage on the Brighton road. S.'s
fondness for this inn is described in
Creevey Papers, i. 58–59.

to the Subscribers,[1] and I have little Doubt of a unanimous acquiescence. You will observe that the Letter assumes Graham to have set the example tho' I have not yet applied to him but of course his previous consent is necessary before the Letters are issued—and Ward takes with him a Letter from me to obtain that object. I cannot express how comfortable this arrangement would make me and what a relief it will be to my mind.—When this is done I have little doubt of obtaining a similar indulgence from Glossip.[2] If I was not perfectly sure that we shall succeed in this arrangement, I would not ask you to send me by tomorrow's Post £20 to Randall's which I shall greatly stand in need of to keep matters *there* on the clear footing we now Proceed on—and, also that you pay a little draft for £5 on Biddulph and Cox for the Landlord here as Ward will explain—I have gone through your Red Book and sign'd the account. I send it by Ward for your satisfaction, and you may give me the Duplicate. If the King should chuse to receive us I shall see you in Town tomorrow I hope Gout gone— | Yours ever | R B S.

I think you told me that something more had been paid to Graham than appears in the account. Pray let that be explain'd to him.—

I have desired Ward to shew you my Letter and Proposal to G.

Strike quick in all this business.

681. To Richard Wilson

Dufferin MS. [Ph.] *Address*: Richd. Wilson Esqr. *Fr.*: R B S. *Dock.*: Sheridan

[*1808?*]
Tuesday
morn

My Dear Wilson,

You will infinitely oblige me by coming to the meeting to

---

[1] The letter (of Oct. 1808) to the contributors to the loan made to S. in 1806 suggested that it would be a material accommodation to Mr. Sheridan if, for the present season, they would have the goodness to 'forego the instalments now becoming due, and taken up by Mr. Graham, for the discharge of the loan . . .' (Winston, 1808–9).

[2] Francis Glossop's letter to Tom S. of 6 Oct. 1808 contains a request that S. should tell Graham to pay Glossop for the goods (candles) he had supplied to the Theatre. See Winston, 1808–9.

be held to day at P. Moore's at 4 of a few principally interested and Adam, and indeed you should. If you cant what
hour can we meet tomorrow? and shall it be at Mrs.
Richardson's?—pray bid Chisom[1] deliver to Peake who will
Guarantee the return of it tomorrow Adam's sign'd trust.
There is not a moment to be lost in selecting names for
immediate application. If you come to Wilson's you will
see[?] communication beneficial to myself and Tom but
which the ill conduct of Hosier and the Renters richly merit.
Besides the Chancellor's order is to be attack'd[2] | yours ever |
R B S

682. [To John Hosier]

Harrow MS.: Rae, vi. 274c. Add. MS. 42720, ff. 147–8, is a copy in
another hand.

Board Room
Theatre
Saturday Evening
Novr. 19–1808

My Dear Sir,
On my return to this Place where I have been dining with
Mrs. Sheridan I learn that my Son had mentioned to you my
wish that Lord Kinnaird could be prevail'd on to accept the
situation of one of our Trustees,[3] but I also learn with great
regret that instead of the idea being most acceptable to *you*,
which I had entirely calculated upon, you seem to state that
I must have been actuated in this proposition by a knowledge
that a difference existed between you and Lord Kinnaird[4] or
that his being your Co-Trustee might create one—I solemnly
Protest that I never heard nor had the slightest idea but that
you and Lord Kinnaird were on Terms of the most perfect
cordiality and confidence, and in wishing to ally him with

[1] William Chisholme?
[2] This might suggest that the letter
belonged to Aug. 1805, when the
Trustees unsuccessfully prayed in the
Court of Chancery that the order of
1802 might be revoked; but the reference
to Peter Moore and the selecting of
names hint at a later date.
[3] A meeting of renters to fill the vacancy caused by Jackson's resignation
was advertised for 21 Nov. See Winston,

1808–9. S.'s nominee was Charles,
8th Lord Kinnaird (1780–1826).
[4] In his reply dated 20 Nov. Hosier
stated that 'there is no difference whatever existing between Lord Kinnaird and
me and I trust never will but that we
shall continue as we are in cordiality and
Friendship' (Add. MS. 42720, f. 149).
Hosier added that he had asked several
men to stand for the office but Houlston
alone had accepted.

you (having suffer'd so intolerably by the scandalous conduct of former Trustees) I thought I should be effecting the thing most grateful to you at the same time securing to my Son and his young Family the Protection in this his only Property of a man of the first Rank Talent and Honor, but certainly also of one most unfit to be suspected of abating one atom of the Duty due to the Trust He undertakes, from any partial biass, or unfair Preference to Private Friendship.

I am confident the subject has never yet been mention'd to Lord Kinnaird,[1] but I am equally confident that it would be a great Grace and Protection to the Theatre if he would consent to the nomination, and should His consent be obtain'd I entreat you to reconsider the subject. I understand a canvass has been made, and that you are to propose a Gentleman[2] whose name even has never been mention'd to me—to myself it is perfectly indifferent who is the Trustee. You must, my Dear Sir, by this time have learnt that my conduct is not only unassailable, but entitled to the fullest Gratitude of the Renters, but suffering as I have done from the egregious Folly and mercenary Knavery of former Trustees I think the choice in the Present moment of infinite importance to my Son and his Family. I wish therefore you would see Tom before anything is finally decided. For my Part I shall not in the least interfere, and as I frankly tell you I mean to place no *half* confidence in you I shall wish the colleague you prefer | yours truly | R B Sheridan

683. To His Son Tom

Add. MS. 42720, ff. 151–2. *Address*: T Sheridan Esqre. | South Audley-St. *Dock.*: On Ld | Kinnaird being | Trustee

[*19 Nov. 1808*]
Theatre—
Saturday Evening

Dear Tom

It was not in my Power to call on Lord Kinnaird to Day

[1] Kinnaird wrote to Tom S. on this subject (from 'Oatlands Sunday') to say that he had no difference with Hosier, and would hesitate about accepting the office of trustee. He had a large interest in the theatre and would prefer to be merely a friend and counsellor, but that if S. and Tom S. wished him to stand and Hosier agreed to it, he would do so. See Add. MS. 42720, f. 153.

[2] William Houlston of Lambeth was elected a trustee on 21 Nov.

tho' I have been at his door three times—but I am sure He is now in Town. I am more than ever convinced of the Protection to be afforded to your Property and Family in the strictest Line of justice were such a young man to accept the situation of Trustee especially in the event perhaps not long distant of anything happening to me; I never heard 'till this evening of Hosier's canvassing for a Dr. Somebody whom nobody ever heard of—a Physician! I send you a copy of a Letter I have written to Hosier which will explain everything to Kinnaird whom pray pray see early in the morning and Hosier too—I shall go out of Town for I will not stoop to meddle in the Election. | yours ever | R B S.

684. To John Hosier

Pub.: S.C., 25 May 1954, lot 278.

[*Nov. 1808 ?*]
Sunday night 12 o'clock

[Mentioning Lord Kinnaird and his acceptance of a trust.]

685. To Lady Ford

Brinsley Ford MS. *Dock.*: 1808 | Mr. Sheridan

5 Dec. 1808
Queen St May Fair
Decr. 5th 1809

Dear Madam,
   I have been extremely sorry and vex'd to learn that there ever could have been a moments doubt of continuing to you and Family the Freedom of D.L. Theatre as heretofore—I have directed the omission to be immediately set right and have the honor to be | Your very sincere and obedient Servant | R B Sheridan

Lady Ford[1]

---

[1] Marianne (Booth), widow of Sir Richard Ford who died on 3 May 1806.

686. To Richard Peake

Harvard MS. *Wm.*: 1808

[*24 Dec. 1808*]
Randalls

My Dear Peake,
I beseech you to urge Graham and Hosier to hasten the assistance I have relied on. I am here without a penny and want to get to Town but cannot move[1] | Your's ever | R B S

687. To Richard Peake

Add. MS. 35118, f. 166. *Address*: Richd. Peake Esq *Dock.*: Mr. Sheridans request to sign Bail Bond Homan

14 Jan. [*1809*]

Dear Peake
Pray sign the Bail Bond with Homan[2] for the Writs issued against him by Henson[3]—on Fairbrothers Bill of Cost for White I had joined Homan in acceptance for—do this on Monday | Yrs ever | R B Sheridan

Saturday 14 Janry.

688. To Lady Bessborough

Pub.: Sichel, ii. 441, with the note: 'To Lady Bessborough most probably from Sheridan, January 1809. It is addressed to "The Countess of Bessborough at Lord Morpeth's, Park Street".' Cf. S.C. 1 Mar. 1955, lot 428.

[*22 Jan. 1809?*]
Brooks's 11 o'clock

Lord Paget[4] is come, they say.—The French attacked us

[1] D.L.Th. Salaries, 1808 to 1809 (Folger MS.) records on 24 Dec. 1808, 'Mr. S. to Randals £10'.
[2] Frederick Homan, a nephew of the Bishop of Killala, was appointed in 1808, by S., as inspector of the money-takers and doorkeepres at D.L.Th. See *Election Reports and Papers, 1806–7*, iii. 466; *The Times*, 21 Nov. 1809.

[3] Homan was in Newgate, having signed a warrant of attorney to Henson on behalf of Fairbrother who had lent money to S. See Add. MS. 35118, f. 121; D.L.Th. Salaries, 1808 to 1809 (Folger MS.): 21 Jan. 1809.
[4] Henry Paget, afterwards 2nd Earl of Uxbridge and 1st Marquess of Anglesey (1768–1854). He 'arrived late

embarking, and Moore killed, your dear Baird lost his arm,
and almost killed. Junot[1] commanded—his troops embarked
and coming away.

Only about 400 killed.[2]

689. To Richard Peake

Osborn MS.

[*29 Jan. 1809*][3]
Sunday morn

Dear Peake
You disappointed me sadly in not sending me last night
what I deem the remainder of P. Moore's draft. £11 is
exactly what I have had from you on the score of this particular Draft but you mix older things with it which is shabby
and not fair and so would leave me in a worse plight than if
I had not had the draft at all. As [for] sending the £10 to
Mrs. S. you must know I have not a penny.

To yourself	£11
Burgess	3
sent me	13
	27 remains £8

And now observe you must be with me uniformly every day.
I shall be always up and at home. Those who neglect to exert
themselves at this crisis are neglecting their own interest |
Yours truly | R B S.

I want as exact a List as possible of the 3,000 Sharers.—

yesterday evening with an account of
an attack made by the French, on
Monday last, on a part of our army at
Corunna. . . . Sir John Moore was
killed during the action, and Sir David
Baird lost an arm' (Ross to Malmesbury,
23 Jan., *Letters of the 1st Earl of Malmesbury*, 1870, ii. 85).

[1] General Andoche Junot (1771–
1813).
[2] Written in pencil.
[3] D.L.Th. Salaries, 1808 to 1809
(Folger MS.) records on 28 Jan. 1809,
'Mr. Sheridan Mr. Moore's Dft. for
£35'.

690. To ——

Harvard MS.

Queen-St.
Januy. 31s: [*1809–11*]

My Dear Sir

Feeling sincerely obliged to you for the kind Pains you have taken to rescue Burgess from the scrape he was involved in on my account—I have sign'd all the securities desired, but not to spoil the Ship for a Little Tar, I have suggested to add £100 to the proposed Loan at the same time giving precedence to your former Loan of £200 to any claim of Mr. Longs.—In borrowing so small a sum as £200 or £300 it never enter'd into my contemplation to add the security of Sir Jasper's . . .!¹ but however take them all—but do not and I am sure you will not refuse the added accommodation of £100 for my private affairs—greatly indeed needing it this moment | your's truly | R B Sheridan

691. To Richard Peake

Salt MS. *Wm.*: 1808.

[*Feb. 1809?*]
Thursday Night.

My Dear Dick

You will see by the enclosed from Hare² that the dirty Fellows at Charing Cross³ will give me no assistance even for £14 tho' you had vouch'd for its repayment. I have given them notice that I remove immediately the Duchy account from their house—for they entrapp'd me into an assurance of my Life pretending to advance me a certain sum and then have cut it down to nothing.

The fourteen guineas to Shepperd if not paid early in the morning strips Mrs. S. of her carriage and plays the devil

---

¹ Illegible.
² Or 'Hore'.
³ S. appointed Thomas Somers Cocks as Deputy Receiver in London of the

Duchy revenue. See Rhodes, p. 261. He was a member of the firm of Biddulph, Cocks, Cocks, & Ridge, bankers, of Charing Cross.

with my domestic quiet—that therefore pray pay at any rate—but stand by me a little more read the enclosed, which by the alter'd date you will see I meant to have sent to you before but hoped afterwards to do without, and return the acceptances keeping £50[1] for present and late advances and as there is Truth in God and Whitbread you can run no risk. I have lodged the order referr'd to in the hands of Moor and Whitbread.

Trust me Whitbread will clear every shilling I can to you. *Shepperd* must have his money in the MORNING *early*. You dont send me the certificate— | yrs | R B S

692. To Richard Peake or William Dunn

McAdam MS. *Address*: Mr. Peake | or | Mr. Dunn *Dock.*: Mr. Sheridan *Fr.*: R B S

[18 Feb. 1809]
Saturday Night

Dear Peake or Dunn—

you must let Gregory[2] have one more £2 this Night[3] and then positively all further demand—shall cease! and the late Driblets be paid on tuesday. | Yours truly, | R B S.

either you or Dunn or Spring[4] must have my Theatre bill which I offer'd to shew Downs that Day in Spring's office I want it particularly

693. To His Wife

Salt MS. *Wm.*: 1806

Saturday
Feby. 25 *[1809]*

My Hearts beloved Hecca,

If I was writing to a Person of an ordinary mind I should

[1] D.L.Th. Salaries, 1808 to 1809 (Folger MS.) records 'Accepted a Bill at one Month for Mr. Sheridan 11 Feby. Value 50'. The date lies between 11 and 18 Feb. 1809.

[2] William Gregory, S.'s servant, 1804–11.

[3] D.L.Th. Salaries, 1808 to 1809 (Folger MS.) records on 18 Feb. 1809 a payment to 'Mr. Sheridan by Wm. £2'.

[4] Samuel Spring succeeded Fosbrook as box-keeper in 1807.

think it incumbent on me to use some circuitous Preface in breaking to you the afflicting Fact of a great worldly calamity —as certainly the world must esteem it[1]—but as I am not greatly moved by it,[2] and owing I am sure to high and good Principles, I mean you no ill compliment in trusting that you will bear it as I do—Drury-Lane-Theatre lies in burning ashes on the Ground. I thought it a Duty and respect I owed to you to come to you with the intelligence myself and I have had a chaise at the Door all the morning—but so many urgencies press on me that I must remain on the Spot.[3] Had I felt this blow as many would have done, so may God judge my Heart if every trace of regret would not have been driven from my mind by the real Pain which your account of yourself has since given me. Only *you* be well and I will yet surmount everything but without you—there is nothing I wish to struggle for.

By all means my Dearest I would have you come to Town, but certainly not this morning—tomorrow morning there shall be a warm chaise at Epsom whence let our Horses bring it to Randalls—then take you back—to Epsom where there shall be Horses ready to bring you to Queen-St: and to your affectionate and unalter'd | Friend and Husband | R B S

Pray give me a Line by to Nights Post—I send this by Fairbrother[4] who will tell you particulars. You may imagine I steal from a croud to write this.

[1] The destruction by fire of D.L.Th. It began at 11.5 p.m. on 24 Feb. and little was rescued from the flames but the books and papers of the Theatre Treasury, and 'articles from Mrs. Jordan's room (*The Times*, 27 Feb. 1809).

[2] He declined the suggestion that Parliament should be adjourned, 'observing that, whatever might be the extent of the individual calamity, he did not consider it of a nature worthy to interrupt their proceedings . . .' (Hansard, 1st Ser., xii. 1105–6). Cf. Farington, v. 142.

[3] S. met the principal actors at Wroughton's house in Gower Street, and told them that his immediate concern was to find a theatre where they could use their patent to put on performances. See Kelly, ii. 254.

[4] He said later that, after the fire, S. was so short of money and credit that he took some workmen to the ruined theatre and, after a search, found 'the remains of a peal of bells, once belonging to the Theatre, which they dug out and sold to a Bell founder in Whitechapel for £90' (Folger MS. T. b. 1, p. 44).

694. To Richard Wilson

Royal Irish Academy MS. 3 D 8, No. 3190. *Address*: Richd. Wilson
Esq. | Lincoln's-Inn-Fields *Dock.*: Sheridan[1]

[*1809?*]
Queen-St.
Monday morn

Domine,
Are you dead or alive? Are you sick or well? Are you in
Town or country?
If in the Land of the Living, if in health and if in Town,
pray give me a call in the course of the Day.—I would come
to you but I am confined by a cold. | Yours ever | R B S

It is of importance

695. [To Richard Wilson?]

Harvard MS.

[*28 Feb. 1809*]
Queen-St.
Tuesday morning

My Dear Friend,
If you can get to Queen St: in the course of the morning
or at any time to Day I need not say how happy I shall be to
see you. Burgess mention'd some suggestions [about] which
I think he must have mistaken you when He said you
approved of them. The Calamity[2] is great and any alleviation
of it even difficult,[3] but I will have nothing to do with any

[1] Accompanied by a cover to Wilson at the same address, and docketed 'Augt. o9'.

[2] 'The total loss was estimated at £300,000, of which only £35,000 were insured; and that sum was instantly attached by the Duke of Bedford as ground landlord' (Watkins, ii. 492).

[3] On 28 Feb. Thomas Hammersley wrote to S. saying, 'Providence is very merciful to you in the great calamity that has befallen Drury Lane Theatre.

It is of all opportunities that have ever happened to you the greatest' (Winston, 1808–9). He suggested a meeting with Peter Moore ('He and I are the best friends you ever had') when he would put forward certain ideas. *The Times*, 3 Mar. 1809, reported that the Dukes of Devonshire, Bedford, and Norfolk, with other friends of S., were to meet to try to alleviate his misfortunes. S. himself thought of raising money by a lottery: see Whitbread MS. 4044.

crooked mode of relief.—But of all this hereafter.—I am writing to Mrs. Richardson. I am much better to Day. | Your's ever sincerely | R B Sheridan

696. [To the Lord Chamberlain]¹

Add. MS. 42721, ff. 9–10. Copy. *Dock.*: Copy to the Lord Chamberlain from Mr. Sheridan.

Queen Street
Mayfair
Wednesday Evening March 1. [*1809*]

Private.

My dear Lord

I confide in your justice and goodness to cause to be suspended any Licence which may be applied for [for] the Lyceum in the Strand, until the unfortunate company of Drury Lane Theatre have had an opportunity of stating to your Lordship the unparallel'd attempts made to deprive them of the only Asylum that is open to them under their misfortune,² and that, if I am rightly informed, by an act of extraordinary treachery on the part of a Person who pretending to act for the company, has taken it for himself

I have been for some days confined by a severe cold, but I trust I shall be able to have the honor of waiting on your Lordship on Friday and to submit to your Lordship such an authentic statement of this transaction as I doubt not will equally interest your Lordships human feelings and justify your strong interference. | I have the honor to be | with the

¹ George Legge, 3rd Earl of Dartmouth (1755–1810), was Lord Chamberlain from May 1804 to his death on 1 Nov. 1810.

² The clearest account of what happened is in Folger MS. W. b. 5, where it appears that on 28 Feb. S. negotiated the use of the Lyceum on the same terms as were earlier offered (and declined by) Arnold, but with the delaying proviso that the consent of the D.L.Th. trustees must be obtained. 'Without however waiting the stipulated time, Mr. Lingham, surprised by Mr. Arnold, who was understood to be treating on behalf of the Drury Lane company, was induced to sign' an authority to his son (Thomas Lingham, Jun.) for the letting of the Lyceum. Arnold then obtained from the Lord Chamberlain a licence for one year. See, also, Arnold's defence of his action, in Add. MS. 42721, ff. 11–15, and his *Observations* (British Museum T.C. 45).

greatest esteem | and respect | Your Lordships Sincere [?] | and obedient Servant | R B Sheridan

697. To Aaron Graham and John Hosier

Add. MS. 42721, f. 28. Copy.[1]

c. 7 Mar. 1809

As to the free admissions etc. etc. I have had an opinion which reconciles me to the total exclusion of them all. So let that be no bar with the performers.[2]

698. To Aaron Graham, John Hosier, and William Houlston

Add. MS. 42721, f. 29. Copy. *Dock.*: 7 March 1809 | The Proprietors to the Trustees. | This has been since signed by Mrs. Richardson. | C. W. W.

March 7 1809

Gentlemen

We hereby authorize and require you if you cannot procure a Lease from Mr. Lingham[3] from the Lyceum to purchase the same from him on the Terms proposed by him in Trust for and to be annexed to the Property of Drury Lane Theatre and to apply such funds belonging to the

---

[1] The extract appears in Graham and Hosier's letter to Wroughton reporting S.'s statement. A draft of their letter (dated 7 Mar.) is in Winston, 1808–9.

[2] The performers wished to act for the benefit of the poorer of them, without their receipts being subjected to the claims of the renters of the destroyed D.L.Th. See Add. MS. 42721, f. 30.

[3] When Thomas Lingham, Sen., found that Arnold did not represent the Proprietors or the company of

D.L.Th., he offered to sell them the remainder of the lease, subject to the one granted to Arnold, for £7,500. On 6 Mar. Burgess and Charles Beazley were sent by S., Graham, and Hosier to Peter Moore's to find out if he would advance that sum. On 7 Mar. Beazley saw Hosier at 10 o'clock, and went with him to Graham's and Lingham's. Nothing came of this proposal. See Winston, 1810–11, 'Charles Beazley's Expenses'; and Folger MS. W. b. 5.

said Property as are in your hands to the above object |
R B S | T S.

To Messrs Graham Hosier and Holston
Trustees of Dy. L. T.

699. To William Taylor

Add. MS. 42721, ff. 38–39. Copy. *Dock.*: 10 March 1809 | Private
letter from Mr. Sheridan to Mr. Taylor.

[*10 Mar. 1809*]
Friday morning

Private

My dear Sir
You will receive a *formal* Letter from the Proprietors of
the late D L Theatre[1] which is sincerely meant in very good
part to you, but which is necessarily formal on account of the
circumstances under which the Proprietors are placed—
pray answer it without delay. It seems to me from what fell
from you the other night and especially from your Letter
since to Mr Graham that the Gentlemen of the Committee
have entirely miscalculated your power and means tho' not
your inclination to accommodate the company in which case
they deceive themselves, us, and the Company and as to the
Lyceum I understand they have no hold upon it whatever.
In short upon the whole I fear that an extension of your last
proposition[2] without putting you to any guarantee whatever
will be the only resource with some additional benefits
elsewhere for that class of the Company who are the real
object of our interest. The mere Servants of the Theatre are
paid up as if the fire had never happened. On this subject the
sooner we meet for half an hour at Grahams the better. | Yrs
truly | R B S.

---

[1] It was written by C. W. Ward from
Queen Street, Mayfair, on 10 Mar., and
asked Taylor to state the number of
nights on which the D.L. company
could play at his theatre. See Add.
MS. 42721, f. 36.

[2] Taylor granted the use of the King's
Theatre to D.L.Th. company for seven
nights in Mar. 1809, and was paid
£628. 2s. 0d. See D.L.Th. Receipts and
Payments. Mar. to June 1809 (Folger
MS.).

700. To George Rose[1]

Winston MS., 1808–9. Copy. *Dock.*: Mr. Sheridans | letter to Mr. |
Rose | March 27, 1809.

> Queen Street
> Mayfair
> Monday Evening
> March 27, 1809.

My dear Sir

I will not affect to apologise to you for the trouble I may
give you by requesting your attention to the inclosed letter,[2]
because I am sure both your public feeling, and some degree
of good will, which I flatter myself you bear towards me
will create an interest in your mind, sufficient to render any
such apology unnecessary.

Mr. Beazleys letter will speak for itself. I really know not
to whom I should address his application unless to yourself.
—I have written however a few lines to Mr. Wilson and
Mr. Wyatt to request them to apply to you for Instructions.

Surely Surely the day must come, in which, we shall be
ashamed to have Somerset House upon which such Sums
have been expended in its present disgraceful ruinous and
filthy State. To remedy this has always been a favourite
object of mine, and unless it can be conceived that this and
every future Government are determined to leave this unfinished Palace as a monument of National Prodigality and
Bankruptcy Mr. Beazley's offer ought in my humble opinion
(putting aside the aid it would afford us, a consideration perhaps not unworthy of attention) to be readily accepted.

I conclude with expressing my confidence that your interposition on this occasion, (as far as you can with propriety)
will be prompted and guided by the most just and liberal

---

[1] Rose (1744–1818) was S.'s successor
as Treasurer of the Navy.

[2] Charles Beazley, architect, was
placed in charge of the arrangements
for clearing the ruins of the D.L.Th.,
and he wished to discharge the rubbish
on to the vacant ground at Somerset
Place. He made many applications to
Rose before this was granted. See
Winston, 1810–11, 'Charles Beazley's
Expenses'.

sentiments | I have the honor to be | Dear Sir | with great regard | Yours sincerely | R B Sheridan

Right Honble.
George Rose.

701. To C. Beazley

Winston MS., 1810–11. *Dock.*: 27 1809 or 1810.

Monday March 27 [*1809*]

My Dear Sir

Indeed I lament to see how slowly a few stupid and apparently sullen Labourers go on at D L Theatre. The weather is invaluable and every Days inaction a loss beyond calculation. I have made a new application to Mr. Rose himself respecting the carting the rubbish to Somerset House. I have entertained a Plan for drawing it out on an Iron rail-way and then carrying it in large and low machines by men on rollers as it is all down Hill to Somerset Place. I am confident of the facility with which this might be effected. I would also open another vent for the rubbish in Drury Lane | Yours etc. | R B Sheridan

(Copy)[1]
To C. Beazley Esq.

702. To John Graham

Pub.: Thomas B. Brumbaugh, 'An Unpublished Letter of Richard Brinsley Sheridan', *The Emory University Quarterly*, iv (Atlanta, 1948), no. 1, p. 57.

Randalls
Thursday April 6th [*1809*]

Most Perfidious!

In what hole in the center of the earth have you been hid? or in what new impure fetters have you been spellbound? Never once at such a crisis to have shewn yourself at head-quarters!—everyone saying have you seen Jack Graham!

[1] All but the signature is in S.'s hand.

I tried to stop the clamour by charitably suggesting that in a fit of despair at the fate of old Drury you had probably hung yourself on one of the oaks in your new plantation, while others less partial to you did not scruple to suspect that you had set fire to the Theatre with the view of selling the timber of the said trees for its rebuilding. But I declared I did not think this likely. However you were actually on the point of being advertised as a Deserter with a reward of fourpence for your apprehension when I was fortunately enabled to assert that you had not abandoned your allegiance, Having received from you a financial plan for raising the supplies necessary for rebuilding the Theatre which in order entirely to acquit you[r] past neglect I fairly stated to be a scheme so laboriously unintelligible, so ingeniously erronious and so extensively miscalculated that I could easily conceive that a man of figures like yourself must have shut himself up Day and Night under unceasing exertion before he could have produced anything so difficult to comprehend and so impossible to execute. Pursuing this friendly line, I soon appeased them.

But if you mean really to be forgiven you must forthwith repair to headquarters, now moved to *this Place*.[1]

Seriously I wish you would come and we will talk over yours and other Plans. You will only find Parke[2] and Ward here and I shall stay till Tuesday next. S. is gone to the warm Baths. | Yours ever, | R. B. S.

703. To Samuel Whitbread

Whitbread MS. 4396. *Pub.*: Moore, ii. 370–2, from a draft.[3] *Dock.*: Mr Sheridan May 28 1809 D L Trust

May 28th. 1809

My Dear Whitbread
    Procrastination is always the consequence of an indolent

---

[1] S. had authorized Fairbrother to dispose of his furniture on 22 Mar. 1809: see *American Book Prices Current* (New York, 1939), xliv. 212.

[2] Peake?

[3] S. did not easily write this letter: see the Yale MS. draft, and cf. S.C., 1 Mar. 1955, lot 430.

man's resolving to write a long detail'd Letter upon any subject, however important to himself, or whatever may be the confidence he has in the Friend He proposes to write to. To this must be attributed your having escaped the statement, I threat'ned you with, in my last Letter; and the brevity with which I now propose to call your attention to the serious, and to me, most important request contained in this.—reserving the greater part of what I meant to have written for personal communication.

I say nothing, but what I sincerely think, when I say, that without comparison, you are the Man living, in my estimation, the most disposed and the most competent to bestow successfully a Portion of your time and ability in assisting the claim of Friendship; provided, that assistance be sought in a case just and honourable; and one, in every respect, entitled to your Protection.

On this ground I make this application to you. You said some time since in my House, tho' in a careless conversation only that you had no objection to being one of a committee to assist in a Plan for rebuilding Drury-Lane-Theatre, if it would serve me—and you kindly suggested that there were more Persons disposed to promote that object than I might be aware of. I most thankfully accept the offer of your interference; and am convinced of the benefits, your friendly exertions are capable of producing. I have work'd the whole subject in my mind; and see a clear way to retrieve a great Property, at least for my son and his Family, if my Plan meets the support I hope it will appear to merit.

Writing this to you in the sincerity of private Friendship, and with the sanguine reliance I place on my own opinion of your character, I need not ask of you, eager and active in Politics as you are, not to be severe in criticising my palpable neglect of all parliamentary Duty.[1] It would not be easy to explain to you, or to any one in prosperous and affluent plight, the private difficulties I have to struggle with. My Mind, and the resolute independence belonging to it, has not been in the least subdued by the late calamity; but the consequences arising from it, have more occupied and embarrass'd me than, perhaps, I have been willing to allow. It

[1] S. did not speak in the Commons from the night of the fire until 6 Feb. 1810.

has been a principle of my Life, persevered in thro' great difficulties, never to borrow money of a private Friend: and this resolution, whatever my embarrassments, I never shall depart from—of course, I except the political aid of Election subscription.

When I ask you to take a part in the settlement of the disorder'd and ill-managed, but by no means desperate state of my affairs, I ask you only to do so, after a previous *investigation* of the past circumstances, which relate to the Trust I wish you to accept in conjunction with others, who wish to serve me, and with whom I think you would not object to co-operate.

I may be again seized with an illness as alarming, at least so to my apprehension at the time, as that I lately experienced.[1] Assist me in relieving my mind from the greatest affliction such a situation can produce—The fear of others suffering by my Death.—

To effect this, little more is necessary than resolution on my Part, and for a short time the superintending advice of a mind like yours.

Thus far on Paper—I hope to see you next, and therefore I will not trouble you for any written reply to this. | Your's Dear Whitbread | most sincerely | R B Sheridan.

S. Whitbread Esqr.

704. To W. James

Harvard MS. *Dock.*: 2d June 1809 | Wm. Geary

2 June 1809
Randalls
Wednesday Evening

My Dear Sir
Every thing will be settled in Sir W. Geary's business

---

[1] The *Monthly Mirror*, New Ser., v (1809), 378, reported that some papers in May 1809 stated that S. was dead, and printed eulogies of him, 'written it is shrewdly suspected by himself'. He 'went down to the House the next day, to assure them that *he was not dead*, but nobody would believe him'.

before tuesday next to your satisfaction and Sir William's who has behaved in so fair and friendly a manner to me. I hear at the same time of something being to be press'd on in chancery tomorrow tho' I really do not comprehend from Burgess by whom—but I am sure it will not be at your instigation. I shall be in Town on Friday when I will immediately wait on you | yours truly | R B Sheridan

W. James Esq

705. To Thomas Perkins

Harvard MS. *Pub.*: Rae, ii. 260.

Tuesday
June 6th [*1809*]

Dear Perkins,

Tho' we have not corresponded, and [I] have been so long [a] stranger to Stafford, I assure you I have never forgot your uniform and generous attachment to me, a remembrance much enhanced by your continuance of it to my son. Your kindness to him has been such that I know you will feel almost as some return for it my informing you that the accounts of him are most favourable, and particularly from the personal observation of a Friend lately arrived from Cadiz.[1] I trust you will receive him and his excellent and lovely wife again at Ricarscourt. I hear you are becoming at Stafford all Purity and Patriotism! never fancy this attainable or men just. Among the better classes[2] of our Friends I have experienced the utmost honor and disinterestedness, but while poor and working men have votes they will '*keep the Borough free*'. | yours most sincerely | R B Sheridan

Thos. Perkins Esqr.

---

[1] Tom S. was tubercular. In March S. accompanied him to Portsmouth, where Tom was 'to embark on board the Audacious man-of-war for Cadiz' (Egerton MS. 1975, f. 164). *Staff. Adv.*, 25 Mar. 1809, stated he had sailed for Madeira, and Tom and his wife met the Hollands at Puerto de Santa Maria on 14 May. See *The Spanish Journal of Elizabeth Lady Holland* (1910), p. 332.

[2] Rae prints 'latter class'.

706. [To Samuel James Arnold][1]

Add. MS. 35118, f. 107. *Dock.*: Copy to Mr. Arnold June 16 1809

16 June 1809
Threasury
D.L. Theatre

Dear Sir

The Proprietors and Trustees are so circumstanced that they feel themselves compell'd to request as speedily as possible the final arrangement of the Terms on which they are to rent the Lyceum Theatre. To prevent Delay on this subject or giving you trouble at so busy a moment I will do myself the Pleasure of visiting you tomorrow at any hour or Place most convenient to yourself

707. To Richard Peake

McAdam MS. *Address*: Mr. Peake *Fr.*: R B S. *Dock.*: Mr. Sheridan
The cover bears a sketch of a man in contemporary dress.

[1809?]
Sunday Evening

My Dear P

Let William[2] have a £1 note or by G—— there will be no fire in this House tomorrow morning.

I will send you the Draft on Wilkie[3] in the morning—which I have settled to have discounted immediately and then you shall deduct old Scores. | Yours ever | R B S

I told Mrs. P. of Shaw's heartiness[4]—pray call in the morning.

[1] Arnold (1774–1852) was lessee of the Lyceum Theatre, at which the D.L. performers had acted from 11 Apr. till June. They reopened there on 25 Sept., under the management of Tom S., Arnold, and Greville. For the proposed terms, see Add. MS. 42721, f. 40.

[2] William Gregory, S.'s servant ?

[3] Thomas Wilkie, bookseller, of 57 Paternoster Row. His relatives J. and G. Wilkie had held the copyright of *The Rivals*, and had published *A Trip to Scarborough* as well as songs from *The Duenna*. He concluded on 4 July 1809 an agreement with S. for a new edition of S.'s works, copy to be submitted by 15 Nov. See Egerton MS. 1975, f. 57.

[4] 'Thomas Shaw's Account rendered to R.B.S.' is among the Salt MSS. and reveals that Shaw was owed £7,983 by D.L.Th. on 31 July 1808. His letters among the Harvard MSS. show that

708. [To General Thomas Graham]

N.L.S. MS. 3605, f. 182.

July 11th 1809.

My Dear General

Mr. Power The Bearer of this is a Gentleman for whom I have a particular regard. He is my Countryman of a good Family, bred in Dublin University, and possesses great Talents as a writer and a Speaker. Had any political means been open to me I should have had great Pleasure in promoting him in an official Line. At present however his spirit and ambition urge him to witness the Scenes in which you are destined to act tho' not the superior Part you merit. Mr. Power is fit to be employ'd in any way where Talents and fidelity are expected. Any countenance it may be in your Power to shew him will greatly oblige me. Health, success and Fame attend you. | Yours | faithfully | R B Sheridan

709. To Sarah Richardson

Harvard MS. *Address*: Mrs. Richardson | 12, Berner's-Street *Fr.*: R B S *Dock.*: Letter from Mr. Sheridan brought to me on Saturday Morning 22 July 1809.

28 July 1809
Friday Evening
9 o'clock.

My Dear Madam—

I always wish to make every communication to you I can. It is thro' hurry or forgetfulness when I do not. I have within this hour received the enclosed.[1] There is absurdity in much of it—but something worth attending to. N.B.

he was thoroughly disillusioned about S., but he may not have been able to withstand S.'s persuasive tongue.

[1] Possibly a letter by Elliston stating that he would act at the Lyceum only if it were opened in virtue of the D.L.Th. patent. See G. Raymond, *Memoirs of R. W. Elliston* (1844), i. 406. S.'s dilem-

ma was clearly put in *The Times*, 26 July 1809: 'The great difficulty, is whether they shall perform under the patent or under a licence. If they use the former, the vast host of Renters etc. will swallow up the whole produce . . .; if they resort to a licence they will . . . reduce the value of patents.'

Palmer[1] has certainly a share or money embark'd in C. G.
Theatre which He has always assisted and preferr'd in spite
of his Professions to me to whom he owes every thing he is
in the world— | yours truly | R B S.

Pray keep the Letter to return to me tomorrow—

710. To Sarah Richardson

Salt MS. Copy. *Dock.*: Letter of Mr. Sheridan | to Mrs. Richardson |
August 5th 1809

Saturday Night
August 5th 1809.

Dear Madam

I am very sorry to inform you that I have this day received
an answer to my application to the Lord Chamberlain which
avows his promise and purpose of licensing the Pantheon[2] as
a Theatre for Dramatic Performances. I have considered and
endeavoured to understand the plan you circulated yesterday
at the meeting.[3] I am sure a few remarks of mine would convince you of its injustice and impracticability. But I fear that
the principle asserted and acted upon by the present Lord
Chamberlain will render all discussion on such propositions
unnecessary. For I see no hope under submission to such an
act of injustice and oppression of accomplishing a successful
endeavour to rebuild the Theatre at all—

I shall call a meeting of the Renters' Committee of which
you shall have due notice. I mean to go to Windsor[4] on
Tuesday. | Yours sincerely | R B Sheridan

[1] According to the letter of 'Another of the Credulous Sufferers' in *The Times*, 17 Nov. 1809, R. Palmer and Wroughton had been dismissed in Mar. once a licence was obtained, but they had forced S. to re-engage them by a memorial to the Lord Chamberlain. Robert Palmer, actor, died in 1818.

[2] To Greville. But S. persuaded him to join in the management of the Lyceum rather than compete with the D.L. Company. See Greville's letter in the *Morn. Chron.*, 23 Jan. 1812, and Salt MSS. D 1788/I. ii/1732–3.

[3] The renters of D.L.Th. met at the Crown and Anchor on 4 Aug. S. proposed that they should accept an annuity of £12. 10s. in lieu of their present £25; and that they should accept a non-transferable admission for the lives of renter and nominee instead of present free admission. See *The Times*, 5 Aug. 1809. 'A Plan for rebuilding D.L.Th.', by Mrs. Richardson, is in Winston, 1810–11.

[4] At the meeting on 4 Aug. S. 'complained of the power assumed by the Lord Chamberlain, in licensing the

711. To Sarah Richardson

Brinsley Ford MS. *Address*: Mrs. Richardson | Berners St. | Oxford Road *Fr.*: R B Sheridan *Dock.*: Letter from Mr. Sheridan | Friday 8th September | 1809.

8 *Sept. 1809*
Friday Evening.

My Dear Madam

Tho' I applaud every Family that follows my example of early hours, I was sorry to Night to find you gone to bed so much before eleven, for as my Son and Daughter are arrived[1] at Randalls I must leave Town tomorrow as soon as it is in my Power. I am therefore compell'd to make you an ungallant request that instead of my waiting on you I may expect the Pleasure of seeing you in Queen St. before two | I am Dear Madam | yours very truly | R B Sheridan

712. To S. J. Arnold

Harvard MS. Draft. *Dock.*: Letter to Mr. Arnold. *Wm.*: 1808

[*Sept. 1809?*]
Monday
Evening

Dear Sir,

When I return'd to Town I expected to find that every thing must have been finally satisfactorily settled between you and Mr. Ward, I have been greatly surprised to learn from him to Day that new Difficulties have been suggested on your Part.

All I require of you is the fair Performance of the Pledge given by you under your hand that you would rent the

minor Theatres. . . . A Committee was appointed . . . to prepare a Petition to His Majesty on the licences granted by the Lord-Chamberlain; and which Petition Mr. Sheridan pledged himself to present to His Majesty himself, as his situation as a Privy Counsellor entitled him to require a personal interview with His Majesty' (*The Times*, 5 Aug. 1809). He had at least once before (25 Mar. 1807) presented a petition to the King, in person.

[1] The *Staff. Adv.*, 16 Sept. 1809, reported that they had arrived in England from Gibraltar, and that Tom S.'s health had considerably improved.

Lyceum to the Drury Lane Proprietors from the usual time of opening the Winter Theatres—the Terms have been since at once agreed to, and all the agreements with the Drury-Lane company have been formed in consequence and the offer of Haymarket Theatre and the Pantheon declined. You wish'd as I understood in friendly compliment to my Son to defer the signing in form 'till his return to which convinced I was dealing with a man of Honor and a Gentleman as I remain confident I am I immediately consented, but declaring my intention with your full consent and approbation to act for him in his absence as if your Proposition in your Letter to me of the 16th of June had become a signed agreement. The Performance of that is all I require. The Proprietors acquiescence in it is liberal I think on our part and I am truly sorry to observe any attempt to depart from it on your's. I need not remind you that it was on the Lord Chamberlains word that He would strictly limit the season of the Lyceum to the usual time of opening the winter Theatres and your pledging yourself to me that it should be so that I withdrew all opposition to your Licence. On the subject of our agreement Mr. Ward as well as myself can testify your avow'd recognition of it— tho' the form of signing was delay'd on account of my Son's absence at your own request. And I understand you saw most of the circular Letters we sent in consequence—which indeed we address'd to your Theatre. I shall request Mr. Ward to send you copies of your own Letters on this subject and I am very sure that the perusal of them will render it impossible that any departure from our agreement will be attempted or any difference arise between us—my Son will *certainly* be here within the week. | your's very truly | R B Sheridan

I have only to add that, should any misapprehension of our contract still remain I am ready to refer the matter to the decision of the Lord Chamberlain[1] or to any fair and honourable arbitration.

---

[1] On 22 Sept. 1809 the Lord Chamberlain granted a licence to T. B. Mash in trust for Arnold, Greville, and Tom S., for 180 theatrical performances at the Lyceum from 25 Sept. 1809. See P.R.O., L.C. 5/163, p. 296; 7/4, f. 479.

713. [To S. J. Arnold?]

Harvard MS.

Monday
September 18th. [*1809*]

Dear Sir,

Tho' it is far from my intention to interfere in the management of Drury-Lane-Theatre yet being very desirous in the present state of my Son's health to save him all the unpleasant trouble I can, I shall be happy to meet you at Drury Lane Treasury tomorrow at four, with a full admission of your Precaution of bringing a Friend with you, however unintelligible to me the motive of such a precaution is, as I understand nothing is ask'd of you but what as a man of honor and an honest man you will assuredly fulfill | R B Sheridan

714. To the Prince of Wales

Windsor MS. 41269.

[*c. 30 Sept. 1809*]

Humbly conceiving your Royal Highness not at leisure to peruse the enclosed[1] now I will have the honor [of awaiting] your commands at half-past three | your dutiful Servant | R B Sheridan

715. To Richard Peake

McAdam MS.

[*1809 ?*]
Randalls
Friday

My Dear Dick

In the first Place I am sorry for your ague—get well for

---

[1] The enclosure is Windsor MSS. 41270–1, a letter from Canning to S. dated 30 Sept. 1809 and sending a paper apparently relating the circumstances leading up to his duel with Castlereagh. Canning remarks, 'I send you the Paper according to your desire; and relying upon its being returned to me without having been shewn to any one except the Prince: as I am by no means anxious to make any general appeal to the world. . . .'

God's sake. Not a Line from Graham—if tomorrows [post] does not bring relief we are undone at Randalls. See by the enclosed[1] the state of the Garrison in Queen St.[2] pray throw in a small supply—my plan is to dine with Tom on Sunday. Mrs. S comes with me. Metcalfe dines with me again tomorrow and we are settling Surry[3] matters well. But here's a pretty Mayor of Salisbury[4] for you! I did not understand your message by Burgess but conceived that you had back a bill[5] for the one lost—it is clear we ought to get quit of him.—So pray send to Bully Raymond[6] *immediately* tell him as much as you please of the past treaty and sound if he can advance a £1000, and pay off the Mayor[7] I am quite well— yours ever R B S.

I don't quite like your receipts but I suppose Convent-Garden would go on—but if they succeed we must return to the alternate weeks.

716. To Sarah Richardson

Osborn MS. *Address*: Mrs. Richardson *Dock.*: Letter from Mr. Sheridan brought to me by Mr. Burgess on Tuesday 17th October 1809

15 Oct. 1809
Randalls
Sunday

My Dear Madam
Again I am prevented from being in Town as I promised.

[1] Not with the letter.

[2] Probably holding the house against bailiffs.

[3] Polesden. Metcalfe wrote to Whitbread on 12 May 1809 justifying his sale of the timber, and reporting a disagreement with S. over S.'s claiming 'a right to cut down any Timber for the repairs of Polesden' (Whitbread MS. 4097).

[4] Mr. Arnold Hare informs me that Thomas Wilkie was Mayor of Salisbury in 1808.

[5] Probably a reference to the £600 paid to S. by Wilkie for the copies of S.'s works. S. had agreed to give him a counter-acceptance for £600 as security.

[6] James Grant Raymond (1771 ?–1817), actor, 'had made an agreement with a bookseller to go into the trade, when the connection was broken off, by his being made acting manager of the English Opera' (*Europ. Mag.* lxxii (1817), 433–5). See p. 72, n. 2.

[7] On 5 Aug. 1816 Wilkie wrote to Mrs. S. proposing an edition of S.'s works and enclosing a copy of the earlier agreement (W.T.). When Murray published the *Works* in 1821, Wilkie was paid £300 'for his share'. See *The Plays and Poems of . . . Sheridan* (ed. Rhodes, 1928), i. xvi.

Mr. Burgess will explain to you how. But on tuesday nothing will prevent my coming to my Son's to dinner—and I will have the Pleasure of calling on you the next morning. I assure you I have not been idle on the Opera.[1] | yours | R B S

717. [To the Editor of the *Morning Chronicle*]

Egerton MS. 1975, f. 129. Draft. *Pub.*: *Morn. Chron.*, 20 Oct. 1809.[2]

20 Oct. 1809
New Grand Imperial incombustable Theatre

Whereas an Advertisement has appear'd announcing a new *national subscription Theatre* the Prospectus whereof is promised in a few Days it is deem'd an attention due to the Public to remind them, without meaning the slightest disrespect to a Mr. Fry[3] the subscribers Solicitor to this supposed speculation, of the palpable Delusion which must belong to the scheme inasmuch as when it first started with the assertion that a great sum had been already subscribed at Lloyd's it immediately appear'd that not a single Merchant or Banker had ever subscribed a single shilling or even heard one word on the subject. But Gentlemen we who now address the Public proceed upon a Principle of a very different character. We are ready to admit that any attempt to defeat or counteract the endeavours said to be earnestly pursuing to re-erect Old Drury and to satisfy in the most just and liberal manner practicable the various and weighty claims of Those who have embark'd their Property on the faith of the Patents would be felt and resented by the Public at large as a base unfeeling and fraudulent endeavour to take advantage of the temporary destruction by the

[1] Mrs. Richardson wrote two tragedies, *Ethelred* and *Gertrude*, but there is no record of an opera by her. Possibly she had urged S. to repair his fortunes by completing *The Foresters* or some other work long expected from him.

[2] Also printed in *Morn. Post*, 20 Oct. 1809, signed 'Gregory Gull'; and reprinted in *Morn. Chron.*, 21 Oct. 1809, with its errors corrected.

[3] Henry Fry, of Critchley and Fry, attorneys, 14 John Street, gave notice in *Morn. Post*, 7 Oct. 1809, that application would be made in the next session of Parliament to bring in a bill to erect a National Subscription Theatre.

calamity of Fire of a great concern, every way entitled to the peculiar Protection of the Public Patronage.—The Persons engaged therefore in the present speculation namely the erection of a new *grand Imperial* and *incombustible Theatre* scorn to attempt to filch any countenance to their Proposition from the momentary present Ferment created by the resistance to the new Prices at Covent-Garden Theatre. They equally scorn to shrink from the admission that if Old Drury can be rebuilt, and that the Report be also true that should there appear a *real* call for a third Theatre, the Dormant Patents belonging to the proprietors of old Drury will be also brought into action to fulfil the Public wish in that respect it would ill become them as Gentlemen and Honest men to persevere a moment longer in their Plan. Should the event however turn out otherwise we are prepared to enter the Lists of competition with Mr. Fry, and are convinced that the discerning Public will even now decree the Palm of superior sincerity to us when we frankly declare, which Mr. Fry and Co. have forborn to do—that the address is by the express order of an ideal committee selected from the general body of non-existing subscribers.— | (Signed) Gregory Grill | First Clerk to Messrs Hum and Hoax | solicitors—No. O[1] Labour in Vain Hill Lower Thames St

N.B. Mr. Grill having great doubts of the actual existence of such a Person as Mr. Fry[2] conceives that he is acting in the fairest manner by thus avowing his own name and those of his respected employers.—

N.B. Such Noblemen and Gentlemen as are desirous of supporting the undertaking, by becoming subscribers, will please to send their names to Messrs. Hum and Hoax, or to any banking-house in London, not receiving subscriptions for the plan of Mr. Fry: in suggesting which restriction

---

[1] The printed versions read '1809'.
[2] Fry replied to this letter, in the *Morn. Post*, 25 Oct. 1809; and when Peake took up the case in the *Morn. Post*, 6 Nov. 1809, Fry's further answer appeared in the same newspaper on 10 Nov. His strongest argument was that if three patents had been granted, surely three theatres had been intended.

Mr. Grill is confident that he does not exclude a single banker in the metropolis.[1]

718. To William Powell

Egerton MS. 1975, f. 21.

Nov. 1809

Mr. Powell deliver the M:S: of the School for Scandal to Mr. Raymond[2]

Novr. 1809

719. To Richard Peake

McAdam MS. *Address*: Mr. Peake *Wm.*: 1808

[*1809–10*]
Randalls
Sunday Night

My Dear Dick—

I have put my name on a Paper you have sent me but I do not understand a word of the meaning of it or a syllable of the Purport of your note—I am sincerely sorry for the illness of your Family—| ever yours most sincerely | R B Sheridan.

I cannot understand a word Fairbrother tells me—or how the devil my signature and Mrs. Richardsons can be necessary to what we have nothing to do with—the accounts being in Arnolds name and not in ours. Mrs. Richardson had never anything to do with my certificates[3]

---

[1] This paragraph is not in the draft but is in the printed versions.

[2] This appears at the foot of an agreement between S. and James Grant Raymond, by which S. sold the whole of his 'Dramatic and Poetical Works' and a general preface to Raymond for £200 in cash on the day when the works were delivered, and various later benefits. The works were never published by Raymond.

[3] Certifying payments: see D.L.Th. Receipts and Payments, 1804 to 1805 (Folger MS.), where there are regular notes reading 'Cash by Certificates brought forward'.

720. To Richard Peake

Harvard MS. *Address*: Mr. Peake | Charlotte-St. | Rathbone-Place |
to be delivered before 9 *Fr.*: R B Sheridan *Dock.*: Mr. Sheridan

[1809–10]
Sunday

My Dear P.

I was in hopes to have seen you this morning as you
promised and did not go out till near one. Pray be punctual
in our appointments or nothing will go right. I thank you
for not deducting from the £50 for every Pound is at this
moment a mint to me.

Send me by Bearer a List of the subscribers to Richardson's
Debentures—marking those who have given them up to
her.[1] I have a Letter from her in which she reprobates your
Letter to the Performers whose Petition she thinks quite
reasonable and moderate[2]—was there ever such an infernal
B.! Send me all of the Balance, you can in the morning and
send a summons to Mrs. R. for three on monday this evening.

Now mind on *no account* fail to pay *Whitehead*[3] fifteen
Pounds on account. Take it from any one's £25 subscription.
It is of the greatest consequence that this should be done
punctually and directly. I have seen Beazley who wants no
money at present | Your's ever | R B S.

721. To ——

Osborn MS. *Dock.*: Feb. 14. 1810

14 Feb. 1810
Queen-St
Wednesday

Sir

I am extremely surprised to receive such a Letter as I have

[1] John, Duke of Bedford, Hugh,
Duke of Northumberland, William,
Duke of Devonshire, and Sackville,
Earl of Thanet, together held twelve
debentures of £500 each. After the fire
of 1809, they made them over to Mrs.
Richardson and her four daughters. See
the 'Assignment of Twelve Debentures
... 1 June 1813' (New York Public
Library MS.).

[2] But she petitioned the King on
8 May 1810, opposing the company's
proposals for a third theatre.

[3] One William Whitehead was owed
an unspecified sum by D.L.Th. in 1801
for 'brick work under the stage': see the
Gilmore MS. 'Abstract of Work done
... 22 Dec. 1801'.

from you if written by your Fathers direction. He very well knows that I have been exerting myself to the utmost of my Power for him, tho' I cannot controul others. I have even offer'd to pay him out of my own pocket what he claims from the Theatre. I am very sorry to hear he is ill, and shall be glad to see you here at 12—tomorrow. | Yours | R B Sheridan

722. To Richard Peake

Harvard MS. *Address*: Mr. Peake | to be taken to him | wherever he is *Fr.*: R B S *Wm.*: 1805

[*20 Mar. 1810 ?*]
Tuesday

My Dear P.
I shall be at home here the whole Day, and in the course of it I *must see you* or *Tom will be crush'd* | Yours ever | R B S

Bring the Star of yesterday with you and some Letter-paper[1]

723. To His Wife

Harrow MS.: Rae, vi. 276. *Pub.*: Rae, ii. 275–6. *Address*: London March twenty eight | Mrs. Sheridan | H B Ogles | Knoyle | Shaftesbury *Fr.*: R B Sheridan

28 *Mar.* [*1810*]
Wednesday
House of Commons

My Dear Hecca
I have but one moment to tell you in one word the good news that the Council[2] have unanimously decided in our

[1] The application of the Lord Mayor of London and his supporters to erect a third patent winter theatre in London was considered by the Privy Council between 16 and 26 Mar. 1810. S. strenuously opposed the application but stated at the meeting on 19 Mar. that he had drawn up his petition (presented on 16 Mar.) in a considerable hurry and now asked for a few days' delay 'in order to lay some papers before them,

which he thought would prove that the patents did give monopoly'. This point had been argued by Randle Jackson (for the D.L. Trustees) on 19 Mar., and a very full account of his speech had appeared in *The Star* of that date. I assume that S. wished to use this account for his submissions on 26 Mar.

[2] The Privy Council, at its meeting on 26 Mar., read S.'s second petition and heard further submissions from

Favor on the Patent right Question and now I shall get my affairs right and you shall never know a plague again—otherwise irretrievable ruin must have been the consequence to me and poor Tom and his Family—it was going against us till I spoke on monday, and is decided entirely on the ground I put the Question on. I spoke for nearly two hours. I was 5 hours in the council and eleven in the House of Commons. I hope you got no cold in the open carriage.
Bless you—and I ever

I am going to make a motion in the House[1]

724. To His Wife

Harrow MS.: Rae, vi. 444.

[*16 Apr. 1810*]

Thanks for your caution! I make no secret of my opinion of Burdett,—I give it roundly in conversation, but as it [is] inexpedient to enlarge the gulf which the opposition has made between itself and the people, I have abstained from saying publicly (I mean, in the House of Commons) that which I feel upon the subject.—I rather agree with him, as to the primitive, constitutional question, but His cruelty and total indifference to the fate of an innocent mob, enthusiastic in his cause[2]—It was barbarous. At this moment six beautiful Regiments of Cavalry are under review in Hyde Park,[3]—This, I suppose, on the part of the Royal Princes,

him. The application for a charter for a third theatre was refused. See *The Star*, 28 and 31 Mar. 1810; and the *Monthly Mirror*, New Ser., vii (1810), 158–9, 315–19, 397–400.

[1] In the debate on whether Burdett had committed breach of privilege in printing his letter in *Cobbett's Weekly Register* of 24 Mar. S. argued that the question was most important and that it ought to be referred to the Committee of Privileges. See Hansard, 1st Ser., xvi. 257–60.

[2] In his letter to the *Weekly Register* of 24 Mar., Burdett deliberately chal-

lenged the right of the Commons to imprison John Gale Jones for the contemptuous nature of a subject discussed at the British Forum. The Commons ordered Burdett's arrest but it was not effected without riots and bloodshed. Soldiers charged the mob on 9 Apr.

[3] 'Yesterday morning, at half-past eight, all the cavalry in and near London, together with a large body of horse artillery, assembled in Hyde Park, on the horse rides leading to Kensington, where they passed in review before the Commander in Chief. The Prince of Wales and all the Royal Dukes were

to give evidence of their military power, Damn them!—The forbearance of the soldiers was exemplary, and quite affecting—Men who have fought, and valiantly fought in Spain, (at Corunna) submitted to have mud thrown in their faces, and patiently endured that the hands that had thrown it, should be wiped upon their cloaths—This must have required more of their manliness than to charge all the hosts of Buonaparte.[1]

Hitherto I have not written to Tal[l] or H. Scott, upon my soul I have been so busied[2] that I have not known which way to turn myself—besides which, I so much dislike writing any thing which may give pain to H. Scott, that I can hardly bring myself to tell him that His hopes, in the Quarter of the Chancellor,[3] seem desperate. Silly thing that you are, going to Law with S. will never do.[4]—Arrangement and conciliation, supported by decisio[n] can alone effect your purpose.

God Bless You!

725. To Richard Peake

McAdam MS. *Address*: Mr. Peake *Fr.*: R B S *Dock.*: Mr. Sheridan | about Petition. *Wm.*: 1807

[17 Apr. 1810 ?]
Tuesday morning

My Dear P.

It is too early for my Papers to be in so I don't know whether the Petition[5] is in others or not—if not money or credit must be had it is of *vital* consequence. Tell Lownds

present. The whole body amounted to about 7000 men.' (*The Times*, 17 Apr. 1810.)
[1] S. has reverted to the events of 9 April.
[2] Over the D.L.Th. petition to the King. See p. 65, n. 4.
[3] S. had appointed Scott Paymaster of the Navy in 1806. Presumably Scott sought some office in the gift of the Lord Chancellor. After S.'s death and as a gesture to S.'s memory, Castlereagh offered Scott the consulship of Bahia.

See Rae, ii. 293, n. 1.
[4] Concerning a separation ? See p. 85.
[5] 'The Petition to the King of the Proprietors of the late Theatre Royal, Drury Lane' appeared in some newspapers on 16 Apr. 1810. It ran over the history of the building, then put the argument that while the drama might benefit from the destruction of the monopoly, the petitioners ought to retain their rights or be compensated for the loss of them. See the *Monthly Mirror*, New Ser., vii (1810), 399–400.

immediately to let me have a proof of the Petition[1] done in a handsome way. If you do not call in the morning pray don't fail to meet me at Peter Moores[2] at half past three— we had better eat our chop together again to Day there is much to be done. You must positively bring with you the enclosed. And it must be proceeded on *immediately* give me my remaining £5 you are well off to get £10 out of the £35 so don't teaze me about twopences just at this moment.— | Your's ever | R B S

I am infinitely better this morning

726. To His Wife

Brinsley Sheridan MS.

Richmond.
April 20th: 1810.

My dear Hester
    I have many Days since burnt a Letter written soon after I received your Propositions in which I express'd more strongly the sentiments and feelings of my Heart upon your conduct than upon reflexion I wish to do or perhaps than I think I ought. Nothing shall ever induce me to utter an unkind or even an expostulatory expression towards you. I ask your Pardon for every embarrassment and distress you have suffer'd in respect to the matters[3] your Letter refers to, and I complain not in the least either of the Purpose or style of that Letter. No[4] one can be in the smaller affairs of the world of a more negligent forgetful and procrastinating habit of mind than I am, united at the same time with a most unfortunately sanguine temper, and a rash confidence that I am capable of exertions equal to any difficulty whenever

---

[1] A copy, printed by Lowndes and Hobbs, is in Winston, 1810–11.

[2] *The Times*, 19 Apr. 1810, states that Moore presented a petition in the Commons (from S. and others) for leave to raise funds to rebuild D.L.Th. This was referred to a committee. Hansard, 1st Ser., xvi. 758, gives the date of the petitioning as 1 May.

[3] Probably concerning lack of money. She refers to this in a letter to the Prince of 1806–7 (Windsor MSS. 42329–30), and in two undated letters (Yale MSS.) begs Peake for money to pay her washerwoman. Cf. also Add. MS. 35118, ff. 169–73.

[4] Rae, ii. 217, quotes at this point from the letter and gives further extracts.

extremity may call for them. To this Frame and Temper
of mind you may trace the ground of every thing you complain of, and not one atom of it to intentional neglect or
indifference to your Comfort and Happiness. Stating this
I cannot avoid making one observation in passing. I cannot
conceive on earth anything more odious than a man's
enjoying comforts and ease himself yet perceiving those he
professes to love or who are dependent on him not sharing
them—on this I have only in one word to say that however
strongly you paint the distresses and mortifications you have
experienced, I am sure you will admit that even, allowing
for the great difference between man and woman, they
cannot be compared with the Privations and vexations which
I have been obliged to submit to, and have submitted to
with more Pleasure when, as *has* happen'd, the result
produced some accommodation to you and upon perhaps
no very important exigency.

I have said before that you do not know me—in truth
you do not in the least—you should judge of my conduct
character and principles upon a larger scale of observation
and not from the defects of daily Life which arise from
the Failings I acknowledge. There is no indelicacy now in
recurring and referring to my conduct in respect to you
before our marriage on the subject of this vile money.—
There was a deliberate and considerate act to be done,
unlike the scrambling duties of an ill-supplied Housekeeper,
and did I then shew an '*entire neglect*' of your future comfort
in the case of my death, being so much older than you? or
an 'indifference to your being able to maintain the independence of a Gentlewoman'?—at that period I was
entitled to consider myself as a Person of very considerable
accruing Property, and so must have been the case or a man
of Honor and correctness like Sir Arthor Pigott would not
after a full investigation of my affairs have reported such
to have been the condition of my affairs to the Dean your
Father, my rashness or madness rather in afterwards
plunging unnecessarily into all the enormous mass of the
Theatre Debt is not to the present Question, but what is
to the present question is that every thing that I could
justly realize or fairly anticipate as my own previous to

that act of insanity I did with the most heartfelt satisfaction devote to *you*. In the course of this arrangement your Father thought it too much that I should bind myself that the Stock should afford me no aid or interest untill it had accumulated £40,000 as I had from the first proposed and accordingly before the settlements were completed He wished to decline this condition as unreasonable, and He wrote to me to this effect, which Letter I have now. I however insisted on abiding by my first Proposition.[1] There was no selfish neglect of you in this at least. Did I in that transaction employ any Law Person on my Part,—no one—and did I not suggest the two Trustees whom I thought your Father and Family would have chosen? there was no neglect of you or care of myself in this. Don't conceive I am mentioning these things as matters to boast of I only state them as a sample of the real kind of instances by which you ought to judge of my deliberate attention or inattention to you, instead of forming a violent opinion upon minor specimens of carelessness, which however I acknowledge carry with them much provocation, and proceed from very vexatious and indolent Habits, but more than all from my own inveterate indifference about what the world calls comforts, and much more its luxuries. This certainly may have led me not to feel so quickly on these subjects for others as I might have done, I wish therefore I had had in my character the admonition of a different Turn, or that we had some proper Person to manage and take care of smaller affairs for us. For after all the Bills do get paid and most of the embarrassments come out to have been unnecessary. All I know is that I never had anything that belong'd to the lesser gratifications or enjoyments of Life that I would not rather have given it up to another than have kept it to my own use, how more than gladly have given it up if that other were *you* I need not say.—

In the same spirit and with the same view with which I have written the above I refer to an other instance by which to judge of me and which relates to Tom. I have all my Life kept free from personal obligation on my own account beyond perhaps any case that has existed under

---

[1] The preceding two sentences are quoted by Sichel, i. 44, n. 4.

the circumstances in which I have struggled thro the world. Yet for the sake of Tom and to gratify his ambition and in the hope of finding him serviceable and creditable occupation I have incurr'd the obligation of the expenditure of not less than eight thousand Pounds on the Part of the Prince in his three attempts to bring Tom into Parliament,[1] I who for myself more than once peremptorily refused the offer even of a modest Loan from Him when I have been in the greatest distress. Of the Princes expenditure for him Tom possesses the account under the Hand of Colonel McMahon. On this subject I must add that my taking up that Bond of Tom's to Carpenter[2] for £1,600 (and how acceptable a present that cancell'd Bond was to Tom when it greeted his last return to England you must remember) deprived me of no inconsiderable personal Resource—while in addition I was obliged to charge my Duchy income, the only source I have at present left to live on, with £60 per annum on the same account. But independent of the Relief I brought to Tom by this effort I had the great satisfaction of taking a heavy load from Peake's mind who had in the most kind and friendly manner join'd in the Bond to Carpenter[3] for Tom's sake and upon whom in the case of anything happening to Tom the Demand would have instantly and unsparingly fallen to the near if not entire ruin of himself wife and seven children. In addition to this I took on myself another Debt of Tom's to the amount of above £500 for which I gave my Bond, while He was abroad the first time,[4] and the settling part Payment of this Bond has since Christmas brought more difficulty on me than I almost ever experienced from any pecuniary embarrassment in the course of my life. This Debt was incurr'd

[1] Apart from his candidature at Stafford in autumn 1806, Tom S. stood for Liskeard in 1802 and 1804. His failure and subsequent petitions are described by G. S. Veitch, 'William Huskisson and the Controverted Elections at Liskeard in 1802 and 1804', *Trans. of the Royal Hist. Society*, 4th Ser., xiii (1930), 205–28.

[2] On 8 Sept. 1809 S. appointed Charles Carpenter of Moditonham,

Deputy to the Receiver-General of the Duchy of Cornwall as Weigher and Prizer of Tin. See Rhodes, p. 261.

[3] On 6 Feb. 1808 S. agreed to pay Charles Carpenter £500, and to give fresh security for the remainder of Tom S.'s debt. He was helped in this by Peake and Graham who were to be repaid over two years by instalments. See Add. MS. 35118, f. 103.

[4] Summer 1809?

by an attempt of Tom's to raise money on bills accepted by Colonel Ogle thro' one Felix McCarthy.[1] Tom was of course cheated out of the money, and he left orders with Burgess to remit the Payment. I took the Demand on myself the night before the Trial was to come on in the Kings Bench,[2] where tho' Tom might have proved He had been made a fool of, I think He had no remedy, and He certainly would have exposed *himself* as well as them, and also Lord Moira's name would have been introduced in an unpleasant way—I rather think Harry Scott knows the whole of this Transaction—for my Part I knew nothing about it 'till officiously and I must add foolishly I took for Tom's credit's sake, the Debt on myself, the Result being that Tom instead of being in the least thankful to me, express'd great indignation to Burgess for allowing the cause to be stopt, tho' He certainly could not have exposed his adversaries without at least an equal exposure of himself, and those with whose alliance he had been acting.—

I bring only one more instance of the *kind of Criterion* by which my conduct ought to be judged—you have remark'd and complain'd that even while I had the assistance of an official income while in Somerset Place, Household matters were equally irregular. To this I answer that not reflecting how brief might be my possession of that situation I did from a principle of honourable Pride take on myself a great Payment to the new renters against the advice of Those even who were to profit by my rashness, and altho' there was no claim on me for a shilling of the money nor the slightest discredit attaching to my leaving the Debt where the Chancellor had placed it with the consent of the Renters themselves, I paid to them the sum of £5,600 from my own means and resources[3] (£2,000 of it coming from my salary). The doing which with the

[1] 'A needy Irish adventurer, but a man of infinite wit,—at the same time destitute of all principle and honour. Still he was received at the table of his Royal Highness, to whom he was introduced by Lord Moira . . .' (Robert Huish, *Memoirs of George the Fourth* (1831), i. 303). McCarthy supported S. on the Westminster hustings of 20–21 May 1807: see *The Times*, 21–22 May 1807.

[2] Possibly 'Ogle' should read 'Ogilvie' for there is extant (Add. MS. 42720, f. 127) a bill from Henry Burgess for £45. 8s. 7d., incurred in the Michaelmas term of 48 Geo. III, in the cause 'Sheridan als Ogilvie'.

[3] Quoted by Sichel, i. 45, n. 2.

expence and loss incurr'd during my short holding the office, left me certainly more than £7,000 poorer than if I had never accepted it. For Brevity sake I send you some vouchers on this subject—which may perhaps put these matters in a clearer point of view than my statements do—

Now as to Polesden were I to calculate the average of my annual loss since Edmonds[1] has had the management of it at £400, I should be very much under the fact, and tho' I have made good Purchases which have greatly encreased the value of the estate, as Charles I trust will one day experience, yet thro' the Blunder or worse of Dunn your Trustees Solicitor these efforts on my Part have occasion'd in their Progress a *Loss* to me of certainly not less than 7 or £8,000.

I have thought it right and necessary to state these preliminary matters and I trust you will not mistake my motives for doing so. And now tho' I come to what might appear the more material matter in discussion between us—I shall be very short indeed both because the subject is a most ungracious one, and because it Turns on Questions of Fact which admit of being very briefly stated.—Your whole conditions and proposed arrangement are founded on the assumption of my Duchy Income clearing to me £1,500 per Annum. I have no such income, The total annual salary or Profit I receive from it do[es] not exceed £940 as the accompanying vouchers will show you[2]—and this is every shilling of income on earth I have *at present* to live upon. Add to this the £200 pin money paid you and the whole will amount to an income of £1,140 independent of the annual £100 or near it left exclusively to you by the Dean. If from this you take £500 to be paid weekly £200 Pin money and £250 for a carriage which you certainly shall have there will remain only £200 for every other expense,— House Rent, Charles's schooling or to get me even shoes to my Feet which God knows I have often wanted! I am willing to give up for the Present having a servant to

---

[1] George Edwards?

[2] The amounts derived from poundage varied from £125 a year to £2,180, but the Duchy of Cornwall office calculated that S.'s income should have averaged in all about £1,402 a year. See Rhodes, pp. 259–60.

myself tho' without dissembling the hardship it will be to me, At my Time of Day, and helpless as I am in this respect, from having been used to have one for nearly forty years. Other *personal* expenses I have none to sacrifice. What I can and will do is this. Your Pin money and annuity shall be entirely relieved and discharged from all claim upon them or any other application of this amount to your own private and personal Purposes.

Your Debts being fully stated and brought together shall be undertaken to be settled by Mr. P. Moore, so that you shall remain subject to no further application on the subject. Should you find yourself fairly enabled to allot any Part of the annuity to help this Object just at present it might be as well.

Mr. P. Moore will engage to pay Mr. Gabell[1] for the full and punctual payment of every expence attending Charles's Education at Winchester—so that nothing on this head can remain to be contributed by you. Mr. Moore either has or will immediately write to Mr. Gabell in this respect.

Mr. P. Moore is already indemnified by me for the rent of our House in Town, and being relieved from Randalls which is all paid for, He will undertake for the carriage.

House-rent Coals Candles Wine Beer Servants wages etc. being amply provided for, Mr. Peake will undertake to pay you five guineas every monday towards Housekeeping in which you need consider only yourself, and you shall have from me £100 bank note in case of exigency but which I trust there never will be occasion to break in upon.

This is what I can do even at present and punctually effect—and you must allow me to be confident that you cannot mean to insult and mock me by requiring impossibilities, or conditions which nothing but your error as to my income could have induced you to propose.

If you ask how from the slender means I *now* possess I can undertake to effect what I have above offer'd—I answer that to satisfy you and to meet as far as I can your wishes I

---

[1] Henry Dison Gabell (1764–1831), Headmaster of Winchester from 1810 to 1823. Mr. John H. Harvey informs me that Charles Sheridan entered the Upper Fifth there in 1810.

have broke thro' the rule of my Life which has formed its Pride also, and have, with a broken spirit stoop'd for the first time to solicit and accept the pecuniary assistance of private Friendship. If you ask on what are my hopes founded that my affairs in future will be improved—I answer that I shall next year be restored to my Theatre income[1] which during 8 months brought me 30 guineas a week,[2] that the arrangements at length making respecting Polesden and the estates purchased by me now under the Direction of Mr. Metcalfe who is fully sensible of the injuries I have sustain'd will yield me a Life assistance of £1,000 more— and I have satisfactory reason to hope that my Duchy income may be increased 3 or £400 more[3]—in addition to this the settlement I am making in Parting with the Theatre,[4] after doing every thing in my Power for Tom and tho' conditioning nothing for myself must at least make my income up £4000 after all Debts paid. And when this shall be the case I shall be able to do more than you require.

I shall have done much if I have obtain'd your dispassionate attention thus far—and now I shall hasten to conclude—you compliment me on my manners, and thank me for my uniform kindness to your Family, especially to Anne—were anything, in the malice of Fortune, to happen to Harry, an event however wholly unlikely, I assure you I could readily walk bare foot to the House of Commons rather than a child of Anne's should want a clasp to its shoe. I say this not to value myself on my Friendship for Anne, but to lead you to conclude, if you believe me sincere, how much stronger must my regard have been for you, Anne's attachment to you having been always with me a main motive to my affection for her. I never in my Life used an expression of kindness towards you by word or writing that went beyond the Truth of what I felt at the time, and

[1] A vain hope.
[2] His income had been five guineas an acting night, totalling twenty-five or thirty guineas a week.
[3] The salary was increased by £100 in 1811. The poundage reached its highest figure in 1809–10. See Rhodes, p. 260.
[4] As early as 12 June 1809 C. W.

Ward had written to Tom S. to say that there was a general feeling that S. 'should retire altogether from the concern'. At first S. refused to consider this, but in talking it over with Whitbread he began to anticipate his affairs settled, a comfortable provision for himself, and 'a secure property for you and the children' (Winston, 1808–9).

in speaking of you I never spoke a syllable but in your warmest praise. How different your conduct in this respect towards me has been I have often regretted but never resented. Some causes of Depression or irritation in your mind, in no degree depending on me, I pass wholly by, This Letter not being probably to be confined to your own Perusal, and I having been long since excluded from any knowledge of the extent of your confidences. All I am sure of is that it will be the best joy of my Life, whatever you may have mistakenly ascribed to my seeming negligence, to see you chearful and in health.

I have mention'd, as I trust I shall always be entitled to do, my confidence in Harry's health, and the Strength of his constitution, but there is another Person respecting whom however painful the sensation it would be folly to endeavour to deceive myself and disguise my apprehensions. I have an ill opinion of Tom's recovery[1] notwithstanding what He may write to Caroline. You will see *then* the Charge that must fall on me—for what has been done for him by a few private Friends[2] would not pay his just Debts. As for my own Life, tho' I feel neither dismay'd nor dispirited at this moment of Time and of exertion on my Part, I can safely swear that I never pass a Day or an hour almost without having present to my mind the probability of one's last hour being nearer than the accomplishment of the most immediate object of our hope and pursuit. That disorder which I have lately had some return of and from which I have been more than once in greater Danger than you have imagined may at any time return and quickly end me—the same may occur from the condition of my veins—for no operation for Life's sake will I ever undergo. Thus circumstanced when you say, as you have in a subsequent Letter—that you are ready to separate if I think it for *my happiness* I plainly answer that such an act would be follow'd on my Part by my instantly taking my Boy with me to some corner of the earth and be no more heard of till my Death should

---

[1] 'Mr. T. Sheridan is returned from Sicily; but, we are sorry to add, not much benefited in health by his foreign excursions' (*The Times*, 20 July 1810).
[2] After the fire the Duke of Argyll organized a subscription for Tom S. The Prince of Wales gave £1,000, and the Dukes of Bedford and Devonshire £500 each.

be by him announced to you, after I should think no very protracted Period, and you should find yourself at least relieved from the embarrassments which had caused our separation. To the Performance of this Determination I add no oaths or protestations, but it is what I should do. With my esteem and affection for you extinguish'd, I should have no motive to commit the mean[n]ess of remaining in an u[n]grateful world an object either of insulting Pity or of by me unmerited condemnation. How you could for a moment bring yourself to look calmly on such a situation has I confess amazed me—can you hold lightly the becoming the Topic of discussion to a deriding malicious and unsparing society all of whom would find their amusement and many their gratification in such an event—do you believe that there is a Human creature out of your own Family who would believe, or at least *admit*, that you had deserted me on account of my Poverty or domestic Distresses however exaggerated or however really afflicting—and can the Pain and disadvantages which such Family schisms always bring on Children never have occurr'd to you as to the manner in which they might operate on a mind so gentle and temper so sensible as Charles's? Should this Question ever again be entertain'd by you, overlook my Feelings and happiness if you will, but do not put aside these considerations

I could say more but were I to pour out all that is in my mind I should never close. I repeat again that you do not know me, nor can you be fairly apprized of the real tests and trials which in my former Life, would more than any observations you have had the means of making have explain'd to you my character. Tho' deeply regretting every moment of uneasiness I may have caused you and again requesting your Pardon in that respect I yet preserve my own self esteem—and hold it beyond all Price or Purchase, nor would I exchange the recollection of acts of kindness gentleness and benevolence which without ostentation I have in my Life done, tho accompanied with all my carelessnesses, for the more imposing character which others may have acquired by more prudent and punctual Habits than I have had the good fortune to cultivate. And sure I am that there is no Person who has been near to me and confidentially acquainted with my private affairs and personal difficulties and who has witness'd my conduct under them that has not been confirmed or improved in principle and integrity in his views and transactions in this Life. You will forgive my having said thus much of myself—it may be egotism but it is Fact.

I ought not to have omitted to mention that whatever have been my embarrassments or however curtail'd my resources I have avoided contracting new Debts—it would be cruel indeed were I compell'd to do so, my former ones are generally speaking all secured as far as I am personally concerned under the Chancellors order and the present one will not be of the Description I dread. But were I personally to involve myself again, and I could obtain no seat in Parliament (a thing infinitely probable) what would become of me? you would be sorry to see me dying in a Jail.

I have only to add, tho' undoubtedly unnecessarily, that the vouchers accompanying this are of course given without an idea to whom they are referr'd, and that it is my earnest wish that your Brother without betraying this may by personal enquiry ascertain the accuracy of the Facts stated.

And now God bless you and as I trust you will have pardoned whatever you have thought amiss in my conduct so do I from my soul forgive you. | Your affectionate | Husband | R B Sheridan

727. To His Wife

Pub.: Rae, ii. 209.

[*1810?*]

. . . You may be assured that if I cannot always immediately meet your wishes in money matters, it is because it is absolutely out of my power, and never from the slightest consideration of myself, or from my ever being disposed to pay anything in preference to any one claim in which you are concerned. The delight of my life is to see you cheerful and without care, and in future we shall have no money anxieties let what will give way; but to follow up my present plan effectually we must be as careful as ants . . . I employed Tom's man to collect for me the bills at Richmond; the amount is frightful, more than four times what I expected, for since the short time we had it, I had twice cleared them off.

728. To Richard Peake

Harvard MS. *Address*: Mr. Peake *Dock.*: Mr Sheridan *Fr.*: R B S *Wm.*: 1804

[*1810* ?]
Theatre
near 5

Dear Peake
I sent all you sent me to Mrs. Sheridan so am penniless again—a supply by Bearer. I wish I had seen you to Day— I have had my own way at last with the committee. Burgess is gone to make my excuse to P Moores—for I am too ill to dine there. He comes back to eat some broth here with me.—I wish you could step down but I shall be gone by 7. | Yours ever | R B S

729. To the Lord Chamberlain, the Earl of Dartmouth

Salt MS. D 1778/iii/489. *Pub.*: H.M.C., *MSS. of the Earl of Dartmouth* (1896), iii. 293.

Tuesday 5 o'clock
May 1, 1810.

My dear Lord
A copy of the Performers Petition[1] having been refused by them to the proprietors I have but this moment received through Mr. Arnold a copy of the same, coming I believe tho' not officially from your Lordship's office. I cannot sufficiently express my astonishment at the contents of this extraordinary Performance which is from the first word of

---

[1] On 27 Apr. the proprietors informed the D.L. company that it would act under the old patent. The company then refused to put itself under the authority of S., Arnold, or Greville, and petitioned the King (on 9 May) to grant it a licence to perform until a new D.L.Th. was erected. See Add. MS. 35118, f. 110; *The Times*, 14 May 1810; *Monthly Mirror*, N.S., vii (1810), 474.

it to the last as devoid of Truth as it is of gratitude and justice. The parties signing having thus most unfairly concealed both the wording and object of their Petition, in order that it might be delivered to his Majesty before their Employers could have an opportunity of exposing their fallacious statements. I do most earnestly, on Behalf of the Proprietors, the Drury Lane Trustees, the Renters and all the other just claimants on the destroy'd Property appeal to your Lordships candour and Justice to allow them a few Days to state their case in order that a paper so injurious and unfounded may be accompanied at the time it is submitted to his Majesty, by a full refutation of all its contents, a statement which will on our Part be dictated under at least as respectful and dutiful a deference to his Majesty's gracious Pleasure as can have influenced the Subscribers to the Petition in Question. | I have the honor to be | My Lord | with great respect and esteem | your lordships faithful Servant: | R B Sheridan

Earl of Dartmouth

730. To the Editor of the *Morning Chronicle*

Pub.: *Morn. Chron.*, 16 May 1810.

15 May 1810

Sir,

A Copy of a Petition to His Majesty, purporting to be signed by a certain number of the Performers[1] at the Lyceum Theatre, forming lately a part of the Company of the destroyed Theatre Royal, Drury lane, having appeared in your Paper of yesterday, you are hereby requested and authorized to assert that an authenticated statement of facts, respecting the same, will forthwith be sent to your paper, after application made to the Lord Chamberlain for permission to publish the documents and petitions trans-

[1] Presented at the levee of 9 May, and signed by John Braham and thirty-one other performers. The passage that S. objected to was probably the following: '. . . [considering] the heavy debt of many thousand pounds now due to performers; and observing the unavoid-able increase of those difficulties and incumbrances from the late dreadful conflagration, a most formidable uncertainty presents itself whether the said Theatre ever can or ever will be re-built.' See the *Morn. Chron.*, 14 May 1810.

mitted to his Lordship's office, or submitted to His Majesty; by which statement it will unanswerably appear, that there is not one syllable of truth in the allegations of the said petition, as far as they relate to the Proprietors of the late Drury lane, or the present Lyceum, Theatres, nor the slightest ground or pretence for the alleged grievances of the subscribing Performers, who, it will be shewn, have been grossly imposed on, and induced to sign what they were falsely assured was not intended to be in any way injurious to the property or interest of Drury-lane Theatre | I am, Sir, your's, etc. | FACT[1]

May 15.

731. To Thomas Shaw

Harvard MS. *Address*: Thos. Shaw Esqr. | Kentish Town | ['Panton-vill' is added in another hand] *Fr.*: R B S *Dock.*: Sheridan | May 21 | 1810 | N.B. | Left at my house | in Penton Str. between | 4 and 5 O'Clock— | Monday Ev | May 21. 1810 | T.S.

19 May 1810
Saturday Evening

Dear Sir

you will do well as an owner of a £3,000 Share[2] to be sure to be with me between 11 and 12 on monday | Yours truly | R B S

732. To Richard Peake

Add. MS. 35118, f. 155–6. *Pub.*: E. M. Butler, *Sheridan, A Ghost Story* (1931), p. 277. *Address*: Mr. Peake *Fr.*: R B S

[7 July 1810 ?]
Oxford
Saturday Night—

My Dear P

I have not had a moment to write to Nowell etc—for the

---

[1] Said to be S. in the *Monthly Mirror*, New Ser., vii (1810), 475, and in Watkins, ii. 498. The performers replied, asserting the truth of their statements, in the *Morn. Chron.*, 17 May 1810.

[2] Shaw owned both this Proprietor's share, and a Renter's share of £500. He gave notice before Richard Warneford,

on 24 Feb. 1810, that he was about to proceed in a Court of Equity for the enforcement of his rights and titles. This was probably inserted in newspapers, for the rest of the notice warns any likely purchaser of D.L.Th. shares to take into account Shaw's claims. (Harvard MS.)

money—nor now a moment but to conjure you by the Love of God to send me by *tomorrow's coach* £15! and then on monday I shall be in Town.

strange things have pass'd but they have ended to my Glory in a way not to be described.[1]

I have not a spare moment etc.[2] | Yours ever | R B S

733. To the Vice-Chancellor of Oxford University[3]

Harrow MS.: Rae, vi. 266. A draft. *Pub.*: Rae, ii. 267–8.

New College
July 11th 1810

Sir

Having been informed by a Friend that an attempt has been made to circulate a report that upon my name being withdrawn from the List of Those to be proposed for a Degree at the Installation, I had express'd myself in Terms of most unbecoming disrespect both with regard to the Honor in Question and those who alone were entitled to confer it, I cannot leave Oxford without so far intruding on your attention as to desposit in your hands my solemn assertion that from me there never proceeded the slightest expression or pretence to give rise to so unjust and false a rumour.[4]

I came here late on monday night or rather the tuesday morning entirely unprovided and in my opinion unentitled to partake of the honorary compliments attach'd to the occasion. Accordingly when I learn't that my name was in the List, but that it was likely to be productive of some

[1] S.'s name was put up for an honorary doctorate in July 1810, on the occasion of Lord Grenville's installation as Chancellor of Oxford University. 'Three gentlemen of Corpus' determined to record a *non placet*, and since S. stated he would not accept the degree if it were not unanimous, no degree was awarded him. When he appeared at the ceremony, the undergraduates created such an uproar that S. was asked to seat himself among the doctors, and took a place next to the Senior Proctor. See *The Star*, 7 July 1810; and C. V. Cox, *Recollections of Oxford* (1868), pp. 64–65.

[2] Butler prints 'so'.

[3] John Parsons (1761–1819), Master of Balliol College and Bishop of Peterborough.

[4] A handbill claiming a degree for him was circulated in the colleges. For its text, see Watkins, ii. 506–7. An original is among the Yale MSS.

degree of contention, I deemed it incumbent on me, without feeling myself entitled in the slightest degree either to be hurt, or to complain of Those with whom the objection originated, to write to Lord Grenville before I went to rest in Terms I trust far different from those which the Report I have alluded to has attributed to me, respectfully to suggest that my name might be withdrawn. Your Polite attention Sir to me on that day follow'd by a similar conduct from the other Colleges entertaining Lord Grenville convinced me that I had judged rightly in avoiding as far as lay in my power any occasion of my name becoming a topic of dispute or the cause of interruption to the Harmony and dignity of proceeding so essential to the High Character of the Convocation.

With regard to what occurr'd on Friday[1] I can only in one word declare to you upon my honor that I was utterly uninformed of any disposition towards the irregul[ar]ity which took place and that had it been referr'd to me no effort on my part would have been wanting to have prevented it.

Again apologizing for the Liberty I have taken in making this address to you I have only to add that with a due regard for your situation and a just esteem for your character and with the most sincere respect for the University | I have the Honor to be| your oblidged and obedient servant| R B Sheridan

To the Vice-Chancellor
of Oxford

734. To Thomas Creevey

J. R. Blackett-Ord MS. *Address*: Thos. Creevey Esq | W Orde Esq | Richmond-Hill | Surrey *Fr.*: R B Sheridan *Dock.*: Poor Sheridan | 1810 *Pm.*: 7 o'Clock | 20 JY 1810.

Friday
July 20 *1810*

Dear Creevey,
Can you receive us if Hester and I mount your Hill to dine and stay with [you until] sunday?

[1] 6 July.

I hope that Mrs. C. and my nieces are in famous health. |
Yours ever | R B Sheridan
Tom is much better since his arrival.

735. To Richard Wilson

Dufferin MS. [Ph.] *Dock.*: 17th Augt. 10 | Sheridan

17 Aug. 1810
Friday Evening

My Dear Dick,
    I was greatly disappointed to find you gone when I started
from my noisy Den on wednesday. I had plann'd in my own
mind that we should go together and stop and sleep at
Sutton—with a late Dinner and a good CASE—and so in
Town early in the morning. This is what I like and practice.
Now tell me where we can meet tomorrow. I have much to
say to you,—I am obliged to dine at Lawrells in Hill-st.
No 4— | yours dear Wilson ever | R B S.

736. To the Rev. Charles Williams[1]

Bodleian Library, English letters, e.i, f. 155. *Address*: Revd. Charles
Williams *Fr.*: R B Sheridan *Wm.*: 1809.

Monday
Oct 22 [*1810*]

My Dear Sir
    Charles has written to Mrs. S. that He is confined by a
sore throat—tho' he makes light of it I am so easily alarm'd
on that subject, especially after [what] was his case formerly
that I shall be greatly obliged to you to see him and favor
me with a Line *by return of Post* should it in the least increase.
I am sure he should be removed from a School Bedroom.
I wish the best Physician to see him about it | R B S.

direct to Queen St.
I send this by the coach.

[1] Presumably C. Williams who matriculated at Corpus Christi College, Oxford, in 1803, aged eighteen; and took his B.A. in 1808. He was made a Fellow of Winchester College in 1819 (Foster). He was among the mourners at S.'s funeral: see *Europ. Mag.* lxx (1816), 46.

737. [To the Rev. Charles Williams ?]

Pub.: S.C., 17 June 1958, lot 476.

Monday 7 Nov. [*1810*]

I shall be much obliged to you to allow him[1] to come immediately in the carriage I send for him.

738. To His Wife

Pub.: Rae, ii. 225.

[*1810 ?*]

[S. has received a letter from Charles in which there is] a *horror* of returning to study which frightens me. If there is not a *sincere* desire to learn and an *ambition* to improve in a boy's mind at a certain age, he will be nothing. *Application, application* without which, says Montesquieu 'there never was or can be a great man . . .' I dislike his using the word *cursed* in his letter to Williams which he wouldn't do in a letter to you or me.

739. To the Prince of Wales

Windsor MS. 41400. *Dock.*: Mr. Sheridan | Novr. 1 1810.

[*2 Nov. 1810*]
November 1st
1810

Sir

I was anxious to have had the honor of reading to your Royal Highness the accompanying Inscription,[2] written at the request of the Corporation of the city of London, while I might yet have had the benefit of any observations your

---

[1] Charles Smyth, pp. 22–24, noticed S.'s tendency to exaggerated worry about the well-being of his son.

[2] This was for Nelson's tablet in London Guildhall. It is printed in *The Times*, 29 Apr. 1811. S. sent a copy to Parr for approval (Parr, *Works*, i. 799), and Parr's opinion of it is given in a letter dated 5 Nov. [1810], in Sir John Soane's Museum.

Judgement and Taste might have suggested. At present I have only to request your very indulgent Perusal of a composition which aims at nothing but plain[n]ness and simplicity which ought I think to characterize every inscription, and which it is more difficult to accomplish than Critics of less Judgement than your Royal Highness may be disposed to admit

I ought to apologize for obtruding on your Royal Highness's attention[1] anything not connected with the superior considerations which must at this juncture so entirely occupy your mind—and referring to this subject allow me to hope that your Royal Highness does not disapprove the Line I took in the House yesterday.[2] There were some, who were connected with the late Government, who were disposed to take objections to the measure proposed. This I thought from the quarter it would have come from would have had a very ill effect and might have been liable to great misconstruction. | I have the Honor to be | with every sentiment of attachment and devotion | Your Royal Highness's | Grateful and dutiful Servant | R B Sheridan.

740. To the Prince of Wales

Windsor MSS. 41481–4. *Pub.*: Moore, ii. 379–82, from a draft.

Barnes-Green[3]
Decr 9th: 1810

Sir

Allow me to express the infinite satisfaction I felt when I was apprized that your Royal Highness had been far from disapproving the line of conduct I had presumed to pursue

[1] The King's insanity had become permanent. 'The Prince resides at Windsor, and conducts himself with very unusual discretion; he has not seen or sent to any person whatever. Sheridan has attempted to see him, but hitherto without success.' (*Journal of Elizabeth, Lady Holland* (1908), ii. 266.)

[2] At the meeting of the Commons on 1 Nov., Perceval proposed that the House follow the precedent of 1788 and adjourn for a fortnight. S. seconded this.

[3] Creevey states that S. used his percentage of a great fine paid for one of the Duchy estates, to take a house at Barnes Terrace 'where he spent all his £1300. At the end of two or three months at most, the tradespeople would no longer supply him without being paid, so he was obliged to remove.' (*Creevey Papers*, i. 52–53.)

on the last question of Adjournment[1] in the House of Commons. Indeed, Sir, I never had a moments doubt but that your Royal Highness would graciously give me credit that I could upon that, as I shall upon every other occasion while I exist, be actuated by no possible motive but the most sincere and unmix'd desire to look to your Royal Highness's Honor and true Interest as the first objects of my Political Life, directed as I am sure your Efforts will ever be to the essential interests of the Country and the Constitution.

To this Line of Conduct I am prompted by every motive of personal Gratitude and confirmed in it by every opportunity which peculiar circumstances and long experience have afforded me of judging of your Heart and understanding—To the superior excellence of both, beyond all I believe that ever stood in a similar relation of rank and Power to Society I fear not to aver my humble Testimony, because I scruple not to say for myself that I have been no Flatterer, and I never found that to become one was the road to your real regard.

I state thus much, because it has been under the influence of these Feelings, thus warmly perhaps express'd, that I have not felt myself warranted, without any previous communication with your Royal Highness, to follow implicitly the dictates of others, however my superiors in Political Pretension, but among whom I can subscribe to no superiority in devotion of attachment or duteous affection to your Royal Highness, or, permit me to add, as to that practical knowledge of the Public mind and character upon which alone can be built that popular and personal estimation of your Royal Highness so necessary to the arduous situation you may so soon be call'd to.

Acting on these Grounds I saw no Policy or consistency in *unnecessarily* giving a *general sanction* to the examination of the Physicians[2] before the Privy-Council, and then

---

[1] In the debate on the King's illness, 15 Nov., S. argued in favour of the adjournment, citing what had happened in 1801 when with such a motion he had prevented an inquiry into the King's state and had been seconded by Pitt. See Hansard, 1st Ser., xviii. 37–39. S. is not named as among the speakers in the debate of 29 Nov. For S.'s refusal to vote for the further adjournment of the Privy Council's examination of the King's physicians, see S.'s letter of 15 Jan. 1811.

[2] In his speech of 15 Nov. S. said:

attempting on the Question of adjournment for a Fortnight to hold that examination as nought. On the same grounds I have ventured to doubt the wisdom or Propriety of any endeavour, if any such endeavour has been made, to induce your Royal Highness at so momentous and perilous a crisis to stir one inch from the strong and high reserved Post you had chosen, or to give the slightest public demonstration of any future intended political preferences either as to men or measures. My Opinion in this respect could not but be fortified by observing the universal admission that the rule of conduct you appear'd to have prescribed to yourself was precisely that which was gaining you the general Heart, and re[n]dering it impracticable for any Quarter to succeed in annexing unworthy and unconstitutional conditions to the Character you might be destined to accept. It is possible, Sir that I may have been guilty of great error in Judgement[1] in both the instances I have referr'd to, differing as I fear I have done from those I highly and sincerely respect, but at the same time I feel it little presumpt[i]on to say that until better instructed I have a strong confidence in the justness of my own view of the subject; and that confidence arises from two considerations—the first that my opinion was not formed on a rash and impatient party view of the subject, and the second that, in forming that opinion I was moved by no selfish object or Political Purpose of my own—[2]

In this respect I am sure your Royal Highness will give me credit. I abstain from Professions.—

Your Royal Highness will I am sure forgive this intrusion, and at the same time attribute to its true motive my having refrain'd from paying my personal Duty to you hitherto, on Tuesday I will attend your commands. | With the most anxious solicitude for | your present situation | but with entire

'If any examination of the physicians in attendance on His Majesty had taken place, he doubted not it would have been laid before the House. But if they had been examined at this period of the disorder, there was reason to believe that they might have been unwilling to pledge themselves to any specific opinion. . . .' (*The Star*, 16 Nov. 1810.)

[1] On 7 Dec. Parr wrote to Holland: 'I have often observed, that the matchless sagacity of Mr. Sheridan is occasionally perverted by a propensity for display, or an affectation of singularity, or a lust of thwarting. Hence I suppose, he did not vote in the second debate. . . .' (Parr, *Works*, vii. 131.)

[2] Moore's extract ends here.

confidence that | you will honourably surmount all diffi-
culties | I am with the truest | sentiments of Gratitude and
Devotion | your dutiful Servant | R B Sheridan

741. To John Graham

Osborn MS. *Address*: John Graham Esqr. | No. 2 Berkeley-St. |
Berkeley-Square *Fr.*: R B S *Dock.*: Sheridan

[*1810 ?*]
Saturday Night

Domine,

The Domus in our Square mention'd by Bates I cannot
find or hear of.—I shall be on the Tramp again tomorrow.
Mrs. S. fancies S. Audley St: much in Preference to this
neighbourhood—I think good abatement might be had—
with good management and our good security.—After
searching laboriously for the enclosed I popp'd upon it
this evening by accident. The acceptor good as the Bank.—
Mayor of Salisbury last year.[1]—Desire Mr.[2] Hindle to
discount it forth with. I am mustering every thing to sweep
our present pests of servants out of the House. I like the
Woman you sent to me extremely—shall see about her
character tomorrow—she is to come to me again on monday
at 12. I send Mrs. Graham a Pheasant hoping she is well,
which is your humble servant | R B S.

742. To Richard Peake

Salt MS. *Address*: Mr. Peake. *Fr.*: R B S *Dock.*: Mr. Sheridan

[*1810 ?*]
Richmond
Tuesday—

My Dear P.

I could not get to Town this morning for the Fact is I
am here in *Pawn*—my money unexpectedly failing me at
Oatlands[3] and I owe for my chaise here etc. Pray fail not

---

[1] Thomas Wilkie ?
[2] Manuscript, 'discuss me'.

[3] Creevey, i. 53, describes how, during the two months at Barnes Terrace,

to send me £5 by Fairbrother whom I send in Purpose and Stevenson['s] Acceptance and you shall positively have it back tomorrow or Thursday morn the discount being promised me. I am going to dine with Lord Sidmouth | Yours ever| R B S

743. To the Prince of Wales

Windsor MS., Addl., Geo. 3

[*11 Jan. 1811*]
House of Commons
5 o'clock.

Sir

I have the honour to inform you that your Royal Highness's answer which Percival[1] read well and fairly at the Bar appear'd to receive the universal approbation of the House. No observation whatever was made. Yet there is an omission in the Copy[2] of the word '*however*' after the words '*deeply impressed*' and this being a conjunctive particle the leaving it out mars the meaning of the sentence. The Speaker[3] and the Chancellor have agreed to correct the error before it is placed on the journals—and I have sent to the Papers.

Mr. Percival wish'd to know whether there was meant to be any Debate on the question of the Great Seal (or the Phantom)[4] Whitbread[5] said He should enter his Protest against it but in a very few words. I said the same and that those who had opposed it in —89 were bound to make their stand by a Protest now but that there was not the

S. 'gave dinners perpetually and was always on the road between . . . Barnes and Oatlands (the Duke of York's), in a large job coach upon which he would have his family arms painted'. But note also three payments to 'Mr. Fairbrother for Mr. S. £5' between 24 and 29 Dec. 1808, in D.L.Th. Salaries, 1808 to 1809 (Folger MS.).

[1] Spencer Perceval (1762–1812), Prime Minister. He read the Prince's answer to the joint address of the two Houses on 'the exercise of the Royal Authority during His Majesty's illness'.

[2] This is in the opening of the fourth paragraph of the Prince's answer. The word 'however' appears in the version in Hansard (1st Ser., xviii. 811), but is omitted in the version in *The Times*, 12 Jan. 1811.

[3] Charles Abbot, afterwards 1st Lord Colchester (1757–1829).

[4] The means of giving royal assent when the King was incapacitated.

[5] See Hansard, 1st Ser., xviii. 815. He would 'declare his dissent by his vote'.

least likelihood of any such debate as would justify his passing over tomorrow. Perceval caught at this and said if there was to be any opposition at all no one could tell to what length it might go—so He proposed to put it off to monday. I again remonstrated[1] and wish'd to divide the House but those near me thought it best not. Thus He has got another Day and his object is clearly delay, and not to hasten on as he pretended to Adam. | I have the honor to be, | Your Royal Highness's | ever faithful and dutiful Servant | R B Sheridan

744. To Lord Holland

Holland House MS. Copy by Mrs. S.[2] *Pub.*: Moore, ii. 394–406. *Dock.*: [by S.] Read and approved by the Prince, January 20 1811.

Queen Street
Jany. 15 1811

Dear Holland

As you have been already apprized by His Royal Highness The Prince that he thought it becoming the frankness of His Character, and consistent with the fairness and openness of proceeding due to any of his Servants whose conduct appears to have incurred the disapprobation of Lord Grey and Lord Grenville, to communicate their representations on the subject to the person so censured, I am confident you will give me credit for the pain I must have felt to find myself an object of suspicion[3] or likely in the slightest degree to become the cause of any temporary misunderstanding between his Royal Highness and those

[1] S. said 'he should feel himself bound in consistency to repeat the opinions he had formerly maintained, upon what appeared to him the greatest and boldest inroad upon the constitution . . .' (Hansard, 1st Ser., xviii. 816).

[2] The signature and four trifling corrections are in S.'s hand. Windsor MSS. 41600–8 are entirely in another hand. See also Sichel, ii. 347.

[3] Grey and Grenville were instructed by the Prince to write an answer on his behalf to the offer of the Regency made by a deputation from the two houses. Grey read the proposed answer to him on 10 Jan., and offered to amend it. The Prince did not like it, and did not like Moira's version. He then compiled his own answer with the assistance of S., and sent a copy of it to Grey, who was displeased with it and with S. See D. M. Stuart, *Dearest Bess* (1955), p. 176; C. Grey, *Life of . . . Charles, 2nd Earl Grey* (1861), pp. 266–74, 433–41.

distinguished characters,[1] whom His Royal Highness appears to destine to those responsible situations which must in all public matters entitle them to his exclusive confidence.

I shall as briefly as I can state the circumstances of the fact, so distinctly refer'd to in the following passage of the Noble Lord's Representation:—

'But they would be wanting in that sincerity and openness by which they can alone hope, however imperfectly, to make any return to that gracious confidence with which your Royal Highness has condescended to honor them if they suppressed the expression of their deep concern in finding that their humble endeavours in your Royal Highness's service have been submitted to the judgement of another person *by whose advice* Your Royal Highness has been guided in your final decision on a matter in which they alone had however unworthily been honor'd with your Royal Highness's commands.'[2]

I must premise that from my first intercourse with the Prince during the present distressing emergency, such conversations as he may have honor'd me with, have been communications of resolutions already form'd on his part, and not of matter refer'd to consultation, or submitted to *advice*. I know that my declining to vote for the further adjournment of the Privy Council's Examination of the Physicians gave offence to some, and was consider'd as a difference from the Party I was rightly esteem'd to belong to. The intentions of the Leaders of the Party upon that question were in no way distinctly known to me; my secession was entirely my own act; and not only unauthorized but perhaps unexpected by the Prince. My motives for it I took the liberty of communicating to his Royal Highness by letter the next day, and previously to that I had not even seen his Royal Highness since the confirmation of His Majesty's Malady.

If I differ'd from those, who equally attached to his Royal Highness's Interest and honor, thought that his Royal Highness should have taken the step, which in my humble opinion he has since, precisely at the proper

[1] Grey and Grenville were expected to lead a new administration.

[2] The full letter of Grey and Grenville is in *Dropmore Papers*, x. 103–4.

period,[1] taken, of sending to Lord Grenville and Lord Grey, I may certainly have err'd in forming an imperfect judgement on the occasion but in doing so I meant no disrespect to those who had taken a different view of the subject. But with all deference I cannot avoid adding that experience of the impression made on the public mind by the reserved and retired conduct which The Prince thought proper to adopt, has not shaken my opinion of the wisdom which prompted him to that determination. But here again I declare that I must reject the presumption that any suggestion of mine led to the rule which the Prince had prescribed to himself. My knowledge of it being as I before said the communication of a resolution form'd on the part of His Royal Highness and not of a proposition awaiting the advice countenance or corroboration of any other person. Having thought it necessary to premise thus much as I wish to write to you without reserve or concealment of any sort I shall as briefly as I can relate the facts which attended the composing the answer itself as far as I was concern'd.

On Sunday or on Monday the 7th Inst. I mention'd to Lord Moira or to Adam that the Address of the two Houses[2] would come very quickly upon the Prince and that He should be prepared with his answer without entertaining the least idea of meddling with the subject myself, having received no authority from his Royal Highness to do so. Either Lord Moira or Adam inform'd me before I left Carlton House that his Royal Highness had directed Lord Moira to sketch an outline of the answer proposed, and I left Town. On Tuesday evening it occur'd to me to try at a sketch also of the intended reply—on Wednesday Morning I read it at Carlton House very hastily to Adam before I saw The Prince. And here I must pause to declare that I have entirely withdrawn from my mind any doubt if for a moment I ever entertained any of the perfect propriety and justness of Adam's conduct at that hurried interview, being also long convinced as well from my intercourse with him at Carlton House as in every transaction I have witness'd

---

[1] As soon as the Regency Bill had been passed.

[2] On 7 Jan. Perceval stated that a deputation must be sent to the Prince to inform him of the resolutions empowering him to assume the government.

that it is impossible for him to act otherwise than with the most entire sincerity and honor towards all he deals with. I then read the Paper I had put together to the Prince, the most essential part of it literally consisting of sentiments and Expressions which had fallen from the Prince himself in different conversations, and I read to him without *having once heard Lord Grenville's name* even mention'd as in any way connected with the answer proposed to be submitted to the Prince: on the contrary indeed I was under an impression that the framing this answer was consider'd as the single act which it would be an unfair and embarrassing task to require the performance of from Lord Grenville. The Prince approved the Paper I read to Him, objecting however to some additional Paragraphs of my own, and altering others. In the course of his observations he cursorily mentioned that Lord Grenville had undertaken to sketch out his idea of a proper answer, and that Lord Moira had done the same, evidently expressing himself to my apprehension as not considering the framing of this answer as a matter of official responsibility any where: but that it was his intention to take the choice and decision respecting it on himself. If however I had known before I entered the Prince's apartment that Lord Grenville and Lord Grey had in any way undertaken to frame the answer, and had thought themselves authorized to do so, I protest the Prince would never even have heard of the draft which I had prepared, though containing as I said before, the Prince's own ideas.

His Royal Highness having laid his commands on Adam and me to dine with him alone on the next day Thursday I then for the first time learnt that Lord Grey and Lord Grenville had transmitted thro' Adam a formal draft of an answer to be submitted to the Prince.

Under these Circumstances I thought it became me humbly to request the Prince not to refer to me in any respect the Paper of the Noble Lords or to insist even on my hearing its contents: but that I might be permitted to put the draft he had received from me into the fire. The Prince however who *had* read the Noble Lord's Paper, declining to hear of this proceeded to state how strongly

he objected to almost every part of it. The Draft delivered
by Adam he took a copy of himself as Mr. Adam read it,
affixing shortly but warmly his Comments to each paragraph. Finding His Royal Highness's objections to the
whole radical and insuperable and seeing no means myself
by which the noble Lords could change their draft so
as to meet the Prince's ideas, I ventured to propose, as
the only expedient of which the time allow'd, that both
the papers should be laid aside and that a very short
answer indeed, keeping clear of all topicks liable to disagreement, should be immediately sketched out and be
submitted that night to the judgement of Lord Grey and
Lord Grenville. This his Royal Highness did not approve
of. The lateness of the hour prevented any but very hasty
discussion, and Adam and myself proceeded by his Royal
Highness's orders to your House to relate what had passed
to Lord Grey. I do not mean to disguise however that when
I found myself bound to give my opinion I did fully assent
to the force and justice of the Prince's objections, and
made other observations of my own which I thought it my
duty to do, conceiving as I freely said that the paper could
not have been drawn up but under the pressure of embarrassing difficulties, and as I conceived also in considerable
haste.

Before we left Carlton House it was agreed between
Adam and myself that we were not so strictly enjoined by
the Prince as to make it necessary for us to communicate
to the noble Lords the marginal comments of the Prince,
and we determined to withhold them. But at the meeting
with Lord Grey at your house, he appear'd to me, er-
roneously perhaps, to decline considering the objections as
coming from the Prince, but as originating in my suggestions.
Upon this I certainly called on Adam to produce the
Prince's copy with his notes in his Royal Highness's own
hand writing.

Afterwards finding myself considerably hurt at an expression of Lord Grey's which could only be pointed at me
and which expressed his opinion that the whole of the
Paper which he assumed me to be responsible for was
'drawn up in an invidious spirit' I certainly did, with

more warmth than was perhaps discreet comment on the Paper proposed to be substituted: and there ended with no good effect our interview.

Adam and I saw the Prince again that night,[1] when his Royal Highness was graciously pleased to meet our joint and earnest request by striking out from the draft of the answer to which he still resolved to adhere, every passage which we conceived to be most liable to objection on the part of Lord Grey and Lord Grenville.

On the next morning Friday a short time before he was to receive the Address, when Adam return'd from the noble Lords with their expressed disclaimer of the preferr'd answer alter'd as it was, his Royal Highness still persevered to eradicate every remaining word which he thought might yet appear exceptionable to them and made further alterations, altho' the fair copy of the Paper had been made out.

Thus the Answer nearly reduced to the expression of the Prince's own suggestions, and without an opportunity of farther meeting the wishes of the noble Lords, was deliver'd by his Royal Highness and presented to the Deputation of the two Houses.

I am ashamed to have been thus prolix and circumstantial upon a matter which may appear to have admitted of much shorter explanation: but when misconception has produced distrust among those not willingly I hope disposed to differ, and who can have I equally trust but one common object in view in their different Stations I know no better way than by minuteness and accuracy of detail to remove whatever may have appear'd doubtful in conduct, while unexplain'd, or inconsistent in principle, not clearly re-asserted.—

And now my dear Lord I have only shortly to express my own personal mortification I will use no other word that I should have been consider'd by any Persons however high in Rank or justly entitled to high political pretensions, as one so little 'attached to His Royal Highness' or so ignorant 'of the value of the Constitution of his Country' as to be held out to HIM, whose fairly-earned esteem I

[1] See M. A. Taylor's account of this second meeting in Moore's *Journal*, iv. 289.

regard as the first honor and the sole reward of my political life, in the character of an interested Contriver of a double Government, and in some measure as an Apostate from all my former Principles, which have taught me as well as the noble Lords that 'the maintenance of constitutional responsibility in the Ministers of the Crown, is essential to any hope of success in the Administration of the public interest.'

At the same time I am most ready to admit that it could not be their *intention* so to characterize me, but it is the direct inference which others must gather from the first paragraph I have quoted from their representation, and an inference which I understand has already been raised in public opinion. A departure my dear Lord on my part from upholding the principle declared by the noble Lords, much less a presumptuous and certainly ineffectual attempt to inculcate a contrary doctrine on the mind of the Prince of Wales, would I am confident lose me every particle of his favour and confidence at once.and for ever. But I am yet to learn what part of my past public life, and I challenge observation on every part of my present proceedings, has warranted the adoption of any such suspicion of me, or the expression of any such imputation against me. But I will dwell no longer on this point as it relates only to my own feelings and character, which however I am the more bound to consider as others in my humble judgement have so hastily disregarded both. At the same time I do sincerely declare that no personal disappointment in my own mind interferes with the respect and esteem I entertain for Lord Grenville —or in addition to those sentiments the friendly regard I owe to Lord Grey.—To Lord Grenville I have the honour to be but very little personally known. From Lord Grey, intimately acquainted as he was, with every circumstance of my conduct and principles in the years 1788–9, I confess I should have expected a very tardy and reluctant interpretation of any circumstance to my disadvantage. What the nature of my endeavours were at that time I have the written testimonies of Mr. Fox and The Duke of Portland. To you I know those testimonies are not necessary, and perhaps it has been my recollection of what passed in those

times that may have led me too securely to conceive myself
above the reach even of a suspicion that I could adopt
different principles now. Such as they were they remain
untouched, and unaltered. I conclude with sincerely declaring that to see The Prince meeting the Reward which
his own honourable nature, his kind and generous
disposition, and his genuine devotion to the true objects
of our free constitution so well entitle Him to, by being
surrounded and supported by an Administration affectionate
to his Person, and ambitious of gaining and meriting his
entire esteem yet tenacious above all things of the constitutional principle that exclusive confidence must attach
to the responsibility of those whom he selects to be his
public Servants,—I would with heartfelt Satisfaction rather
be a looker on of such a Government giving it such
humble support as might be in my power than be the
possessor of any possible situation either of profit or ambition to be obtain'd by any indirectness, or by the slightest
departure from the principles I have always professed and
which I have now felt myself in a manner called upon to
re-assert.

I have only to add that my respect for the Prince, and my
sense of the frankness he has shewn towards me on this
occasion decide me with all duty to submit this letter to
his perusal before I place it in your hands, meaning it
undoubtedly to be by you shewn to those to whom your
judgement may deem it of any consequence to communicate
it.[1] | I have the honor to be | My dear Lord | With sincere
esteem and affection | Yours faithfully | R B Sheridan

To Lord Holland.

745. To Thomas Creevey

Pub.: *Creevey Papers*, i. 138.

Friday night, Jany. 18th. [*1811*]
My Dear Creevey,
    It is determined in consequence of the earnest Desire of

[1] Grey forwarded it to Grenville on 20 Jan.: see *Dropmore Papers*, x. 108.

high authority to have *a last debate and division* on the Regency bill[1] on Monday next. Here is a Conclave mustering all Hands, and I am requested to write to you as it is apprehended you mean to leave Town to-morrow. I conjure you at any rate to be with us on Monday. | Yours ever faithfully, | Bly.[2] Sheridan.

746. To Lord Holland

Holland House MS., S. 85. *Address*: Lord Holland. *Fr.*: R. B. Sheridan

Sunday January 20
1811

Dear Holland

I will explain to you what has delay'd your receiving the Letter[3] which I had apprized you some days since I had address'd to you—but I am in haste that you should have it now. If there appear any expressions in it of much soreness in my mind I have to observe that I wrote this Paper before I had any reason to surmise that the impressions I complain of had been in any degree removed. At all events I wish it to be shewn to those to whose representation it is in part intended as an answer, and to be deposited in your hands as an humble record of my conduct and of those principles which it cannot but be satisfactory to find the Prince entirely approves of.[4] | Your's ever faithfully | R B Sheridan

Lord Holland.

747. To Lord Holland

Holland House MS., S. 86.

[*20 Jan. 1811 ?*]
Sunday Night

My Dear Lord

I forgot to say to Day that it will be but fair that the

---

[1] It had been debated on 18 Jan., when S. had spoken. In the division of 21 Jan. the administration was victorious by 212 to 190.

[2] Unique. A misreading of 'R B'?

[3] Of 15 Jan. 1811 (Holland House) MS.

[4] Holland acted as intermediary between Grey and Grenville and Carlton House.

Paper I left with you, if you see no reason to the contrary, should be communicated, not only to Lord Grey and Lord Grenville but to Those also to whom *their representation has been shewn*. I particularly wish that Adam Ponsonby and Whitbread should also see it. The Prince has desired a copy of it from me which it is really not easily in my Power to give him. Will you, who have always a hundred Scribes about you, enable me with as little delay as possible to obey his orders. | Your's ever | R B Sheridan

748. To the Speaker

P.R.O. MS. 30/9. Copy. *Pub.: Colchester Corr.* ii. 309.

[*24 Jan. 1811*]

. . . particularly sorry that it will *not be in his power* to have the honour of waiting on the Sp[eaker] on Sunday.[1]

749. To His Wife

Yale MS. *Wm.:* /02

[*27 Jan. 1811*]
Sunday Night

My Dearest
    Our great Dinner to Day[2] at C. House went off extremely well, and the Prince very pleasant and entertaining—He is delighted with my Epigrams.
    I think 'My Trunk'[3] might amuse your Mother and Henry[4] and the Epigrams too.[5] Alter in the Line,—'my

[1] This excuse irritated Charles Abbot because S. had led him to suppose that the Speaker's parliamentary dinners took precedence even over the Prince's commands. See *Colchester Corr.* ii. 309.

[2] The Prince, Duke of Devonshire, Lord Keith, Lord Moira, Lord Yarmouth, Lord Hampden, Colonel Bloomfield, and S. were present. See the *Diaries of Sylvester Douglas* (1928), ii. 120.

[3] See Moore, ii. 477–8, 393–4.

[4] The occasion of these lines is to be found in *The Times*, 4 Feb. 1811:

'A few evenings since, as Mrs. Sheridan was coming to town in her carriage from Barnes to her house in Queen-Street, Mayfair, a portmanteau, containing lace, silk, and valuable articles to a considerable amount, was cut from behind the carriage, with which the robbers made their escape.'

[5] Probably the three epigrams that appeared in the *British Press*, 30 Jan. 1811, and *Morn. Chron.*, 31 Jan. 1811, above the name of 'No Toad-Eater'. One was 'In all humility we crave . . . .'

Fibars are shrunk'—to 'my Figure's quite shrunk' and in the next Line write instead of *'the loss' 'this* loss of' etc.—

Perhaps it might be better to say 'Who rifle fair Ladies while handling their Trunks,' but it would be more indecent. Bless you my heart I would rather write ten Lines to divert you than a dispatch as Secretary of State | —S

You let me go away without my own copy of the Epigrams— pray bring it—

750. To the Prince of Wales

Windsor MSS. 42526–8.

[*Jan. 1811 ?*]
Barns
Wednesday night

Sir

I find myself impell'd before I rest to night to express my grateful acknowledgements for the gracious and friendly tone and manner your Royal Highness was pleased to resume towards me this morning.[1]—Forgive, Sir, the freedom I take in using the word *resume*, for your countenance and nature are too ingenuous and sincere for me not to have perceived some degree of alteration, and abatement of cordiality in your reception of me in a former interview. Perhaps I may be over jealous and apprehensive on this subject in proportion to the value I place on your esteem and confidence, The possession of which *has* been for so many years of proof, and *does* now constitute the first Pride and happiness of my Life.

I am aware, Sir, how many there are who from various motives, are anxious to discolour whatever I say or do—and especially where they think they have an opportunity of making an impression on your Royal Highness. I think too highly of Lord Grenville to suppose him capable of encouraging these curious[2] misrepresenters, but there are in truth round him many Persons of vulgar and narrow

[1] Ward (*Memoirs of R. P. Ward* (ed. cit.), i. 367) reported on 28 Jan. 1811 that S. was 'dismissed from all confidence or management at Carlton House'. This dismissal must have been a very brief one.   [2] Or 'envious'.

minds who take upon themselves to resent that any individual who ranks as a party man should presume on any
occasion to prefer *your* honor and interests to the protection and patronage of their political Leader. From any
lasting impression resting on your Royal Highness's mind
from their insinuations I feel a certain shield in the first
hour of your Royal Highness's recurrence to your own
excellent Heart and superior understanding.

But there are circumstances in the present crisis which
require more from me than the sincere expression of the
grateful and affectionate duty I owe you. I am most sensible
of your long and unalterable friendship towards me and
conscious that you are at this moment desirous to give me
an additional Proof of it. The only fit return I can make is to
free your Royal Highness from any embarrassment or obligation on my account, and therefore it is that I have firmly
formed my resolution not to accept any office or situation
whatever from those whom your Royal Highness has in my
humble Judgement most prudently and from the most
noble motives destined, under circumstances, to be your
future ministers.[1] I will not intrude on your Royal Highness
with further explanations at present. To two Persons only,
two men with whom it would be the highest honor of my
Life to vie in ardo[u]r and sincerity of attachment and
devotion to your Royal Highness have I made this communication I need scarcely say I mean Lord Moira an[d]
McMahon.

No, Sir, allow me to cherish the animating conviction
that I shall to the last moment of my Life retain and merit
the esteem of your heart and the happiness of your society
and I gain all that is left in my bosom of public or private
ambition. | I have the honor to be | with the justest admira-
tion of your | Character, and the most zealous | attachment
to your happiness | Your Royal Highness's | most dutiful
Servant | R B Sheridan

[1] On 22 Jan. Grey noted that the
Prince wanted S. to go to Ireland as
Chief Secretary, and was still pressing
this a week later. Grey opposed this as
'sending a man with a lighted torch
into a magazine of gunpowder', but had
no objection to S.'s having a place [i.e.
Treasurer of the Navy] with large
emoluments. See C. Grey, *Life . . . of
Charles, 2nd Earl Grey* (1861), pp.
273–4.

751. To the Prince of Wales

Windsor MS. 41642.

Tuesday¹ Night
Feb. 1st 1811

Sir

It is impossible for me to express the Gratitude I feel for the gracious manner in which you were pleased to accept the opinions I ventured to urge to Day² against the Decision you had previously adopted.—But that Question being over, allow me to assure you that every effort of my heart and intellect shall be directed most earnestly and honestly to prevent or parry all attacks which may follow that Decision.

As I shall have the Honour of seeing your Royal Highness tomorrow I say no more at present—but only to add that General Fitzpatrick will call at Carlton-House between 12 and one, and that for reasons you will at once anticipate He is perhaps the Person above all others to whom it may be *useful* to open your mind. | your Royal Highness's dutiful Servant | R B Sheridan

752. [To John Graham?]

Osborn MS.

[*1811 ?*]
Saturday Night

Citizen G——³

I find it will be better to settle your application *after* I have seen *W.* at two tomorrow when I shall immediately come to you—boundless riches (I mean independence of

¹ This was a Friday, but S. has written 'Tuesday' quite clearly.

² Sir Henry Halford and the other physicians led the Prince to believe that the King's recovery was probable. On 1 Feb., therefore, the Prince decided not to bring in a new administration, and sent a message to this effect to Grey and Grenville. S. tried to dissuade him from this course but, as usual, some reports suggested that S. 'had played

false'. See Roger Wilbraham's letter in A. M. W. Stirling, *Coke of Norfolk and his Friends* (new ed., 1912), pp. 345–7, and cf. Rose, ii. 478, *Memoirs of R. P. Ward*, ii. 371, and *Creevey Papers*, i. 138.

³ This suggests a letter to Grubb of the period 1795–7, but the reference to 'your application' seems to fit in with the letter to Graham that follows this one.

poverty) are pouring into your reluctant Lap.—But never lend yourself to the disgraceful office of dodging or watching or pumping or pimping on the subject you mention'd to me to Day—or I have done with you. Tell those who apply to you again for such a Purpose that your Lord and Master would despise you if you listen'd even to their application | R B S

753. To John Graham

Osborn MS. *Address*: J Graham Esq | Berkeley-St | Berkeley Squar[e]
Fr.: R B Sheridan

[*1811* ?]
Wednesday Night

My Dear Colonel
I have seen Whitbread—settled every thing in your matter.—*Read* and send the enclos'd *early* in the morning—never mind expence of Porter—let me see you in the morning. I was in the House of Commons to Day—a most good humour'd reception in the *Lobby*—| yours | R B S

rely on it no other tone to be taken about Shaw—yet accompany my note with one expostulatory from *you*.
Forward *positively* the enclos'd with a note from yourself.—

754. [To John Graham ?]

Harvard MS. *Dock.*: Sheridan

[*1811* ?]
Tuesday Evening

Private
My Dear Colonel—
The Answer to P. Moore's Letter from the *Dowager*[1] was that her Grandson Mr. Colville (the young man you saw)[2] should call on him at half past three to Day. Peter

[1] Probably Lady Asgill. She married the banker, Sir Charles Asgill, Bart., in 1755. Their son, General Sir Charles Asgill, Bart. (1762–1823), married Mrs. S.'s cousin, Jemima Sophia Ogle, in 1790. See Ogle, p. 153.

[2] Lady Asgill's daughter, Amelia, had married Robert Colville (1763–99) and had four sons. The oldest was afterwards Sir Charles Henry Colville (d. 1833).

says He was back from the city in time, and that he never came now I cannot help thinking there is some mistake perhaps of his Servants. We have more than ever set our Hearts on the House[1] Mrs. S. especially. What I wish you to do is to be in Wimpole St. by 10 in the morning as from P. Moore stating how he is press'd for time and that you believe he is then staying at home for Mr. Colville so at least you will learn where the Hitch lies. For all which this shall be your sufficient warrant— | R B S

Pray call here after

755. [To His Wife]

Pub.: Rae, ii. 273.

[*Feb. 1811 ?*]

As to politics nothing can be worse. I am doing and shall do nothing but what is honest and disinterested. At the same time it is a mortifying situation to endeavour to promote the views of persons who have treated me as they[2] have done, and are entitled to no service from me to find them returning from their confidential meeting with Tierney, Whitbread, etc., and confidently expecting every co-operation and common cause from me. But no matter. I act as in my conscience I think is best both for the Prince and the country. . . . since writing the above Perceval is confirmed.[3]

756. [To His Wife]

Pub.: Rae, ii. 273–4.

[*Feb. 1811 ?*]

Pray, pray never suspect or decry the Prince. He is acting as honourably as man can do and gives me his entire and unqualified confidence. . . . I wrote his answer to

[1] In Cavendish Square ?
[2] Grey and Grenville ?
[3] Rae's note is ambiguous and this

sentence may not belong to the rest of the letter.

Perceval's communication.[1] I must feel a little proud to see the turn my *friends'* opinions have taken on my conduct.

757. To His Wife

Pub.: Rae, ii. 273–4.

[*c. 14 Feb. 1811*]

I must dine at Carlton House to settle a paper for the Prince, not a political one you may be sure for never will I have anything to do with double advice. Pray copy the Prince's reply to Perceval and Perceval's answer. . . . Perceval's reply is mean and miserable.[2]
. . . The rascally Minister tried to put an infamous speech in the Prince's mouth to the City Address.[3] He should turn them out rather than speak it.

758. [To Samuel Parr?]

Bodleian Library Western MS. 25448, f. 100.

[*1811*]
Cavendish Square[4]
Thursday

My dear Sir
I have found Mr. Montague's Pamphlet[5] and other Papers relative to the poor young man—I think his statement quite convincing, and the testimonies ought by no

[1] See Moore, ii. 408. Probably the Prince's letter of 4 Feb. For S.'s draft, see iii. 286–7.

[2] The Prince's letter to Perceval on 4 Feb. and Perceval's reply of 5 Feb. are both given in R. Huish, *Memoirs of George the Fourth* (1831), ii. 29–30, and in *Colchester Corr.* ii. 316–18.

[3] On 14 Feb. the Prince received the address of the Corporation of the City of London on his being appointed Regent. It charged ministers with mismanagement and usurping the royal authority. The Prince's reply contained his thanks for their attachment and his statement that the happiest moment of his life would arrive when he could resign the powers delegated to him, to

his father. See *The Star*, 15 Feb. 1810.

[4] Lady Bessborough had a house in Cavendish Square for many years; and, in Feb. 1811, noted that the Sheridans had taken a house 'in C. Sq., and we shall live together, I suppose' (*Leveson-Gower Corr.* ii. 382). The Bessboroughs lived at No. 2; the Sheridans at No. 6.

[5] In 1810 Basil Montagu (1770–1851) wrote a pamphlet called *The Case of Denis Shiel, condemned to die, and now transported for life to Botany Bay,* but suppressed it before publication. Shiel had been indicted at the Old Bailey on 29 Sept. 1809 for stealing calico from his employers. Montagu argued that Shiel had taken the goods by mistake.

means to be suppress'd. I wish I could have the Pleasure of seeing Mr. Montague—| Yours truly| R B Sheridan.

759. To John Walter, Junior[1]

Pub.: *The History of 'The Times': 'The Thunderer' in the Making, 1785–1841* (1935),pp. 92–93. *Address*: John Walter, Esquire, Junior.

[*Mar. 1811 ?*]

Dear Sir

I confess my surprise at being shown on my return to day to Town a letter in your liberal Paper, containing a gross attack[2] on me personally, and a very foul attempt to obstruct our endeavours to rebuild Drury Lane Theatre— The whole is a string of most impudent falsehoods—and addressing you, not as an Editor, but, on the footing of the fair and friendly intercourse, which, as a private man, I have always met you and your Father, I must regret, that you could have permitted the publications of such Libels—A proper answer will be sent—tho' not from me—And, I hope, I shall have the pleasure of finding you at home between three and four tomorrow—| Dear Sir Yours truly | R. B. Sheridan

760. To Thomas Shaw

Harvard MS. *Address*: Thos. Shaw Esqr. *Fr.*: R B Sheridan *Dock.*: Sheridan | March 17 | 1811 *Wm.*: 1810

Cavendish-Square[3]
Friday Evening
March 15th. *1811*

My Dear Sir

I shall be obliged to you to favour me with a call tomorrow

---

[1] John Walter II (1776–1847), manager of *The Times* from 1803.

[2] A scathing attack on S. appeared in *The Times*, 15 Mar. 1811, when 'a Correspondent' claimed that, in 1810, S. had stated that arrangements had been made for the speedy rebuilding of D.L. Th. Having 'silenced those whom he is pleased to call his opponents . . . his splendid abilities fell again into their wonted lethargy, and we hear no more of the rebuilding of Drury-lane, 'till he is roused a second time by those unwearied petitioners renewing their application to Parliament; and now, again, we perceive the effects of his genius in the public prints, and in the rumours which he so well knows how to create. . . .'

[3] 'No. 6' has been written in.

morning before 12 or if more convenient to you on sunday¹
at the same hour | Your's truly | R B Sheridan

T Shaw Esq.

761. To His Son Tom

Osborn MS. Copy in W.T. *Wm.*: 1805.

[*1811 ?*]²
Hertford-St.
Friday Evening—

My Dear Tom,
My decided opinion is that you will not be touch'd. I
have done every thing on my part short of any act of
mean[n]ess which I am confident you would not expect
from me for any advantage to yourself—I am myself in a
very embar[r]ass'd situation (I don't mean in the little
petty matter of money which we will yet ride thro') but
politically and I speak with especial reference to the Prince.
But by whom I must and shall stand—doing everything I
can honourably by Party—but I will not sacrifice myself
or you—to those who only court me or profess to deal fairly
by me when they find they want me | Ever your | R B S.

suppose you step here if at home   kindest love to Caroline

762. To Samuel Whitbread

Whitbread MS. 4108 *Dock.*: Sheridan recd. May 1[1]811 £200

[*30 Apr. 1811*]
Tuesday Night
My Dear Whitbread,
I ought to write you a long Letter and such was my
intention, but under the present Feelings of my mind,

¹ Shaw replied on 17 Mar. (Harvard
MS.), saying that he had just received
the letter and asking S. to put any
proposition he had to make in writing.
Did S. suspect him of being 'a Correspondent'?

² Sichel, i. 70, quotes the last sentence of this letter and dates it '1811
(March 7)', without giving reasons. His
date is open to objection because it falls
on a Thursday.

asking you to grant me a favor at the precise moment when you have very just reason to be out of humour with me and to deem me ungratefully negligent of the kind and friendly interest with which you exert yourself to serve me,¹ I must pursue my purpose with the utmost abruptness —Lend me for six weeks two hundred £ or even one hundred Pounds—I make this request with a degree of Pain and mortification which it cannot be possible for you to conceive. I can say from the sincerity of my soul that the most unobliged man on earth in this way, strug[g]ling with distress thro' his Life is myself. It is the only application of the kind you will ever receive from me. And I pledge you most solemnly my word, and stake every title to your esteem that the Drafts I enclose shall be punctually answer'd—

What has caused this pressing exigency, I cannot now pause to detail— | your's ever| most gratefully| R B Sheridan.

763. To Sir Charles Bunbury²

University of Rochester Library MS. [Ph.] *Address*: Sir Chas. Bunbury Bart. | 110 Pall Mall. *Fr.*: R B Sheridan *Dock.*: Richard Brinsley Sheridan May 5th 1811

Sunday May 5th *1811*
My Dear Bunbury
Your early attendance at the House to morrow³ will greatly oblige me⁴| Yours etc.— | R B Sheridan⁵

¹ Whitbread was the chairman of the sub-committee of management and was virtually responsible for the rebuilding of D.L.Th.

² Sir Thomas Charles Bunbury, 6th baronet (1740–1821), M.P. for Suffolk, 1790–1812, was a shareholder in D.L.Th.

³ The delay in rebuilding D.L.Th. led to an attempt by 'a few speculators' to obtain parliamentary sanction for the erection of another playhouse. The second reading of their 'New London

Theatre Bill' was deferred, through the opposition of the D.L. committee, from 25 Mar. to 6 May, then to 9 May.

⁴ The message and date are in Mrs. S.'s hand. The address is in another. Salutation and signature are by S. Clearly S. was circularizing his supporters.

⁵ The letter is summarized in the *Catalogue of the Autograph Collection of the University of Rochester* (comp. R. F. Metzdorf, Rochester, 1940), p. 128.

764. To the Attorney-General[1]

Harrow MS.: Rae, vi. 274. Copy. *Dock.*: 8 May 1811 | Mr. Sheridans Letter to the Attorney General

Cavendish Square
Wednesday Evening May 8th. [*1811*]
Dear Sir

In every instance of the little accidental intercourse I have had with you, I have been imprest with a conviction of the fairness and impartiality of your Character. With this conviction I take the liberty of making a short appeal to you on the subject of a Bill now before the House, call'd the third Theatre Bill,[2] and even this I should not presume to do had I not, failing to find you in the House of Commons, this day asked Mr. Percival whether there was any impropriety in my so doing. I have not the least apprehension of the new Speculators being able to succeed in their Plan to destroy the means now successfully arranged for constructing Drury Lane Theatre and satisfying all the just claims thereon, but in my humble judgement their Bill ought not to be thrown out merely on the score of its private injustice, but principally upon the superior objection of its unprecedented attempt to encroach on the prerogative of the Crown, and to insult and rebuke the Committee of privy Council by whose advice his majesty refused to grant to them, by his prerogative, the boon they now seek to wrest from him by an Act of the Legislature.

If I understand anything of the practice of the constitution, nothing is more clear than that neither House of Parliament will entertain any application which has for its object to do that by legislative enactment which the King is enabled to do by his establish'd P[r]erogative.

The new Projectors seek to establish a new Theatre in Westminster, for to prevent the declared opposition of

[1] Sir Vicary Gibbs (1751–1820).
[2] Or 'New London Theatre Bill', debated in the Commons on 9 May, when Whitbread said there was now the strongest probability that D.L.Th. would be rebuilt. Peter Moore's amendment, that the second reading be given in three months' time, was carried. S.'s speech embodied many of the objections made in the above letter. See Hansard, 1st Ser., xix. 1141–7.

the City of London, they have agreed that London shall be put out of the question.—By the 10th. of Geo. 2nd. and other acts, the power of granting Patents or Licences for dramatic representations in Westminster rests with the King alone. Last Year these Gentlemen applied to Parliament to make them a Corporation, but they had the decency to apply to the Crown for the Patent or Licence necessary to their purpose.—This upon a full hearing and investigation before the Privy Council was refused to them and they come to Parliament appealing against the decision of the King in Council and require a perpetual Patent by a Legislative Act!

I am sure I need not add a word more to induce your attendance tomorrow as the first legal Protector in our House of the Rights of the Crown than to request your attention to the particular Paragraph which I have referr'd to and mark'd in the Bill which I take the liberty of sending to you with this.

Trusting you will pardon this intrusion on your valuable time | I have the honor to be | with great Respect and Esteem | Your obedient Servant | R B Sheridan

Sir Vicary Gibbs

765. To the Prince Regent[1]

Windsor MSS. 18055–6. *Dock.*: Mr. Sheridan | May 24 1811

May 24th. 1811

Sir

I address a few Lines to you on the decision only this Day known to me respecting the re-appointment of his Royal Highness the Duke of York by your Royal Highness to the Station He is so eminently entitled to fill.[2] I always feel confident that your Royal Highness will graciously excuse any intrusion of mine while you are convinced it

---

[1] The Prince of Wales became Regent on 5 February 1811.

[2] The Duke of York had been removed from the office of Commander-in-Chief in 1809, following the parliamentary inquiry into the taking of bribes by his mistress, Mrs. Clarke, from persons seeking promotion in the army. The Committee found that the Duke knew of these transactions, but did not profit by them himself.

can only proceed from my unqualified attachment and devotion to your Royal Highness's Honor and Happiness. Whatever may have been my *doubts* respecting the *timing*[1] of this act of magnanimity and Justice on the Part of your Royal Highness and which doubts you have most condescendingly allow'd me frankly to express, I feel yet so implicit a deference to your superior Judgement, justified by so many recent instances, that I do not hesitate to express my conviction that your decision is wise as it is just: and that my apprehensions of its abating anything, at this moment, from your high estimation in the Public mind have proceeded from a timidity founded however on no unworthy motive. But be this as it may, The act being done, I have only with the utmost sincerity to beseech your Royal Highness to consider me as the Person on earth among the numbers attach'd to your Royal Highness and to the Duke who will with the most dutiful and affectionate zeal exert every faculty of my mind in all possible ways of just effort to maintain the act, and beat down all attempts to injure your Royal Highness or the Duke on this occasion come they from what quarter they may

I have felt it a relief to my mind to address these few lines to you this evening, as I have lately fear'd you might misunderstand me on this subject. | I have the Honor to be| with every sentiment of gratitude and Duty| Your ever faithful Servant | R B Sheridan

766. To His Wife

Osborn MS. *Wm.*: 1809.

[*24 May 1811 ?*]
Friday

My Dearest Hecca,
I own I am glad you stay another day in the country. I

---

[1] C. W. Wynn suggested, in a letter of 1 April 1811 (N.L.W. MS. 2791D), that S.'s recent eulogy of the Duke of York was meant to sound opinion concerning the Duke's taking up command again. But it is evident from a letter of Lord Lauderdale to S. (a copy of which, dated 'April 21, 1811' is Windsor MS. 17948–9) that S. now thought that 'a few months hence' would present a better opportunity for 'bringing His Royal Highness forward'. Lauderdale argued that it would be wiser to make the move as soon as possible and at a time when Parliament could discuss it.

think you wanted it—we have material business to Day in the House of Commons—but tomorrow dine with you I will.—I am very grateful for Henry's anxiety about Charles —yet on reflexion I cannot help thinking there must have been some misrepresentation or misconception, For I never saw anything approaching to malice in our dear Beastie—and where there is a total absence of that rely on it there must be the ingredient of some degree of dulness in the mind of anyone man or boy, who is easily hurt at goodhumour'd and playful ridicule any retort of which I am sure Charles would bear with the most perfect chearfulness. I hope you spoke to him however—of course I have not said a word. It is however the precise subject perhaps respecting which I may be of the greatest service to him—a Talent for ridicule even to bitterness and severity has not been wanting among such as I possess—but a certain Portion of good sense and more of good nature very early decided me to forego the use of it, and I may say, without feeling it much of a boast, that a more inoffensive companion among the various classes it has been my lot to mix with has scarcely been found.—You shall see I will now apply myself to Charle[s]'s mind and Taste—his heart I confidently believe admits of no amendment—and so I think also of his temper.—

The creature went off this morning in a very safe long coach for Winchester. He had £2 stock from Brand and I gave him £6 more so if his stage costs him two, He will have £6 in pocket—

I send you a little mot[1] and cards and Letter for Anne— my Love to her. I am no dealer in Professions—but it shall go hard if something shall not be done for Harry. Pray now don't dislike the House in C. Square—you wanted some Place where you could have a little musick of an evening and upon my soul I do not pay so much for it as Tom receives for his mansion in South Audley St.[2]

no particular news. I am going to the House—where I shall probably be obliged to speak—on the Irish Papers[3]—

[1] Kiss? In dialect a mark at quoits (O.E.D.). [2] No. 11. [3] S. spoke on duties on advertisements in Irish newspapers in the debate of 24 May 1811. See Hansard, 1st Ser., xx. 312–13.

so you ought rather to thank me for this Letter—but in Truth Charles is nearer to my heart than any Political consideration.—Bless you again and let me find mots upon your cheeks | S

767. To Richard Peake

McAdam MS. *Address*: Mr. Peake *Dock.*: Mr. Sheridan *Wm.*: 1811

[*1811*]
Grosvenor Place
Tuesday Night

My Dear Peake

Pray send me a bill of two months drawn on and accepted by Wilkie leaving a Place for my name as the Drawer—

I had no conception the other one was near due and pray oblige me by sending me two Pounds by William[1]—Whitbread has now settled to advance the money 1 want and you shall have all these scraps returned in the cours[e] of this week. | God bless you | R B S

768. To Richard Peake

Osborn MS. *Address*: Mr. Peake *Dock.*: Mr. Sheridan

[*Before June 1811*][2]
Friday Evening

My Dear Dick—

Deducting *only* £10 in part *for the present* (and you shall have plenty more presently) you should have sent me £30 the other Day instead of £17 odd. I have since had £4 from you and Gregory £3—so there would remain about £6—which pray send by the Bearer—it is a pity I should be teaz'd about twopences just now. I am sorry to find myself compell'd to expose Ward as a most determined Knave—but I must and will do it.—| yours ever | R B S.

[1] Gregory, S.'s servant.
[2] William Gregory left S.'s service in June 1811: see his statement of 6 July 1813 in Winston, 1813–14. His name first appears in D.L.Th. accounts in 'Salaries, 1804–06' (Folger MS.), on 22 Dec. 1804.

769. To Eleanor Creevey

J. R. Blackett-Ord MS. *Pub.*: *Creevey Papers*, i. 39. *Address*: Mrs. Creevey | Park-Place *Fr.*: R B Sheridan

[1811]
Grosvenor Place
Saturday morning
12 o'clock

My Dear Mrs. Creevey

I left Hester about two hours ago—she violently expects you—remember we have a bed for you, and fishing rod for Creevey on monday morning. If you will stay over monday Hester and Richmond Hill will make you quite well and there are not cockney but classical Lions[1] for Creevey to see.

I hope you are quite well. Hester has been ill too. | Yours truly | R B S

770. To Sir Robert Barclay

Harvard MS. *Pub.*: *P. & S. C.*, 29 July 1861, lot 1134. *Dock.*: From R. B. Sheridan 1811 June. *Wm.*: 1809

June 1811
Friday
4 o'clock

My Dear Barclay

I am just returned from Holland House where I slept last Night and having hasten'd to the Bankers lo! to my confusion I am come from thence Re infectâ. I can't tell you how this embarrasses me—having so confidently relied on finding the thing done that I had given drafts for Payments tomorrow. Pray pray see it settled in the morning, and give me a few lines by bearer which I may send to Hare tonight | Yours ever | R B S

---

[1] The royal gardens at Richmond contained 'a collection of curious foreign and domestic beasts' that was open to the public in summer on Sundays: see *Leigh's New Picture of London* (4th ed., 1820), p. 489.

771. To Thomas Shaw

Harvard MS. *Address*: Thos. Shaw Esqr. *Fr.*: R B S *Dock.*: Sheridan | July 4th. | 1811

3 July 1811
Cavendish-Square
Wednesday Evening

Dear Sir

When and where can I have the Pleasure of seeing you[1] tomorrow? | Yours truly | R B S.

772. To Lord Holland

Holland House MS., S. 91. *Address*: Lord Holland *Fr.*: R B S

[July 1811]
Wednesday Evening

The exhibition of the two Models is unavoidably put off to Friday at three. The first at Benjamin Wyatts[2]—Foley-Place[3]—then Phillips at Carlton-House | ever yours | R B S.

Tom writes a note to you on a subject which poor Fellow he is very anxious about, and which I will explain when we meet.

773. To William Adam

Adam MS. *Dock.*: Mr. Sheridan

[Aug. 1811][4]
Thursday Night

My Dear Adam

I sought you in vain yesterday in Bloomsbury-Square

[1] In May S. promised to pay half his private debt to Shaw in a fortnight. Now Whitbread claimed that S. was 'without money and without resources', and offered five shillings in the pound to cover Shaw's arrears of salary, £12. 10s. per annum for his £500 share, and £1,000 outright for his £3,000 share. Shaw refused the offers in his reply of 15 July 1811 (Harvard MS.).

[2] Architect (1775–1850?). Philip Wyatt was his brother.

[3] *The Times*, 22 July 1811, reported that the Committee for the Rebuilding of D.L.Th. had seen Benjamin Wyatt's model of a new theatre at his home, 22 Foley Place.

[4] Mr. D. E. Ginter notes that the letter was one of a bundle docketed 'Aug. 1811'.

misinformed by P. Moore but I understand you are to be in Town tomorrow—send me a Line to say where I can meet you. I have something of importance to say to you *Theatrically*—but something of more importance *politically*| yours ever| R B S| could we not eat a mutton chop together? there is a committee at P Moores at 3, but I want to see you alone

774. To Sir Robert Barclay

Harvard MS.

[*10 Sept. 1811*]
Tuesday Evening

My Dear Barclay
the Model at Carlton-House will be lit up tomorrow for Lord and Lady Holland the Duke Infandado[1] etc.—come if you can but I entreat you not to fail a committee on Thursday at 3 at P Moores| Yrs ever| R B S.

775. To Thomas Shaw

Harvard MS. *Address*: T. Shaw Esq | No. 1 Temple-Hall *Fr*.: R B Sheridan *Dock*.: Sheridan Sep 13 | 1811

12 Sept. 1811
Thursday

My Dear Sir
I shall be much obliged to you to meet me at Peakes[2] tomorrow a quarter before two. I shall be on my road to Mr. Whitbreads—| yours truly| R B S

---

[1] The Duke of Infantados was Ambassador Extraordinary from the Spanish Cortes. Accompanied by Lord Holland and Lord John Russell, he saw Philip Wyatt's model for the new D.L.Th. in the Gold Room at Carlton House, on 11 Sept. See *The Star*, 13 Sept.

1811.
[2] Shaw was anxious to become leader of the band at the Lyceum Theatre and obtained S.'s support for his application. On 4 Oct. Peake wrote to Shaw (Harvard MS.) to say he had been unsuccessful.

776. To ——

Pub.: Rae, ii. 277.

[*1811*]

The first general meeting of our theatre grand corporation is on the 4th[1] of October, and every exertion of my mind and every hour of my time must be employed to meet that occasion. Oh! how I long to be fairly and honourably freed from all connexion with this to me disagreeable property! Yet in the new hands in which it will be placed it will be their own fault if it does not prosper.

777. To John Wilson Croker[2]

Text from a transcription by Sir Shane Leslie, of the original formerly at Lowther Castle.

[*14 Oct. 1811*]
Cavendish Square

Lieutenant W. Stevenson of H M Ship Egmont has had the good Fortune I understand to have been for some time noted by Mr. York[3] for Promotion for services performed. And having a high opinion of his character, and personally wishing him well I cannot resist his Father[’s][4] sollicitation to give him this Letter altho I have so little pretention to suppose that my recommending can be of use to him. But so it is that many will have it that I retain some privileged influence at the Admiralty which the Practise and kindness of Lord Melville[5] and Lord Mulgrave[6] I apprehend has contributed to countenance. It is on this account that as

[1] 'The first general assembly of subscribers to the rebuilding of the Theatre-Royal, Drury Lane' was held on 14 Oct. 1811.

[2] Croker (1780–1857) was Secretary to the Admiralty.

[3] Charles Philip Yorke (1764–1834), First Lord of the Admiralty.

[4] One John Stevenson agreed to lend

S. £100 on 29 Aug. 1811: see Harvard MS. docketed 'Proposal'.

[5] Henry Dundas, 1st Viscount Melville (1742–1811), was First Lord of the Admiralty 1804–5.

[6] Sir Henry Phipps, 1st Earl of Mulgrave (1755–1831), was First Lord of the Admiralty 1807–10.

I have not the honor of sufficiently knowing Mr Yorke to justify my intruding on him I beg you to pardon the Liberty of my thus addressing you. I have the Honor to be, with great esteem and respect your obedient servant | R B S

778. To the Prince Regent

Windsor MS. 18727. *Dock.*: R. B. Sheridan | Sept. 16 1811

17 Oct. [*1811*]
Cavendish-Square
Thursday Oct 16th:—

Sir

The unvaried and protecting Kindness with which you have so long regarded my private situation and circumstances (placing wholly out of the question all political considerations) induces me address to you these few frank Lines. I hate to intrude myself upon you respecting small matters especially when they relate to myself, but the Truth is that while I am on the point of parting with my Theatrical Property on an arrangement which would leave me discharged from a single Debt to any one [on] earth,[1] and give me what remains of my Life to the exertions of my own freed and I trust active exertions in your Royal Highness's service, I find my Hopes thwarted by disputes in the Committee under the act of Parliament; the main cause of which is a difference of opinion respecting the merits of the candidates for building the new Theatre, a Difference and a difficulty which I am confident your Royal Highness's interference would immediately settle, but your's alone[2]—

[1] Whitbread saw the Prince Regent on 18 Oct. and informed him that £400,000 had been subscribed for rebuilding D.L.Th., 'out of which £40,000 is made applicable to the purchase of the old patent interest' (*Gent. Mag.* lxxxi (1811), pt. 2, 478). See Moore, ii. 410, for the terms accepted by the Sheridans: £12,000 by Tom S., and £24,000 (with £4,000 for the fruit offices and reversion of boxes) by S.

[2] Benjamin Wyatt wrote to C. W. Ward on 13 Aug. 1811 (Winston, 1810–11) to say that McMahon had remarked that Philip Wyatt's design would be accepted. In a letter to McMahon [?] of 15 Oct. (Windsor MSS. 18706–8) Whitbread said that the Committee ought not to have to decide the dispute between the brothers. Cf. Farington, vii. 12, 130. Eventually Benjamin Wyatt's design was accepted.

The Particulars I cannot presume to trouble your Royal Highness with in writing, but I will have the Honor of attending your Commands in the morning— | Your Royal Highness's | most devoted | and grateful Servant | R B Sheridan

779. [To Thomas Shaw]

Osborn MS. *Dock.*: Impudent—I have as much common sense as | Mr. Sheridan tho' most certainly *not* | so much uncommon knavery.

[*1811*]
Cavendish-Square
Friday Evening

Dear Sir,
I am very sorry that thro' the Blunder of my Servants I did not see you when you call'd to Day in Cavendish-Square. I shall be glad to see you on Sunday here or at Peake's.— There is no common sense but in your frankly disclosing to me what is the settlement you want. From your old and long Friendship[1] with my Father in Law Linley you must be assured of my good-will to you.—If you have thought your character attack'd by Mr Arnold or my Son[2] you know I am no party to that but, that on the contrary my sincere opinion is that you are an honest man and a true Friend to old Drury and | Yr | R B Sheridan

780. [To Thomas Shaw?]

Osborn MS.

[*1811* ?]
Tuesday Evening

Dear Sir,
Whether by the fault of the Post or the neglect of my

[1] Mentioned as early as Nov. 1785.
[2] In a draft of a letter to Whitbread, Shaw wrote on 22 Oct. 1811: '. . . I will here say nothing of the Calumnies spread abroad against my Name and Character, because Mr. Sheridan has most solemnly denied himself to be the Author (tho' he admits them to have been reported by one of his Family) because he has pledged himself to his Belief in their untruth and to my Integrity. This is the only act of justice he has done me.' (Harvard MS.) The pledge was given when S. called on Shaw at Shaw's chambers 'about two months back'.

servants I did not receive your note untill long after the hour named in it.—I will however call on you tomorrow about the time you mention—my wish is to propose something very grateful respecting the feelings you have express'd on the attack you conceive to have been made on your character and that consideration I presume induced you to call on me | Your's very truly | R B Sheridan.

781. To Samuel Whitbread

Harvard MS. Copy in Mrs. S.'s hand. *Pub.*: Moore, ii. 412–17. *Dock.*: Mr. Sheridan to Mr. Whitbread *Wm.*: 1808

[Late Oct.–Early Nov. 1811]

My Dear Whitbread,

I am not going to write you a controversial[1] or even an argumentative letter but simply to put down the heads of a few matters which I wish shortly to converse with you upon in the most amicable and Temperate manner, deprecating the impatience which may some times have mix'd in our discussions and not contending who has been the aggressor.

The main point you seem to have had so much at heart you have carried, so there is an end of that, and I shall as fairly and cordially endeavour to advise and assist Mr. Benjamin Wyatt[2] in the improving and perfecting his plan as if it had been my own preferable selection, assuming as I must do that there cannot exist an individual in England so presumptuous or so void of common sense as not sincerely to solicit the aid of my practical experience on this occasion even were I not in justice to the subscribers bound spontaneously to offer it.

But it would be unmanly dissimulation in me to retain the sentiments I do with respect to *your* doctrine on this subject and not express what I so strongly feel—That doctrine was to my utter astonishment to say no more first promulgated to me in a letter from you written in Town in

[1] There is a further copy in W.T. Here it reads 'conventional'.
[2] The agreement with H. R. Rowles for the building of the new theatre to the design of Benjamin Wyatt is dated 18 Oct. 1811.

the following terms.—Speaking of Building and Plans you say to me '*You are in no way answerable if a bad Theatre is built it is not* YOU *who build it, and if we come to the* STRICT RIGHT *of the thing you have* NO BUSINESS TO INTERFERE' and further on you say '*Will* YOU but STAND ALOOF, *and every thing will go smooth*, and a good Theatre shall be built'[1] and in conversation you put as a similar case that '*if a man sold another a piece of land it was nothing to the seller whether the purchaser built himself a good or a bad House upon it.*'

Now I declare before God I never felt more amazement than that a Man of your powerful intellect, just view of all subjects and knowledge of the world should hold such language or resort to such arguments, and I must be convinced that, altho' in an impatient moment this opinion may have fallen from you, upon the least reflexion or the slightest attention to the reason of the case you would 'Albeit unused to the retracting mood'[2] confess the erroneous view you had taken of the subject, otherwise I must think, and with the deepest regret would it be, that altho' you originally engaged in this business from motives of the purest[3] and kindest regard for me and my family, your ardour and zealous eagerness to accomplish the difficult task you had undertaken have led you in this instance to overlook what is due to my feelings, to my honor, and my just interests. For supposing I were to '*stand aloof*' totally unconcern'd, provided I were paid for my share, whether the new Theatre were excellent or execrable, and that the result should be that the subscribers instead of profit could not through the misconstruction of the house obtain one per cent for their money, do you seriously believe you could find a single man woman or child in the Kingdom out of the Committee who would believe that I was wholly guiltless of the failure having been so stultified and proscribed by the Committee (a Committee of *my own nomination*!) as to have been

---

[1] On 5 Nov. 1811 Whitbread wrote to Tom S.: 'It is unquestionably hard and galling that you should be in the sort of proscription there is on the name of Sheridan, as connected with the New Theatre. . . . The Question asked before any Man or Woman will put down their Names is this "Has Mr. Sheridan anything to do with it?" a direct Negative suffices. . . .' (Add. MS. 42721, f. 79.)

[2] Cf. *Othello*, v. ii. 349: 'Albeit unused to the melting mood.'

[3] W.T. reads 'truest'.

compell'd to admit as the condition of my being paid for my share that 'it was nothing to me whether the Theatre was good or bad' or on the contrary can it be denied that the reproaches of disappointment thro' the great body of the subscribers would be directed against me and me alone? So much as to *character*, now as to my feelings on the subject I must say that in friendship at least if not in *'strict right'*, they ought to be consulted even tho' the Committee could neither prove that I had not to apprehend any share in the discredit and discontent which might follow the ill success of their plan, [n]or that I was entitled to brave whatever malice or ignorance might direct against me. Next and lastly as to my just interest in the property I am to part with, a consideration to which however careless I might be were I alone concern'd, I am bound to attend in justice to my own private creditors. Observe how the matter stands, I agree to wa[i]ve my own *'strict right'* to be paid before the Funds can be applied to the building[1] and this in the confidence and on the continued understanding that my advice should be so far respected that even should the subscription not fill I should at least see a Theatre capable of being charged with and ultimately of discharging what should remain justly due to the Proprietors. To illustrate this I refer to the size of the Pit, the number of private Boxes and the annexation of a Tavern—but in what situation would the doctrine of your Committee leave me and my Son? 'It is nothing to us how the Theatre is built or whether it prospers or not'. These are two circumstances we have nothing to do with only unfortunately upon *them* may depend our best chance of receiving any Payment for the Property we part with—it is nothing to us how the ship is refitted or mann'd only we must leave all we are worth on board her and abide the chance of her success. Now I am confident your justice will see that in order that the Committee should in *'strict right'* become entitled to deal thus with us and bid us *stand aloof* they should buy us out

---

[1] 'The two Messrs. Sheridan ... expressly declined receiving anything until the Theatre should be built, and appeared disposed to abandon their claim rather than prevent the rebuilding of the Theatre' (*The Times*, 31 Oct. 1811): Whitbread's statement at the general meeting of 30 Oct.

and make good the Payment. But the reverse of this has been my own proposal and I neither repent nor wish to make any change in it.

I have totally departed from my intention when I first began this letter for which I ought to apologise to you, but it may save much future talk—other less important matters will do in conversation. You will allow that I have placed in you the most implicit confidence—have the reasonable trust in me that in any communication I may have with B. Wyatt my object will not be to *obstruct* as you have hastily expressed it, but bonâ fide to assist him to render his Theatre as perfect as possible as well with a view to the public accommodation as to profit to the subscribers, neither of which can be obtain'd without establishing a reputation for him which must be the basis of his future fortune—and altho' I cannot approve of his conduct in the contest, my manner to him shall be just the same as it would have been to his brother, or to both of them had they join'd[1]

And now after all this statement you will perhaps be surprised to find how little I require—simply some resolution of the Committee to the effect of that I enclose.

I conclude with heartily[2] thanking you for the declaration you made respecting me and reported to me by Peter Moore, at the close of the last meeting of the Committee.[3] I am convinced of your sincerity—but as I have before described the character of the gratitude I feel towards you in a letter written likewise in this house, I have only to say that every sentiment in that letter remains unabated and unalterable | Ever my dear Whitbread | yours faithfully

P.S. The discussion we had yesterday respecting some investigation of the *Past* which I deem so essential to my character and to my peace of mind and your present concurrence with me on that subject have relieved my mind from great anxiety, tho' I cannot but still think the better opportunity has been pass'd by.—One word more, and I

---

[1] The words, 'and altho' . . . join'd', are omitted by Moore.

[2] W.T. 'hastily'.

[3] The committee met for the first time on 1 Mar. 1811. At the close of the second general assembly of subscribers on 30 Oct. 1811, S. and Tom S. were thanked for their liberal conduct in the adjustment of their claims.

release you, Tom inform'd me that you had hinted to him that any demands not practicable to be settled by the Committee must fall on the Proprietors. My resolution is to take all such on myself, and to leave Tom's share untouch'd.[1]

782. To His Son Tom

Add. MS. 42271, ff. 132–3. *Dock.*: [by Tom S.] My Father.

[*Nov. 1811*]
Thursday Evening

My Dear Tom,
    I call'd at 7 this evening in South-Audley St. having heard a strange rumour that you had been seen in Town in the morning—![2] I thought it impossible that you could have returned to your house yesterday without *sending* at least to me!
    I think Theatre matters at least as far as relates to *you* are going on very fortunately. I take on myself all the stray claims, heavy enough in pretension, which the committee cannot liquidate and YOU will have your £12000 *clear* which from my soul I believe will be the last money in the shape of profit any man will ever get out of a THEATRE[3]
    I am very anxious to know how you are   beg Caroline at least to write.
    I could not keep my engagement to see you before you left Town, my business with Whitbread demanded my staying at Southill after the Duke of Glocesters departure—[4]
    write and tell me about Oatlands | Yours ever | R B S

I will send you a copy of a correspondence between me and Whitbread while at Southill this last time.

---

[1] Whitbread wrote to Tom S. on 5 Nov. 1811 informing him that 'Your Father says he will not suffer your share to be diminished. He will be the only eventuall Sufferer. . . .' (Add. MS. 42721, f. 80.)
    [2] Tom S. was at Lymington when Whitbread wrote to him on 5 Nov.

1811. See Add. MS. 42721, f. 82.
    [3] The debts of D.L.Th. were said to have increased by £90,000 between 1812 and 1819. See Add. MS. 27831, f. 110.
    [4] *The Times*, 4 Nov. 1811, reported that the Duke had lately visited Whitbread at Southill.

783. To S. Jernyngham[1]

Salt MS. *Pub.*: Rhodes, p. 230.

Cavendish-Square
Monday 25th Novr. 1811.

Private

My Dear Sir,

In consequence of Sir Oswald Moseley having publicly declined[2] to stand for Stafford at the next general Election I have been strongly solicited by the leading Party in the Town to *return* again to *my old farm*—I had promised Sir Oswald as a party Friend and a *Friend to the Catholic Rights* every Support in my Power, and He now I am sure will do the same by me. Many motives *under the present circumstances* lead me to accede to and pursue this offer—and none so much as my ardent wish to support the catholic Claims in an *independent* seat. This is the sole political object now near my heart, and that which I wish resolutely to support both in the House of Commons and with whatever humble influence I may possess with the Prince Regent.[3] I am sure of my Return again for Ilchester and even of the second seat for my Son. Yet perhaps you may surmise—and pardon me at the same time for not being more explicit—my motive is to stand the master of my own motions in the ensuing session of Parliament, especially on the *Question of the Catholic Claims*.

The constant support which I am indebted for to your Family in Stafford, and the kind alacrity with which *you* offer'd to accompany me to that Place on a former occasion from Carlton House are remember'd by me with just Gratitude. I have now only to request you to communicate

---

[1] Probably Edward Jerningham (1774–1822), who was a barrister and became secretary to the British Board of Catholics. See the *Annual Biography and Obituary . . . 1823*, vii. 446. His eldest brother was prevented by attainder from succeeding as 8th Baron Stafford, but the reversal was achieved in 1824, and he assumed (1826) the name of Stafford-Jerningham.

[2] Reported in *Staff. Adv.*, 16 Nov. 1811.

[3] On 1 Sept. Grey reported to Lord Grenville that S. had 'very lately been expressing so much discontent at the Prince's conduct, as to talk of resigning his place and his seat in Parliament' (*Dropmore Papers*, x. 167).

this Letter to your Brother—sanguinely confiding that He will continue on the present occasion the same cordial support which I have so long experienced from your most respected Family—| I have the Honor to be| My Dear Sir| Your's most sincerely | R B Sheridan

S Jernyngham Esq.

784. To Sir Oswald Mosley

Harrow MS.: Rae, v. 259. *Pub.*: Moore, ii. 422–4.

Private and confidential

Cavendish Square Nov. 29 18[*11*]

Dear Sir Oswald

Being apprized that you have decided to decline offering yourself a Candidate for Stafford when a future Election may arrive, a Place where you are highly esteemed, and where any humble Service in my power, as I have before declared to you, should have been at your command I have determined to accept the very cordial invitation I have received from *old friends* in that quarter, and (tho entirely secure of my Seat at Ilchester and indeed even of the second seat for my Son, thro' the liberality of Sir Wm. Manners) to return to the old Goal from whence I started thirty one years since! You will easily see that arrangements at Ilchester may be made towards assisting me in point of expence to meet *any Opposition*, and *in that respect* nothing will be *wanting*. It will I confess be very gratifying to me to be again Elected by *the Sons* of *those* who chose me in the year 80 and adhered to me so stoutly and so long. I think I was returned for Stafford seven if not eight times,[1] including two most tough and expensive contests,[2] and in taking a temporary leave of them I am sure my credit must stand well, for not a Shilling did I leave unpaid. I have written to the Jerninghams who in the handsomest manner have ever given me their warmest support,[3] and as no Political object

[1] Six times.
[2] 1784 and 1790? Cf. Moore, i. 405, and *Shrewsbury Chronicle*, 25 June 1790.

[3] Indicated in Edward Jerningham's letter to Lady Bedingfield: 'I have declared open hostility against every

interests my mind so much as the Catholic Cause, I have
no doubt that independent of their personal Friendship I
shall receive a continuation of their honorable support.
I feel it to be no presumption to add that other respectable
Interest in the Neighbourhood will be with me.

I need scarcely add my sanguine hope that whatever
Interest rests with you (which ought to be much) will also
be in my favor | I have the honor to be with great esteem and
regard | yrs most sincerely | R B Sheridan

I mean to be in Stafford from Lord G Levisons[1] in about
a fortnight

785. To Thomas Perkins

New York Public Library, Berg MS. *Pub.*: Rae, ii. 259–60. *Wm.*:
1810

Cavendish-Square
Thursday 29 Novr. 1811

Private
Dear Perkins,

I have really been so incessantly engaged that it has not
been in my Power to keep my Promise of writing to you by
last monday's Post. I have now to say that upon mature
consideration, and reviewing other accounts I have received
of the disposition of your Borough I have decided in my
own mind to embrace the present opportunity of declaring
again for Stafford—I am not only secure of *Ilchester* for
myself but also of the *second seat* for *my son*—yet I pant for
my old *independent* seat—and my own means, as well as
the assistance I can receive if necessary from *another* Quarter
enable me to *meet any opposition.*—You are a Sportsman[2] and
as all lovers of Field Sports must be more or less friendly to

tenant who holds, and against every
Man who expects to hold land, and who
opposes Sheridan—I think by great
personal exertion I can muster near one
hundred votes. . . .' (*The Jerningham
Letters* (ed. E. Castle, 1896), ii. 23–24.)

[1] Possibly the visit to Tixall did not

take place then, but S. stayed there
after his defeat in Oct. 1812.

[2] 'T. Bateman Perkins, Stafford,
Gent.' is named in the list of Staffordshire gentlemen with certificates for
killing game, in *Aris's Birmingham
Gazette*, 22 Sept. 1788.

Poetry I may refer you to Gouldsmith for my Feelings on the present occasion.—

> And as a Hare whom Hounds and Horns pursue
> Pants to the Goal from whence at first she flew
> I still have hopes my long vexations past
> There to return—and die at *home* at last.[1]

Political Death, mind I mean—but even before that I trust that we and the few surviving old Friends may yet spend some pleasant Days together.

I have secured the Jernyngham Interest and am writing to Sir Oswald Moseley and shall also to Monckton—and Lord Granville Levison—application will be made to Lord Talbot[2] from the Properest quarter. Let me know if there are any others to whom you think it would be useful to apply. Pray communicate this to our old Friends Drakeford[3] and Horton to whom I also will write as also to my Friend Dr. Knight[4] to whom I feel much obliged. I shall be anxious to hear from you| Your's Dear Perkins| most sincerely| R B Sheridan

786. To General T. H. Turner[5]

Windsor MS. 18933. *Dock.*: 29 Dec 1811 | Mr. Sheridan | Police

> *29 Dec. 1811*
> Cavendish—
> Square
> Sunday Evening

My Dear General,

I wish'd very much for an opportunity to have spoken to the Regent on the subject of the Police[6] conceiving the present to be an occasion when great Popularity may

---

[1] *The Deserted Village*, ll. 93–96, slightly paraphrased.

[2] Charles Chetwynd, 3rd Earl Talbot of Hensol (1777–1849), Lord-Lieutenant of Staffordshire, 1812–49. A moderate Tory.

[3] Edward Drakeford of Charnes Hall (1750–1814). 'He was through life the

steady and uniform friend and admirer of the Rt. Hon. R. B. Sheridan' (*Staff. Adv.*, 5 Mar. 1814).

[4] A physician at Stafford, who organized S.'s meeting there in May 1812.

[5] Tomkyns Hilgrove Turner (1766 ?–1843). Deputy secretary at Carlton House. Knighted, 1814. [6] See p. 147.

originate from him—but I have not left my room and
scarcely even my Bed since I saw you on sunday last.[1] I
find you have seen Arnold. I send you his Letter to me and
his Plan. I hope to be able to get out on tuesday when I will
come to Carlton-House | yours ever sincerely | R B Sheridan

General Turner

787. To Dr. Ward

Osborn MS.

[*1811–12*]
Cavendish-
Square
Sunday Evening

Private
My Dear Doctor Ward,
  I am confident you will not have attributed it to any want
of regard and respect towards you that you have not heard
from me before on the subject of my returning to Stafford,[2]
but I have been in a state of indecision in my own mind
which has prevented my communicating with you 'till I
had finally formed my determination. That Determination
is now taken and I shall be in Stafford in a few Days, where
I hope to have the Pleasure of seeing [you]. I am secure of
both seats at Ilchester—but I wish for my native Home
and I find such a concentration of Interest in my favor that
I doubt not of success | yours truly | R B Sheridan

788. To John Kenderdine

Yale MS. *Pub.*: Moore, ii. 424.

[*1811–12*]
Cavendis[h Sq]³uare
Sunday Night

Dear King John,
  I shall be in Stafford in the course of next week and if

---

[1] Lady Bessborough stated on 31 Dec.
that S. was 'very ill with a fever and
inflammation on his lungs' (*Leveson
Gower Corr*. ii. 429).
  [2] Announced in the *Staff. Adv.* of
7 Dec. 1811: 'Mr. Sheridan, who
represented this Borough in Parliament
for so many years, has declared his
intention of again becoming a candidate
at the next election.'   [3] Torn.

your Majesty[1] does not renew our old alliance I shall never again have Faith in any Potentate on Earth. | your's very sincerely | R B Sheridan

Mr. John Kenderdine[2]

789. To Richard Peake

Salt MS. *Address*: Mr. Peake *Dock.*: Mr. Sheridan

[*1811-12* ?]
Monday
Night.

My Dear Dick

you must make the 10s a £1 for lo! and behold! just after you were gone came the *enclosed* with a Parcel of Game from Norfolk and William was obliged to put the man off till tomorrow. I send you one of the *ares* (stafford). The more I think of Stafford the more I am determined to proceed. I shall have money plenty by and bye tho' none out of my Pocket will ultimately be wanted. In consequence of old Dudleys hint what think you of my taking down *Bell*[3] my old and attach'd Friend as a fourth in Ironmongers Barouche with *a contract in his Pocket* for £3000 worth of Shoes to be fairly divided among the Masters. I think also of putting forth an advertisement or an authorised Handbill by tomorrows Post—so that my intentions shall be known on *thursday* and I appear at least the *first* in the Field, for I see clearly the intention of the *Friday's Dinners*. I forget the Stafford Editors name[4] who has always been a friend of mine tho I have neglected him and is a devilish clever Fellow and one Tom greatly esteems—but I will trace you out in the morning and settle all this— | yours ever | R B S.

What's Drakeford's direction? I will shew you the additional

[1] The Stafford poll-book of 1812 reveals that John Kenderdine voted for S. Nine other Kenderdines also voted, six of them for S. Cf. i. 134.

[2] Another hand has corrected 'Kenderdine' to 'K'.

[3] Present at a meeting of the master boot and shoe makers at the Crown and Anchor on 17 Apr. 1812: see *The Times*, 18 Apr. 1812. Cf. Rhodes, p. 234.

[4] Joshua Drewry was the publisher of the *Staff. Adv.* and had considerable influence in the town. Cf. *Staff. Adv.*, 13 Apr. 1809.

Letters I have written tonight   my heart is in the Thing and
if I start *I will not be beat by God*! | R B S
Forward this to Bell—I think Greek St.[1]

790. To the Reverend H. Rathbone[2]

Osborn MS.

[*1811–12*]
⸚ Cavendish-Square
Sunday Night.

Dear Sir
    Having heretofore been honor'd with your support, and
having now decided to comply with the wishes of many most
kind and attach'd old Friends by offering myself once more
to represent the Borough of Stafford (the Goal from which
thirty one years since I first started in my Parliamentary
Career) allow me to express the satisfaction I shall now feel
in now experiencing a continuance of your Goodwill and
interest in my favour.— | yours most sincerely | R B
Sheridan

Reverend Mr Rathbone

791. To Richard Peake

Harvard MS. *Dock.*: Mr. Sheridan

[*1811–12* ?]
Tuesday

My Dear Dick,
    By Heaven I can do nothing with the enclosed. I must
entreat your endorsement—Whitbread knows every thing[3]
and will take care of everything— | ever yours | R B S.

Ironmonger will be here early on wednesday morning.
I will send you a Letter presently to take to Monkton—

[1] Thomas Bell's address was 47 Dean
Street, Soho.
[2] He was Mayor of Stafford, and took
the chair at S.'s meeting on 13 May
1812 at the Town Hall. See the *Staff.*
Adv., 16 May 1812.
[3] About the decision to stand for
Stafford ?

792. To Richard Peake

Salt MS. *Dock.*: Mr. Sheridan *Wm.*: 1810

[*1811–12* ?]
Saturday Night

My Dear Dick
In answer to your last by G—d I will never rest 'till I se[e] you safe and beyond the reach of their jealous Despotism.[1] I know them now—and mark the end.—
As to Stafford I am decided to set out for it on *wednesday*[2]—we will have a very jolly jaunt of one week—make a fair copy of Monctons enclosed Letter—done in the *middle* of a sheet Paper and not in your vile way of beginning at the Top.—And sign 'a true Copy—and that the lines scored are as in the original by Mr Monkton.'[3] I send Lord G. Levisons answer—bring me back these tomorrow morning before eleven. I have an answer for Sir O. Mosely pledging himself to the most energetic support| yrs | R B S.

793. [To a Stafford Supporter]

Yale MS.

[*1811–12* ?]
Monday Night.

My dear Sir,
Something particular has delay'd our coming—but we shall have the Pleasure of being with you on *Thursday*—and then you will dispose of us. I am convinced for reasons too long for the present that Drakeford is wrong in thinking I had better not come now—but of this when I have the Pleasure of seeing you.| yours truly,| R B Sheridan
you must not alter your Plan of coming to Town a Day on our account.

[1] The Committee for rebuilding D.L.Th.? Peake remained in office as Treasurer from 1812 to 1815.
[2] S. paid a visit of six days to Stafford in 1812, arriving on Friday, 8 May, and speaking with Sir Oswald Mosley at the Town Hall on 13 May. See the

Staff. Adv., 9 and 16 May 1812.
[3] Possibly a letter of support. Edward Monckton's letter to the burgesses of Stafford, notifying them that he would not stand again for election to Parliament because of his advanced age, was printed in the *Staff. Adv.*, 8 Feb. 1812.

794. To Thomas Perkins

Salt MS. *Dock.*: Note of R. B. Sheridan to Perkins Esq of Rickerscote, Stafford.

[1811–12 ?]
Friday

My Dear Perkins

We had the Carriage at the Door yesterday certain of being in Stafford—but a political circumstance which I have not now a moment to explain compells me to postpone my visit for a very short time—when I fix the Day I shall be punctual to an hour. Peake writes and I will again tomorrow[1] | Your's truly | R B Sheridan

795. To Richard Peake

F. W. Hilles MS. *Address*: Mr. Peake *Dock.*: Mr. Sheridan *Fr.*: R B S

[1811–12 ?]
at P. Moore's
past 8—

My Dear P.

For G—d sake do something for me—try Spring close—and leave the Note with him—and I'll get it discounted tomorrow or thursday—there is not one halfpenny in C. Square for breakfast tomorrow.— | Your's ever | R B S

796. To J. Willoughby Gordon[2]

Pub.: Maggs Catalogue 433 (1922), item 3696.

[1811–12]
Cavendish Square

. . . I make it a rule not to presume to make any direct application to the Prince on any matter that ought to go

---

[1] Princeton University Library contains a cover addressed by S. to Perkins at 'Ricardscourt' and dated 'London May five 1812', a Tuesday.

[2] General (afterwards Sir) James Willoughby Gordon, Bart. (1773–1851). In 1811 he was Commissary-General.

thro the proper official channel—I believe it would be pleasing to him, if a request could with propriety be complied with. . . .

797. To Sir Robert Barclay

Pub.: S.C., 26 Nov. 1891, lot 307.

[*1811–12*]
Sunday evening

Since we parted circumstances have occurred which induce me to adjure[1] you as a man of Principle and honor, and (no weaker motive I trust) as MY FRIEND to give your mind and attendance to the Committee *at last agreed to by Whitbread* himself, namely to enquire into the causes of the Debts and embarrassments of the late Theatre, and to investigate and decide impartially whether blame or merit are ascribable to the Proprietors in that respect your share in the execution of this *Duty* I require from your situation as a member of the Committee, but I solicit it with more confidence from you as *my private and confidential Friend* come and assist favourably and fairly (for nothing but the most impartial fairness do I require) and Whitbread *now* confesses he will be rejoiced to receive your report, tho' he certainly has browbeat the committee into almost a nonentity, but browbeat or subdue me he cannot and shall not. Send me back the *correspondence* which I think must have *surprised* and even *affected* you, follow my fortunes while you think me right and you will never repent it.

798. To M. Edmondson

Osborn MS. *Dock.*: Mr. Sheridan | to Edmondson.

[*1811–12*]
Cavendish-Square
Thursday Evening

Sir,
After repeated messages to Dean St: etc. etc. I sent you a few Days since a very civil note to Welbeck St: to request

[1] Printed 'abjure'.

you to call on me early the next morning you came at 5 or 6 in the evening and then left a very rude message to desire I would send some Person to you to inform you what I had to say.—What I had to say, was, to apprize you of the repeated notices I had sent to Dean St: of the scandalously dilapidated state of the House[1] I hold of you at so enormous a rent and so punctually paid, expecting that you would have immediately caused what was necessary to keep out the weather to be done, I also meant to propose that if you would cause to be clean'd the filthy Furniture and put the House into habitable repair I was willing to continue in it thro' the winter and give it up at the end of the summer when you would have time to put it into condition fit to be let again—This I thought to be a proposition greatly for your advantage, but as you have thought proper to behave with such incivility not to say impertinence I now give you notice that I shall order the necessary repairs to be made to keep the wet and weather out during my short remaining time and deduct the charge from the rent, and that I shall quit your house at the expiration of my year of which take notice | I am, Sir | your's etc. | R B Sheridan

Mr. M. Edmondson.

799. To Lady Holland

Holland House MS., S. 87. *Address*: The Lady Holland *Fr.*: R B S *Wm.*: 1809

[*Early Jan. 1812*]
Thursday

I am always infinitely grateful for your kindness—I was seized with a violent cough the Day after I left Holland-House—such a one as I have not had for these fourteen years Past, and had two nights a pain in my side which I hate above all things. I have been walking for an hour to day but of course I did not go out till the Sun had gone in and the Fog had risen. I am getting quite well, only, I have lost my voice, which next to one's memory perhaps is at present no

[1] See William Gregory's statement that the house was very damp and that the beds were in dirty condition, in Winston, 1813–14.

bad thing to be rid of. I attribute my cold entirely to anger and vexation on *private* subjects—Theatrical I mean[1] tho' perhaps a little assisted by an east wind and having got wet thro'. The message to me was that you desired a *written account*—I hope you will admit that I have been tolerably circumstantial.—

I trust you and Holland have observed the conduct of the Magistrates at Shadwell.[2] Their sole object is, and that of the Government of course, to fasten by any means, perjury or otherwise, the late murders on *Irishmen* and to have it believed that there exists a Popish P[l]ot to massacre all the protestant Publicans![3] When they allow'd Williams to hang himself they thought he was an Englishman—and now they are sorry and try to screen themselves by making a theatrical exhibition of the Wretches body. Assuming that He was the convicted murderer yet under that conviction they allow'd him for three days the certain means of making away with himself—never ordering some one not to leave him. They might just as well have directed the jailor to have a Razor and a loaded Pistol on his Table, indeed I rather believe they did so but the Fellow shrewdly anticipating that the iron bar and the neck-cloth would do quite as well took it on himself to neglect their orders. You know I suppose that their own Runners have strict orders to bring no one before them who does not '*speak with an Irish brogue*' or any witnesses whose examination they cannot commence by asking if they are Papists and bidding them cross themselves —Williams was no more an Irishman than He was a Laplander[4]—and his comrade and certain associate in the murders they allow'd to escape the moment they found He was a Dane.[5]—All this you may depend on.

---

[1] S.'s wife wrote to Lord Holland on 5 Dec. 1811: '. . . I never can see him as *deeply wounded*, as I have seen him lately. . . . The disagreement between him and Whitbread hurts me more than I can express.' (Sichel, ii. 359.) The disagreement is described in detail in Moore, ii. 418–22.

[2] The murder of the Marr and Williamson families in Ratcliffe Highway and Gravel Lane in Dec. 1811 led to great public alarm. 'Strong evidence has been adduced against an Irish sailor named John Williams, *alias* Murphy' (*Gent. Mag.* lxxxi (1811), pt. 2, 582–4). Williams committed suicide in his cell in the Cold Bath Fields prison.

[3] S. repeated this in the Commons on 18 Jan. 1812. See the *Staff. Adv.*, 25 Jan. 1812, and Hansard, 1st Ser., xxi. 216.

[4] He claimed to be a Scot.

[5] One Allblag.

The Idea of a military Police is seriously entertain'd in high quarters.[1] I fear you will not in a hurry ask me again to put pen to Paper—| your faithful Servant | R B S. I will take a morning walk to H. House.

800. To His Wife

Price MS.

[3 Feb. 1812 ?]
House of Commons
Monday

My Dear Hecca,

I was much disappointed at not hearing from you to Day your account of Tom makes me particularly anxious to hear more[2]—I wish to go and see him, and it would be in my Power towards the end of this week and to bring you back I trust to a new house and rid of the Devils.[3] I am very unwell myself and have lost all power of sleeping and yet upon my soul I drink little wine[4]—but you know not the grounds I have for being deeply irritated—or you would make every allowance. I will send money tomorrow. Tell Charles I shall never ask him to write to me again.

The Country is going to the Devil—I have resisted every effort to induce me not to vote for the Catholic Question to Day[5]—under the shabby pretence that it was premature

[1] At the inquest on the Williamsons the coroner suggested that soldiers should patrol the area during the night. See *Gent. Mag.* lxxxi (1811), pt. 2, 584. In his speech on the state of the metropolis S. referred to his motion for the reform of the police, brought forward in 1781 (cf. *Speeches*, i. 6–17); and recommended members to read Henry Fielding's book on the subject. This was on 18 Jan.

[2] Tom S. wrote from Itchen Ferry to Mrs. Wilmot to say, '. . . I am ill in health and spirits, and as thin as a Highland crop of oats . . . Mother and Charles are here . . .' (Barbarina, Lady Grey, *A Family Chronicle* (ed. G. Lyster, 1908), p. 27).

[3] The state of the house in Cavendish Square led to much disagreement with

the owner. John Graham gave back the key 'about a fortnight or a month after Feb. 1812', according to William Gregory's statement of 6 July 1813.

[4] This sentence is quoted by Rae, ii. 214, as belonging to Jan. 1809.

[5] S. said in the debate on the state of Ireland that the real question was 'whether Ireland should be preserved in her allegiance to the British crown by conciliation and justice, or driven into the arms of the enemy. . . . The claims of the Catholics . . . formed only a part of a mass of grievances of which Ireland had to complain.' Morpeth's motion favouring conciliation with the Catholics obtained S.'s vote but was heavily defeated. See Hansard, 1st Ser., xxi. 601, 669–70.

and ill-timed a ground which some real Friends to the Catholic Cause mean to take to make court to the Regent, and it is the worse court for him that can be taken.—It has been a toss up whether I should not have taken the Chiltern Hundreds and been out of Parliament this Day[1]—but I shall continue to consult nothing as a Public man but my own self-esteem.

Whenever Wind permits news will come from the Peninsula of a bloody Character I fear. Ciudad Roderegue will have been assail'd by *Storm* on the 17th Ult, a Desperate business and Graham I should bet will command the assaulting Column[2]—a practicable breach was made on the 15th. On the 16th. Lord W.[3] was battering with 21 twenty four Pounders within 250 yards of the walls which are very thick but low and scaling Ladders were ready and of course there will be great slaughter—tho' success is not doubted. Marmont will arrive with his Army on the 22d. and what's to follow The God of War only knows[4]—(This for Tom and Harry)

tell Ironmonger I have received his letter yet hope not to see him quite so soon—

Tell Arnold He has not written to me at all and that the Lyceum was burn'd down this morning,[5] I should send him the Particulars but many others of course have written to him | God bless you | R B S

I will write to Tom tomorrow

[1] Tierney reported on 3 Mar. that S. meant to secede from Parliament and 'vote no more, except for the Catholics' (*Memoirs of R. P. Ward* (1850), i. 450).

[2] Thomas Graham had no share in the storming of Ciudad Rodrigo. News of its capture was reported to Lord Liverpool on 4 Feb.

[3] Wellington.

[4] Thomas Graham wrote to R. Graham from Gallegos on 20 Jan., reporting the taking of Ciudad Rodrigo on 19 Jan. and adding, 'Marmont and Dorsenne are to be at Salamanca tomorrow on their way to relieve the place' (*H.M.C., Supplementary Rep. on the MSS. of R. Graham of Fintry* (ed. C. T. Atkinson, 1940), p. 160).

[5] This is not true. It may be a joke or possibly S. had heard some rumour to this effect. A cutting in the British Museum (Th. Cts. 44), with the manuscript dating of 27 Feb. 1812, reports an unfounded alarm of fire at the Lyceum and the confusion that took place.

801. To His Son Tom

W.T.

Monday Night
March 7th: [*1812*][1]

My Dear Tom,

You have indeed good cause for reproaching me for not writing, but a sullen humour has for some [time] taken possession of me which has utterly indisposed me to communicate with any one, I mean on *public* affairs which has been the subject you have appear'd most anxious to hear from me upon,[2] and yet upon which I felt particularly that I could say nothing that would be satisfactory to you especially did I enter into explanations of my own views of circumstances and characters. I hate disagreement with you in opinion or principles—it warms and agitates you and leads to altercation, and I have left off being warm'd or agitated about anything. I especially shunn'd replying to a former letter of your[s] on the longstanding vexatious topic of past *Election-grievances* tho' I felt only increased regret and astonishment that you should persevere to hold that perverse opinion on this subject which has always appear'd to me so contrary to the natural justice of your Character—I put gratitude out of the question—but it is a subject upon which you are literally infatuated—so let us have done with it for ever—tho' having for the last time touch'd on it—one word with respect to Stafford.—I am certainly desirous of returning there.—The dread of the expense only retards my declaring myself. Why you ever made any mystery of your transaction with Sir O. M.[3] (I mean with respect to me) I cannot conceive.—There was nothing in the slightest degree improper in your share in the business, as I understand every shilling of his £1000 went among the Burgesses[4]—After

[1] S.'s '9' is sometimes mistaken for a '7'. I believe the above letter was begun on 9 Mar. and completed soon after 17 Mar.

[2] In a letter of 26 Feb. [1812] to Mrs. Wilmot Tom S. declared, 'I am mad about politics. The Catholic Question will be carried by those who were heretofore its opponents. ... the Opposition have acted like a pack of noodles' (Barbarina, Lady Grey, *A Family Chronicle*, pp. 29–30).

[3] Mosley.

[4] Tom S. may have been referring to this in his letter to R. Peake of 29 July 1812: '. . . it appears the Sum

this resignation however which *he never noticed* to *me* 'till after *I* wrote to him on the subject He narrates to me this history offering to meet me in Stafford and canvas for me with all his interest, *but* stipulating that I should *first repay* him that thousand Pounds towards which I had not nor have one thousand Pence! the result was that I never answered his Letter, for certainly your explanation of the transaction did not raise my estimation of his conduct—and I understand He has since threaten'd to put [up] some one else.—Another thing that threw cold water on my wishes as to *Stafford* was the Princes confess'd dislike to my declining to continue to be brought in by *him*—This observe, months before his decision to continue his present ministers—but while he continues them array'd against the Catholic claims they cannot have a vote in their support from me and therefore I ought not to continue to owe my seat to their Master.—Of Stafford I certainly *could* be *sure*—but the expense must curtail the means of my doing justice to my existing creditors, and diminish the hope of my lessening the discomfort of my latter Days. I feel it however very generous and disinterested in you to wish my risking to stand for Stafford at any rate.

I scarcely know when I began this Letter—but I have carried it about with me with your two Political Letters always *meaning* to answer both fully—but I give that up for the present and shall send what I have scribbled. One word only to your first apprehension that I had endeavour'd to persuade Lord Moira to disgrace himself by accepting the Blue Ribband[1] I rely on my assurance that you have been misinformed—I was merely the conveyer of explanations between them and the Prince and I gave the Prince my Frank opinion that Moira was right the moment He, The Prince declined giving him the explanation he required respecting Ireland.[2]—As to St. Patrick's Day it is a long

Norton received from me is £1082, I well remember at the time *thinking* I had provided for all *my* expenses.—Nor did I think so many as a 143 Burgesses had been on the List . . .' (Add. MS. 35118, f. 117).

[1] 'It is reported that the Earl of Moira has refused one of the vacant Blue Ribbands, offered to him, by the Prince Regent as a mark of his high personal regard' (*Staff. Adv.*, 22 Feb. 1812).

[2] Moira refused to support Perceval. 'No consideration will ever induce his Lordship to unite with any Administration, that refuses to accede to Catholic emancipation. . . . The Prince sent for him; an expostulation ensued . . .;

story and had been totally misrepresented—I assure you I had not drunk too much wine nor regret or would retract one word I *really* said.[1] On the whole I would not change my present political position for that of any of the mercenary and factious Phalanx[2] who fancy themselves entitled to my implicit devotion, because I think it enables me to do more real good than they *can* or *mean* | God bless you | R. B. S.

802. To His Son Tom

W.T. At the foot of the letter are the words: 'M.C. | 26, Abercromby Place | Edinr. N.B.' Possibly this was Tom Sheridan's forwarding address.

Friday Night
1812

My Dear Tom,

I must catch moments when I can write to you a few lines and it is all I can do—I continue very unwell and the progressive state of my varicose veins, my secret alarming complaint, preys on my hopes and spirits for I never will have to do with any operation. I have two letters of yours to notice—the last a short one, I will dispose of first. I consider it as a great compliment your being disappointed by my silence in the Catholic Debate—I was too ill even to be able to remain in the House—and it was settled at 12 when almost no one had spoken that the debate should be adjourn'd to Monday and then I gladly gave the matter up—as to saying a few words it would have been foolish. I had the Day before said enough in presenting the county of Wexford Petition to make that at least unnecessary but

suffice it to say that His Royal Highness has since flinched on the Catholic question.' (W. A. Miles, *Correspondence . . . 1789–1817* (1890), ii. 371.)

[1] Irish disappointment at the Regent's lack of support for Catholic emancipation was shown at this meeting, on 17 Mar. S. said that he 'knew well the principles of the Prince Regent, and that so well satisfied was he that they were all that Ireland could wish, that he [S.]

hoped, that as he had lived up to them, so he might die in the principles of the Prince Regent. . . . He could only assure them, that the Prince Regent remained unchangeably true to those principles' (*Morn. Chron.*, 18 Mar. 1812). S. himself was applauded, but every mention of the Prince Regent drew hisses.

[2] The supporters of Grey and Grenville.

on this subject as far as relates to me put your mind at rest there is a better opportunity coming and of my own creating for my regaining all the credit you think I have lost.

Now as to your long letter agreeing as I do with all the general sentiments of it I yet could were I in the mood show you how you err in the particulars on which they are grounded—particularly for instance as to Moira. As for myself when you say 'what a situation would yours be could you now stand between the Prince and the People possessing The confidence of both' etc.—this and the remainder of the sentence is a very excellent and eloquent suggestion only it is exactly what I considered to be the case when I said I would not change my Political Position etc. etc.[1]—the event shall justify me. I will add more on this point if I can tomorrow. On Election matters—I see the Bulletin must be his Majesty King Tom remains nearly in the same state.[2]

God bless you I am as tired as a dog.

803. [To Richard Fitzpatrick]

Add. MS. 47582, f. 262.

[*1812* ?]
Brook[s]'s
Monday six oclock

My Dear Richard,

However long and cordial Friendship may have been among men in this world in asking a favor the fewer words or Professions are used the better. I am driven by a sudden emergency to want for a Payment £100 by ten o'clock tomorrow morning. The ill consequences of the failure to me and consequently the obligation of the accommodation are beyond what I can describe—I want the money only for a fortnight. Perhaps no one ever more rigidly avoided receiving favors of this sort from private Friendship than

---

[1] In the last sentence of Letter 801.
[2] Without a chance of a parliamentary seat? Writing to S. on 23 Sept. 1812 James Wallis remarked, 'Happy should I be, if the health of your amiable Son permitted of his ... offering himself for the County of Wexford.' (Salt MS.)

myself and such an application can never be renew'd by me to anyone but it is an occasion of a most pressing nature which alone could induce me to apply to your perhaps straighten'd and precarious circumstances. The Theatre bills being finally pass'd next week[1] I commence to be in receipt of a very considerable sum of money for my share. This circumstance enable[s] me to assure you by *everything that is sacred* in the *word* or *honourable* in the *heart of man* that the enclosed check at a fortnight shall be as punctually paid as a bank note, I would not apply to you on any other condition | yours ever | R B Sheridan

on a word from you here they would advance me cash on it. Whitbread is at Southill.

804. To Colonel John McMahon

Windsor MSS. 42524–5. *Pub.*: *Letters of Geo. IV*, i. 70. *Dock.*: Rt Honble R B Sheridan

Saturday Night
April 25th [*1812*]

Private

My Dear McMahon
    The Statement made at the close of the Debate last night[2] in the House of Commons, respecting the Prince's *authorised Pledge* to the Irish catholics under the Duke of Bedfords administration, *must not* remain uncontradicted or at least unexplain'd. I cannot describe the mischief it will do to his Honor and Character while a statement of the *Truth* can only do him honor.
    I have had a long conversation with G. Ponsonby on the

---

[1] Whitbread reported to a meeting of subscribers, on 11 Apr. 1812, that 'the new bill, which the Committee had found it necessary to introduce, having passed into law', the new theatre would be opened in Oct. See *The Times*, 13 Apr. 1812.

[2] In the adjourned debate on the Roman Catholic question, George Ponsonby declared that Bedford, as Lord-Lieutenant, and he himself, as Secretary, had received commands from 'the illustrious person alluded to' [the Prince] during their term of office to communicate to the Roman Catholics of Ireland the message that he would never forsake their interests. See Hansard, 1st Ser., xxii. 1010–11.

subject this evening, and I shall entreat a few minutes audience of his Royal Highness tomorrow on a subject, in my humble Judgement, of such consequence to his Character, which there is a manifest combination to endeavour to destroy.[1]

I have been in unaccountably bad Health and Spirits for the last ten Days or you should have seen me. I enclose you a Letter from Adam which will shew you that waiting for my *Brief* it was not my fault that I only[2] gave a vote on the last Question respecting you.—[3] | yours my Dear Friend | ever | R B Sheridan

805. To Sir Vicary Gibbs

Mitchell Library MS., Sydney. [Ph.]

Tuesday
May 5th: 1812

Dear Sir

Having satisfactorily arranged with the Drury-Lane-Theatre Trustees The very slight alteration I had required in the making out of the renew'd Patent, and which I thought I was in justice bound to persevere in requiring, I take the Liberty of informing you that all objection on my Part is withdrawn—as Mr. Mash[4] will have the Honor of explaining to you.

I must trust to your indulgence to excuse the trouble I have given you and I beg you to believe that | I am with great esteem and respect | Your oblig'd | and obedient Servant | R B Sheridan.

Sir Vicary Gibbs

---

[1] In a letter to Tom S. of 7 May 1812, Moira wrote of the Regent: '. . . it is not his heart which has been defective but his conceptions have been completely bewildered by the representations of the invidious and mercenary set in whose Toils he is unhappily involved. This your Father sees perfectly, Alas! he sees also that there is no chance of retrocession from the erroneous paths . . .' (W.T.).

[2] 'Only' may have been cancelled.

[3] C. W. Wynn's motion, on 14 Apr., concerning the appointment of McMahon as Private Secretary to the Prince. See Hansard, 1st Ser., xxii. 332.

[4] Thomas Mash, Paymaster in the Lord Chamberlain's department.

806. To the Prince Regent

Windsor MSS. 19688–90. *Pub.*: *Letters of Geo. IV*, i. 81–82.

Bruton St.
Thursday Evening May 21st
1812

Sir

I cannot but be aware that at a moment so critical as the present[1] and while so many important public considerations must press upon your Royal Highness's time and attention, any intrusion upon either from the suggestion of private Feelings, however dictated by duty and attachment, requires the gracious indulgence of your Royal Highness to pardon it.—Not to trespass a moment longer than necessary I have only frankly to say that my object in now taking the Liberty of addressing you is to express my extreme concern that your Royal Highness could for a moment, if I understand McMahon right, have thought me capable of the vanity and silliness of being Party to the misrepresentations in the Newspapers which stated me to have mix'd in the recent consultations at Carlton-House.—There is nothing more repugnant to my temper and nature than to be characterized as a medler of that description, and I had myself authorized the contradiction of the Paragraphs alluded to before I had the honor of calling at Carlton-House.[2]

Undoubtedly Duty would require of me, as of every other Privy-Councellor to submit my humble opinion at the

[1] The assassination of Perceval on 11 May led to negotiations between Liverpool, Canning, and Wellesley for the formation of a new government. Their correspondence was published in the *Morn. Chron.*, 21 May 1812. The same day an Address was carried praying the Prince Regent to make sure of an efficient administration. On 22 May Liverpool and his supporters resigned from office.

[2] On 17 June 1812 S. stated in the Commons, 'I have spoken to His Royal Highness only once within the last two months, which I did with his own permission. I purposely abstained from having any communication . . . and I had only one audience since I came back from Stafford, which I requested for the purpose of explaining my motives for going to Stafford. His Royal Highness was then pleased to ask my opinion with respect to the negociations that were going on; and I gave him my opinion . . .' (Hansard, 1st Ser., xxiii. 555).

express'd command of your Royal Highnesss upon any subject regarding which it might be required—and I only humbly take the Freedom of adding that I can lay my hand on my heart and declare that that opinion never has in a single instance, nor ever can be, if ever again required been formed or given but upon grounds and motives proceeding from the most sincere, grateful and ardent attachment and devotion to your true interests Honor and Happiness.

My object in presuming to have wish'd to see your Royal Highness on tuesday last was, as I explained to my most esteem'd Friend and your Royal Highness's most faithful servant Colonel McMahon, to prevent the possibility of my canvass at Stafford[1] being misrepresented as being in any way a declining on my Part still to have the honor of [o]wing my seat in Parliament to your gracious Protection and partial recommendation.

To continue to be your servant with unalter'd and unalterable zeal anxiety and affection is the hope and Pride of my private wishes and ambition—but I feel confident that I can in no way be usefully so but by preserving the independence and consistency of my public course and political character, now doubly endear'd to me since allow'd and sanction'd by your Royal Highness's gracious approbation.

I wish to avoid giving way to gloomy thoughts respecting the possible results of the present aweful crisis of unprecedented difficulty and Danger—but I can from my soul aver that under any condition of calamity, public or private I should find a degree of consolation in the very worst events in proportion as they af[f]orded me an opportunity of proving the true sincerity with which I am and ever will be | Your Royal Highness's | most dutiful grateful and devoted | Friend and Servant | R B Sheridan

To
  The Prince Regent

---

[1] 8–13 May. Burgess's letter of 11 May, describing Perceval's assassination, was received by S. there. It recalled him to London with the words, 'it is an excuse for leaving Stafford. I congratulate you on your success in the canvass' (Add. MS. 29764, f. 13).

807. To Lady Holland

Holland House MS. S. 88. *Address*: Lady Holland | Holland-House
Dock.: Mr. Sheridan *Wm.*: 1804

[24 May 1812 ?][1]
Sunday morning

There is a perverse fatality attends me which often makes
me appear most negligent where I am anxious to pay the
greatest attention. I shall most gladly accept your invitation
for to Day, and then endeavour to make out that I have not
been so much to blame as I must appear to have been, but
I must rely on your good-nature to assist me

I conceive Fitzpatrick must have neglected to transmit
to you my Letter to him as I desired—if so it is very provok-
ing and makes me appear worse | I have the Honor to
be | your sincere and obedient Servant | R B Sheridan

can I stay the evening?

808. To the Marquis Wellesley

Add. MS. 37297, f. 29. *Dock.*: 1812 Mr. Sheridan | D 26th May

26 May [1812]
Bruton St.
Tuesday Evening

Private

My Dear Lord
Having it in command from the Prince to have a conversation with Lord Moira this evening[2] I should be happy
afterwards to do myself the honor of waiting on you—There
being matters I wish to communicate to you.

[1] S. and Fitzpatrick were at Holland
House with Lord John Russell and
others on this day. See *Creevey Papers*,
i. 157.

[2] Wellesley approached Liverpool as
well as Grey and Grenville, but received
no definite promises of co-operation. On
26 May Moira accepted his suggestion
that he call at Carlton House, and a

reconciliation between the Regent and
Moira duly took place. On 27 May
Moira wrote to Wellesley to say that
the Regent intended 'to give a fresh
authorisation to Lord Wellesley as soon
as his Royal Highness had satisfied himself on some points necessary towards
his decision' (Add. MS. 37297, ff. 27
and 31).

Shall I find you at Apsley-House between 10 and 11? |
ever Your Lordships | most faithfully and sincerely | R B
Sheridan

Marquis Wellesley.

809. To the Prince Regent

Windsor MSS. 19783–4. *Pub.: Letters of Geo. IV*, i. 104–5. *Dock.*:
R. B. Sheridan | June 1. 1812.

Monday Evening
June 1st: 1812.

Sir
I should think myself deficient in the respect and duty
I owe to you were I to close this day without conveying to
your Royal Highness in a few words my humble congratu-
lations on the wisdom and magnanimity of the Part you have
taken in giving to Lord Wellesley the Powers with which
you have invested him this morning[1]—At the same time I
should be insincere if I attempted to dissemble the deep
regret I have felt at an apparent alteration in your manner
towards me—produced solely I must believe by my expressing an opinion that a Proscription of Lord Grey in
the formation of a new administration would be a proceeding
equally injurious to the estimation of your Personal
dignity and the maintenance of the Public Interests.

Long indulgence, Sir, on your Part in allowing me to
speak the Truth to you leads me not to hesitate, or consider
it as presumptuous to say that you grievously wrong'd me
if you supposed I ventured to press this my opinion on you
from any undue Partiality to the noble Lord in Question

[1] S. referred to this in his speech in
the Commons, of 17 June 1812: 'I knew
it from the marquis Wellesley, who did
me the honour to call in his carriage on
me at my own house, in the face of day,
on the morning on which he was authorized by the Prince Regent to form an
administration, for the purpose of shewing me the written terms which he
proposed to offer. I knew by the noble
marquis coming again to me about an
hour afterwards, offering me a situation
in his arrangements, when he received
from me a most disinterested denial of
accepting of any official situation. I
knew afterwards from a noble earl . . .
I mean the earl of Moira.' (Hansard, 1st
Ser., xxiii. 556.) He also referred to the
above letter in the speech.

or any of those with whom He is allied. I have never profess'd or affected any such motive—and with great submission I must express my surprise that your Royal Highness could for a moment have entertaind this notion. My object I can with the utmost sincerity declare was founded on what I considered best *for your Honor and your Interest* and *the general Good of the Country.*

Junius says in a public Letter of his address'd to your Royal Father 'Fate that made you a King forbad your having a Friend'[1] I deny his Proposition as a general Maxim. I must feel confident that your Royal Highness possesses qualities to win and to secure to you the attachment and Devotion of private Friendship in spite of your being a Sovereign at least I am entitled to make this declaration as far as relates to myself—and I do it under the assured conviction that you will never require from me any proof of that attachment and devotion inconsistent with the clear and honourable independence of mind and conduct which constitute[s] my sole value as a public Man and which have hitherto been my best recommendation to your gracious Favour confidence and Protection.[2] | I have the Honor to be | Sir | with unalterable Duty | and attachment | your faithful Servant | R B Sheridan.

810. To His Son Tom

Osborn MS. *Address*: London June second 1812 | T Sheridan E | Itchen | Southampton *Fr.*: R B Sheridan

2 June 1812
Tuesday
My Dear Tom

Nothing yet settled it would have [been] worse than useless to have attempted to give you the details or any account of the various intrigues that have been going on— Grey and Grenville will this evening decline having

---

[1] 'The fortune, which made you a king, forbad you to have a friend' (*The Letters of Junius* (ed. C. W. Everett, 1927), p. 148).

[2] This paragraph is quoted by Moore, ii. 429, who summarizes the earlier part.

[anything] to say¹ to the new set²—and Lord Moira and Wellesley will form an administration without them. They have both been most attentive and confidential to me—you may have anything you like | R B S

I am in a fury[?] with Caroline

811. To Colonel John McMahon

Windsor MSS. 19845–6. Pub.: M. Roberts, *The Whig Party, 1807–12* (1939), p. 418. *Dock.*: R. B. Sheridan | 17 June 1812. | N.B. Recd. at 10 oClock A.M. | Wedny. 17th June.

16 June 1812
Bruton St.

My Dear McMahon
Unquestionably I shall obey the Prince's commands by waiting on him tomorrow at the time he is pleased to command—but I am really so ill that I have not left my bed to Day³ but to receive Lord Yarmouth⁴ for an hour to night—between whom and myself there remains not a shade of difference⁵ and further I do most humbly hope and implore that his Royal Highness would press no more that I should submit to the attacks so foully levell[ed] at me and forfeit my pledge to vindicate myself.⁶ To act [thus] would render me the most disgraced and dishonour'd man living and I could never shew my Face again. Surely surely

¹ They were offered a minority of seats in Wellesley's proposed Cabinet, but declined them on the ground that differences of policy would lead to a weak administration. See *Dropmore Papers*, x. 279–80; and G. Bennet's diary quoted in P. Fitzgerald, *Life of George the Fourth* (1881), ii. 99.

² Wellesley, Canning, and Moira.

³ Yet in his speech in the Commons on 17 June S. declared, 'Now the fact is that I was very well yesterday . . .' (Hansard, 1st Ser., xxiii. 552).

⁴ Francis Charles Seymour-Conway, afterwards 3rd Marquis of Hertford (1777–1842), was Vice-Chamberlain. He claimed to have informed S. that the

Household would resign on a change of government. S. did not give this information to Grey and Grenville.

⁵ Confirmed by Brougham, who saw some correspondence between Yarmouth and S. on the subject. See Grey Bennett's diary, quoted by P. Fitzgerald, *Life of George the Fourth*, ii. 105.

⁶ Moira had already sought to 'limit definitely the substance of what he is to address to the House'. See his account of their discussion in M. Roberts, *The Whig Party, 1807–12*, p. 417. S. gave his parliamentary explanation of what happened, on 17 and 19 June. See Hansard, 1st Ser., xxiii. 552–9, 606–13, 622–5.

my Dear Friend I may be trusted with the discretion that my devotion to the Prince will guide me thro' the whole of the *very little* I shall have to state and that I shall not utter one word that will not be in maintenance of his honor. I am aware of the Points he dislikes my touching on and of my anticipating Part of the Lords Debate, not one word that I shall utter can lead to any such result. Pray let me have another Line. Upon my honor I can scarcely hold the Pen I am scrawling with. | Ever faithfully yours | R B Sheridan

I mean a line graciously dispensing with my attendance tomorrow

Right Honourable Col. McMahon

812. To One of His Sisters[1]

LeFanu MS. *Pub.*: Rhodes, pp. 268–9.

Friday night
July 24th. [*1812*]

My Dearest Sister
   Homan makes such a Point of being the bearer of a Line from me to you that I cannot refuse him, tho' I am ashamed to say it can only be of a single Line to assure you that you shall hear from me in the course of next week and that in future I shall endeavour to make up for past seeming neglect | ever yours most affectionately | R B Sheridan

813. To Lady Holland

Holland House MS.

[*1812*]
Bruton St.[2]
Thursday Evening

I received a very kind message from you yesterday by Tom and to Day a card to dine at Holland-House tomorrow. I

---

[1] Probably Alicia. See Rhodes, p. 268.   see Maggs Catalogue 522 (1929), item
[2] He took a house there on 4 Apr.:   1189.

assure you, tho' it may surprise you, that I should with great readiness have obey'd your summons, if I had not been previously engaged to a farewell dinner with my son previously to his setting out for that state of Banishment[1] which the exquisite wisdom and justice of the Leaders of opposition have among other lovely exploits consign'd him to, no doubt for the Benefit of his health, in the Highlands of Scotland. One talk I shall wish with Holland and then farewell Politics | but yours ever gratefully | R B Sheridan

814. [To W. A. Downs ?][2]

Pub.: Lady Charnwood, *An Autograph Collection and the making of it* (1930), p. 185. Cf. Maggs Catalogue 417 (1921), item 3139.

[*Aug.–Nov. 1812 ?*][3]
Isleworth
Tuesday.

Timid Miscreant,

I have received your Flabby labour'd epistle. *You* presume to affect to read Bacon's Essays—what do you learn there but that *Courage* is the first virtue in private as well as in Public affairs. I shall cashier you from my Bodyguard— '*a cottage in Wales*'—because your *innocent, unsuspicious* soul has *at length* discovered that attorneys may be knaves! sweet simplicity! I'll tell you shortly that I will have those two Fellows struck off the Rolls if not put on the Pillory— mark my words. | R. B. Sheridan.

I shall see you perhaps *before* this arrives—but I cannot delay rebuking your stupid pusillanimity.

[1] On 29 July 1812 Tom S. wrote to R. Peake, 'I go on Sunday to the North and immediately after *I* shall probably sail for Madeira. I am very ill Dick . . .' (Add. MS. 35118, f. 117). The *Staff. Adv.*, 19 Sept. 1812, reported he had gone to Scotland with Lord Kinnaird and would embark at Leith for Madeira.

[2] From the irony of the letter and the reference to '*Courage*'. On 10 Nov. 1813 Downs wrote to Whitbread (from the Custom House, Edinburgh) saying 'as

Mr. Sheridan holds me in such contempt as not to take in my letter I am determined through the press to let the public know how he has swindled me '(Whitbread MS. 4122).

[3] S. lived at Isleworth from 1791 to 1795, but does not appear to have known Downs at that period. From the *Leveson Gower Corr.* ii. 444, and a letter of Tom S. (N.L.I. MS. 7373, f. 15), it seems likely that S. also lived there between Aug. and Nov. 1812.

815. To Samuel Whitbread

W.T. Copy. *Pub.*: Moore. ii, 431–3.

Cooks Hotel[1]
November 1st.
1812.

Dear Whitbread

I was misled to expect you in Town the beginning of last week, but being positively assured that you will arrive tomorrow I have declined accompanying Hester into Hampshire as I intended and she is gone to Day without me—but I must leave Town to join her *as soon as I can*. We must have some serious but yet I hope friendly conversation respecting my unsettled claims on the Drury Lane Theatre Corporation.—A concluding paragraph in one of your last letters to Burgess[2] which He thought himself justified in shewing me leads me to believe that it is not your object to distress or destroy me. On the subject of your refusing[3] to advance to me the £2000 I applied for to take with me to Stafford out of the large sum confessedly due to me (unless I signed some paper containing I know not what—and which you presented to my breast like a cocked pistol on the last day I saw you) I will not dwell. *This and this alone lost me my election*. You deceive yourself if you give credit to any other causes which the pride of my friends chose to attribute our Failure to rather than confess our Poverty. I do not mean now to expostulate with you much less to reproach you but sure I am that when you contemplate the positive injustice of refusing me the accommodation I required, and the irreparable injury that refusal has cast on me, overturning probably all the Honor and independence

[1] Albemarle Street. S. stayed there occasionally between 1 Nov. 1812 and Oct. 1814.

[2] Possibly Whitbread's letter of 19 Dec. 1811, where he wrote, '. . . I grieve for the sad state of Mr. Sheridan's affairs. I would contribute my mite to their temporary relief...' (Moore, ii. 421).

[3] See Whitbread's reasonable letter of 25 Sept. 1812 (Harvard MS.), printed in Moore, ii. 433–5, and Q. Skinner, 'Sheridan and Whitbread', *Theatre Notebook*, xvii (1963), 76. The stipulation was that S. should take a large part of his balance in bonds, and should leave the bonds 'in trust to answer events'. This was naturally galling to S., who needed ready money, and thought Whitbread was excluding him from Parliament.

of what remains of my Political life, you will deeply reproach yourself.

I shall make an application to the Committee when I hear you have appointed One, for the assistance which most pressing circumstances now compel me to call for, and all I desire is, thro' a sincere wish that our Friendship may not be interrupted, that the answer to that application may proceed from a *bonâ fide Committee* with *their signatures*, testifying their Decision. | I am yet | Yours very sincerely | R. B. Sheridan

S. Whitbread Esq.

816. 'To the Committee for Re-building Drury Lane Theatre'

Seven Gables Bookshop MS., New York. Text from Mr. Michael Papantonio's transcription.

Cooks Hotel
Nov. 3. 1812

Gentlemen

I shall be obliged to you out of the monies due to me to pay a Draft of mine for Five hundred pounds in favor of Mr. Martin Wright of Stafford[1] and also to lodge in the hands of Mr. Peter Moore the sum of Fifteen hundred pounds in addition to the Fifty Shares of One hundred pounds each which I have already made over to him for which I will give a proper discharge— | R B Sheridan

817. To Colonel John McMahon

Windsor MSS. 41700–1. *Pub.: Letters of Geo. IV*, i. 365–6. *Dock.*: Mr. Sheridan

[*1812* ?]
Cook's Hotel
Sunday Evening

My Dear Friend,

Tho' since I last had the Honor of paying my Duty to the Prince Regent I have been often in Town I have

---

[1] Wright seconded the vote of confidence in S. at the Stafford meeting on 13 May 1812. I surmise that the sum of money covered some election expenses.

purposely abstain'd from attending at Carlton-House. The anxiety express'd by his Royal Highness that I should avoid all possible risk of personal insult on the score of Debt[1] made, I need not say, a most grateful impression on my mind, but when his Royal Highness proceeded to offer me an apartment in his own Palace, with the same benevolent view to my Protection, I can only say that *Gratitude* is too weak a word to express the Feelings which that offer has indelibly planted in my mind—

And now my dear Friend I come to the real Purpose of this short Letter. The very Graciousness of the Prince's conduct towards me was the Spur that made me apply myself to a strict examination of my own circumstances and I am confident that you will hear with Pleasure, and with Pleasure communicate the Fact to our Royal Master that I am free from every personal difficulty or embarrassment of Debt[2]—except the Debt of Gratitude I owe to him, which it will be the object of my Life honourably and faithfully to discharge— | ever yours, my Dear Friend | R B Sheridan.

Rt Honble
Col. McMahon.

818. To ——

Butler Library MS., Columbia University. *Pub.*: *Sheridan's Comedies* (ed. B. Mathews, Boston, 1885), facing p. 56. *Dock.*: R B Sheridan *Wm.*: 1806

Cook's Hotel
Sunday
Decr. 3d. [*1812*]

Dear Sir,
I will return to Town[3] on purpose on tuesday and come

[1] S. had not been elected at Stafford, so he no longer enjoyed parliamentary immunity.

[2] If, as the Prince alleged to Croker, S. used the money given him to buy a seat in Parliament to pay his own debts, the above letter may belong to late in 1812. The Prince added that S. later obtained £2,000 from Whitbread on condition that he (S.) did not re-enter Parliament. See J. W. Croker, *Correspondence and Diaries* (ed. L. J. Jennings, 1884), i. 306–9. There is some confusion in the stories, and S.'s letter may belong to a later date. S. was never free from debt during the rest of his life.

[3] S. went to Hampshire on 11 Nov. See *Letters of Geo. IV*, i. 180.

to you between 4 and 5 when I have no doubt we shall immediately and satisfactorily conclude for the House in Saville-Row | your's truly | R B Sheridan[1]

819. [To Thomas Metcalfe]

Cornell University Library MS. [Ph.]

[*1812 ?*]
Sunday Evening
Cook's Hotel

My Dear Sir
Here I am but just arrived from Southill and Mr. Whitbread comes tomorrow—and now you shall see that we will proceed with a smoothness and velocity respecting Polesden[2] which I confess past events have not given you reason to expect. I hope Mrs. Metcalfe and her most pretty little ones are quite well—Mrs. Sheridan comes with the Whitbreads —and on wednesday we shall move into a House whose Lease I have bought in Saville-Row— | ever your's | R B Sheridan

820. To ——

Harvard MS.

Itchen[3]
Sunday Decr. 13th. [*1812*]

My Dear Sir,
I had the Pleasure of your's yesterday—but no Post went from hence or I should not have delay'd expressing my satisfaction at everything you state.—I see I shall have the Pleasure of giving you and Mr. Hudson some mutton at Polesden in less time than you will believe I can build a chimney—
As to Williter He has been plundering me ever since I bought Polesden beyond anything you can form an idea of

---

[1] This letter is listed in S.C., 21 July 1883, lot 156, as from the 'Carolus Hotel'.

[2] A newspaper cutting of 9 May 1813 (among the Widener MSS.) notes: 'Mr.

Sheridan has recommenced the rebuilding of his seat at Polesden, in Surrey.'

[3] Harry Scott's house at Itchen Ferry, Southampton.

so much so that it is my intention to file a bill against him for an account. It has been no fault of mine that He has not been turned out anytime these 12 years—. I like the notion of Mr. Hudson[1] much and it will suit my other Plans. I leave this Place for Leatherhead on tuesday before the Post comes in. | ever your's | R B Sheridan

821. [To Colonel John McMahon]

Windsor MS. 41702. *Pub.*: *Letters of Geo. IV*, i. 157. *Dock.*: Rt. Honble. R. B. Sheridan *Wm.*: /12

[*1812–13*]
Saville Row
Wednesday Night

My Dear Friend
   I will call on you tomorrow—and, our gracious master willing, I shall be glad to be honor'd with an audience of ten minutes. I grieve to observe the existing mismanagement of his honor and character.—At five in the evening I set off with Attersol[2] for Wotton-Basset[3]—most reluctantly incurring the expence,[4] but with a hope that my presence in the House may afford an opportunity for being useful to the Prince | ever yours, | R B Sheridan

[1] See Clayden, i. 139–41, for S.'s dealings with Thomas Hudson, and the note: 'There is coming to me for land etc., I sell him full £3000. H. rents near £700 per ann. of me.' After S.'s death, Hudson bought the manor of West Humble with Chapel Farm and Phœnice.

[2] John Attersoll was a London merchant of 66 Portland Place. See J. Sinclair, *Correspondence* (1831), i. 113.

[3] Wootton Bassett, near Swindon, was made up of about 250 electors, and in 1807 the price of votes was 45 guineas a man. 'At the general election in 1812, Mr. Kibblewhite and Mr. Attersol were chosen; but soon after the meeting of Parliament they both vacated their seats, and Mr. Ellison and Mr. Rickards were returned by the same interest' (T. H. B.

Oldfield, *The Representative History of Great Britain and Ireland* . . . (1816), v. 231–2).

[4] For a detailed explanation, see Rhodes, pp. 234–9. One not cited by him is given in the *New M. Mag.* (1827), pt. i, pp. 222–3: the Regent presented S. with £4,000, 'giving him the choice of putting that sum to his private uses, or of enabling him to be returned for Wootton Bassett. Although S. had a great desire to resume his seat in Parliament, he could not well stomach the idea of exchanging the representation of a populous and respectable town like Stafford, for that of a rotten borough. After some hesitation, therefore, he declined it.' Cf. *Staff. Adv.*, 30 Apr. 1814: S. would not now be 'a dependant member'; and see *Letters of Geo. IV*, iii. 194–7.

822. To ——¹

Harvard MS. (Amy Lowell collection).

[*1812–15*]
Saville Row
Monday

You are a most faithless Sylph. How well you sent me what you promised!

I shall shew my superior punctuality by requesting you to present my Homage to my Lord and Lady and to announce that not having received any counter notice from you I shall have the Honor of finding myself at Brocket² tomorrow—| R B S.

823. [To Colonel John McMahon]

Windsor MS. 42519. *Pub.*: *Letters of Geo. IV*, i. 157. *Dock.*: Mr. Sheridan. *Wm.*: 1811

[*early 1813 ?*]³
Leatherhead
Thursday

Private

My Dear Friend

I have received this morning a Letter from Burgess repeating a conversation you have had with him—I say little now because it will bring me to Town tomorrow—with the utmost frankness I am compell'd to declare that it has not been in my Power to make any effort with respect to a seat, and that after our last conversation I should have thought it disrespectful to our Royal masters declared intention if I had busied myself on the subject even had I had an opportunity. The very Place however which Burgess mentions to me has been voluntarily offerr'd to [me] and I

¹ Lady Caroline Lamb (1785–1828)? She was Lady Bessborough's daughter. She had married William Lamb in 1805.
² The Hertfordshire home of Viscount Melbourne.

³ The *Staff. Adv.*, 30 Jan. 1813, reported that 'Mr. Sheridan is again become a resident of Surrey, having taken the mansion at Leatherhead lately occupied by Mr. Grimstead'.

requested it might be kept open which has been promised me—.[1] Apart from personal motives I confess I am on *political* grounds anxious to be in Parliament an[d] to take a line which I think the Prince Regent will not disapprove of. No more now, I shall see you tomorrow | ever most faithfully Yours | R B Sheridan.

824. To George Colman the Younger

Egerton MS. 1975, f. 56. *Wm.*: 18/

[*1813 ?*]
Leatherhead
Feby. 11th.

My Dear Sir
   If you can extend your Protection to the young man who writes the enclosed you will very much oblige me. I hear a very good account of his professional abilities as a subaltern, as well as of his general Character. I hope you will excuse the Liberty I take in making this application. Never interfering in any Theatrical matter you[2] are the only Person I should have consented to apply to. | yours sincerely | R B Sheridan

G. Coleman Esr.

825. To Lord and Lady Holland

Holland House MS.

[*1813*][3]
Sunday

My Dear Lord and Lady
   I am obliged to go out of Town to day and cannot return till wednesday—I regret it very much, for I am most sincere in saying that there is no Place I am ever ask'd to that I go to with so much Pleasure as to Holland House | yours faithfully | R B S.

---

[1] The *Staff. Adv.*, 13 Feb. 1813, stated that S. had had 'an offer from some of the most respectable persons in the Corporation, to stand in the present vacancy for Salisbury'.

[2] Colman was manager of the Haymarket Theatre until 1813.

[3] So on the manuscript in another hand.

826. To ——

Osborn MS. Draft. *Dock.*: Copy of a letter from Mr. Sheridan relative to Polesden.

[*1813 ?*]

my[1] Plans of compromises and exchanges unless I manifest to you that I am entirely determined to build a thorough good House near the Spot where the shameful ruin stands for which I paid I believe a shameful Price. And that I will instantly set about it, and following your example and expedition positively have it cover'd in before winter. My motives for this are nothing giddy or ostentatious[2]—I know the Place and its allurements—and how infinitely the value of the whole estate would be encreased by a House of good Taste and convenience belonging to it and the grounds disposed and the Farms repair'd and allotted as they ought to be.[3] If I live and prosper at all I shall delight to inhabit Polesden. Were I to die a year after the House shall be finish'd and the Farms arranged I feel confident that I shall have better'd the estate were it to come to sale fifty[4] per cent. On this Ground I have taken my Determination, and I make this communication freely to you that you may not be influenced by any loose rumours that I am too poor to keep the Place, or that I am easily to be tempted to sell what immediately belongs to myself, as is the case with the Farm you offer to buy from me. At the same time I assure you, and I am convinced you will readily give credit to it, that I am incapable of a Desire to possess a mere extent of acres where the possession of a distant part of them would give any friend or Neighbor very superior satisfaction to what I could derive from them.—

I have only to add that this communication being sufficient to open my mind and purposes generally tho' not in as distinct and detail'd a manner as I at first intended—I

---

[1] The text begins at the head of a page marked '4' by S.

[2] 'Gaudy' is deleted: S. disliked puns.

[3] Lord Broughton noted (*Recollections of a Long Life* (1909), i. 208) S.'s 'great delight in talking of his estate at Leather-head, where he said he has 1,500 acres, and shall have 2,200 by an approaching purchase. He is going to take out his dedimus to act as a Justice in Leather-head'. This was on 16 Feb. 1815.

[4] Substituted for 'forty'.

shall most readily now meet you at your own convenience to pursue the subject in the same spirit of frankness and goodwill which has induced me to trouble you with this long Letter—

The haste in which I have written this disjointed scrawl induces me to ask Mrs Sheridan's assistance to send it to you in a legible Form and you may assure Miss Delancey that tho she doats on Polesden and everything connected with it and is very partial to the Spot of Barnets's cottage She yet has the same feeling with me on the whole subject and should our arrangements take Place we'll endeavour not to envy Miss Delancey's making it the very prettiest cottage in the country which I take to be all that can be required from female magnanimity.

827. To W. J. Denison

Shuttleworth MS.

[*1813 ?*]
Saville-Row
Monday Evening

My Dear Denison

I call'd on you to Day and was glad to hear you were in Town and likely to remain.—

There is a Solicitor at Dorking, a new comer I believe, of the name of *Willet*.[1] He has been recommended to me with the addition in his favour that you protect and employ him—pray tell me if I am rightly informed?—or if I knew when I should find you I would call—I don't care how early—| most truly your's | R B Sheridan.

828. To His Stafford Supporters

Pub.: W. F. Rae, 'More about Sheridan', *Nineteenth Century*, xliii (1898), 257.[2]

Gentlemen,—   [*Apr. 1813*]

The kind and partial terms in which my friends at Stafford

[1] Wilmer Mackett Willett is noted as an attorney at Dorking, in Clarke's *New Law List* (1816), p. 130.
[2] Rae states: 'I have found among Sheridan's papers the rough draft of his reply in 1812, to an address from several of the Stafford burgesses.'

have been pleased to express themselves respecting my character and conduct in the Address I have now the honour of receiving are truly gratifying to my mind, and more than compensate for the unexpected disappointment I experienced there at the last election[1] . . . All I wish to be forgotten is the conduct of those who were hastily misled to withdraw their promised support from me. I could not have complied with their wishes without a breach of faith towards those most respected friends to whom I have pledged myself in my canvass to stand singly and not to propose a second candidate.

It is, however, a consoling circumstance to us all that the great majority of these persons were either young burgesses who scarcely knew me, or newcomers who had never known me at all. It is with heartfelt pride I have to boast that of my old and early friends who really had known me not a man deserted or failed to make exertions in my behalf, which, to the end of my life, will be remembered by me with the deepest gratitude.

With regard to the general regret the addressers are pleased to express at my absence from the nation's councils at this momentous [crisis], I can only thank them for their confidence in me, feeling it no presumption to say that during the thirty-two years I possessed a seat in the House I am not conscious of having given a vote against my conviction, or of having failed in any instance, according to the best of my talents, to support the liberty and constitution of my country—a simple duty, for they are one; but not to stain my past course of conduct, if I am in the House of Commons at all, I must sit there free, unfettered, and independent, or I hold [it] no exile to be excluded.

I have only to return you, Gentlemen, who have brought me this Address, my sincere thanks for the flattering preface

[1] After S.'s defeat in the Stafford election of Oct. 1812, his friends in the borough 'resolved to present him with a Gold Cup, as a small tribute of their admiration, esteem, and gratitude' (*Staff. Adv.*, 17 Oct. 1812). On 14 Apr. 1813, a deputation called on him at Saville Row and presented him with 'a superb Golden Cup, with an appropriate in-scription, accompanied by an address which was signed by the Mayor, in the name and on behalf of the burgesses. . . . Suitable speeches were made by Messrs. Turner and Wilkinson, who presented the Cup, and Mr. Sheridan delivered a most eloquent and animated reply.' (*Staff. Adv.*, 24 Apr. 1813.) The cup was actually of silver gilt.

with which you have introduced it, and to entreat you to convey to our friends the sentiments of ardent gratitude with which I have received it.

829. To His Wife

Pub.: Rae, ii. 276.

[*Before 5 May 1813*][1]

I have been arranging and winding up all my affairs and accounts as if it were certain I could not outlive the next three months. . . . My settlement with the theatre is an *arduous* and *complicated* business; it requires reference to many written documents exchanged through the course of three years, my share of which, though I have not lost or destroyed them, gives me no small labour to search for and produce. Then come discussions and communications with individuals of the Committee, who mean me well, and who are no longer disposed to bow implicitly to the nod of Kehama.[2]

830. To Richard Peake

McAdam MS. *Address*: Mr. Peake | *R.S.V.P.* | *Thursday* | To be delivered to night or very early in the morning *Fr.*: R B Sheridan

[*1813 ?*]

Saville Row
Thursday Evening

Dear Peake

I wish very much you would meet P. Moore and Ward here at dinner tomorrow at six. I am sure you would assist in the Paper I am drawing up. And I have a rare Turkey and Chine.

I want also to know about Wroughton—I have heard nothing about him [since] I know not when!— | Your's truly | R B S

---

[1] When the 'Assignment and Release' of his interest in D.L.Th. was made.

[2] Rae notes that Southey's *Curse of* Kehama had appeared in 1810, and that S. referred to Whitbread under this name.

831. [To S. J. Arnold ?][1]

Berg MS., New York Public Library *Wm.*: 18/

[*13 May 1813 ?*]

past 9

Private

My Dear Sir,

Send me word how the Play[2] has gone off *truly and sincerely*—

perhaps you will do me the favour to look in here for *two minutes*—after it is over—I am most anxious for its success—but I have received contradictory accounts—I am here at *Mollards Hotel* close to *the Theatre*—but shall be going when the Play is over—you know I do not enter your d——d Theatre[3]— your's truly | R B S.

832. To His Son Charles

N.L.I. MS. 7373, f. 1. *Pub.*: W. F. Rae, 'Sheridan's Sons,' *Temple Bar*, cxvi (1899), 423.

Saturday May 15th. [*1813*]

My Dear Charles,

I meant to have written you a longish Letter but I have been so engaged this morning that the Post time is come so I write now chiefly I believe for the sake of not wasting a Frank.—However I cannot omit to say how very much I was pleased by your last Letter—as was your mother. I am sure you are now working in earnest.—Which gives Hester the greatest delight—she is certainly improving but very slowly.—I grieve to say I can learn nothing of your Foils—I rejoice to say your Blackstone and three more books are come from Peter Moore. I will send them forthwith. You shall hear from me again very soon.— | most affectionately | your's | R B Sheridan.

You write a much better hand which pleases me much

[1] Manager of the new D.L.Th.

[2] Tom S.'s *The Russian* ? This melo-drama was give at D.L.Th. on 13 May 1813, and on ten further occasions before the end of the season.

[3] S. had vowed not to enter the new D.L.Th.

833. To His Son Tom

Price MS. *Address*: Thos. Sheridan Esq | Lord Kinnairds[1] | Rossie
Priory | Inchture | Perthshire | N.B. *Fr.*: R B Sheridan *Pm.* 31 JY
1813; AUG 3 1813.

Fetcham
Friday July 30th [*1813*]

My Dear Tom
It is in vain for me to account for my long silence[2]—I
cannot myself even guess at the cause of it. It has proceeded
from anything but an abatement in the affectionate interest
I take in you, or of my anxiety respecting your health—but
there is a perverse fatality in my nature which has often
made me seem most negligent to those I most love.—

One excuse however may be added to this infirmity—
that of having no pleasant feeling to express on any of the
subjects you most naturally might have expected me to
touch on. Politics I am sick of. The Prince I know nothing
of. Party is a Cheat, Stafford worse, and the Theatre and
the Conduct towards me I hate to think of. In addition to
all this there is one subject which has heavily weigh'd on
my mind for these last six months—watching by a sick
couch with the most gloomy apprehensions which my
desponding temper always fix in my mind, was hard work
to my nerves even in my stout Days.—The plain Truth is,
whatever you may have heard from others that Hester has
been for the last six months and *is* in a very dangerous way.[3]
They say she is better—but I fear not essentially. But no
more of this at present as I shall see you so soon—and
sooner I trust than perhaps you had intended. You will

---

[1] 'From one friend Sheridan received
a useful mark of affection: Lord Kinnaird built in his park "a very elegant
cottage" expressly for his use.' (P. Fitzgerald, *Lives of the Sheridans* (1886),
ii. 246.)

[2] There are two letters from Tom S.
to Mrs. S. that appear to belong to 1813.
Writing from Phoenix Park on 25 May,
he asked, 'Is it true that my Father has
had a violent quarrel in Public with the

Prince ?—a Letter from London so informs me, but I do not credit it.'
Writing from Rossie Priory on 25 July,
Tom S. stated that he had sent his father
'several little messages' but had 'never re-
ceiv'd the slightest notice in return, is
this his neglect or yours ?'. See N.L.I.
MS. 7373, ff. 7–11, 16–18.

[3] She suffered from cancer for five
years, before dying on 27 Oct. 1817.
See Sichel, ii. 388, n. 2.

wonder why I say that—it is because I now come to something that is comparatively good news to tell you. McMahon informed me of your application to the Prince respecting some situation at the Cape. I think you were right, and right also in not saying anything to me about it. However reliance on the Prince we can have none[1] and it has so turn'd out that I have effected your object in a way and with a Quarter which I think will be infinitely more grateful to you. I have the Duke of Yorks solemn word and pledge that your desire shall be immediately accomplish'd.[2] The whole Patronage is *his exclusively*—you will owe no atom of obligation either to the Prince or his ministers. I will only now say further that it is absolutely impossible to describe the cordial earnestness shewn by him on this occasion and his kind zeal to serve you.—More of this tomorrow. And now my dear Tom you see my motive for wishing you to come up *immediately*. I have room for you and any number of Chicks at this Place—where you will all be very comfortable—and from hence you may visit Oatlands—and when business calls you to Town there are rooms for you there. Write pray by return of post—and beg Caroline to write too. I send you a box of Papers about I know not [what] that were forced on me from your Father in Law. | ever your's | most affectionately | R B Sheridan

Hester and Charles's kindest Love
Canning has broke up his Party[3] and with Wellesley, Pole[4] etc etc is coming into office.—

[1] In a letter to Tom S. of 23 Jan. 1813 (F. W. Hilles MS.) Moira reported that he had tried to remove the grudge the Regent felt against Tom S. for the language he 'had held on the Expiration of the Restrictions'. Moira added, 'The Duke of Cumberland and Lord Yarmouth beset the Prince with such jealous vigilance and keep him in such trammels that the opportunity of suggesting to him any thing congenial to the kindness of his heart most rarely occurs.'

[2] When Tom S. was about to set off for the Cape of Good Hope, the Duke wrote (6 Nov. 1813) to wish him well and to deplore the uncertain nature of his new post. He added, 'You may depend upon my doing every thing in my power to obtain a situation for you there' (F. W. Hilles MS.). See also *Letters of Geo. IV*, i. 264–5.

[3] But on 9 Aug. Canning mentioned to Abbot that he had separated from Pole and Lord Wellesley. See *Colchester Corr.* ii. 453–4.

[4] William Wellesley-Pole, afterwards 1st Baron Maryborough (1763–1845).

834. To Messrs. Robins and Reid

Historical Society of Pennsylvania MS. *Address*: Messrs Robins and Reid | Warwick St | Golden Square | London *Fr.*: R B S *Pm.*: 2 AU 1813

[*31 July 1813*]
Fetcham
Saturday Evening

My Dear Sir

I am sorry that I miss'd seeing you the other Day and that it was not in my Power to return as I proposed—I assure you upon my solemn word that my agreement with Jacob Campbell was that the whole of the Glass China and earthen ware which he show'd us should be left—his master having removed every thing that was to be taken away—I paying for anything that should be broke. Mr Ironmonger and Mr Ward who were present will attest this to you tomorrow for your more entire justification.—

I am much obliged to you respecting the House in Saville Row but my poor Son is coming there previous to his going to Madeira.[1]—I shall be in Town on tuesday evening. | yours truly | R B Sheridan

835. To His Wife

Pub.: Rae, ii. 226

[*1813*]

It would half break your heart to see how he is changed. I spend all the time with him I can as he seems to wish it, but he so reminds me of his mother, and his feeble, gasping way of speaking affects and deprives me of all hope.[2] He tries to suppress the irritability of his temper in a very amiable way which makes me fear he thinks ill of himself. . . .

[1] Tom S.'s visit to Madeira did not take place until he set out for the Cape in the autumn, but on 25 May [1813] he wrote to Mrs. S. 'In September I shall be in town, on my road to Madeira or elsewhere—what a God send it would be, could I get some appointment at the Cape.'

[2] Tom S. wrote to Mrs. S. on 25 May [1813], 'I cannot walk or ride a foot's pace, from the oppression instantly brought on by my breathing—I am miserably thin and weak.' (W.T.)

This,[1] poor fellow, was so unlike what in his stouter days would have occurred to him that the very kindness of it grieved me.

836. To R. B. Peake[2]

Add. MS. 35118, f. 119–20. *Address*: Mr. R. B. Peake junr. | Charlotte-St. | Fitzroy Square | London. *Fr.*: R B S *Wm.*: 1812.

[*1813*]
Fetcham
Sunday

I am surprised to learn from Mr. Ward that you never received the Letter I sent to you by Graham junr. Ward being present. Pray find him out at Somerset Place and know the reason of this—for if you had received it Mr. Heath (with whom after so long and intimate acquaintance I should be very sorry seriously to dispute) would have known that I never thought of asking him to take the Shares in Payment, only to have them made out in his name, 'till in the course of a few Days I turn'd them into ready money for him. I shall be in Town on wednesday when I will do this—Yours truly | R B S

837. To Viscount Sidmouth

Pub.: Birrell and Garnett Catalogue 16 (1927), item 674. *Address*: Viscount Addington, one of his Majesty's Principal Secretaries of State etc. etc. etc. *Fr.*: R. B. Sheridan.

13 Aug. 1813[3]

My Dear Lord,
Some time since I took the liberty of recommending to your Protection my friend Mr. Burgess as a person I was particularly anxious to serve . . . my present application tho' still connected with Mr. Graham[4] is of a different

[1] He insisted on S.'s going in the chaise: see Rae, ii. 226.
[2] Richard Brinsley Peake (1792–1847), Richard Peake's eldest son. He appears to have been assisting his father at this time, for Tom S. wrote to R.

Peake on 29 July 1812 to say, 'Your son behaved like a lad of sense'. He afterwards achieved fame as a writer of farces.
[3] Cf. S.C., 4 Mar. 1935, lot 177, where it is described as from 'Fetcham 1813'.
[4] Aaron Graham ?

character,—it is that your Lordship would allow Mr. Graham to appoint Mr. Burgess, during his illness to be his *Deputy*—I am confident this would be a very healing indulgence to poor Graham's mind, who has been a very meritorious public servant, as it would show that his recovery is not considered beyond hope. And with respect to Mr. Burgess I pledge myself to be responsible for his ability diligence and integrity. . . .

838. To Henry Burgess

Pub.: Birrell and Garnett Catalogue 16 (1927), item 673.

[*1813 ?*]
Wednesday 8 oclock

Dear Burgess

I ought to have been very angry at your addressing me with 'SIR.' but let the past be forgot. You ought to have known me better than ever to have doubted for a moment my sincere desire and persevering efforts to serve you whenever I could. After our long and intimate connexion nothing can be so foolish as doubt or complacency on either side, but you often allow your temper to get the better of your reason— however as I said before, let us look to the future. I wish particularly to see you to night. I shall be alone the whole evening. | Yours truly | R. B. S.

839. To Richard Wilson

Robert E. Keighton MS. [Ph.] *Address*: Richd. Wilson Esqr. Craven Cottage, Fulham[1] *Fr.*: R B Sheridan *Dock.*: Given to me by Mr. Wilson 13 Nov. 1813. J.D.

[*1813 ?*]
Saville-Row
Thursday Night

My Dear Domine,

How and where are you? and where can I see you in the course of tomorrow— ? | Ever your's | R B Sheridan

I eat a chop at the Piazza Coffee-House.

---

[1] Wilson and his wife held 'rural déjeunes' here in 1812 and 1814. See the *Morn. Chron.*, 14 July 1812; 30 June 1814.

840. To Graham, Ward, and Morland

Pub.: Maggs Catalogue 386 (1919), item 3034.

October 6th., 1813

I hereby make over to Messrs Graham, Ward and Morland jointly or separately to indemnify them for byeing in my Pictures now on sale at P. Cox's,[1] the ten shares of Drury Lane Theatre now in the hands of Mr. Ward belonging to me, also the £350 coming to me from Mr. Moreland. . . .

841. To Lady Holland

Holland House MS. *Pub.*: Sichel, ii. 373. *Address*: Lady Holland *Dock.*: Mr. Sheridan

[*1813–14 ?*]
Tuesday

Will you give me shelter and concealment for to Day in my quiet Tower? I am going to walk after my messenger and shall receive your answer at H. House door[2] | faithfully yours | R B S

842. To Charles Ward

Harvard MS. *Address*: *Private* | Charles Ward Esqr. | Secretary's Office | Drury-Lane-Theatre | London *Fr.*: R B Sheridan *Pm.*: 3 J/ 181/ BIGGLESWADE

[*2 Jan. 1814*]
Southill
Sunday

I beg you my Dear Sir on receipt of this see Frost and Moreland.[3] The latter after we thought every thing settled

---

[1] Two Gainsboroughs, Nos. 808 and 809 in E. K. Waterhouse, *Gainsborough* (1958), p. 104.

[2] See Moore, *Journal*, ii. 187, for an amusing account of S.'s habits at Holland House. [3] See p. 211, n. 1.

seems to want to shirk from doing anything. Pray send me every thing in your Power by return of Post that I may get away tho scarcely recover'd enough. If you are forced to borrow I will replace in two Days after my return— | ever yours | R B S

843. To Charles Ward

Add. MS. 27925, f. 43. *Wm.*: 1813

> [*19 Jan. 1814 ?*][1]
> Saville-Row
> Wednesday Jany. 15th

My Dear Sir

I hear you are canvassing on the occasion of a vacancy of some office in St. Pancrass Parish in favor of my old and constantly respected Friend John Frost. No one is better informed with respect to the unjust political oppression under which he has suffer'd than myself—I see among the List handed to me the name of my brother Dramatist *Reynolds*[2] and I am informed He is a friend of your's if in your approach to him you may think it right to take the Liberty of expressing my wishes to him, you may add that I shall feel personally obliged by his supporting my Friend *John*. Yours ever | R B Sheridan

C. Ward Esqr.

844. To James Heath

British Museum MS., bound in Byron's *Poetical Works* . . . (ed. Moore), xv, unfol. (Press mark: C. 44 e). *Address*: James Heath Esq | Russel Place | Fitzroy Square | London *Fr.*: R B Sheridan *Pm.*: 29 JA [B]IGGLESWADE *Wm.*: 1812.

> [*27 Jan. 1814 ?*]
> Southill
> Thursday

Dear Sir

I will not disguise that I did take extremely ill the Letter

[1] Or 25 Jan. 1815.   [2] Frederic Reynolds (1764–1841).

you sent to me some time since—and I was especially hurt
that you should have dictated it to the Person who signed it—
A name that ought not to have appear'd to such a Letter
address'd to me. I have not received my means from the
Theatre or our account should have been settled at the time
I hoped—but I am now coming to a setttlement with Mr.
Whitbread.¹ With respect to your dispute with the committee
I cannot conceive that the difference can continue respecting
so small a sum—I will pay the £100 myself sooner than it
should. I shall be in Town on sunday and shall be glad to
see you | yours truly | R B Sheridan

845. To Charles Ward

Pub.: Maggs Catalogue 445 (1923), item 2874.

[*1814 ?*]
Saville Row

What I particularly resent in Mr. Heath's conduct is
his causing a letter² to be written to Mr. Bouverie after I
had written to Mr. Heath before the St. Cecilia³ was put in
the Exhibition authorising him to consider his lien on that
Picture to continue the same as before, and so to this hour it
remains—therefore his application to Mr. Bouverie could
only proceed from an unworthy determination personally
to insult me. I authorise you to pay Mr. Heath £100 in
money on my account tomorrow. . . .

---

¹ S. made an assignment of his interest in D.L.Th. on 5 May 1813. The
document is in New York Public
Library.
² R. H. Evans's Catalogue, 10 Mar.
1841, lot 1538, lists a letter 'of Heath to
Sheridan threatening to sell Mrs. S.'s
portrait', but gives no text. *The Post
Office Annual Directory for 1814*, p. 152,

lists Heath and Hawkins as brokers of
12 Water Lane, Tower Street.
³ Reynolds's portrait of the first Mrs.
S. was exhibited at the Royal Academy
in 1775, and at the British Institution in
1813. See A. Graves and W. V. Cronin,
*History of the Works of Sir Joshua
Reynolds* (1899–1901), iii. 887–90.

846. To Charles Ward

Osborn MS. *Pub.*: *The Dramatic Works of . . . Sheridan With a Memoir of His Life by G.G.S.* (1852), p. 196. *Address*: Charles Ward Esqr. | Secretary's Office | Drury-Lane-Theatre | London *Fr.*: R B Sheridan *Pm.*: BIGGLESWADE 5 FE 1814

4 Feb. 1814
Southill
Friday

Dear Ward

Beg borrow steal forge £10 for me and *send by return of Post* then I am with you—| your's truly| R B S

What do you think of Kean[1]—I am glad He is to play Richard and not of Post[2]—How is Brinsley?

847. To Charles Ward

Harvard MS. *Address*: Charles Ward Esqr | Secretary's Office | Drury-Lane-Theatre | London *Fr.*: R B Sheridan *Pm.*: 11 FE 1814

10 Feb. 1814
Southill
Thursday

Dear Ward

I was very much obliged and pleased with the contents of your Letter. The style is brief but admirable. I cared not if I received such communications six times a week—

but Here is the case seriously. I got by the same Post such an account from Fetcham that I was obliged to dispatch what you sent me immediately to that Quarter![3] now what is to be done?—I'll tell you and I will do as much for you on a similar occasion. You must take the trouble to *see Mr. Hudson* YOURSELF with the enclosed—and I have no doubt He

---

[1] Edmund Kean (1787–1833) had excited great interest as Shylock at D.L.Th. from 26 Jan. 1814; and went on to add to his reputation by his performance in *Richard III*.

[2] G. G. S[igmond] reads 'note of post'.

[3] Mr. John H. Harvey's transcriptions from the Great Bookham Church Rate Books show that S. was a defaulter in the amount of £58. 17s. 6d. for rates due in 1813–14.

will advance the £50 I require—I write to him by this Post, but tho He will have a considerable sum to pay me when we have compleated our settlement yet there has been so much delay on my Part in deciding what I mean to sell him, (and indeed I have had so little opportunity of looking over the Ground and Farms sin[c]e Micklemas as you know) that it will be a favour his advancing any thing further. All this you must palliate and enforce with your wonted eloquence and ingenuity.—Now assuming you have got the £50 pray send to my coachman. I should think £10 would extricate him—and then let him pack off with the Horses to Fetcham —Citizen Frost will help to manage him—and send me £30 by Post. | ever yours | R B S

Pray write me a long letter and tell me of Kean. Mrs. S is better and will be able to travel on sunday

848. To Charles Ward

Osborn MS. *Pub.*: *The Dramatic Works of . . . Sheridan With a Memoir of his Life by G.G.S.*, p. 197. *Address*: Charles Ward, Esqr. | Secretary's Office Theatre, Drury Lane | London *Fr.*: R B S *Pm.*: BIGG[LES]W[A]DE 18 FE 1814

17 Feb. 1814
Southill   Thursday

PRIVATE

Dear Ward,

Thou art a trusty man, and when I write to you I get an answer and the thing done if it can be—and you don't write or want to receive *long* Letters—which are my horror. I have been very ill with a violent attack of bile—kept my bed three days[1]—but *don't say this to a soul*, it always does harm in my situation. I am now quite well, and the better for it. Pray let two or three Theatre chaps or their con- nexions put up a little scaffolding in my Hall that may serve to wash the walls and white-wash the ceiling *as soon as you receive* this. I will explain my motives when I arrive

---

[1] S. stayed with Whitbread at Southill for over a month, and report said that he was busy with a comedy: see Egerton MS. 1975, f. 168.

on Sunday—as I suppose I have replaced the last £10 you stole for me, I trust you may reputably renew the theft when I arrive should it be again wanted, as I greatly fear it will. I have had a very civil letter from Hudson—from whom I have great resource coming. There are *political* events (*home*) *brewing*. One letter more will catch me here. | Ever yours, | R B S

849. To ——

Folger MS. *Dock.*: Sheridan

[*Feb. 1814*]
Southill
Friday

My Dear Sir
    I am truly vex'd at the trouble and dilemma you [have] been brought into by my having been unluckily so long detain'd here. Mrs. Sheridan is now so much better that she will be able to accompany me on sunday or monday next at farthest. In the mean time I have written to my Friend P. Moore to make out the Security for Sir George as well as to see or write to him. I shall also write to him myself before I leave this Place.| I am your sincere and obliged | Friend | R B Sheridan
I will come to you the moment I get to Town.—

850. To Thomas McGrath[1]

Osborn MS. *Address*: Dr. McGrath | Biggleswade *Fr.*: R B Sheridan *Wm.*: 1810

[*1814 ?*]
Southill—
Friday

My Dear Sir
    I beg you will do me the favour to accept enclosed for your most attentive attendances on Mrs. Sheridan and myself with many thanks from us both.

[1] Mr. W. R. LeFanu informs me that Thomas McGrath was admitted M.R.C.S., London, 1 Feb. 1811; and appears to have been a general practitioner at Biggleswade throughout his life. He died *c.* 1842.

Mrs. Sheridan informed me that she has requested you to send the medicine account to Saville-Row—which she will immediately discharge— | Believe me Dear Sir | your very sincere well wisher | and COUNTRYMAN | R B Sheridan

851. To Samuel Whitbread

J. R. Blackett-Ord MS. Copy in the hand of Whitbread.[1] *Pub.*: *Creevey Papers*, i. 190, where from a misreading of the signature it is ascribed to Thomas Sheridan.

[*9 Apr. 1814*]

Bonaparte has signed his resignation—Bourbons proclaim'd—Victor[2] Ney[3] Marmont[4] Abbe Sieyes[5] Caulincourt[6] etc. etc. have sign'd. The Emperor has a Pension of 200,000 per Ann.: and a retreat in the Isle of Elba. The Archduchess late Empress goes with him. She is gone with an Austrian Escort to join him at Fontain[e]bleau—there are to be immense rejoicings on Monday. White Cockades and tremendous illumination. Carlton House to blaze with Fleurs de Lis, etc. The Royal Yatch is ordered to take the King. The Admiral of the Fleet the Duke of Clarence to command her—all true honor bright. I am just come from the Prince.[7]—R. S.

852. To Charles Ward

Pub.: Maggs Catalogue 266 (1911) item 503.

Saville Row, April. [*1814 ?*]

My Dear Ward

The unfortunate absence of our friend P. Moore from

---

[1] Enclosed with Whitbread's letter of 10 Apr. 1814, and docketed in Creevey's hand 'Sheridan's letter to Whitbread upon the Peace—with Whitbread's answer'. For the answer, see *Creevey Papers*, i. 190–1.

[2] Claude Perrin Victor (1764–1841), Marshal of France.

[3] Michel Ney (1769–1815), Duke of Elchingen and Marshal of France.

[4] Auguste de Marmont (1774–1852), Duke of Ragusa and Marshal of France.

[5] Emmanuel, Abbé Sieyès (1748–1836).

[6] Armand-Augustin-Louis de Caulaincourt (1772-1827), Duke of Vicenza.

[7] The *Staff. Adv.*, 23 Apr. 1814, reported that S. had 'an audience with the Prince Regent on Saturday' [9 Apr.].

Town till Monday prevents my obtaining the aid of the £100 which you know to be so essential to me. . . .

You know the whole of my means and difficulties; *raise the money*, and I hereby authorise Mr. P. Moore to use the means in his hands to discharge the said £100.

853. To Samuel Whitbread

Whitbread MS. 4126. *Address*: S. Whitbread E[sq.]

[*May 1814 ?*][1]

Wednesday evening—

Burgess is very properly gone to clear his Character with the Solicitors for the Plaintiff. They assert He was well apprized of the whole business. He swears not—and I hope He is right—I never heard Burgess admits a word on the subject for the last 8 years—Debt contracted eighteen years back.—Fraudulent enough—but I find it has nothing to do with the Theatre | R B S

you surely will not let me be kept here tonight

854. To Samuel Whitbread

Whitbread MS. 4128. *Pub.*: Moore, ii. 442–4. *Dock.*: Sheridan May 1814 *Wm.*: 1812

May 1814

Tooke's Court[2]

Cursitor St

Thursday past two

I have done every thing in my Power with the Solicitors

---

[1] There are three other occasions on which S. is said to have been arrested for debt and taken to a sponging house. Rae, ii. 277–8, states that this one happened in Aug. 1813 but I have not found his authority for the remark. Farington, vii. 229, mentions on 30 Mar. 1814 that S. had lately been 'kept for two days in a Lock-up House'. Wraxall declares that S. was shut up for three days with Sir Watkin Lewes in a sponging house in Fetter Lane in Aug. 1815: see *Posthumous Memoirs* (2nd ed., 1836), i. 55.

[2] 'Follett, the Clown . . . was one day locked up at Hirst's, the sheriff's officer, in Took's-court, when Sheridan was brought in' (*New M. Mag.* (1835), Pt. I, p. 85).

White and Fownes[1] to obtain my release by substituting a better security for them than their detaining me—but in vain.

Whitbread, putting all false professions of Friendship and feeling out of the Question, you have no right to keep me here. For it is in truth *your* act. If you had not forcibly witheld from me the £12,000 in consequence of a threatening Letter from a miserable swindler[2] whose claim *you* in particular knew to be *a lie*—I should at least have been out of the reach of *this* state of miserable insult—for that and that only lost me my seat in Parliament. And I assert that you cannot find a Lawyer in the Land, that is not either a natural born Fool or a corrupted Scoundrel who will not declare that your conduct in this respect was neither warrantable or legal. But let that pass for the present.

Independently of the £1000 ignorantly with[h]eld from me on the Day of considering my last claim, I require of you to answer the draft I send herewith on the Part of the committee, pledging myself to prove to them on the first Day I can personally meet them that there are still thousands and thousands due to me both legally and equitably from the Theatre—my word ought to be taken on this subject, and you may produce to them this document—if one among them could think that under all the circumstances your conduct required a justification. O God! with what mad confidence have I trusted your word—I ask justice from you and no boon.—I enclosed you yesterday three different securities which had you been disposed to have acted even as a private Friend would have made it certain that you might have done so without the smallest risk.—These you discretely offerr'd to put into the Fire, when you found the object of your humane visit satisfied by seeing me safe in Prison.[3]—

---

[1] Richard Samuel White (*ob.* 1817) and James Somerville Fownes. For Beckford's comments on them, see *Life at Fonthill, 1807–22* (ed. B. Alexander, 1957), pp. 50, 102, 120.

[2] W. Taylor claimed £20,000 from D.L.Th. 'altho' not a shilling was due'. In 1811 S. had offered to allow Taylor's claim to go to arbitration. Whitbread

was alarmed by Taylor's threats and, in 1814, still held back S.'s money from D.L.Th. to meet a possible demand. See *Reports Presented to the First and Second General Assemblies of Subscribers to the Re-building . . .* (1811), p. 33; and *Letters of Geo. IV*, iii. 195.

[3] J. G. Lockhart, in the *Quarterly Review*, xxxiii (1826), 585–6, stated that

I shall only add that, I think, if I know myself, had our Lotts been reversed, and I had seen you in my situation, and had left Lady E.[1] in that of my wife[2] I would have risk'd £600 rather than have left you so altho' I had been in no way accessory in bringing you into that condition. | R B Sheridan

S. Whitbread Esr.

855. 'To Mr. Graham'

Pub.: S.C., 22 July 1908, lot 278.

[*1814*]

Kean most kindly came to Saville Row on Sunday and read Othello to Mrs. S.[3]—He exceeds all I have heard.

856. To John Graham

Berg MS., New York Public Library. *Pub.*: Maggs Catalogue 386 (1919), lot 3036. *Address*: John Graham Esqr. | Cranford Bridge | Middlesex *Fr.*: R B Sheridan *Dock.*: Sheridan *Pm.*: 22 JU 814

Saville Row
Wednesday June 22d *1814*

Dear Graham
I cannot but thank you most cordially for the Letter you have written to Ward and which He has put into my hands. It breathes in every sentence the true spirit and gives me

Whitbread left his dinner table to go to S. but found that he had been liberated by the 'unsolicited interference' of the Prince Regent. He noted, however, that S. 'may have been twice delivered . . . and that on one of the occasions Mr. Whitbread *was* the deliverer'.

[1] His wife, Lady Elizabeth.

[2] Her letter to Whitbread reads: 'Sheridan's state of mind kills me—all I can say to him seems to poison his mind. Clarke has given me leave to go

and see him . . . tell me then where I am to direct the Coachman—Do not refuse this, for you will only do me harm—and above all do not go to him yourself. . . .' (Whitbread MS. 4131.)

[3] Mrs. S. was too ill to go to D.L.Th. Kelly, ii. 285, states that S. 'had once studied the part of Othello himself, to act at Sir Watkin William Wynn's private theatre in Wales; and that Kean's conception of Othello was the precise counterpart of his own'.

the greatest satisfaction—for I must sincerely assure you that nothing could hurt me more than the continuing to believe that you had given me just cause to break off our old friendship. I am now convinced that you have been grossly belied to me—but of this when we meet.—For now I have only to accept your most friendly offer and to entreat that you will come to Town on receipt of this and dine with me tomorrow. | truly Your's | R B Sheridan.

857. To Colonel John McMahon

Windsor MS. 21472. *Pub.*: *Letters of Geo. IV*, i. 458–9. *Dock.*: R. B. Sheridan | 1814

[*1814*]

Saville-Row

Monday Evening

Private

My Dear Friend

I have *decided* to stand for Westminster.[1] I have the Whig *support* made known to me thro' the Duke of Norfolk.[2] This will enable me only to be a more powerful and efficient Friend to the Prince.—After what has pass'd between me and Lord Sidmouth I cannot doubt the support of Government. Without a Boast depend on it no man can beat Brogham,[3] but myself and against me I think He will yet shrink to stand. How hateful the ground of his mob popularity would be to the Prince I need not state | ever your's | R B Sheridan

[1] The *Staff. Adv.*, 25 Dec. 1813, stated that 'in the event of the death of Lord Dundonald, father of Lord Cochrane, Mr. Sheridan is expected to become the representative of Westminster'. Cochrane, however, was unwarrantably accused of being a party to a fraud on the Stock Exchange and was expelled from Parliament on 5 July 1814.

[2] S.'s candidature is mentioned as early as 30 May, and Norfolk's support on 11 June: see Add. MS. 27850, ff. 281–2. The assistance of some Whigs, of Carlton House, and of Lord Liverpool, is suggested by Brougham in *Creevey Papers* (i. 195) on 29 June.

[3] Henry Brougham (1778–1868), later Lord Chancellor and Lord Brougham and Vaux, was adviser to the Princess of Wales.

858. To the Duke of Norfolk

The Duke of Norfolk, Arundel Castle MS. Text from Mr. F. W. Steer's transcription. *Pub.*: Rhodes, pp. 242–3. *Wm.*: 1812

Saville Row
Tuesday, July 5th [*1814*]
My Dearest Lord
    On the subject of the Westminster Election I was compell'd to make my decision before I had an opportunity of again consulting your Grace.—The messages I have received from you the words which you have utter'd in my behalf in short your whole conduct in this business impress on my mind the deepest sense of unalterable gratitude.— This Crisis and last effort is the winding up of my political exertions and perhaps the last gratification remaining to my public or even private Feelings.—I feel very sanguine of success but I protest I think I shall owe that success principally if not solely to *you*. | Your Grace's | ever most faithfully | R B Sheridan.

His Grace the Duke of Norfolk.

I will wait on you tomorrow if returned to Town.

859. To Arthur Morris, High Bailiff of Westminster

Pub.: *Morn. Chron.*, 15 July 1814. The version printed by P. Fitzgerald (*Lives of the Sheridans* (1886), ii. 230–1) appears to be from a draft.

Saville Row, Sunday Evening, July 10, 1814.
Sir,
    Observing that you have called a meeting to-morrow,[1] to be held in Palace-Yard, to consider of a fit person to fill up the present Vacancy in the Representation of the City of

---

[1] The High Bailiff read S.'s letter from the hustings on 11 July and it was received with great applause. Burdett said that 'an act more graceful or more politic he [S.] could not have performed at the present instant'. See the *Morn. Chron.*, 12 July 1814.

Westminster, and having myself received very earnest applications from numerous and independent bodies of its Inhabitant Householders, requiring that I should meet their wishes, by proposing myself as a Candidate:—I take the freedom of addressing these lines to you, to say, that I absolutely decline to put in Nomination in opposition to Lord Cochrane.

I send you this, my determination, without concert or communication with the respectable persons, to whom I have above referred, and towards whom, I must ever continue to owe the utmost gratitude.

I trust I need not declare, that I should have felt greatly honoured by having been again returned the Representative of Westminster:—my title to aspire to that distinction is simply, that, after, more than 31 years' service in Parliament, I can, without fear of successful contradiction, assert that I never gave a Vote that was not in support of the Truth of Liberty, and in Assertion of the People's Rights; duly respecting, at the same time, the just Prerogatives of the Crown, and revering the Sacred Principles upon which are founded and maintained, the glory and security of our unrivalled Constitution.

Holding these opinions, as a public man, have I hitherto sat in the House of Commons; and never will I accept a seat there, but on the sole condition of being the master of my own vote and voice—the servant only of my conscience.

As to the present question, which occasions your Meeting tomorrow, I enter not into it. No man feels more the reverence due to the seats of justice, or the confidence due to the verdicts of juries. But under the circumstances of an expulsion from the House of Commons, I do not hesitate to say, that I have a decided opinion, that the expelled Member has a right to appeal to his Constituents; with a view to the restitution of his seat, and rescue of his character.

On these grounds, Sir, I will not allow myself to interfere with the present appeal made on the part of Lord Cochrane, and to which I conceive him to be so justly entitled.

In adopting the determination, I beg leave distinctly to state, that I wa[i]ve my claim to solicit the suffrages of the

Electors of Westminster in favour of Lord Cochrane alone.[1]
| I have the honour to be, Sir, | With sincere respect and
esteem, | Your very obedient and humble servant | Richard
Brinsley Sheridan.

860. To Arthur Morris

Clements MS. [Ph.] *Dock.*: Mr. Sheridan

Saville Row
July 12th 1814

My Dear Sir
    As I take it for granted there will be employment for a
Hustings at Westminster you will greatly oblige me by
appointing Mr. T. Smith to be one of the Poll Clerks.[2] He
is strongly recommended to me and I am confident will
not discredit your patronage.
    I take this opportunity of returning you my sincere thanks
for your uniformly friendly attention towards me. In declining to stand on the present occasion I feel assured that
I have acted rightly under all the circumstances.[3] I have not
a copy of my Letter to you—could you favour me with
one? | very truly your's | R B Sheridan
A. Morris Esqr.

861. [To Colonel John McMahon]

Windsor MSS. 21492–3. *Pub.*: *Letters of Geo. IV*, i. 472. *Wm.*:
1814

Saville-Row
Wednesday July 27th [*1814*]

Private

My Dear Friend
    I have done exactly as you wish'd and seen Lord Liverpool
as well as Lord Sidmouth—I said every thing to the former
you advised, avowing your previous communication with

[1] Apart from S. and Brougham, Major John Cartwright, the radical reformer, also thought of standing. All three withdrew and Cochrane was re-elected on 16 July.

[2] See S.C., 11 Nov. 1929, lot 765, where part of this sentence is quoted.

[3] See S.C., 12 May 1851, lot 720, where this sentence is quoted.

me and what I said was under the impression of very sincere gratitude—

I have grieved, and so I believe I express'd myself to you the other night at the Fête,[1] to hear from different quarters that the Prince was dissatisfied at my giving way on the Westminster Election.—Against Brogham I would have stood 'till I dropt, for that was a *personal assault* on the *Prince*—and meant to have produced the most mischievous effects. The other was a very different case, and one in which the *Prince* had no *personal* concern. Had I persever'd in being a candidate look for a moment to what my situation would have been. I should have had to encounter a popular yell for three weeks, (for observe *during the contest* no *pardon of the Pillory* could have been granted) which I would not do for any seat, and *that*, while my best attentions were due to another tho' a domestic Quarter—but how would I have maintain'd the conflict when I found my Friend the Duke of Norfolk despairing of the supplies he hoped for, and feeling the cause unpopular, desirous of beating a retreat.— I was left myself personally in debt £1700 after the last Westminster Election which has press'd upon me grievously —what could I have done *now* when I found not a shilling subscribed to support me—I told both Lord Cholmondeley[2] and Lord Yarmouth when I found the thing desperate the Line I meant to take—and I think I had their concurrence that it would be right to signify that I *would not have given way to Brogham* which I think the last sentence of my advertise-ment[3] very intelligibly intimates—I have no wish to be member for Westminster but as that seat would furnish me in these precarious Days a more independent opportunity of being of service to the Prince, nor have a wish to be in Parliament at all but for the same object—even in opposing Brogham it is lamentable to think that I now find He would have been espoused and supported by the *leading Talents* against me—Grenville Grey and Whitbread etc. I cared not for—but it was a grief to my heart to find Tavistock,[4] with

---

[1] At Carlton House on 21 July.
[2] George James, 1st Marquess of Cholmondeley (1749–1827), was Lord Steward of the Household.

[3] Letter 859.
[4] Francis Russell, afterwards 7th Duke of Bedford (1788–1861), was M.P. for Bedfordshire.

whom I had been living on such intimacy, and the name
of Russell pledged to the same cause!—with others whom
I will not name! ! but Adam who can only act in one line,
and that is the line of perfect honor can ascertain the fact
to you, and perhaps deplored it more than I do. It would be
gross affectation in me if I did not confess that I write this
Letter with a sanguine confidence that you will communicate
its contents to the Prince—I am sure He has only to glance
his eye over it to be convinc'd, that Those who have told
him that in declining Westminster at this moment I have
fail'd in duty to him or regard to the Public, have not
judged well.

Now my Dear Mac, I must conclude this long letter—I
shall do it with a short but sincere sentence. The Prince
is an excellent Critic in every thing and in nothing more than
in his insight into political character. I believe He gives me
credit for honourable and independent political Principles
and I trust for sincere personal attachment to him—but
He places no confidence in my judgement to apply these
well—and there, if I dare use the phrase He is mistaken—
but I yet feel confident that it would require a very strong
effort to dislodge me from his Good-will, | R B Sheridan

862. [To Colonel John McMahon]

Windsor MS. 42626. *Wm.*: /14

[*1814 ?*]

Saville Row
Wednesday Evening

My Dear Friend
My influence at Carlton House being overrated I am
press'd by Ladies lovely for six tickets—for which I must
be indebted to your ever friendly exertions—| truly your's |
R B Sheridan

I open this note [to] say that when you have read my
Letter to the Prince and seal'd it I need not say I wish him
to see it before I come to the Levee. I am a poor but proud
Devil

863. To John Wilson Croker

Lonsdale MS. Text from transcriptions by Sir Shane Leslie and Dr. Arthur Aspinall.

Saville Row Friday 29 July [*1814*]

Private

My dear Croker,

You ought to be surprised if not indignant at my making a new application to you and that upon a matter comparatively frivolous—but all I want is an answer to prove to a Lady fair that I have obey'd her commands in making the application. I believe my shortest way will be to enclose to you her letter and to tell you who she is. She is the elder sister[1] of my daughter, Tom's wife, Fanny[2] is the youngest sister and the very prettiest creature I believe in the united Kingdoms, and Brinsley is my eldest Grandson now with them. So you have the history of my application. The poor woman seems a most decent Person—but I know the difficulty of discharges.

I will not mix with this my thanks or expressions of unalterable gratitude for your kindness respecting Mrs Sheridan's voyage, but I cannot omit to mention, that I have this day heard from my son and that she is safely arrived at Cowes after a most pleasant sail, which has done her infinite good. I never saw anything more perfect in accommodation than the Vessel and the master and crew have been most obliging | yours truly R B S

864. To Thomas Shaw

Harvard MS. *Address*: Thos. Shaw Esq *Fr.*: R B S. *Dock.*: Sheridan | Sepr. 10 | 1814. | By Mr. Farebrother

August[3] 4th. *1814*

At a considerable distance from Town where my Letters

[1] Georgiana Callander died unmarried.

[2] Fanny Callander married Sir James R. G. Graham, 2nd Baronet, on 8 July 1819, and died in 1857.

[3] Possibly a mistake on S.'s part for September.

have not follow'd me as I was expected back I have just received yours you shall hear from me fully tomorrow | Yours etc. | R B S

865. To Anna Maria Ogle

Osborn MS. *Address*: Mrs. N. Ogle *Fr.*: R B S

[1814 ?]
West Cowes
Marine Hotel
Tuesday Evening

My Dear Malty
Here we are after a delightful sail—and an excellent Dinner on Board. John sprung up here in his search after Lord Craven.¹ He has persuaded Ephriam to stop to take him to Ryde. I have nothing to do with this and remonstrated against it—as it will lose Ephriam the tide. Hester is going to a vile Lodging and Charles and I have got beds here for to Night. What is to become of us all tomorrow I know not, for I can find no decent Place empty—² | God bless you | R B S

866. To Anna Maria Ogle

Pub.: Rae, ii. 264.

[1814 ?]

I have scarcely closed my eyes since I have been in this infernal noisy hotel.³

867. To ——

Pub.: *Catalogue of the Collection of Autographs belonging to the Estate of the late Lewis J. Cist, Esq.* (Bangs & Co., New York, 1886), pt. 1, p. 160, no. 1835.

[1814]

Mrs. S. has received the £20, but for want of the remainder

¹ William, 1st Earl of Craven (1770–1825).
² Great increase of company was reported from Cowes on 13 Aug. By 3 Sept. 'houses and lodgings of every description were in much requisition': see the *Hampshire Courier*, 15 Aug. and 5 Sept. 1814.
³ The Marine Hotel at West Cowes.

to pay off the dirty, noisy hole she is in, we have miss'd a neat little, clean and cheaper lodgings. I rely on you to-morrow.

868. To Sir John Cox Hippisley[1]

Pub.: *The Era*, 26 May 1878: 'For the use of the original we are indebted to Mr. W. C. Day of Bedford Square.' Cf. S.C., 23 Feb. 1856, lot 29: 'Confidential'.

Cowes, Friday Night, September, 1814

(Confidential)

My dear Hippesley,

You will, perhaps, be surprized at receiving this letter, but not more than I am at writing it, and, perhaps, thro' life no man that has not always stood free from embarrassments has so resolutely and perseveringly stood free from personal obligation as I have done. In making this application you are the second person in the world I ever asked a pecuniary favour from. I am induced to it by words you once uttered tending to more service than I wanted. But to the point. I ask you to advance me £100 upon the enclosed draft, which I *pledge my solemn word of honour* to you shall be most punctually answered, and as such you may send it into your bankers.

My good old friend, if you have mark'd, as I am sure you have, the independence of my public and private character and conduct, you will readily believe that it is a great exigency that suggests this application. | R. B. Sheridan.

869. To Anna Maria Ogle

Osborn MS. Pub.: Rae, ii. 264. *Address*: Mrs. N Ogle *Fr.*: R B S

[*1814 ?*]

Beloved Malty

You save my Life by offering me a quiet bed to Night—

---

[1] Hippisley (1748–1825) was created a baronet in 1796, after 'important negotiations in Italy'. He strongly supported Catholic emancipation. His 'buildings' were at the north end of the parade at Cowes: see the *Hampshire Courier*, 19 Sept. 1814.

for an Inn kills me and I have lately been sleeping in none
but Quiet Rooms—| Yours truly | R B S

I will come early—

870. To Charles Ward

Dufferin MS. [Ph.] *Address*: Charles Ward Esq | Secretary's Office |
Theatre | Drury Lane | London *Pm.*: COWES 12 SE 1814

11 Sept. 1814
Cowes   Sunday
Confidential

Dear Ward
    Thank you for every thing you do. I am clear we should
avoid paying Frost the dividends on those Shares. He may
be truly told that I have pledged my word to Fowell[1] that
those Dividends should be held sacred for him till He had
received his £140—that is on giving up the shares which
would relieve everything Frost and all—at all events post-
pone till I get to Town which you may assure Frost will be
on wednesday with Charles—too long kept from Bloomfield—
    I shall send you by tomorrows Post a most absolute
security to cover every risk. | ever yours | R B S.

What the Deuce brought Whitbread to Town

871. To Thomas Metcalfe

Osborn MS. *Address*: T. Metcalfe Esq | New-Square | Lincoln's Inn
Fr.: R B S *Dock.*: 19 Septr. 1814 | Mr. Sheridan *Wm.*: 1811

Monday
Sepr. 19th [*1814*]

My Dear Sir
    I am extremely anxious to know how Mrs. Metcalfe is.
I hope you are able to send me a good account.
    I am just come to Town leaving Mrs. S. in the Isle of

[1] An undated note among the 'Fowell for Fairbrother for White
Harvard MSS. contains the item: Horses—£70'.

Wight and I am sorry to say but very little if at all better,—
which after a year and a half's suffering and confinement
is a hard case.

I am rather in lag at this moment but if you are in Town
tomorrow I will get to you or shall you be in the evening in
Keppell St. ?—| most truly your's | R B Sheridan

872. [To John Young?]¹

Princeton University Library MS.

[*1814 ?*]

Saville Row

Monday Evening

Sir

The Pictures I have sent I wish to be thus designated—

    Landscape   Gainsborough
    —   Do.   Girl and Cat
    — Mr. Thos. Sheridan when a Boy —²
    —The late Mrs. Sheridan and her sister the late
        Mrs. Tickell —

I have just been told that this Picture is to be described
in the catalogue as Mr. W. Linley's³—This is an Errour—
The Picture is *mine*—I beg the catalogue may be corrected
—or the Picture not exhibited— | R B Sheridan

873. To Charles Ward

Pub.: Maggs Catalogue 547 (1930), item 1728.

19 September 1814

[An interesting letter referring to his financial difficulties,

¹ (1755–1825), engraver and Keeper
of the British Gallery. He advertised in
The Times, 8 Apr. 1814, that works by
Hogarth, Wilson, and Gainsborough
would be exhibited shortly. For S.'s part
in this, see W. T. Whitley, *Art in
England, 1800–20* (1928), p. 230. A
franked cover (Osborn MS.) is extant
and is addressed by S. to '— Young
Esqr. | Secretary to the National
Institution | or if absent | To the Keeper

of the Gallery.'
² See E. K. Waterhouse, *Gainsborough*
(1958), p. 89, no. 612.
³ Linley appears to have been given
the picture temporarily as a security
against (or as he claimed, a payment for)
a loan of £100. He still possessed it on
7 Nov. 1825, when he wrote to Thomas
Moore mentioning it: see his letter in
Notes and Queries, 11th Ser., x (1914),
62.

and mentioning a legacy left to him. The legacy referred to was one of £1,200 left to him by a Burgess of Stafford,[1] and arrived most opportunely, when Sheridan was in great financial difficulties, having been arrested for debt in 1813.]

874. To Anna Maria Ogle

Osborn MS. *Address*: Mrs. N. Ogle | Orchard-Place | Southampton
Fr.: R B Sheridan *Wm.*: 1811

[*Sept. 1814*]
Cowes Sunday

Dear Malty

How are you? where are you? what are you about? give me a Line—where is Nat?[2] Hester is I think much improved since she came here—Harry Anne and all the Children in unbounded Health. Are the Miss Callanders at Southampton? I wish I could hear from them—

We are going to have a grand Christening on board the Blue-eyed-Maid (Owen Williams) on tuesday—if you could purchase for me a little *good Fruit* and lay Hands on any *Red mullets* I should be an important contributor to the Feast—You know I suppose that poor Mrs. Charles Ogle is dead[3]—She was an excellent creature. | truly yours | R B Sheridan

875. To Georgiana and Fanny Callander

Dufferin MS. [Ph.]

Cowes
Sunday Octr. 2 [*1814*]

Ladies fair

I rely on your not having left Southampton—and that you will not without making us the promised visit for which

---

[1] Edward Drakeford left S. money 'as a mark . . . of respect for the distinguished talents and public virtues of that enlightened Patriot and Statesman' (*Staff. Adv.*, 19 Mar. 1814).

[2] Son of Nathaniel Ogle, who had died in May 1813.

[3] 'Lately at her mother's, Hon. Mrs. Gage, Great Cumberland Street, the wife of Capt. Ogle, R.N.' (*Gent. Mag.* lxxxiv (1814), pt. 2, p. 404. Cf. ii. 224.

Hester bids me say she is most anxious—we are now going into a House where we shall have perfect room for you. Write pray by return of Post, and I will fix the Day to fetch you—I believe you rather shirk'd the blowing weather the other Day. | truly Your's | R B Sheridan

876. To His Wife

Robert H. Taylor MS.

[*15 Oct. 1814 ?*][1]
Saturday Evening

Dearest,

I enclose you a Letter and a Newspaper professing to *publish* for the *first time some* verses of mine to Mrs. (now Lady) Crewe. They are inaccurately printed but on the whole I certainly wrote them but had for*gotten* (Capt. B) them, which is not common with me. From what Quarter they can have been sent to a Newspaper at this late date I cannot surmise—and I certainly have no means of furnishing the remainder of the Poem were I disposed to do it. I hate anything thus surrept[it]iously publish'd to be attributed to me—I never yet own'd or allow'd the printing of anything Play Poems or Speeches but two things to both which I put my name—viz. The Critic and a Political Pamphlet on the affairs of India[2]—I put Pizzarro out of the Question— but this Winter I am determined to give my Friend Rogers[3] full Power to put together and publish all my Scrib[b]lings —and he offers to ensure me four thousand Pounds if done by my Authority. When I look at these ver[s]es Oh! how it reminds me what an ardent romantic Blockhead nature made me!

[1] Rhodes says 'A Portrait' appeared 'surreptitiously in print in 1810, but in what form is unknown': see *An Ode to Scandal* (Oxford, 1927), p. vi. Sichel, i. 94, dates the letter 'about 1812'. They seem to have ignored a newspaper cutting in Egerton MS. 1975, f. 169, which contains a 'Fragment of a Portrait | By the Right Honourable R. B. Sheridan | (Never before published) | Addressed to a Lady, with the Comedy of THE SCHOOL FOR SCANDAL.' The first sixty-one couplets of 'A Portrait' are printed here (with six minor changes in the wording), and the cutting is dated in manuscript 'Oct 12 1814.' This was a Wednesday, and I assume S.'s letter was written on the following Saturday.

[2] See ii. 222, n. 1.

[3] He delayed doing so.

They were sent with a M.S. copy of the Play finely bound etc. N.B. I was not then 25—by the way She was in truth the Handsomest of the set.

Monday

I have lost the Paper with the verses. I'll get it tomorrow. I shall drown myself if I miss my Scotts

My Dear Harry—having been out of Town yesterday I did not get yours till this moment and only one moment have I to say you shall hear from me. Don't mind losing one Day| God bless you | I must hear by return of Post from every one| Annie dear write from Hecca| S.¹

877. To Samuel Whitbread

Whitbread MS. 4133. *Dock.*: Mr. Sheridan. Nov. 6. 1814 Money

6 Nov. 1814
Sunday Night

Dear Whitbread
A Spell of stupid Pride ties my tongue and prevents my speaking frankly face to face on the subject of any pecuniary obligation. Burgess came to see me at your house this evening in great distress—He wants £100 (on my affairs certainly) very early indeed in the morning—but He *will himself engage to return* it to you *tomorrow sen'night.* Pray give this temporary aid on a very great emergency—As to the Pictures I shall certainly sell them before *thursday*—and I shall grieve to see them pass into strange Hands—for I part with them at all most reluctantly. The Good you can do me is to speak to some fair men like Baring² or Angerstein³ etc etc who will deal liberally that I may not be forced to take half their value for them—Rising⁴ estimates the two upright Gainsboroughs⁵ at much more than I have put them

---

¹ His arrival at Cook's Hotel 'from a tour' was noted in the *Morn. Chron.*, 24 Oct. 1814.
² Alexander Baring (1774–1848), financier, was M.P. for Taunton, 1806–26, and became 1st Baron Ashburton in 1835.
³ John Julius Angerstein (1735–

1823), merchant and art collector.
⁴ John Rising (1756–1815), painter.
⁵ Identified as 'A Boy at a Cottage Fire and a Girl Eating Milk' and 'A Boy with a Cat—Morning', by E. K. Waterhouse in 'Gainsborough's "Fancy Pictures"', *Burlington Magazine*, lxxxviii (1946), 140.

at. Mark my words you shall see me clear of every difficulty.
What will you give me for my heavenly piping Fawn?[1] |
truly yours | R B S.

878. To Samuel Whitbread

Whitbread MS. 4134. *Address*: S. Whitbread Esq *Dock.*: Nov. 7 |
1814 | Mr. Sheridans | Pictures

7 November 1814

	£
Two upright Gainsboroughs	300
Landscape with Cows[2]	200
Two Morelands[3]	120
Boys robbing apple-Stall	40
	660

H Burgess will return at six.

879. To G. Watkins[4]

Salt MS. Copy. *Address*: G. Watkins Esqr. | Lincoln Inn Stone |
Building

Guildhall Chambers
Nov. 7 1814.

My Dear Sir
I am just arrived and have received both your Letters.

[1] In a letter of 15 Aug. 1816 (Osborn MS.), John Graham declared that S. on his death-bed (actually on 29 June) had charged Graham to deliver the bronze faun, given to S. by H. C. Combe, into the hands of S.'s son Charles.

[2] If this were a Gainsborough, it may have been the picture, 'Woody Landscape with Girls with Milkpails, Cattle, etc.', described as possibly being in S.'s possession in 1814, by E. K. Waterhouse, *Gainsborough* (1958), p. 115.

[3] A note (Shakespeare Memorial Library MS.) by Alfred Bunn reads: 'Morland the painter lived in Graham's Lock-up house for years; whereby Graham got some of Morland's finest paintings, subsequently brought to the hammer at George Robins's. Sheridan was well aware of the collection, while in Graham's possession, desired to possess a particular specimen thereof. This came to the notice of Phillips of Grosvenor Place, the celebrated lottery contractor, who, to complete his good feeling to Sheridan resolved to buy this picture ("Sir Joshua's Kitchen and Morland's Garret") and present it to him. Sheridan unaware of this had employed Billy Dunn to buy it; and the consequence was Dunn and Phillips outbid one another.'

[4] George Watkins was an attorney of 2 Stone Buildings.

As you are so well acquainted with the whole transaction and have Mr. Richard's advice I trust all is right. I have not really time even to call upon you. I have sent all I can conveniently spare which you will have the goodness just to acknowledge | I am truly yours | R B Sheridan

G. Watkins Esqr.   £30
  Lincoln['s] Inn   5
                       5
                    40

880. [To Douglas Kinnaird ?]

Price MS.

Monday Novr. 7th: [*1814*]

My Dear Sir

General Gordon[1] just arrived from Madeira where He has been inexpressibly kind to my Son and Daughter dines with me to Day and I have promised that He should meet Brinsley. He pledged himself, on the beach as he was embarking, to his Parents that this should be one of his first objects. I shall be much obliged to you to allow him to come up immediately in the carriage I send for him

I am sorry to say that the General's account of both my son and Daughter is very disheartening— | I have the Honor to be | with great esteem | truly yours | R B Sheridan

881. To His Wife

Harvard MS. *Wm.*: 1810

[*Nov. 1814*]
Wednesday night or rather
Thursday two in the morn.

I am struck by a little circumstance which escaped my notice when I first open'd the Letter from Beaumaris

[1] Major-General H. M. Gordon, 'on his return from Madeira and appointment to the York Chasseurs', was presented to the Prince Regent at the levée on 10 Nov. at Carlton House. See *The Star*, 11 Nov. 1814.

namely two Pencil lines of *your's* in the cover about its going free, and not one word to tell me how you are—this convinces me that you could not give me a good account for after so much silence I am sure you would not have been so unkind as to omit the only thing that in my present state of mind can bring me the slightest consolation. O my Hecca how tenfold is my dejection from such an apprehension. I[1] have endeavour'd to escape from despairing of Tom as long as my sanguine heart would hold a hope. But now and you must think so too all hope is over—it is a heavy stroke and the long postponing of it led to a habit of irrational confidence on the subject, for his malady seem'd to have become a part of his constitution and unable to conquer Life. Yet heavy as the affliction will be the anxiety with which I look to your Health and Life almost extinguishes what I ought to feel on the occasion. Be this just or not so judge me God it is the fact. But if you were well I would go to him tho' the scene would crack what nerves I have left.—What a situation is her's—and Gordon their sole Prop gone. I would not say these things but I know they are all in your mind. I have tried to avoid writing to you in my present most gloomy mood—but as I told you I had slept so much in the day I cannot think of bed so here have been trying by reading and looking at business Papers to fly from aching thoughts and bitter recollections all mix'd with much self reproach—self reproach clear of anything my *Heart* ever entertain'd or suggested. I never have done a dishonest or a base act. I never have omitted to do a generous or a benevolent one where I had the Power—but sins of *omission* —Oh me—senseless credulity, destructive procrastination, unworthy indolence, all abetted by one vile habit, somewhat perhaps to be palliated by an original infirmity of constitution (an occasional and unaccountable dejection of Spirits without a cause and a constant inability to sleep) but never to [be] excused. Let me fly from the regrets these reflections altogether inflict on me—and to do that let me try to talk with you, for now I have begun I cannot quit you, on some less dark matters and even try to resume a ray of hope of

---

[1] The passage, from this point to 'blessed circumstance' is printed by W. F. Rae, 'Sheridan's Sons', *Temple Bar*, cxvi (1899), 420.

thee my Son! for observe what she says of '*his Spirits being still excellent*'. And that in all events is a blessed circumstance.

You told me lately in one of your Letters that I was too apt to eat the calf in [the] Cow's belly, apologizing for the homeliness of the Phraze, and dared me to deny it. I do not wholly deny it, but I do assert that in most of the great cases in which I have sufferr'd by eagerness of anticipation the cause has been more infinitely in the roguery and insincerity of others than even in my own credulity and indolence.—But I will not enter into this matter now but I will pursue the subject in my next and produce you *three instances* in which my loss of justly expected receipt has not been less than *sixty thousand Pounds* without fault on my Part but the rashness of misplaced Confidence.—I will prove this to you my Hecca—Poor Dan!—very much cheated—

I will try to sleep. Heaven bless thee above all things—don't shew my Letters.—

Thursday—O Heaven no Line. I should set off directly, but it would be at a distressing risk when I arrived in the Island till I have settled a matter here now on the point of being settled,[1] as is every thing else. You may surmise what I mean. Open a letter of mine to W. if gone. A long interview with General Gordon—O sad sad!—what shall I do

882. To His Wife

Harrow MS.: Rae, v. 211.

[*1814 ?*]
Friday

My Dear Hecca

I am very much disappointed at not hearing from you to Day and I scarcely know where to direct to you. If you were to see how I am labouring from seven in the morning 'till ten at Night you would think that I need and merit every encouragement | God bless you for all | S

[1] His claims on the D.L.Th. were not yet settled, but he was busy drawing up a full list of them.

883. To Henry Burgess

Yale MS. *Pub.*: Birrell and Garnett Catalogue 16 (1927), item 671. *Address*: Mr. Burgess *Fr.*: R B S *Dock.*: R B Sheridan Esq | acceptances and Cognovit | Radford. Reeve[1] 169.4 | Pictures

[1814 ?]
Monday

Dear B
  The only resource I can see at this moment for meeting this days difficulty is your accepting the enclosed which I can get discounted to take up the other but on the sole condition that He is put into the situation of the present holder that is that the cognovit shall be made over to him as a new one given—so that you will stand precisely in the situation you do now without a shilling more risk; send me word where the bill is? Wm: Fairbrother is returned from Smallpeice[2] who will finish his business tomorrow and be in Town on wednesday morning to meet Mr. Metcalfe and me—you had better be with us | Yours | R B S

W. F. will tell you why I dont go out.

884. To Henry Burgess

Pub.: Moore, ii. 441.

[1814]

Dear Burgess,
  I am perfectly satisfied with your account;—nothing can be more clear or fair, or more disinterested on your part;— but I must grieve to think that five or six hundred pounds for my poor pictures are added to the expenditure. However, we shall come through!

---

[1] James Reeves, attorney, of Union hall, Southwark?
[2] John Smallpiece, Treasurer for the County, was an attorney at Guildford, Surrey. See *Clarke's New Law List* (1814), p. 126.

885. To Henry Burgess

Yale MS. *Pub.*: Birrell and Garnett Catalogue 16 (1927), item 672.
Dock.: 1814 | R B Sheridan Esq | £157–10 to Revd. Mr. Blomfield
Fr.: R B Sheridan *Pm.*: 22 NO[?] *Wm.*: 1813

21 Nov. [?] 1814
Farnham
Monday Evening

Dear B.

I entreat you to bear uppermost in your mind the 150
Guineas for the Revd. S. Blomfield[1] Dunton, Winslow
Bucks. I shall pant for the Hour of your transmitting me
the receipt for that to Northcourt[2]—

pray write to me constantly as I will to you—I will write
by tomorrows Post to Driver[3] and Metcalfe.

I am happier in my own mind for the measures taken and
I thank you sincerely for the alacrity and zeal you have
shewn in the business.

Polesden look'd most beautiful to Day—thank God the
three Farms are not in sight of it![4] I have two Teams at
work on Polesden itself and Wood is doing quite right at
Yew Trees. Hudson chearfully guarantees Ironmongers
Rent and Taxes[5]—but you must advance him £50 for
Stock. I shall take as little as I can. I don't want the Cows—
The Lillies are *close* to the High Beeches[6] | truly yours |
R B S

[1] Charles James Blomfield (1786–
1857) was Rector of Dunton from 1811
and took resident pupils (among them
S.'s son Charles) there: see A. Blomfield,
*A Memoir of Charles James Blomfield,
D.D.* (1863). He was afterwards Bishop
of London.

[2] At Shorwell, ten miles from Cowes.
It was the seat of Capt. Richard H. A.
Bennet, R.N. (*c.* 1771–1818), M.P. for
Launceston, 1802–6, 1807–12.

[3] Abraham P. Driver, of Kent Road,

acted as valuer for S. in his sale of land
to Hudson. See his valuations in Clayden,
i. 139–41.

[4] Mr. John H. Harvey suggests that
these may be the Home Farm, Phoenice
Farm, and Carters Farm.

[5] Ironmonger let S. take his furnished
house at Leatherhead, while he went
abroad.

[6] The Lillies and High Beeches were
part of Carters or Carthouse Farm.

886. To Samuel Whitbread

Whitbread MS. 4136. *Dock.*: Mr. Sheridan Nov 28 1814 *Wm.*: 1812.

[*Nov. 1814*]
North-Court
Tuesday Morn

Dear Whitbread

I have only one moment to write one line—but my Letter to Ward is sufficiently explanatory. I enclose it—can you doubt of accepting my *notice* and *warning* in this manifest attempt at a gross Fraud who accepted a hoaxing Letter from a poor crack'd man[1] known to be in my debt yet for which, (tho' the nonsense of this imaginary claim of twenty years standing was evident to yourself) you thought fit to tie up £12000 of my Property, by which I *lost my seat in Parliament*, God forgive you! and more than £4000 besides God d——n you! but as these form the 79th and 86th articles of the impeachment[2] no more on that subject now | truly yours notwithstanding | R B S

I can't mix another subject had I time in this letter—but I am doing all thats right—and setting Hecca right as to you and Lady E.—I will write on this tomorrow.

She is *much better*. I quite well.

887. To Charles Ward

Robert H. Taylor MS. *Address*: Charles Ward Es[q.] | Theatre | Drury Lane | London *Fr.*: R B Sheridan *Pm.*: 2 DE 1814

30 Nov. 1814
North-Court
Wednesday morning 9 o'clock

Private

Dear Ward,

you will see that the other Letter is that to be communi-

[1] See p. 188, n. 2. Whitbread was praised in the *Morn. Chron.*, 7 Sept. 1814, for his successful negotiation with the proprietors of the Opera. 'That he should have obtained from them £3500 for a *fragment* of Killigrew's patent, which cannot be divided, and which is not worth a farthing when entire, does infinite credit to his address and firmness.'

[2] His claims upon D.L.Th.

cated to Frost—I can trust no one to deal with him but yourself for you know my feelings—to avoid dispute with him and to have done with him, submitting to be moderately cheated, but not plunder'd by wholesale. You have temper and at the same [time] steadiness—Burgess and He fall directly into a blackguard wrangle—and there is the greatest personal animosity between them—especially on the Part of Burgess. I always like to hear from you—Mrs. S. is much better and I am in high health— | ever your's | R B S

never mind postage
—anything going on in the political world?
don't let the Letter out of your hands
I hope my official one of yesterday answer'd

888. To Charles Ward

Shakespeare Memorial Library MS., Stratford-upon-Avon.

[1814]
North Court
Friday

Private and most confidential

Dear Ward

I think Burgess either from heinous negligence or what He thinks a crafty maneuvre for my good is forwarding the Plan of Plunder impending on Saville-row. Moreland and Popkin[1] want the quarter's rent not £80 or with taxes £100—in the state I left Burgess and after my assignment to Devon it is infamous to pretend they can have the slightest difficulty in raising it!—but for fear of Tricks I send[2] Jack with this tho' to my great inconvenience. Burgess

---

[1] Alfred Bunn attached a note to the manuscript reading: '. . . Morland and Popkins here named were Morland, the brother of the painter, who kept "Morland's Coffee House" in Dean Street, Soho, and Popkins was Morland's lawyer, also resident in Dean Str: Morland was a money lender. Devon to whom the assignment was made was an auctioneer in Hill Street Berkeley Sq: and assignee to Chambers Estate and the Opera House. "Jack" was Sheridan's confidential valet. Hindle was partner with Graham, the auctioneer . . . and Crook was a farmer near Pollesden: he had lent Sheridan money, and a good deal of it. . . .' Parr Popkin lived at 20 Dean Street. [2] Possibly 'sent'.

says He is dealing with *Hindle* to stand in Crooks shoes—
this will only do mischief—so I send means by Jack that
will raise the money if indispensably necessary and he will
act by your directions. B I know will thwart *you* if he can—
but if anything can urge him to do right it will be his
jealousy of you | ever yours | R B S

write write

889. To Charles Ward

Folger MS. *Address*: C. Ward Esq. *Fr*.: R B S

[*1814 ?*]
Saturday Evening
½ past 7

Dear Ward
   I hope you have not waited dinner—Collier's coach[1]
came in and no Charles nor a single Line since tuesday!—
this worries me and [I] was upset 7 this morning after no
sleep last night. I am now going to bed fearing sharp
twi[t]ches of Lumbago
   —pray give Bob[2] £5 for *Wright*—and send me what you
can in the morning—there is mischief abroad still, tell me
what is your Plan for tomorrow | ever yours | R B S

890. To Charles Ward

Pub.: S.C., 26 Nov. 1891, lot 308; and Parke-Bernet Catalogue,
8 Oct. 1963, lot 204. *Fr*.: R. B. Sheridan. *Pm*. 7 Dec. 1814[?]

[*5 Dec. 1814 ?*]
North Court, Monday

   Of all the Rascalls we have been dealing with depend on
it our Friend Moreland and his Click are the worst and yet
that is saying a great deal. . . . I am becoming a perfect
misanthrope, but a very good humour'd one—which is a
new character.

---

[1] Probably Collier's Southampton coach.
[2] Fairbrother.

891. To Charles Ward

Widener MS. *Address*: C Ward Esq | Secretary's office | Drury Lane Theatre *Fr.*: R B S

[*1814 ?*]

a tremendous Fire pray at your Banqueting House—I send you some heavenly Spratts
Dinner ½ past five | R B S

892. To Charles Ward

N.L.I. MS. 3901, ff. 11–12. *Address*: Charles Ward Esq | Secretary's Office | Drury Lane Theatre *Fr.*: R B S *Pm.*: EPSOM 20 1814

[*1814*]
Leatherhead
Friday Evening
Caitif[f] Deserter—
    You must not leave Town but return with me to this place on tuesday and so on to Portsmouth—I have been excessively diverted by a Letter of yours to Ironmonger this morning—it is quite too good to be all your own—whence did you take the hint from?—meet Frost and me at the Piazz[a] to a late and cheap dinner tomorrow at half past seven at the Piazza—honor bright— | Yours ever | R B S.

893. To Charles Ward

Pub.: S.C., 24 Apr. 1876, lot 323. *Address*: To Charles Ward Esq.

Northcourt, Dec 23 1814

[On private affairs. Speaks of his intention to pay his just debts but desires to rescue himself from] the oppression of the grossest impositions that fraud ever practised on credulity and carelessness.

894. To Lord Holland

Holland House MS. *Wm.* : 1815 *Dock.*: Shew the Duke | the 6 days

[*1815 ?*]
Saville-Row
monday—

I have business to settle with John and Henry Ogle respecting Mrs. Sheridan's abode in the Isle of Wight. So I do the virtuous thing and forego the pleasure of waiting on you and Lady Holland to day.—May I come tomorrow? | faithfully yours | R B S

895. To Georgiana Callander

Dufferin MS. [Ph.]

Saville-Row
Saturday Jany. 28th: [*1815*]

My Dear Miss Callander

By some miscarriage of a Letter from me to Douglas Kinnaird I have not been apprized whether my Grand-Children[1] are come up from Scotland or not or what is to be their Destination. Now thus stands the case. I have most fortunately the means of accommodating you and them (if this is to be the Plan) and most materially saving Tom's Pocket, and every shilling we can save him is the same as profit to myself—and this I can do without the smallest expence or inconvenience to myself. The case is this. Iron-monger is gone abroad for two years. I had an opportunity of doing him a *particular service*—He has made over his

---

[1] When Tom S. and his wife and daughter Helen went to the Cape of Good Hope, they left their other children at the home of the Callanders, Ardkinglass, in the custody of Georgiana and Fanny. See Jane G. Perkins, *The Life of Mrs. Norton* (1910), pp. 2–3.

furnish'd House[1] to me for the Time, Mrs Ironmonger sojourning with her Brother at Clapham, and He thanks me for keeping it up for him. I have merely bought the wine and Cows—and there is every comfort with cream Pigs Hens eggs Chickens most excellent vegetables and Fruit and every thing particularly comfortable for a Family with small Brats. My object of course in accepting is its vicinity to Polesden where I have a great deal to settle. It is close to Leatherhead. I should keep *one* room which I have alway[s] been in the habit of sleeping in, and perhaps be down once in ten Days. The air the best in the wor[l]d. Then is there also a little chaise and Poncy for you—and you would be in no solitude unless you wish'd it—There is sweet Mrs Hankey[2]—there is a fine Pew in the Church—heavenly walks and drives and the house Garden and fields the safest for Children that can be—and then too you might come up with me when you liked (and here is Mrs. S's apartment for you) and see the gay world. If Caroline's plan is what I understand there cannot be a more wise pleasant and œconomical way of executing it.[3]

I will write again on monday but let me have a line by return of Post to ascertain that you are at Southampton. There is an excellent Apothecary in the Village—of which I am King and of the Hills beyond. The Children are known there when I lived at Randalls and poor Tom much esteem'd. Think of my going thro Southampton not know[ing] that you and Brinsley were there! my kindest love to Fanny—| affectionately Your's | R B Sheridan

I shall be soon at Southampton   excellent accounts lately from Mrs. S. but I am uneasy at having heard [nothing] these three Posts. I expect Charles to night. I have charged him to see you

---

[1] At Leatherhead. For Peter Moore's version of what happened, see Moore, *Journal*, iv. 221–2. Moore suggests that S. artfully got possession by advising Ironmonger to go abroad and (when Ironmonger soon returned) was very reluctant to give up the tenancy.
[2] Mr. H. M. J Barnard-Hankey suggests that this refers to Elizabeth de Blacquiere, who was a daughter of the Duke of Chandos, and who married John Barnard-Hankey of Fetcham Park in 1807. She died in 1870.
[3] On the need for economy, see H.M.C., *MSS. of Earl Bathurst* (1923), p. 443.

896. To Mrs. Ironmonger

Victoria and Albert Museum MS. [Press mark D. 26 E. 6]. *Dock.*:
R. B. Sheridan to Mr[s]. Ironmonger

Saville-Row
Monday Feby 6th. [*1815*]

My Dear Mrs. Ironmonger
Pray remind Parish to have the little mare exercised twice
a Day in some light cart. If you would have the goodness
to send me a List of any little matters that are wanting for
me I will provide them before my next visit. Is there a Tea-
chest there, or can I bring one. Pray where was the Honey
I tasted there bought in London? We landed Anne safe—
but Mr. Shettlewell was out—we propose dining there on
thursday. I should wish at *four* precisely as I mean to go on
to Leatherhead. If I can execute any commissions for you
in Town command me—I hope Blake is hard at work—I am
very desirous to engage Parish *permanently* | truly your's |
R B Sheridan

897. To His Wife

Osborn MS.

[*Feb.–Mar. 1815*]
Thursday

My Dearest I just hear from Anna that Henry leaves you
this Day—and who is coming my Dear one? I was in hopes
of a little Pencil note to tell me your plight and who is
coming to you. Mrs Randolph[1] (Sally Wilson that was)
says that Mary Ogle is coming to them in Hampshire—
They have a small cottage close to Leckford. He is a young
Clargie[2]—Son of the late Bishop of London—and they are
all very well pleased with him—surely Mary would not lose
time in getting to you. I see no soul so I can send you no

---

[1] Sarah, Richard Wilson's elder
daughter, married the Rev. J. Hony-
wood Randolph, second son of John
Randolph (1749–1813), on 30 Aug. 1814.

[2] 'Clargy': clergyman, in the dialect
of Northern Ireland. See J. Wright,
English Dialect Dictionary (1898), i. 618.

news. I have not even seen the Whitbreads—Anna says she thinks Mrs Bouverie very far from well. There is an Irish Countess brought to bed of a black child solely from looking very often at a black Servant in the Family—and there is a Duchess who has a grown up Daughter with the Head of a Pig[1]—those I understand are the chief Topics in the fashionable world. I shall go to Leatherhead again on Saturday—and if I hear from you tomorrow that you are all alone I shall come to you tho' a few Days Hence would be better for me. The Actors wanted to give me a fine Dinner but I declined it—it would have been great Dudgeon to Whitbread. I have not been near Carlton House—I ought to have gone to the Levee to Day but I am fast turning into a Hermit and like nothing but shade and solitude—

How I do long to hear from you and not a little to see you. Does the Cub write to you. At Easter I understand there is more than [a?] weeks Holidays. But I should not think of his coming but for his ear. I know nothing of the Callanders —Cavendish Bradshaw[2] told me yesterday that He had seen a Letter from Harry Scott, which states them to be very comfortable and now much pleased with their situation.

I am going to dine with Wilson and the married People. I am too late for the Post. So more tomorrow. God thee bless.

Saturday

I could not get home to send this yesterday—but I wrote a Line from the Theatre.

Not a Line again to Day! And no Post tomorrow! However I have seen Henry! I am just setting off for Surry

898. To His Wife

Pub.: Sichel, ii. 375.

[c. 1 Mar. 1815]

Whitbread has been on the verge of a duel from words in the House of Commons, as you will see by the papers.

---

[1] Cf. *The Scourge*, ix (1815), 273–5.
[2] Augustus Cavendish-Bradshaw (1768–1832) was M.P. for Honiton, 1805–12, and for Castle Rising, 1812–

17. He was at the christening party of Brinsley Sheridan on 26 May 1806, and was a member of the Committee for Rebuilding D.L.Th.

All parties say that he is coarse and vulgar, overbearing, and is become past endurance. I neither see him nor Lady Elizabeth.

899. To His Wife

Osborn MS.

[*c. 1 Mar. 1815*]

Davis[1] was very sulky in giving his word to the Speaker that the matter should go no further and said He did it with the greatest reluctance—He was quite in the wrong. He is Brother in-Law to General Whittingham whom He supposed Whitbread to have attack'd unwarrantably. I have seen very little of Whitbread, and her Ladyship I have not seen at all—She is certainly disgruntled (as old Tony says) at something. They have never once ask'd me to Dinner tho they knew I was alone and had no resource but a chop house when uninvited but no matter.—A final Theatrical settlement, by *arbitration*, with Whitbread is one of the important things that ties me by the Leg—it must be settled before He resigns his Dictatorship,[2] and it will depend upon his conduct in this settlement whether we are enemies or Friends for the rest of our Lives.—I grievously doubt him. His Vanity is infinitely stronger than his regard for Truth or Justice. If I am fairly dealt by the difference will be very many thousand Pounds to me. And looking to my Grand-Chicks I am bound not to allow myself to be fool'd if I can help it.

Mentioning dining out I dined last Sunday with Lord Lynedoch to meet Mrs Broderick (Miss Graham that was[3])

[1] 'The unpleasant altercation between Mr. Hart Davis and Mr. Whitbread, which attracted the interference of the Speaker and of the House on Wednesday night, took place in the lobby during the division. It originated in some remarks which Mr. Whitbread thought it his duty to make in his place, on the conduct of General Whittingham, who is a relative of Mr. Davis.' (*The Times*, 3 Mar. 1815.) See the Speaker's account of the incident in *Colchester Corr.* ii. 259.

[2] Whitbread resigned from the D.L.Th. Committee in May, without having satisfied S. On 12 Oct. 1815 an answer to a letter from S. to Peter Moore was sent to S. by the Committee. It asked him to give the Committee a detailed statement of S.'s 'unsettled claims in Equity' (Winston, 1815–16).

[3] Anne, daughter of Robert Graham of Fintry, had married General John Brodrick (1765–1842) in 1809. She died in 1852.

she is looking extremely well and more than ever engaging
and interesting in her manner. She has been to the West
Indies and God knows where—she has one little Girl—Her
Father you know is dead. All the rest of a Large Company
(except my Lady Patroness) were military men, and new
to me which I hate. However I think I have lately taken a
new turn among strangers—and try *to be agreeable*[1] God
forgive me. Mrs. Broderick enquired most kindly and
earnestly after you. No more my Dearest to night I fear I
write too much—but I will get some green Paper.—And
when Mary is with you I shall not fear to write at any length
if it amuses you.—

900. To His Son Charles

N.L.I. MS. 7373, f. 4. *Pub.*: W. F. Rae, 'Sheridan's Sons', *Temple Bar*, cxvi (1899), 423–4. *Wm.*: 1811

Saville-Row
Saturday March 4th [*1815*]

My Dear Charles
    Being on a ramble from Leatherhead your Letter did
[not] reach me in Town 'till yesterday—pray tell me by
return of Post what money is wanted for your entrance at
Trinity[2]—and then I will write to Mr. Blomfield which I
have shamefully delay'd doing. I am greatly gratified by
your account of his *manner* towards you, for I am sure, as
you justly confess, everything else on his Part was always
perfect.—O my dear Boy exert every energy of your mind
to take the utmost advantage of the short time you have to
remain with him—it may be decisive of all your future
Pretensions to Fame and Distinctions as well as of the
chance of realizing the fond expectations which those who
love you best have formed of your future character and
rank in Life.
    I enclose a mot[3] of money which I think you must want.
God bless you | R B S

[1] On 1 July 1804 Horner had thought
S. 'rather too attentive to strangers': see
F. Horner, *Memoirs and Correspondence*
(Edinburgh, 1849), p. 141.

[2] He was admitted pensioner at
Trinity College, Cambridge, on 13 Mar.
1815.

[3] 'Mort'? Dialect for a great quantity.

901. To Samuel Whitbread

Whitbread MS. 4425. *Dock.*: Mr. Sheridan March 7 1815 | Richard II

7 Mar. 1815
Leatherhead
Tuesday Evening

Dear Whitbread

I read Richard the second this morning—I see, beyond what I had recollected, infinite opportunity for Kean[1] to make a great impression, but that is not my point in writing this.—How the Play is alter'd I know not—but I find a number of passages in it, which if not *judiciously moderated*, are open to application which may produce the most inflammatory effect on the audience at this *peculiar* and perilous Crisis[2]—look at the scene between the Gard[e]ners and others that I have mark'd. Beware, and listen to the wise. Keep politics out of the Theatre.[3] Any mischief arising from the allusions I have stated will be laid at your Door. I will call on you when I get to Town on thursday, if I find your house standing which I scarcely expect. I have a hatful of Polesden violets on the Table while I write and three samples of Lambs wool.—God forgive you all in your curs'd City—| R B S

902. To His Wife

Price MS.

[Mar. 1815]
Thursday

Oh my Dear one, O HEAVEN no Line again to Day!

If I don't hear tomorrow I shall set off immediately to come to you tho' my absence will be most detrimental to my affairs. Henry has ask'd Charles to spend the Easter week at Owen William's[4]—but that I think out of the question. If

[1] Kean acted Richard at D.L.Th. on 9 Mar. 'His address to Bolingbroke, on his abdication, drew immense applause' (*The Times*, 10 Mar. 1815). For the alterations, see H. N. Hillebrand, *Edmund Kean* (New York, 1933), p. 143.

[2] Anti-Corn Bill riots took place from 6 to 8 Mar., and the houses of Sir Joseph Banks and Lord Castlereagh were attacked.

[3] A lifelong opinion: see Watkins, ii. 333, and Kelly, ii. 33.

[4] Owen Williams (1764–1832) was

there are any *real* holidays which I don't believe in such a tiny establishment I would bring him to you—and He might see Stevenson twice.

So all is over in France and Napoleon again Emperor![1]—God! what an event! If I can come to the Isle of Wight (indeed I will) I shall settle something with Sir John Doyle[2] whom I am to see tomorrow on the subject to send a Guernsey Vessel to meet Scot if necessary at St. Maloes. | ever Dearest yours | R B S.

Not observe that I apprehend the least danger to any English who chuse to remain

903. To Anna Maria Ogle

Osborn MS. Text from Mr. Alastair Wood's transcription.

Leatherhead; March 31st. [*1815*]
Dear Malty

I thought to have been at Southampton on wednesday last but I find Mrs. Sheridan is not in Solitude and there would have been no room for either Charles or me, so I defer my journey—pray sen[d] me word by return of Post whether the Miss Callanders are still in Southampton, or if gone their present address.—Rare events in France! I shall see you soon— | sincerely Yours | R B Sheridan direct to Saville-Row

904. To W. Hartley[3]

Hyde MS. [Ph.] *Address*: W. Hartley Esqr. | 26 New-Bridge St *Fr.*: R B S

Saville-Row
Wednesday April 5th: [*1815*]
Sir

In your absence I received a very civil note from Mr.

M.P. for Great Marlow, 1796–1832 (Judd). His country home was at Temple House, Great Marlow, Bucks.
[1] Napoleon landed in France 1 Mar. 1815, and reached Paris on 20 Mar. but did not resume the throne until 1 June.

[2] Sir John Doyle, Bart. (1750?–1834), was Lieutenant-Governor of Guernsey, 1804–15.
[3] Probably James Hartley, attorney, of 26 New Bridge Street, Blackfriars. See *Clarke's New Law List* (1812), p. 65.

Fisher—acknowledging the receipt of £10 on account of your client—but declining my post-dated draft for £15 as subjecting the Parties to Penalties if used. Certainly so is the letter of the act, but I have always found it universally neglected—and no penalty incurr'd. I am very sorry therefore to find that the draft has been presented as had I not conceived that you considered it as a nullity I would certainly have provided for its due payment—in a very few Days however be assured you shall receive the balance in money. Mr. Fisher says that the Client is 'very honest and poor'.— He could use no stronger argument to induce me to hasten a settlement and to make him compensation if He has suffer'd by delay on my part in the smallest degree—but tho' perhaps you may think it odd I really do not know who your client is—your obedient Servant | R B Sheridan

905. To His Wife

Osborn MS.

[*25 Apr. 1815*]
Tuesday

My own dearest Hecca

There is a long Letter from me to you in Saville-Row begun on Saturday and continued thro' sunday and monday. No small Part of it you may imagine relates to poor Bab's play[1]—but I cannot get home in time to send it—so I scrawl a Line from hence that you may not wonder at not hearing from me. She has been cruelly treated—I did not think I could have been so interested in any Theatre matter while I lived, or so mortified at the result—! Henry wrote yesterday. My kindest love to Mary—how glad I shall be to see you and Mary dear—but with regard to the exact time of your selling[2] They repeat to me that you must listen to the voice of the weather-wise | God thee bless | R B S

I had a very dear Letter from Charles Yesterday

---

[1] Mrs. Wilmot's blank verse tragedy, *Ina*, was presented at D.L.Th. on 22 Apr. 1815, with Kean as Egbert. It was damned. See *Journals and Corr. of Miss Berry* (1865), iii. 48; H. N. Hillebrand, *Edmund Kean*, pp. 145–6.

The tragedy is printed in Barbarina, Lady Dacre, *Dramas, Translations and Occasional Poems* (1821), ii. 1 seq.

[2] S. probably meant to write either 'sailing' or 'setting off', and fell between them.

906. To His Wife

W.T., but a photograph of one passage from the original is in Rae, ii, facing 234.

[Early May 1815]
Sunday evening

I dine again by my ownself, as indeed I do every Day, so I will scribble a little now for fear business should prevent me to-morrow—I was infinitely delighted to get your letter by Henry and in *your own* pencil hand too Ma'am! and the direction by *pen and ink* and in your best copper-plate—! You may imagine I hasten'd to find out Henry and to ask no few questions about you. I was tolerably satisfied with his answer, but I don't like your living lower than ever, and avoiding any attempt to walk,—for you could walk a little without hurting yourself when I left. Then I grieve at your not letting your maid come to you—tho' I enter into your reasons—but do let us leave the *Puffin's nest* and get into a *house*—I think settl'd fine weather will come now—tho' *yesterday* and I dare say you did not notice the difference, was as detestable a day as ever nipt the nose of April—but still, ad interim, (you know you are a perfect latin Scholar) let Bloxham send you a substitute—my Mary dear can't do everything. Henry diverted and pleased me extremely by his account of your joint cheerfulness—no two little swallows in their mud tenement under a friendly Pent-house I fancy ever twitter'd more gaily. Henry says you want the new Novel by the *author of Waverley*.[1] I shall send it to you and when you [are] done with it make it a present to Mary. —I spent near three hours this blessed morning, for mind I don't hop step and jump thro' a book as some certain people do, in reading the third volume of Waverley—having read the first at Leatherhead and the second at intervals since I came to Town. I am enchanted with the work. I class it above any book of its character and description that I ever met with in my Life—to a Highland Scotsman it must have a tenfold recommendation. Henry tells me you have read it, I wonder at your not having mention'd it to me.—What relates to the subject of education in the early part of the first

---

[1] *Guy Mannering, or The Astrologer* (1815).

volume and the account of Edward's half idle and desultory reading must have brought Charles to your mind. Charles confess'd it did most strongly remind him of himself. He read the book at Leatherhead.—We had it Ma'am from our *Leatherhead circulating Library*. I will positively find out the Author. I abstain from beginning his new work, for the present—it would keep me from business—but I will send it you and Mary will read it to you—and dear Mary if you have not read Waverley, do.

Now a word of Tom and Caroline.—Colonel Graham[1] a Cousin I think of Lynedoch's, goes to the Cape in a weeks [time] where He also is appointed to an office. He will take everything to Tom whom he already knows, pray thro' the *instrumentality* of Mary write to Caroline—enclose your letter under cover to Lord Lynedoch or Peter Moore. Shall I send her a little remembrance keepsake in your name? There can be no doubt of their having left Madeira.[2]

And now a word of the Scotts—indeed you may dismiss every fear about them—tho' war or no war is quite *in nubibus* —but Buonoparte's Manner is to be all that's kind to the English—indeed had he the will he has not the Power to be otherwise For He is extremely in the hands of good Republicans and Friends to real Liberty—and they have brought about and contrived this new revolution and not Buonoparte. So Ma'am I was rather surprised at your saying that you rather expected Napoleon's return to the Throne, unless you have been in correspondence with Carnot[3] and Fouche[4] which I rather suspect. Lord Kinnaird arrived this morning from Paris leaving Lady Kinnaird there and to Paris he means[5]

[1] Captain John Graham of Fintry informs me that his family manuscripts include a letter from Lord Bathurst to Lord C. H. Somerset, dated from Downing Street on 9 May 1815, and containing the sentence, 'Col. Graham whom I had occasion to recommend . . . is on the point of embarking for the Cape.' He was Colonel John James Graham, 13th of Fintry, and had gone with Baird's expedition to the Cape in 1805. He raised the Cape Regiment of Hottentots, and was commandant of Simons Town. Grahams Town was named after him.

[2] On their way to the Cape. Caroline Sheridan's letter to Fanny Callander from Madeira on 15 Feb. [1814] is among the Dufferin MSS.

[3] Lazare-Nicolas-Marguerite Carnot (1753–1823) capitulated at Anvers on 16 April and recognized Louis XVIII.

[4] Joseph Fouché, Duke of Otranto (1763–1820).

[5] The transcription breaks off at this word.

907. To Richard Wilson

Salt MS. *Pub.*: Rhodes, pp. 271–2. *Address*: Richd Wilson Esqr. |
Lincoln's-Inn-Fields. *Dock.*: May 1815 | Sheridan

Saville-Row
Saturday May 27th [*1815*]

My Dear Domine
    Having been from Town I did not get your note 'till last
Night. I should be most happy to be of your Party to Day—
but I have a formal engagement of a fortnights standing to
dine with Lord Essex.[1] You are wrong as to St. *John's*—it is
Trinity Charles goes [to]. Do I read aright in the newspaper[2]
that there is a Grand-daughter produced in Lincoln's Inn?
if so I wish you and Mrs. Wilson joy. Why would you not
be a fifth in the new direction[3] of old Drury? by the way I
wish to see you on matters connected with this subject. I
will call in a day or two. | ever yours | R B Sheridan

908. To His Son Charles

Harvard MS. *Pub.*: W. F. Rae, 'More about Sheridan', *Nineteenth
Century*, xliii (1898), 257. *Address*: Mr. C. B. Sheridan | Revd. Mr.
Blomfield | Dunton | Winslow | Bucks. *Fr.*: R B Sheridan *Pm.*:
6 IY 815 *Wm.*: 1810

6 *July 1815*]
Saville Row
Thursday

My Dear Charles
    I have to apprize you of the Deplorable event of Whit-
bread's sudden death[4] at ten this morning in Dover St:—it

[1] George Capel-Coningsby, 5th Earl
of Essex (1757–1839). Cf. Moore, ii.
445–6.
[2] 'Yesterday, at her father's house,
in Lincoln's Inn-fields, the Lady of the
Rev. J. H. Randolph, of a daughter'
(*Morn. Chron.*, 27 May 1815).
[3] This was eventually made up of
Lord Essex, Lord Byron, Douglas
Kinnaird, George Lamb, and Peter
Moore. See *Morn. Chron.*, 14 Oct. 1815.

[4] He cut his throat. This was partly
caused by worry over the debts incurred
by D.L.Th. under his management,
and by the threats of legal proceedings.
For a view (hostile to S.) of S.'s relations
with Whitbread, see Q. Skinner,
'Sheridan and Whitbread at Drury Lane
Theatre', *Theatre Notebook*, xvii (1962–
3), 40–46, 74–79; and cf. Lord Holland's
Further Memoirs of the Whig Party (ed.
Lord Stavordale, 1905), p. 214.

is a sad task for me to break it to your mother in her most weak and nervous state—She is herself something better—I will write again tomorrow | ever Yours | R B S

909. To His Son Charles

N.L.I. MS. 7373, ff. 2–3. *Publ.*: W. F. Rae, 'More about Sheridan', *Nineteenth Century*, xliii (1898), 257 *Address*: Mr. C. B. Sheridan | Revd. Mr. Blomfield's | Dunton | Winslow | Bucks *Pm.* iy 10 815

10 July 1815
Saville-Row
Monday

My Dear Charles
I have sent you yesterdays Sunday Paper which will give you the clearest account of the deplorable end of our poor Friend. I only add a Line to mention a circumstance in which his Family and Friends find a melancholy consolation. On the Head being open'd by Cline[1] part of the Skull and brain were found in such a state that it is impossible he could have kept his senses, or indeed have retain'd a painful existence but for a very short time.[2] I know my dear boy you will regret him feelingly—He was always very partial and kind to you. | God bless you | R B S

Here is another lamentable event a sailing boat off Bognor upset, and Mr. Poyntz of Cowdry with his two sons are drown'd. Also two Miss Parrys[3]

[1] Henry Cline (1750–1827), the Whig surgeon.

[2] On 8 July Cline and Sir Henry Halford reported that they found 'the dura mater had become thickened and ossified to the extent of a quarter of an inch in length'. See the full report in the *Annual Biography and Obituary* . . . *1817*, pp. 87–88. Cf. Farington, viii. 23.

[3] 'As Colonel Poyntz, his two sons, and their tutor, Miss Parry and Miss Emily Parry (daughters of the late Admiral Parry of Fareham), a fisherman and his son, were returning to land, at Bognor, in a pleasure yacht, a sudden gust of wind upset the boat, when the whole party, except Colonel Poyntz and the boatman, were drowned.' (*Gent. Mag.* lxxxv (1815), Pt. ii, 79.)

910. To Thomas Grenville

Add. MS. 41858, f. 213. *Address*: Right Honble: | Thos. Grenville
Fr.: R B S *Dock.*: Mr. Sheridan | July 1815

July 1815
Sunday
past six

Dear Grenville

I want to request you to ask a favour for me of Lord
Grenville. It relates to a Mr. Mulholland, a countryman of
mine of course, who is in Lord Grenville's office and is a
Surveyor and Architect to boot. I turned away from your
Door just now finding it was later than I thought—shall you
happen to be at Brook's or Lady Jersey's this evening?

a single word only. I write this from Brook's | truly
Yours | R B Sheridan

911. [To Georgiana and Fanny Callander]

Dufferin MS.

[*c. Aug. 1815*]
Saville Row
tuesday—six o clock

My Dear Ladies

I have but one moment to say that I have this instant
received a letter from Tom of the date of May *19th*.[1] with
an exceeding good account indeed both of him and Caroline.
The latter is quite recovered—I will write again tomorrow—
you must make us a visit in Town—according to solemn
promise | faithfully your's | R B Sheridan

912. To His Wife

Osborn MS.

[*Aug. 1815*]

think[2] you care about any. The Hollands are arrived.[3] The

[1] The death of one C. Bishop at the
Cape on 5 Jan. was reported in *The
Times*, 26 Mar. 1815. On 20 Aug. 1816
the Duke of York acknowledged (Yale
MS.) a letter from Tom S. dated 18
May. Ninety days is a fair estimate.

[2] The opening pages of the manuscript are missing.
[3] 'Lord and Lady Holland and family
arrived Tuesday at Holland, house,
Kensington, from Brussels' (*The Pilot*,
10 Aug. 1815).

joyous dear manner in which *He*, seeing me coming up Berkley-Square yesterday *ran* like a Schoolboy, lame as he is, to catch me by the hand quite affected me—He is an excellent creature and the single Public man I have any attachment to. My Lady I understand is grown thin and amiable.—So says Lady Melbourne.—I am to go to Holland-house on monday, being engaged to repeat my visit to Cassiobury[1] in the interval. The Bessboroughs will arrive in a few Days in Town[2]—poor Ponsonby[3] I fear not recovering from his wounds in the favourable way that was hoped. My Friend the Duke of Norfolk is I fear in a very bad way—indeed likely soon to die.[4] He had just settled a plan to give me a seat without expence before the next meeting of Parliament—and He is nearly the only one I would accept one from because he knows my condition of being my own absolute master—and in Politics no difference has existed between us.—But poor Dan He meet[s] with many disappointments lately—but no matter—I shall come thro'. On the subject of Whitbread I am deeply surprised at many things I hear. There is a strange mystery thrown over the whole state of his own affairs—(*but say not this to a soul*) and odd circumstances as to the Theatre are daily out. My—

I stopt last night and have not now a moment to say more than Heaven bless thee and send me a good account— | S

Charles write write

---

[1] Cassiobury Park, near Watford, Herts., was the seat of the Earl of Essex.

[2] *The Pilot*, 16 Aug. 1815, reported that the Earl and Countess of Bessborough had arrived at their house in Cavendish Square, from Brussels.

[3] Lady Bessborough's second son, Colonel Frederic Cavendish Ponsonby (1783–1837), cavalry leader, received serious wounds at Waterloo. See the description of them on 10 Aug. by Surgeon Hume, in J. Ponsonby, *The Ponsonby Family* (1929), pp. 225–6.

[4] He grew seriously ill during the autumn and died on 16 Dec. 1815.

913. To Georgiana and Fanny Callander

Dufferin MS. [Ph.] *Address*: Miss Callander | Petersham | Surry
Fr.: R B S *Pm.*: 8 o'clock 25 AU

August [*1815* ?]
Saville Row
Thursday

Ladies dear and fair
  Being anxious to know whether I have anything in the
shape of a Grandchild alive I propose calling

914. [To James Henry Earle?]¹

Osborn MS.

[*1815* ?]
Leatherhead
Tuesday Evening

Friend Earl
  When I saw you last in Saville Row you voluntarily
pledged to me your solemn word that you would allow no
further Law Proceedings in the matter between us, as Mr. R.
was entirely paid of[f]. I told you then of the cause of the
interruption of the installments owing to Mr. Whitbreads
death but that the Payments due to me were only delay'd
and that you should be one of the first considered.—I have
since received to my great surprise a threat[e]ning notice
from Mr. Hurst² the Officer which on receipt of this I trust
you will immediately remove. I shall be in Town in a week
or ten days when I doubt not to be able to settle everything—
| yours truly | R B Sheridan

915. [To Viscount Sidmouth]

Viscount Sidmouth MS. *Wm.*: 1814

Leatherhead
Friday Night
Oct. 6th [*1815*]

My Dear Lord
  I very much fear you must have thought me most

---

¹ An attorney of 4 Gray's Inn Square.   ² Joshua Hirst, the Sheriff's officer,
See Clarke's *New Law List* (1812), p. 58.   of Tooke's Court: see op. cit., p. 228.

strangely and most improperly negligent in not having noticed your Letter sooner. The Truth is I have been lingering in the Isle of Wight in attendance on Mrs. Sheridan and joining in sailing excursions for this Fortnight past yet meaning positively from day to day to return to Town—so no Letters follow'd me. At last I muster'd up a peremptory determination to be at my house here on Saturday last—and here I am this moment only arrived and find your Letter![1]

I shall be in Town tomorrow and will immediately have the Pleasure of waiting on you | most sincerely and faithfully | your's | R B Sheridan

916. 'To Viscount Sidmouth'

Viscount Sidmouth MS. *Pub.*: *Letters of Geo. IV*, ii. 117–18, from a copy in Windsor MSS. 21805–6.

Saville-Row
Thursday night Oct 19th: 1815

Private

My dear Lord

I saw Colonel McMahon on tuesday morning as I promised you I would, and He has shewn me the correspondence you wish'd me to see respecting this most delicate and dangerous Business with Sir William Manners. The result in my mind is a still more confirmed conviction that be the course taken what it may on the Part of the Prince Regent or his ministers this unfortunate transaction must

---

[1] On 13 Sept. Liverpool stated that he intended to ask Sidmouth in the next week to see S.: 'I think it but just that as Sheridan was the person who profited by this ill-advised measure, and as he will be supposed therefore as the person who advised it, that he should be apprised of the state of the Transaction before it becomes public.' (Add. MS. 38262, f. 59.) This concerned a written promise by the Prince to Sir William Manners (patron of the Ilchester seat), of 14 July 1807, that he would convert a promise of 1784 to make John Manners or his eldest son into an Irish peer, into an English barony for Sir William or his eldest son 'whenever the opportunity may offer'. On 1 Feb. 1815 Manners wrote to McMahon to say that he would circulate 500 copies of the promises if they were not fulfilled. The administration's refusal to listen to these threats with the correspondence that ensued are among the Sidmouth MSS. For Manners's earlier approaches to Pitt and Perceval, see *English Historical Documents*, xi (1959), 208–9, and Add. MS. 38191, f. 220.

not meet the Public eye.—The two contracting Papers with the Prince Regent's own signature to them, must surely be withdrawn from Sir Wm. Manners, upon almost any Terms, unless the most fatal mischief to the Prince and to the Monarchy itself be regarded as a matter of slight consideration.

Your Lordship informed me[1] that it was the particular wish of Lord Liverpool that I should see his correspondence with Colonel McMahon on this subject and the communications contained in it. In one of his Lordship's Letters He states (what you had before apprized me of) that 'as *I* had profited by this Transaction I should be suspected of having been the adviser of it'—or words to that effect.—Now my dear Lord I must not I think repeat what I averr'd to you on Sunday that so far from being the adviser of His Royal Highness's signing any such Papers I never even knew that the Prince had actually put his name to them till you assured me that you knew it to be a Fact.[2] At the same time if I did not greatly misunderstand you, you added that Lord Liverpool as well as yourself were perfectly sure that I could never have been the adviser of such an inadvertence, however friendly and kind the object of his Royal Highness might have been towards me personally, and do not think it presumption in me to add that I am not in the least afraid of any public ill opinion attaching to me on this occasion. Believe me that in bestowing the obligation of a seat on me The Prince was too generous and liberal to make me any Party to the Terms upon which it was to be obtain'd.—

In offering his seats to the Prince Sir Wm. Manners in a letter, which I have no doubt is remaining, says that without presuming to recom[m]end—He should be gratified[3] if his Royal Highness's nomination should happen to fall on Mr. Sheridan.—And afterwards while I was standing for Westminster (having been already returned for Ilchester)

---

[1] Sidmouth refers to this in his letter to S. of 21 Oct. as of 'Sunday last at Richmond Park': i.e. 15 Oct.

[2] Sidmouth replied to S. on 21 Oct.: 'Lord Liverpool's wish that I should see you, did not arise from an Idea that you had any Share in advising *the*

Promise; but from an opinion, that as you were concerned in its Consequences you ought to be made acquainted with what had recently passed ...' (Sidmouth MS.).

[3] In 1806 Manners was one of the Gentlemen of the Privy Chamber.

He wrote me a very handsome Letter, announcing that if I succeeded for Westminster He would return my Son for Ilchester,—with respect to Sir Wm. Manners himself I not only never had any negotiation or communication with him but to the best of my knowledge I never saw him in the course of my Life.

Now I have nothing to add but to explain my Purpose in having said so much on my supposed share in this business.—It would greatly mortify and hurt me to be misunderstood on this Point.—I have said what I have with regard to myself from the sole apprehension that Lord Liverpool might misconstrue my extreme and encreasing anxiety and eagerness that this unlucky transaction should not be brought before Parliament and the Public as proceeding in the slightest degree from any apprehension or consideration as to myself,[1] and on that account alone I have shewn how little concerned am I in the business. But at the same time I must declare that in whatever light the malice of some or the rashness of public suspicion might implicate me I should deem it base and ungrateful if I shrunk for a moment from taking my full Part in the whole transaction—What might be said[2] of me I hold to be of such comparative insignificance that I would not make the slightest effort to prevent it.

I do solemnly repeat therefore that I am solely influenced by my peremptory conviction that the publication of the documents in question would infallibly bring on the most fatal results to the Prince the Throne and the Constitution.

I am aware, and I am sure your Lordship is also, how unfit this whole discussion is to be committed to Paper however confidentially.—If I did not mistake you intimated that Lord Liverpool might wish to meet me after I had seen the correspondence—I shall be most ready to wait on his Lordship and yourself whenever you shall please to appoint me.—

If in the course of this Letter I have used strong expressions, or appear'd to have given too peremptory an

---

[1] Sidmouth replied, on 21 Oct., 'It cannot, I trust, be necessary for me to assure you, that the Motives of your Conduct are secure from the slightest Imputation, or Suspicion on the Part of Lord Liverpool.' (Sidmouth MS.)
[2] Manuscript torn. The words 'might be said' are taken from the Windsor copy.

opinion,[1] I am confident you will excuse a warmth not to be attributed to any unworthy motive | I have the honor to be | my Dear Lord | with sincere esteem and respect | your's faithfully | R B Sheridan
P.S. I ought to have added that I can perceive no decisive difficulty in settling the matter.—
Viscount Sidmouth etc etc etc

917. To Thomas Dibdin[2]

Pub.: Thomas Dibdin, *The Reminiscences of* . . . (1827), ii. 84.

Dear Sir,

[1815]
Saville-row, Friday evening.

This is the first application I make to your new Directory; I am very earnest in urging it: it is in favour of Robert Fairbrother, an old and true servant to me and to the theatre, though latterly discountenanced. I will pledge my life for his zeal, integrity, and ability in whatever he may be employed. What the line is in which he may be made most useful, Mr. Ward is most competent to explain. I say nothing of his large family, many of whom are qualified to give fair assistance to the theatre. I have only to add, that your kind attention to this will oblige me more than I can express. | Yours, | R. B. Sheridan.

918. [To Colonel John McMahon]

Windsor MSS. 21807–8: a copy. *Pub.*: *Letters of Geo. IV*, ii. 119–20. *Dock.*: This is a Copy of a rough and imperfect Draft in Mr. Sheridan's Handwriting, which together with other Papers, I, by Sir Wm. Knighton's desire, returned to Mr. Burgess in the presence of Mr. Marrable on Thursday the 13 Septr. 1827. Geo M

Saville Row
Saturday, Octr. 21, 1815

Private

My dear Friend,

When you showed me at the desire of the two noble Lords the Correspondence between you and Lord Liverpool I

---

[1] Manuscript torn. The words 'peremptory an opinion' are in the Windsor MS.

[2] Thomas John Dibdin (1771–1841) was assistant stage director of D.L.Th.

mentioned to you that I had promised to write to Lord Sidmouth after I had seen you, principally for the Information of Lord Liverpool, having as far as I knew of the Case, already frankly given my opinion to Lord Sidmouth.—I also told you that under all the Circumstances I considered it proper that you should see my Letter to him.—In consequence I shall enclose a Copy of it, together with his Lordship's Answer received this Evening.—

Notwithstanding the superior official knowledge, and political Abilities of both the noble Lords which no Man is more ready to admit than myself, as well as my Conviction of their honorable Attachment to His Royal Highness, I yet deem it no presumption to say that I know the Character of the English People, and the Composition of publick Feeling better than they have had the Opportunity of knowing them.—Therefore with all Deference and Submission I feel that I should trifle with the Sincerity of my own Mind if I hesitated freely to declare that my opinions as expressed in my Letter to Lord Sidmouth remain not merely unaltered but if possible strengthen'd.

You will see in Lord Sidmouth's Answer that he will forward my Letter to Lord Liverpool by this Night's Post, so that I suppose Lord Liverpool is at some distance from Town.—However it is apparent to me that they have made up their Minds on the Subject, and that no good[1] can arise from any further humble Efforts on my Part.—I discontinue therefore my Application to the Quarter I mention'd to you and shall return to the Isle of Wight in a few days—deeply regretting the Situation in which this important business remains.

The alternative we spoke of, and which had been before noticed to me by Lord Sidmouth (I speak with reference to Lady M)[2] I should have thought expedient and practicable.

[1] A note, here, reads: 'On a scrap of Paper pinned on to this Part is the following in Mr. S.'s handwriting— "state why I clear myself—Send back Lord S's Letter—Note my Words—Privy Councellor." '

[2] Sir William Manners's wife was formerly Catherine Grey (1766–1852); his mother was Louisa, Countess of Dysart (1745–1840). Sidmouth wrote to Liverpool on 22 Oct., to say: 'As far as I can discover S's meaning, it is, that the Proposal respecting the Lady ought to be accepted, which H.R.H. seems fully satisfied is inadmissible' (Add. MS. 38262, f. 107).

—The Fact is that enough on the Subject in question has long since been more than w[h]ispered abroad so that general Expectation is in a great Measure prepared for something being done relative to it, and I believe that the Arrangement I refer to would be even regarded as a satisfactory Compromise, contemplating the admirable Conduct, Character and accomplishments of the Lady.—

But even this Arrangement it may be said would be liable to be arraign'd on the Score of a Title bestowed in return for parliamentary Support.—From whatever quarter it might come I should now, as I should at all times have done, applaud the Grounds of such an objection,—Having been from the Commencement of my political Life a pledged opposer of corrupt Influence in either House of Parliament,—but alas, what has been the practice? I should be happy to see the Minister conscientiously competent to declare (placing of course Peerages conferred for military Service out of the Question) that three fourths of those he has recommended to seats in the Upper House have not acquired the Government Patronage to which they owed their Advancement, by the Weight of their Parliamentary interest, or the previous performance of due Service in the House of Commons—I know of no such Minister—I wish I did—and therefore I cannot fancy that extreme prudery on the present occasion, however founded in principle, will excite any very serious admiration in the Public Mind.— Yet could no failure of Effect in this respect in the least diminish the Clamour and Indignation which would assuredly follow the publication of the bare Fact of the Sovereign having affixed his Signature to an unconstitutional Engagement without precedent or Parallel.—

Certainly the best Thing of all would be that Sir W. M. himself should decide not to venture further in this Business[1] —for he is miserably misinformed if he conceives that he can bring his alledged promises forward without incurring the most serious penal Consequences to himself.—But should he be so vindictively wrong-headed as to persevere in his present Determination, remember my Words, my dear McMahon, note what I have written and mark the result.—

[1] Manners was styled Lord Huntingtower from 1821 to his death in 1833.

You will see in my Letter to Lord Sidmouth the grounds on which[1] [I wish?] him to consider me as giving at least disinterested Advice.—And his Answer does me Justice— otherwise feeling the Importance of the Subject as I do, I should have had no hesitation to have claim'd the privilege of a privy Councillor most humble to have.

919. To Sir William Beechey[2]

Lehigh University Library MS. *Address*: Sir Wm. Beechey | Harley-St. *Fr.*: R B Sheridan *Dock.*: Mr. Sheridan

Saville-Row
Saturday Evening Oct 28 [*1815*]

My Dear Sir William,
Shall I have the Pleasure of seeing you for ten minutes if I call in Harley-St. tomorrow between three and four? | truly Yours | R B Sheridan

920. To the Lord Mayor of London

Osborn MS. *Fr.*: R B Sheridan

Saville-Row
November 9th 1815

Mr. Sheridan presents his Respects to the Lord Mayor[3] and Sheriffs, and begs leave to express his very particular regret that He was unexpectedly prevented by indisposition[4]

921. To Kate Ogle

Osborn MS. *Address*: Mrs. J. S. Ogle | The Close | Salisbury *Fr.*: R B S *Pm.*: 22 NO 815 *Wm.*: 1811

Saville-Row
Wednesday Novr. 22d *1815*

Dear Kate
One line only in three weeks is hard measure. I am sure

---

[1] There is a marginal comment here in the same hand as that of the transcript: 'so in the Paper. Geo M.'

[2] Beechey (1753–1839) made a copy of Reynolds's portrait of S.'s first wife as St. Cecilia, and S. retained this after the original had passed into Burgess's possession.

[3] Matthew Wood (1768–1843), police and prison reformer. Baronet, 1837.

[4] From attending the Lord Mayor's banquet?

your good nature would prompt you to do otherwise, unless you are hinder'd, or what would be worse have only a bad account to send me. I am writing to Hester but cannot finish in time for the Post—bitter weather! yet cannot the cold with you be so bad as here—for we have besides a constant horrid Fog—perhaps John would write a line— | Your's affection[a]tely | R B S

922. To His Wife

W.T.

Saville Row
Wednesday Novr 22d [*1815*]

On Servants

You will scarcely believe that there is at this moment a Letter in Progress of being written to reach[1] you the Day after Charles arrived in Town—yet so it is—and in this Letter among other matters I meant to have said a good deal on the above subject which causes so much uneasiness to so many Families.—As to maids, especially your own, I uniformly not only abstain from giving an opinion but even from forming one respecting them.—With regard to Edward I own I am sorry you dismiss'd him—I think he was in many respects the very thing you wanted and particularly because docile and controulable by your own women. I have no doubt but that an awk[w]ard country bred Lad might often appear not ingenuous[2] in his answers, and so Charles certainly thought, but that might have been corrected and in other matters in my life I never saw a Lad so improved in so short a space of time as he appears to be.—However of course I gave up all idea of him the moment I knew your wishes—but there is one thing more on this subject of servants which has vex'd me to the heart— I have often been in terror lest you should listen to any evil suggestion or take any distaste against *Cary*—He is the best—that is saying little—He is the only good servant I ever had in my life, nor had any Master in any country ever

---

[1] W.T. reads 'of been written to begun you'.
[2] 'Ingenious'?

a better—He is as nearly perfect as ever servant was.—As
to his taking the £10 out of the Letter, it happens that he
never saw the letter, nor was ever near it, for I sent it from
Mr. P. Moore's who gave me the Frank and at his house
I put the note into it—but as for his honesty I would trust
him alone, had I such a freight, with a barge-load of untold
Banknotes from the mouth of the Thames to its source. It
was also an early recommendation of him to me to observe
the respectful willingness with which he endeavour'd to be
of any use to you—to Charles the same.—He is not
particularly shrewd or sharp—so much the better—but He
is attentive beyond measure and never leaves the House
for ten minutes without asking me and even that happens
very rarely indeed since I have been ill He has never left
me for a minute—He is sobriety itself, very reputably
looking, and uncommonly clean in every respect—in his
accounts he is accurate with proof of a farthing, but what
has won my earnest good will beyond all this is that I have
had an opportunity of knowing that he is capable of that
sort of affectionate attachment which sometimes lays quick
hold of an Irish Heart—this I have *proved* tho' unaccom-
panied by any Irish palaver or professions. I wish to Heaven
you had his like in a female. At my time of day I ought to
know how to suit myself in a Servant, and under the alarming
state of my recent and possible new infirmities the thought
of any change would distract me—No—should what's
amiss with me turn out serious at any near or distant time
I feel assured that I should not be deserted on a sick bed—
and if the worst came, I am content that he should lay the
weight on my eyes, and probably I think with tears in his—

As for my health why should I speak to you about it who
do not think it worth enquiring after—Yet in my gloomiest
moments, when I feel most desponding as to what remains
of my life it must be gratifying to me to reflect on what I
have done for my Sons in spite of all my carelessness and
prone[ne]ss to be imposed on. This consideration cannot but
be consoling under every difficulty and deprivation attaching
to myself. But I have written more of this in the Letter
forthcoming—because I mean to impress Charles with a
just notion of the very superior terms on which He will

start into Life,[1] from those of his poor Father's state at twenty.—I have said more perhaps than I needed respecting Cary, but not more than I feel—

Tho' I hear nothing from Salisbury I hear good accounts of you from others—I do not like my last account of Tom tho' He has written to others in good Spirits

well good night Hecca and God thee forgive and guard | R. B. S.

Thursday Gracious God! not a single line—if a voice from Heaven had told me that any Human Being would have treated me thus I should not have believed it!—no matter.—

923. To Thomas Grenville

Add. MS. 41858, f. 239. *Dock.*: Mr. Sheridan | 1 Dec. 1815

> Saville-Row
> December 1st: 1815

Private

My Dear Grenville

I doubt you will be surprised at receiving this Letter. I am at writing it—tho' to so very old a Friend and one whom I have never ceased to regard and esteem. In one word it is to ask a favour of a most unusual character for me. For a man who has not been exempt from knowing what pecuniary difficulties are, I can say without a boast that no one has more steadily abstain'd from incurring personal obligations on that score from private Friendship than I have done. I learn'd accidentally that you arrived in Town yesterday. A difficulty of so sudden and pressing a nature has come upon me that the accommodation of the amount of the enclosed will at this moment be an essential service and favour confer'd on me.—I will say no more than solemnly to assure you that the cheque I enclose for the same will be punctually answer'd at its date. | ever truly your's R B Sheridan

---

[1] At the time of the marriage settlement of 1795 S. had insisted that the income as well as its capital should not be touched. Consequently, when Mrs. S. died in Oct. 1817 she left over £40,000. See Sichel, i. 44; ii. 272-3.

924. To Kate Ogle, and to His Wife

Osborn MS.

Saville-Row

Thursday night Decr. 7th [1815]

My Dear Kate

I should not have fail'd to have written by to Day's Post, having seen Baylie but having lain awake the whole night with eight hours incessant Coughing—I kept my bed to Day trying for a doze and am only up now while They do the room—I will get rid of myself first with Baylie before I speak of what is of more importance—Dear Hecca—. I could not help making the best of matters to him knowing He is so blunt a man I fear'd his giving me some terrifying opinion. I went thro' all my cases with him which are four. Would you know them—1st my poor veins—my first terror!—2d the inflammation, which caused my going into that infernal hot Bath, and which still continues—3d my total loss of appetite—I fear beyond remedy—and 4th. this racking cough which seized me last saturday sennight, and seems resolved to scoff at the other three maladies and carry me off his own self. If for six weeks you find a Person never eating four ounces of solid food altogether nor obtaining through the whole times six hours of sound sleep—if I cannot walk I can have no exercise, if no exercise no sleep—and besides other drawbacks how can I have the least appetite? and how can this last? But Kate my Dear don't imagine I shall ever write in a moaning or melancholy Tone about myself—I will hope for the best. And I should add that Baylie left me with very encouraging words—He ha[s] gotten my two guineas tho'. Tho' do him justice he was very reluctant to take them but I spoke of his kindness and generosity to Hester and that I could not admit of a double intrusion—and He prescribed something which has done me good. As to my veins He would not let me undo what Cline had bound up so in fact He did not see the worst part—however he approved of what Cline had done in whom I have implicit confidence and whom I could very hardly prevail on to touch a fee either and only on the condition of notoffering him another. Baylie says that by all he can judge you *certainly are better*. Good! O here is too much about myself.—

And now my Dear Hecca a word about your cottage. Can you suppose for a moment that I can wish to thwart you in anything you seem to set your heart so much on as quiet and seclusion, and that which you deem indispensible a facility of seeing Baylie. You describe how eagerly you desire to recover your health, by Heaven not more eagerly than I do—my own condition I value as little to it.—But I must make you *smile* another time at your idea of this cottage and 'Place'. Such a cottage as I believe never enter'd into the head of any human being before, and such a cottage as I am sure no human head ever enter'd into yet. Such a cottage as I believe Middlesex cannot produce nor I suspect all England. But my dear nummy you calculate erroneously even as to your principal point the seeing Baylie as I thought from the first—Baylie takes his turn in going to Windsor[1]— but is far from settling at his Place in the neighbourhood, when I ask'd him when he thought of going there again He answer'd 'at my usual time the beginning or middle of August' so that Hecca after getting out of the reach of me and poor Charles, would have got nearly out of the reach of Baylie too. To say truth I never much believed in Baylie or any Scotchman retiring from a most lucrative Profession without some very strong cause.—However I will assist in accomplishing your scheme rely on it with all my means and all my whole veins because I see your heart is set on it, and under modification it may be the very best. Baylie and I jump'd together on the same idea—and you may be in truly lovely air, aye in a flower Garden in a month—not a 100 yards out of Baylie['s] road, and the Bishop passing the door![2] but no more now I am tired to death.| God thee bless and good night| R B S

I do long to hear what you think of Cub's[3] account

Friday   O disappointment! I did think Charles['s] Letters must have extracted one line!

[1] Mrs. S. may have lived at Windsor for a short period, for she was buried in Old Windsor churchyard in Oct. 1817.

[2] 'The Bishop of London ... is a near relation of Mrs. Sheridan' (Watkins, ii. 529). He was William Howley (1766–1848), and was present at S.'s deathbed.

[3] Charles Brinsley Sheridan's.

925. To Henry Cline

Osborn MS. *Wm.*: 1814

Saville Row
Sunday Evening
Decr. 31—[*1815*]

My Dear Sir

When I saw you last I had previously prepared a little Paper containing the vulgar remuneration of *fees*—but your frank and friendly manner put my offering it even out of the question—so you must accept a little token of my goodwill hereafter instead.—I certainly was infinitely better many days after we parted—but I am sorry to say that has gone off again—and the sooner you can favour me with a call the more I shall be obliged. | very truly yours | R B Sheridan

S Cline Esq.

926. To His Wife

Pub.: *Dublin University Magazine*, ix (1837), 694.

[*1815–16*]

. . . Never again let one harsh word pass between us during the period, which may not be long, that we are in this world together, and life, however clouded in me, is mutually spared to us. I have expressed the same sentiment to my son, in a letter I wrote to him a few days since, and I had his answer—a most affecting one—and, I am sure, very sincere; and have since cordially embraced him. Don't imagine that I am expressing an interesting apprehension about myself which I do not feel.

927. To Thomas Howard[1]

The Duke of Norfolk, Arundel Castle MS. Text from Mr. F. W. Steer's transcription. *Pub.*: Rhodes, pp. 246–7.

Saville Row,
Monday, Jany. 22d 1816

My Dear Sir

I sincerely condole with you on the Death of our noble

[1] Of Corby Castle. He was the 11th Duke's executor.

Friend.¹—After an indisposition which had confined me for more than six weeks I went out for the first time on saturday when I did myself the Pleasure of calling on you. The particular subject I wish'd to mention relates to some private Papers and M.S.S. of mine which I left in the Duke's care ever since He lent me his house at Dibden² and I know He preserved them safely for me³—having the Honor only of a slight acquaintance with the present Duke⁴ I take the Liberty of applying to you, and I will take my chance again of finding you at home in the course of the morning or I will attend any appointment convenient to you— | Your's truly | R B Sheridan.

928. [To Frederic Reynolds?]

Add. MS. 27925, f. 45

[*1816 ?*]
Saville-Row
Saturday Evening

My Dear Sir

At our Dinner at Mr. Robins's⁵ you may recollect your introducing me to a Friend and Relation of your's, whose manner and conversation I had taken a Fancy to, you may also recollect that we had some conversation on the subject of publishing all I had written, when I promised to have further communication on the subject.⁶ With the exception

¹ Lady Holland wrote to Grey on 9 Jan. 1816: 'Poor S. is really very unwell. . . . What a calamity the loss of the Jockey [the Duke of Norfolk] has been to him, as he was to have brought him into Parliament . . .' (Grey MS.).

² Since the Duke sold it to Burrell in 1791, S. must be referring to an occasion some twenty-five years before he wrote the letter: cf. i. 199, n. 1.

³ One of them was S.'s speech on the Begums (1787). A cutting in a 'Drury Lane Scrapbook' (Folger MS.) reads: 'The Duke's papers were extremely numerous. Two waggon loads . . . were searched in vain for it. A third cargo

was impatiently waited for, and in that it was fortunately found. Mr. Sheridan afterwards valued it so highly, that he kept it in his bed-room, and was gratified when some parts of it were read to him.' Cf. Rhodes, p. 247.

⁴ Bernard Howard, 12th Duke of Norfolk (1765–1842).

⁵ At dinner at Robins the auctioneer's Byron heard S. reproach the Whigs for boasting of resisting office and keeping to their principles when some of them had thousands of pounds from sinecures and public money.

⁶ On 4 Feb. 1816 Lady Holland wrote to Grey thus: 'Lord Byron and Mr. Rogers have undertaken to publish

243

of two or three Days I have been confined by illness ever since—I am now recovering fast and eager to pursue my object—could you favour me with a call between three and four tomorrow? perhaps Mr. Longman[1] would accompany you? | yours truly | R B Sheridan

I hope my old valued Friend your Father is well

929. To John Taylor[2]

Pierpont Morgan Library MS. *Dock.*: This Letter was sent me by the late Richard Brinsley Sheridan. John Taylor.

[*1816 ?*]

My Dear Taylor
    I am not as well as I ought to be for this work[3]—but very sound in Spirit and sanguine in hope—
    Thank you a thousand times—and for the enclosed— | Yrs ever | R B S

930. To Mrs. Richard Wilson

University of Indiana Library MS. [Ph.] *Dock.*: Mar. 1806[4] | Sheridan

[*Mar. 1816 ?*]
Saville-Row
Thursday Night

My Dear Mrs. Wilson,
    Mrs. Sheridan who has been obliged to make a rule to write to no one, not even to her Sisters desires me to convey to you her sincere thanks for your kind and obliging note. She would with the greatest Pleasure have forwarded your recommendation to Mrs. J. Ogle but that they have for some weeks been provided with a Governess with whom Mrs. Ogle is entirely satisfied.

forth a preface of Sheridan's plays and poetry, in order to give him a little Money of which alas! poor fellow he stands in great need' (Grey MS.).
   [1] Thomas Norton Longman (1771–1842), the publisher.

[2] Journalist and playwright, 1757–1832.
   [3] Preparing an edition of his works?
   [4] Address and theme prove that the docketing of this letter is incorrect.

When does that Truant Husband of your's return? I
want to see him very much.

—I am getting well but slowly—Mrs. S. is certainly
materially better.

With kindest remembrances to all the Sallies and Elizabeths[1]
etc. | Your's truly | R B Sheridan

931. [To Georgiana and Fanny Callander]

Dufferin MS. [Ph.]

Saville Row
Saturday Evening March 30th. [*1816*]

Upon my word you are very fine Ladies, and a poor
forgotten Friend may continue confined for four months
by severe and serious illness without your once condescending to enquire after him. It is a fact that nearly for
that period with the exception of three or four Days I have
been so confined and for the most part to my bed or room.
I was going to send to Petersham to enquire whether it was
true that you were gone to the Cape and that three of my
Grandchildren had been drown'd—when the newspaper
reports of the public Balls announced your being in Town.
I send this only to endeavour to ascertain the Fact and where
you are. | affectionately yours | R B Sheridan

932. To John Murray

Pub.: Anderson Auction Co. Catalogue, New York, 1 Feb. 1905,
lot 768.

Apl. 9 1816

[Asking him to send] Lord Byron's last verses.[2]

---

[1] Wilson's daughters, Sarah Randolph and Elizabeth Oxenden, wife of
the Rev. Montague Oxenden, Rector
of Middenham, Kent. See *Notes and
Queries*, 12th Ser. ii (1916), 74; Kelly,

ii. 252. Rhodes, p. 271, is wrong.
[2] Byron's *The Siege of Corinth* is
reviewed in the March number of the
Gent. Mag. lxxxvi (1816), 241–2.

933. To John Graham

Osborn MS. *Address*: John Graham Esqr. | Cranford | Middlesex
Fr.: R B Sheridan *Dock.*: Sheridan | May 9. 1816

Saville-Row
Thursday May 9th *1816*

My good Friend
Fail me not tomorrow—Dinner at three—remember
never between you and me is any favour whatever but a
litt[l]e of your time and advice to be in Question. That dirty
Thief Hindle[1] the moment you were gone laugh'd and
offered to bet you never thought of coming again. Thank
God I have means to get rid of all the Scoundrels—| ever
your's | R B S.

934. To Samuel Rogers

Pub.: Moore, ii. 454–5. This differs in two details from the version in
Clayden, i. 216–17. The manuscript may be that listed in the
Merwin-Clayton Sales Co. Catalogue, New York, 17 May 1911,
lot 636.

[*15 May 1816*]
Saville-Row.

I find things settled so that £150 will remove all difficulties.[2] I am absolutely undone and broken-hearted. I shall
negotiate for the Plays successfully in the course of a week,
when all shall be returned. I have desired Fairbrother to
get back the Guarantee for thirty.
They are going to put the carpets out of the window,
and break into Mrs. S.'s room and *take me*[3]—for God's sake
let me see you. | R. B. S.

[1] A poster in which George Hindle
advertised a sale by auction of S.'s
furniture and effects, at 14 Saville Place
on 10 and 11 May 1816, is in the
Osborn collection.
[2] Moore was with Rogers when the
note was received at between twelve and
one at night; and took Rogers's draft
for £150 to S. next morning. For his
reception, see Moore, ii. 455–6. S. died
on 7 July 1816.
[3] For his fear of bailiffs, see Farington,
vii. 229.

935. To William Chisholme

Liverpool City Library MS.: Boaden, *Memoirs of Kemble*, i. 11
(HL 18–4). [Ph.] *Pub.*: S.C., 27 Nov. 1889, lot 211.[1] *Dock.*: 25th
May, 1816 | Mr. Sheridan | Died 7 July 1816. I was | with him for
some time. | 27th May 1816 | On calling I found him ill and confined
to his bed, he however rallied a little and told me some anecdotes
as to Cannings having prevailed on Queen Caroline to leave the
country by which he got into great favour with the Regent—
Sheridan was at this time in considerable pecuniary difficulties and
very much neglected by his former friends—he never I believe
left the house after this and died on 7 July following.

25 *May 1816*
Savill Row
Saturday Evening

My Dear Sir
   Don't let it be said I am fallen from the frying Pan into
the Fire—but I am again ruin'd by Delay—it is of the utmost
importance I should see you in the course of tomorrow.
I fear Wilson is still out of Town | your's truly | R B S

936. To Georgiana Callander

Dufferin MS. [Ph.] *Address*: Miss Callender | No: 2 Harley Street

[*1816 ?*]
Saville Row
Thursday Evening

   I wrote my note to you last night and gave it to my Foot-
man to be given to you at ten this morning—the Fool
confesses he forgot it—but no more excuses. Mind I am
dying[2]—and so tell Toms [children?]. I have a carriage at
your command

---

[1] Mentioning another to Chisholme,
written in S.'s last illness. Both came
from the collection of 'William Chisholme, Successor to Lord Stowell as
Literary Executor of Dr. Johnson'.
   [2] The newspapers suggest this condition only from 28 June onwards.

937. To A. Chateauneuf[1]

Pub.: A. Chateauneuf, *Infidélité conjugale ou École de Médisance*, Paris, 1834, p. [5].

[*1816*]

Monsieur,

La suppression du tiers de mon dialogue dans *School for Scandal* m'a causé un peu de déplaisir, je vous l'avoue. Mais la réflexion m'a ramené à votre avis. Il me semble que vous m'avez délivré d'un poids, et puisque me voilà naturalisé Français, je dois avoir plus de légèreté. Le chevalier Makintosh,[2] qui parle, écrit dans votre langue comme s'il était né à Paris, a trouvé votre prose d'un naturel et d'une pureté remarquables.

Je vous remercie du dessein d'imiter en vers ma comédie des RIVAUX (*la Dot de six millions*). Vous m'écrivez qu'il vous faudra deux ans pour que le plan, l'intrigue, les caractères et le style soient bien français. J'ai moi-même employé trois années à la corriger.[3] Je ne peux donc que vous louer d'un si long travail. Je crains bien que la mort ne me prive du plaisir de vous lire;[4] je suis toujours souffrant, et ce n'est que le soir que j'éprouve un peu de calme. Si donc vous venez me voir, nous causerons en prenant le thé, etc. |
SHÉRIDAN.

---

[1] Agricole Hippolyte de Lapierre de Chateauneuf translated and adapted several English plays for the French stage, including *The School for Scandal* as *Londres au dix-huitième siècle* (1824), *The Rivals* as *Les Trois Rivaux* (1824), and *The Duenna* as *La Duègne et le Juif polonais* (1827).

[2] Sir James Mackintosh (1765–1832) returned to England in April 1812 after eight years in India. Cf. Moore, *Journal*, ii. 315–16; iv. 267–8.

[3] For these three sentences and comment on S.'s statements as well as Chateauneuf's text, see F. W. Bateson, 'The Text of Sheridan', *T.L.S.*, 28 Nov. 1929, p. 998.

[4] Chateauneuf notes, 'Je vis ce grand homme dans son lit de mort; il me dit "J'ai protégé le malheur et l'enfance de Mademoiselle d'Orléans. Si j'invoquais la bienfaisance de son frère! mais quel sujet de honte pour notre régent qui m'abandonne! non, je vais mourir et je lui pardonne."' S. died at noon on 7 July 1816, and was buried in Westminster Abbey on 13 July. Cf. ii. 257, n. 2.

SUMMARY OF OTHER LETTERS

A. *Letters to His Wife, Hester*

1. Rae, ii. 205.
   His zeal for politics has cooled: 'I think a great deal more of two great china jars I have bought for our dairy—and such a bargain.'

2. Rae, ii. 211.
   'By Jove, I will see my emeralds on Friday.'

3. Rae, ii. 211.
   He reassured her about her sight: 'as for your emeralds, I will guarantee them.'

4. Rae, ii. 212.
   'My cold is going, but I am not well! "I see a hand you cannot see." '

5. Rae, ii. 229. 1806.
   'Only one thing on the subject of Grey. Believe me that there never can be misapprehension or coldness on my part, nor I think on his.'

6. Rae, ii. 231.
   'I am very much pressed to come into Parliament: but of that hereafter.'

7. Rae, ii. 367.
   His wife is to have ready on his arrival: 'a boiled knuckle of veal and bacon and greens.'

B. *To John Grubb*—Harvard MSS.

1. *Wm.*: 1794. Sunday
   S. recommends Grubb to get the original shares from Troward, who claims that he never refused to give them up. The new ones, made by desire of Grubb and Richardson, seem as difficult to obtain from Jones, and should be destroyed.

2. *Wm.*: /94. Thursday
   'I am really compell'd to nurse my cold. I wish if possible you would call here in the evening.'

3. *Wm.*: /794. past 5
'Don't wait for me. I am at work with Carpenter and eating a Chop. And I will be with you before you have done your cheese—and hobb-nobb with Wroughton.'

4. *Wm.*: 1795.
'Pray compleat Richardson's Shares—the other Trustees have sign'd so it is all right and clear that neither you nor They have executed more than you stated last Night. It must be done to Night'

5. [*December 1795*].
S. advises Grubb how to answer a letter of 1 Dec. 1795 from Joseph Hardy, in which Hardy threatened to go on with legal action if S. did not pay the rest of the money owing to him. Grubb was to reply that the proprietors were taking measures to liquidate all the old claims against the theatre.

6. [*1796–7 ?*]. Monday Evening
'Remember I expect the Pleasure of your company to Dinner tomorrow. The Party Richardson Westley Carpenter and your Honor. I have sent to each Paper the Speech Wroughton *ought* to have spoken.'

7. [*1797 ?*]. Also signed by Richardson.
'We have settled to pay Messrs Wright and Graham £30 per Night which we are sure you will see punctually executed.'

8. *Wm.*: 1797
Has successfully provided for the Renters on Monday and secured a reprieve for the security until Tuesday. Entreats Grubb to find £50 'for the Carpenters tomorrow—and all will go on creditably'.

9. [*1797 ?*]. Friday
'I am so worried that I find I shall not be able to get to you till Dinner—I am now going to that thief Sadler.'

10. [*1798 ?*]. Polesden, Thursday
'Pray either make Wroughton come with you on sunday—or detain him a few Days—or settle with him as you like. He may take this in his way to Bath and my chaise shall put him into the Andover Road.'

11. n.d. Polesden, Monday
Is 'in a Sad Scrape' and wants £100 without delay. 'Peake and I will rummage among the Tenants to assist for wednesday and Saturday and I have no dou[b]t of reducing the money in Wrights hands.'

12. n.d. Wednesday
Westley's acceptance for Richardson must be paid tonight or Westley will be arrested. Put to Richardson's account.

13. n.d.
'Such a cursed Headach[e] I have not been able to reason—I have written an apology to White. Will return tomorrow Night and be with you early tuesday morn pray manage with Holland and Cabanall tomorrow.'

14. n.d.
'I will come to you at half past eight.'

15. n.d. Thursday
Asks him to dine at Hertford Street tomorrow to meet friends and attend, with office-keeper and door-keeper, a Board at three.

16. n.d. Monday
Hopes he will be disengaged for dinner on Wednesday. 'Would your Brother do me the favour of meeting you'

17. n.d. Monday
'You will oblige me by taking care of Miss Arne in the Ticket way.'

18. n.d.
Is to settle with Miss Mellon as she proposes about the tickets. 'it is best for all Parties'

19. n.d.
'In order to get quite well I am this moment going to bed. But at half past 12, tomorrow I am at your command'

20. n.d. Wednesday Evening
Had hoped to see Grubb or Birch 'at the House to Night' to apologize for absence from the Piazza this evening and ask Grubb to take his place. 'It is something *very particular.*'

21. n.d.
'I have a bad cold—perhaps you will look in on me.'

22. n.d. Saturday
Is obliged to put off their party for that day to Tuesday.

23. n.d.
'I hope we meet at Dinner—by God many things will come right if we do not divert ourselves. I have made an arrangement with

Burchell which gives us six days grace, and I shall have a Promise of assistance tomorrow.'

24. n.d.
'We had better give this man the above Draught which I have dated monday. as to the rest of the Trustees unless He would let us have the whole (*including the additional five*) for £200, for which we would give him a bill I think we had better have nothing to say to them   I am nursing my cold. I am cursedly vex'd about Church but in less than a month every difficulty shall be extinguish'd.'

25. n.d. Tuesday morning
'Unless I am peremptorily wanted, I had best nurse my cold here tomorrow, and then I can come for good. And by Heav'n all the difficulties shall cease.   I shall have the Power to profit of the enclosed immediately.'

26. n.d.
'Mr. Cust has been very patient and is much distress'd. After these two fifty, I will settle with Hammersley to take on him the Remainder of the Debt.'

27. n.d. Monday morning
Grubb Must settle Westley's business before he leaves town and draw up an indemnity from S. to Grubb and Richardson to protect them 'against the loss of the annuity becoming payable from any Fund but that of the Theatre'.

28. n.d.
'I will be with you in a quarter of an hour   I wish much to see you and have nothing but *good* news'

29. n.d. Sunday morning
'Can you dine with me to Day?—I will call on you in half an hour'

30. n.d. Tuesday
'Tomorrow at 12 I am at your command—a bad cold is now sending me to bed.'

31. n.d. Polesden, Monday
Has been seriously at work and will be at Richardson's tomorrow at eleven without fail. Begs Grubb to be present then.

32. n.d. Saturday Evening
'Do the wise thing and come with R. tomorrow to me at Polesden and [we] will return together monday'

33. n.d. Saturday
'Mrs. S. not going shall I drive you in my Curricle.'

34. n.d.
'For God's sake send my Stipend by the Bearer. I'll see you in the Evening'

35. n.d. Thursday morning Also signed by Richardson
'A Cross Event unavoidably postpones business 'till tomorrow. Then the whole Day at the Theatre.'

36. n.d.
'Pray let our Farewell Speech be in all the *Papers tomorrow*'

37. n.d.
'I am so unwell We can't be of the Griskin Party which is a great disappointment to Mrs. S. as well as to me—tho' we shall try to look in at the Play. Pray issue some vigorous orders to make them attentive at the Doors and keep back the 2d. account 'till the end of the Farce Will you meet Richardson and the Linleys in Hertford St. to dinner tomorrow?'

38. n.d. Saturday Evening
'A Board at my House pray tomorrow at 12'

39. n.d.
'excuse my Paper. You will find in my account the Theatre is still in arrear to me—but I will give you a Lift this week by Heaven—but by all the Gods I beg you for G. Edwards £25 this Night.'

40. n.d.
From Saturday's receipt of £270, and Monday's of £365, S. deducts £220 for the Trust, £200 for 'Taylors bill', £50 for Sadler, £25 for Jordan, and £92 for others. This leaves £48. S. notes, 'assistance by discount from my bill must be paid by Saturday'.

41. n.d. Thursday Evening
'It is of *the last importance* that you should meet me at the attorney general's tomorrow morning at nine precisely for God's sake don't fail.'

42. n.d.
'I'll get to you as soon after Dinner as possible my needful for the Lord's sake by the Bearer'

43. n.d.
'I shall soon be back I have disengaged myself for Dinner—and should like the Cold Pye-party at B. much. I have order'd my chaise at Hyde park Corner at five.'

44. n.d. Friday
'I will see you without fail on monday, but I am really compell'd to go out of Town. Pray pacify Wroughton till then. Richardson surely may do a £300 Bill with Palmer.'

45. n.d. Monday
'For God's sake send two £50 Draughts to Kemble to Night. *Date on.* And then he shall blood-suck no more.'

46. n.d. Friday Evening.
'Something very urgent Stops my coming to you to Night—I will be *early* tomorrow—and we will assail Troward—What was in the House to Night?'

47. n.d. Decr. 21st:
'The enclosed two Draughts which I have taken care shall be provided for will take up a company bill overdue for Canvass Old Debt to Mr. Evans.'

C. *To Willoughby Lacy*

1. *Wm.*: /96. Shuttleworth MS.
'Upon my Soul I have not one shilling in the House but I will make Peake produce some to Night, and you may rely on the enclosed being paid.'

2. *Wm.*: 17/. Shuttleworth MS.
'If you will send up to me at eight o'clock you shall not be disappointed.'

3. *Wm.*: 1801. Shuttleworth MS.
'By Heaven this is all I can scrape but tomorrow at this time you shall have material assistance—I have spoke to my Friend to call in at Bow St.'

4. [*1803–8*]. Friday morning Shuttleworth MS.
'Pray meet me in G. St. tomorrow at one o'clock. I am very sorry you have been so neglected in my absence I was promised it should be otherwise.'

5. n.d. Thursday Evening Egerton MS. 1975, f. 118.
'You may positively assure your Landlord that the Rent shall be paid him without fail on tuesday Evening and if necessary in my Name request his patience 'till then.'

6. n.d. Monday Shuttleworth MS.
Is vexed on Lacy's account at having to disappoint him, but sends all the money he has. S. is sure of money on Wednesday, and Lacy must send for some that evening.

7. n.d. Shuttleworth MS.
'I am worried to Death and have not a halfpenny more—I will meet you at Earl's tomorrow at 4.'

8. n.d. Shuttleworth MS.
'I am truly mortified to put you off—but I can no ways help it—but if you will call or send tomorrow at four you shall not be again disappointed.'

9. n.d. Saturday Shuttleworth MS.
'By all that's good I have not 5 shillings or you should have it. I will see this paid to Day—I will accept the bill if you will send it, and take care it shall be punctually paid, for when neglected they run me to the devil and all of expence.'

10. n.d. Shuttleworth MS.
'Certainly next season your income will be restored and on Thursday I trust to be able to do something for the present.'

11. n.d. Shuttleworth MS.
'I beg you not to stop me now—I shall be at the Theatre at $\frac{1}{2}$ past 3 precisely.'

12. n.d. Shuttleworth MS.
'Send to me at the Theatre at ten to Night and by G— I'll not fail you.'

13. n.d. Shuttleworth MS.
'Having been kept out of Town till the House of Commons yesterday, I must beg to see you tomorrow—when I will without fail'

14. n.d. Shuttleworth MS.
'I am going to send Dunn to Peake—and He shall call on you before 7 with whatever Peake can spare. The Draught shall certainly be paid this Night'

15. n.d. Harvard MS.

'By Heaven I have not another halfpenny—but shall tomorrow.'

16. *Wm.*: 1794. N.L.S. MS. 3218, f. 2.

Promises to pay the note next week, and asks Lacy to make S.'s excuse to Landel.

17. Wednesday N.L.S. MS. 3218, f. 1.

'You may rely on the enclosed. In a few Days we will [have] a couple of hours together.'

D. *To Richard Peake*

1. [*c. 1791–4*]. Friday Night. Egerton MS. 1975, f. 49. *Address*: Mr. Peake | Gerard St. Soho.

S. must see Peake at twelve tomorrow. Peake must deliver 'this' by nine.

2. [*c. 1791–4*]. Isleworth, Tuesday. Egerton MS. 1975. f. 97. *Address*: Mr. Peake | Gerard-St.

'Pray do not fail to meet me at the Theatre tomorrow at one.'

3. *Wm.*: 1793. Add. MS. 35118, f. 127.

Begs him to settle Lacy's arrears and pay him in money this week.

4. *Wm.*: 1794. Thursday. McAdam MS.

'By what ever means you come by it, you will *infinitely oblige* me and by God I can't do without it—by giving Edwards 8 or ten Pounds. It is of the very utmost consequence and Westley has not a guinea.'

5. *Wm.*: 1794. Treasury, Friday Evening. Add. MS. 35118, ff. 144–5.

Has missed him tonight, but must see him before he goes to pay the company tomorrow. Burgess must be repaid £20 of the money given to Baddeley's widow.

6. *Wm.*: 1794. Osborn MS.

'*Thirty Pounds must* be sent this Night to Mr: Nowell in Essex-St: and Dunn must bring me [mine] to Night.'

7. [*c. 1792–5*]. Wansted, Sunday Night. Add. MS. 35118, f. 154. Wants £20 by bearer. S. is overdrawn at Hammersley's by £20. Peake is to call and settle that draughts for £50 shall be met and 'assure them the difference shall be paid in on Wednesday'.

8. Tuesday, 9 o'clock. *Dock.*: 'Sent by his Servant 7th Novr. 1797.' Osborn MS.

Must see him tonight or Peake must send £20 by bearer. S. will make it up tomorrow if necessary.

9. *Wm.*: 1797. Egerton MS. 1975, f. 32.

Must send S. £20 by tomorrow's post to get S. back on Sunday. Peake should not have left without the advertisement being ready:' no advertisement to Day looks sad disgrace.'

10. *Wm.*: 1797. Friday. Egerton MS. 1975, f. 40.

Entreats him to send £20 by return of post. 'I come in health and spirits.'

11. *Wm.*: 1797. 7 o clock. Egerton MS. 1975, f. 101.

They must meet at Steevens's, Bond Street, instead of Cocker's. Peake not to fail to be there at ten 'that we may be secure for tomorrow'.

12. [*1797?*]. McAdam MS.

'Pray let me see you without fail tomorrow at 12. And for the Love of Heaven bring £20 with you.'

13. Saturday 6th Jany. 98. Harvard MS. Copy [Signature only by S.].

S., Grubb, and Richardson authorize Peake to accept bills in favour of James to the amount of £50, for last season's canvas.

14. London January sixth 1798. Harvard MS.

Renewing the authorization in the preceding letter.

15. *Wm.*: 1798. Charlotte St. ½ past 5 Add. MS. 35118, ff. 129–30.

'They assured me you were to dine at home which has put me horridly out of my way.' Peake is to send Tom S. £10 at once, under cover to C. Taylor, Esq., M.P., Liphook, Hants.

16. [*3 February 1798?*]. McAdam MS.

'Save me £100 you must by God, and send it in the morning— I'll settle. Now—*send* it by bearer.'

17. [*1798?*]. Egerton MS. 1975, f. 90.

'We find it best to sup here with Kemble—with whom we have settled every thing most smoothly. Let us meet in the morning in H. St. and then go to Polesden why not take Watkins and Downes.'

18. *Wm.*: 1798. Add. MS. 35118, f. 128.

Wants five £1 notes. Has settled with James. Burgess has gone off to Sir W. Geary.

19. [*1799?*]. June 4th. Egerton MS. 1975, f. 116. *Dock.*: Mrs. Tirrell.
'The Bearer is to be placed on our Chorus List.'

20. Dec. 28th 1799. Brinsley Ford MS.
Peake is to pay Mrs. Hamilton the one-fifth (that Kemble and King thought her entitled to) of the £200 'or thereabouts received by Mr. Fosbrook for Tickets beyond the whole receipt paid into Messrs Hammersleys for the Benefit of Mr. Palmers Family'.

21. [*1799?*]. ½ past 7 Shakespear Egerton MS. 1975, f. 104.
Since S.'s note, something has occurred which makes it necessary for him to see Peake immediately. 'I send a Coach with the Porter.'

22. *Wm.*: 17/ Friday Harvard MS.
S. must see Peake as soon as possible. 'I just find from Richardson that Things are driven to extremity in Wroughtons business for want of £25 installment and £19 cash and all this while there is a sum of £280 we may have for holding up a finger.'

23. *Wm.*: 17/ Monday Evening Egerton MS. 1975, ff. 30–31.
'Faith with Burgess for the £100 above all things—honor bright. We will work assistance for saturday never fear.'

24. *Wm.*: 18/ Wednesday Osborn MS.
'Give £1 each to William and Richardson—and pray let me see you tomorrow-morning.'

25. [*1800?*]. Wednesday Dec. 10th Egerton MS. 1975, f. 111.
Peake must send word that S.'s draught for £20 is to be given to Lanza and a receipt for it obtained from him.

26. *Dock.*: 1800. Wednesday Evening Egerton MS. 1975, f. 12.
S. wants that night Mr. Richardson's £20, Wood's £15, Goldsmith's £5, and Thomas Serjeant's £20; and will replace these amounts before Saturday.

27. Thirtieth September 1800. Egerton MS. 1975, f. 9. Copy.
Cocker has lent S. a Newcastle Bank Bill for £240, and £10 in cash, to pay the renters. Peake is to repay this at the rate of £20 a night.

28. 22 October 1800. *Pub.*: Maggs Catalogue 417 (1921), item 3140.
'By all that's sacred Graham must have One hundred pounds in payment from me on Tuesday morning next.'

29. [*13 November 1800 ?*]. Egerton MS. 1975, f. 117.
   'Mr. Burgess must positively have his £100 *this Night.*'

30. [*1801 ?*]. Henry E. Huntington Library MS.
   'Reinstate Miss Voyer.'

31. Novr. 29th 1801. Egerton MS. 1975, f. 16.
   'Put Miss Jacobs on our List at three Pounds per week.'

32. [*1801 ?*]. Sunday Evening Egerton MS. 1975, ff. 36–37. *Address*:
   Mr. Peake | Brumpton.
   'Pray don't fail to call in H. St. tomorrow the moment you get
   to town.'

33. *Wm.*: 1801. Charlotte-St. Friday Osborn MS.
   'Don't leave the Treasury. Mr. Heath and I will be there at
   ¼ past three.'

34. *Dock.*: 3 January 1802. Sunday. Osborn MS.
   'Positively pay Mrs. Friar [Ellen Ferrears] ten pounds immediately.' She had been extremely ill used.

35. Monday 20 December [1802]. Osborn MS.
   'Give Peter the remainder of the week I have had £20 including
   £10 to Burgess.'

36. March 14th 1803. Add. MS. 35118, f. 85.
   'Put Miss Palmer on our Pay-list at the Salary which I will settle
   with Mr. Richardson this morning and apprize you of in the
   Evening—and pay her from the first inst.'

37. *Wm.*: 1803. Saturday March 2 Add. MS. 35118, ff. 139–40.
   'You must give Peter £5 for me.'

38. *Wm.*: 1805. Osborn MS.
   'I conjure you to get the enclosed done for me and send it to me
   at S. Whitbreads Esq. Southill Biggleswade.'

39. *Wm.*: 1806. Add. MS. 35118, f. 136. *Dock.*: Sent by Richardson.
   'You must leave £5 with R for me. I will settle all to Night.'

40. *Wm.*: 1807. McAdam MS.
   'Mrs. S. is distress'd for £2 that I cannot help dunning you tho we
   must come to a stop and a settlement. Pray send me word the
   moment you hear from Carpenter. I have heard from the *Trustees*
   and the *Committee.*'

41. Monday Decr. 5th: 1808. Osborn MS.
'Pay Mr. Mackay of Wardour St: or Bearer £5 on wednesday morning next and five Pounds in the course of the ensuing week.'

42. *Wm.*: 1811. Thursd[a]y Night Osborn MS.
'give the Bearer £2. I will return it to you within the week as I did the £4—I am in fact sustaining you all in the present Plan and these little accommodations should not be grudged.'

43. n.d. Friday Evening Add. MS. 35118, ff. 146–7.
Peake's malady is not of serious consequence. S. called at the bankers and missed Grubb, who cannot 'exert himself for the Security'. Peake can manage it without difficulty.

44. n.d. Add. MS. 35118, f. 151.
Must send £25 tomorrow before ten to answer a draft to Long. S. wants to see Peake at Felton's at twelve.

45. n.d. Wednesday Evening. Add. MS. 35118, ff. 152–3.
Before Peake goes to the bankers next morning, he must bring S. the five accounts and S.'s 'direction of the appropriations copied'.

46. n.d. Saturday Evening Add. MS. 35118, ff. 157–8.
S. must have £5 by the bearer, West, for Lacy, whose situation is shocking. 'Put it down to his account.'

47. n.d. *Pub.*: American Art Galleries Sale Catalogue, New York, 24–25 Jan. 1918, lot 466.
'Send me word that all is right—and that Jordan plays—send all you can muster to the Bankers or my private account.' There were some small things which must be honoured if the theatre was to avoid discredit.

48. n.d. *Pub.*: *A.P.C., 1916–17*, ii. 179.
'You forgot to give me pound note.'

49. n.d. Saturday Evening Egerton MS. 1975, f. 53.
'I find this has miss'd you at the Theatre. You must not fail to let me see you tomorrow.'

50. n.d. Egerton MS. 1975, ff. 65–66.
'Don't let them wait Dinner for me only save me a chop and have means of making Tea for Mrs. S.' Peake is to see Vines, give him two guineas, and tell him to call at the theatre again at seven.

51. n.d. Saturday Evening Egerton MS. 1975, ff. 71–72.
'What's the receipt? and pray don't fail to be here at 12 tomorrow.'

52. n.d. Dec. 24th: Egerton MS. 1975, ff. 73–74.
Peake must take up his acceptance for Lacy—'it distresses him beyond measure.'

53. n.d. Monday Jan 19 Egerton MS. 1975, f. 80.
'Be the consequences ever so you must send me £20 by the Bearer.'

54. n.d. Monday Evening Egerton MS. 1975, f. 81.
'twenty one Pounds to go by nine in the morning to Hammersleys to answer my Draughts given to Day to the St Patricks Society.'

55. n.d. Egerton MS. 1975, f. 84.
'Get the £100 from H—then make up the Deficiency and send [to] the Trust and return to me here at *one*—it is indispensable.'

56. n.d. Egerton MS. 1975, ff. 82–83.
Reserve money to pay Lacy weekly, and accept £20 for arrears.

57. n.d. Egerton MS. 1975, ff. 88–89.
'You must [let] Lowe have some money he is in very great distress—see him yourself.'

58. n.d. Egerton MS. 1975, ff. 95–96.
Wants Goldsmith's bill[1] punctually answered. He will explain the immediate necessity.

59. n.d. Monday Egerton MS. 1975, ff. 108–9.
Will see him in half an hour. Dunn is to put aside £60 for S. from that night's receipt; it can be replaced on Monday morning from Fosbrook's bill. S. has seen Drewe. '£300 still remaining on the old Renters account.'

60. n.d. Jan 31 Egerton MS. 1975, f. 112.
'take the £10 which Mr. Lacy must have to Night out of this Night's receipt.'

61. n.d. Fosbrooks, Sunday Evening Egerton MS. 1975, f. 120.
'After the Letter you enclosed me this evening, I did think you might have left word how I might have traced you—we must not go on in this manner. Frankly speaking I have heard many things that surprise and offend me. I shall be here tomorrow at two with Mr. Richardson—when I hope you will fail to meet us.'

62. n.d. Monday Evening ½ past 8 Egerton MS. 1975, ff. 125–6.
'Don't fail to bring me £20 to the Garrick's Head before ten.'

---

[1] D.L.Th. Nightly Accounts 1799 to 1800 (Folger MS.) contains the entry: '14 January 1800—Goldsmith Dft. dated 17th. Mr. S. £20.'

63. n.d. Monday Brinsley Ford MS.

Does not want Peake to miss country air this holiday but must see him tomorrow at twelve; then, not until Easter Monday.

64. n.d. Thursday Harvard MS.

'I am not going out and wish much you would give me a call in the course of the Day. Don't make up Kelly's account 'till I see you'.

65. n.d. Tuesday Evening Harvard MS.

'Say nothing to the Bankers 'till I see you and call on me early.'

66. n.d. Monday Evening Harvard MS.

'It really vexes me that I can no way get a sight of you.—I wish very much you would come to me either to Night when you have made up the account or litterally at *ten* tomorrow morning.'

67. n.d. Thursday Evening Harvard MS.

Must see him tonight or by eleven tomorrow morning. Peake is to discount Glossop's draft for S. and send S. the money from the theatre this evening.

68. n.d. Harvard MS.

'Let my Lad have £5 for the Draft I send. You may rely on its being punctually paid—and let me see you at one tomorrow.'

69. n.d. Sunday Night Harvard MS.

'Send me what you can as *early* as you can in the morning as Mrs. S. is going with H. Scott to her sister for a fortnight and I must furnish her with money.'

70. n.d. Tuesday Night Harvard MS.

Graham has promised to return £50 tomorrow. This must be sent by the bearer, Peter, to Biddulph and Cox, by nine tomorrow morning.

71. n.d. Harvard MS.

'You must see Graham tomorrow morning—I find him in very good disposition.'

72. n.d. Wednesday Evening Harvard MS.

Is to give the bearer £25, and to be with S. between 11 and 12 tomorrow.

73. n.d. Polesden Wednesday McAdam MS.

'You may judge of my distress here when I send a man on Purpose to bring me ten Pounds from [you], which he must have *to Night* and be back with me by *ten* in the morning. I conjure you not to disappoint me. I rely you will not. I shall be at Carlton house at eleven precisely on Friday morning.'

74. n.d. Friday McAdam MS.

What Peake recommends about G. is what S. proposes and hopes for. Wants Richardson to bring back with him sheets, napkins and towels from the linen draper in Russell Street. 'God bless you. I hope your Gout is gone.'

75. n.d. Hertford St. 7 o'clock McAdam MS.

'Here I am at last, and just swallowing a Mutton-Chop. I hope Grubb is returned—and where shall we meet for an hour this Evening—and Burgess. If you can all come here you shall have Partridge for Supper and part at ½ past eleven to be early in the morn.'

76. n.d. McAdam MS.

'£2 Honor bright as day.'

77. n.d. Mond[a]y McAdam MS.

'Another £1 note 'till wednesday—my cold has been so bad I have not been able to leave the Room to Day.'

78. n.d. Monday morning McAdam MS.

'Pray send me the enclosed to take me to Town for my Xmas Dinner it shall be [met] most faithfully honor bright let me know how you are.'

79. n.y. Novr. 4 McAdam MS.

'pray scramble me £10 and send it by return of Post and I shall set off for Town instantly.'

80. n.d. Thursday McAdam MS.

'By G—d you must give B. £10 to Night—it is for a Matter of moment to me it is but one Days anticipation of Saturday—I never will exceed the Weeks advance.'

81. n.d. Friday Evening near 9 o'clock McAdam MS.

'it is dismal to be as ill as I am alone here and not one penny in the house. Pray give two pound to James. Burgess will without fail receive the draft from P Moore in the morning when you shall take Eleven pounds out of it and Burgess three. I wish to see you in the morning before I go to the meeting.'

82. n.d. Thursday McAdam MS.

'send me £5 by the Bearer—move Heaven and earth for the subscription. There will be near £400 to be repaid to me and I will give you the first order for your £50 acceptance and other advances. I have arranged this with P. Moore.'

83. n.d. *Pub.*: Maggs Catalogue 445 (1923), item 2875.
S. is vexed by 'the bitter contempt with which my directions are treated by you the moment my back is turned'.

84. n.d. Polesden Saturday morning Osborn MS.
'I don't understand your Letter—I wrote to *you*—still less do I understand Mr. Grubb's calculation. However I shall be in Town tomorrow *Sunday*, but do not fail to give the Bearer my Thirty Guineas for this week.'

85. n.y. April 1st Osborn MS.
'Pay John Edwards twenty pounds for me out of Evan's money.'

86. n.d. Osborn MS.
'I am astonish'd there can arise any new difficulty respecting Mr. Lacy's Payments. I beg he may have his arrears immediately.'

87. n.d. Friday 6 o'clock Osborn MS.
'I conjure you not to fail to give the Bearer 3 Pound Notes for me.'

88. n.d. March 20th. Osborn MS.
Peake is to pay £14. 7s. 0d. for wine before next Wednesday.

89. n.d. Wednesday evening Osborn MS.
'You send me a gloomy Letter which I don't see the use of—and with Saturday Nights Receipt unless the Bankers have advanced nothing your account must be wrong—as for Drewe etc there is always harm done when any one speaks to them but myself. Pray make no Payments however but as we settle.'

90. n.d. Monday Osborn MS.
Mrs. S. is in distress. Peake must give R. money and a £10 bill stamp, and can deduct these amounts when S. sends on Earl's acceptance.

91. n.d. Wednesday Osborn MS.
'On second thoughts see Monckton *to Night* he goes in the morning. Sound if He will *advance* a little. I never yet have been obliged to him for a shilling but have paid more than my share often.'

92. n.d. Winchester Tuesday Osborn MS.
'By all that's good you must send me £20 by return of Post.'

93. n.d. Sunday Osborn MS.
'you must absolutely give G. Edwards £50 this Day to bring to me at Polesden by nine in the morning or I am disgraced there *forever*—I will answer it to Grubb. I shall be in Town by 12. He must have it *to Night*.'

94. n.d. Osborn MS.
'The Bearer must *positively* have ten Pounds.'

95. n.d. Theatre Osborn MS. *Dock.*: Mr. Sheridan £5.
'It is indispensable I should see you to Night. I am going to Fairbrother's where Graham will meet me.
[P.S.] At Fairbrothers
I cannot conceive how this could miss you at the Treasury after I spoke to Dunn—if you cannot come you must send me by West £5 till we meet with Graham tomorrow.'

96. n.d. Thursday Osborn MS.
'Pray let Fairbrother have £1 in silver.'

97. n.d. *Pub.*: P. & S. C., 15 July 1853, lot 90. Cf. I. K. Fletcher's Catalogue 192 (1960), item 116.
'Pay away to the company to the last farthing.'

98. n.d. *Pub.*: S.C., 7 July 1931, lot 168.
'I find several people were at my door and nobody to let them in.'

E. *To Various Correspondents*

1. To J. Adolphus. *Pub.*: S.C., 4 July 1892, lot 523. No text given.

2. To J. Aikin. Sunday. *Pub.*: S.C., 5 Mar. 1877, lot 289. No text given.

3. To James Aikin *Wm.*: 1796. Thursday Harvard MS.
'Mr. Richardson and I shall be glad to see you at the Theatre between two and three tomorrow.'

4. To James Aikin. Jan 7th 1798. Dufferin MS. [Ph.]
'Mr. Read being positively promised that the play of Dido written by the late Mr. Reed should have a Trial at Drury-Lane-Theatre, I shall be obliged to you to pay every attention to the subject, and to fix the best opportunity for its Performance.'

5. To James Aikin. [*1798–1800*]. *Pub.*: S. C., 21 July 1883, lot 157.
Calling him to a meeting with the proprietors of D.L.Th.

6. To James Aikin. [*1798–1800*]. *Pub.*: S. C., 1 June 1891, lot 300.
'For God's sake do not fail to have this Comedy out this week; wait for no alterations, and pray write *this Day* to Mr. Linley, and put this afterpiece into immediate rehearsal.'

7. To an Actor. Tuesday. *Pub.*: Anderson Auction Co. and Metropolitan Art Association Sale Catalogue (New York), 22 March 1915, lot 494. *Dock.*: 'Mr. Sheridan's answer to my terms—£25 each night, played 5 nights.'
In regard to the production of one of his plays

8. To J. Bannister. Sunday morning Osborn MS. Cf. S. C., 4 July 1892, lot 523.
'When I call'd yesterday I am afraid I said to Day when I meant tomorrow at half past 12.'

9. To Sir Robert Barclay. Sunday Night Harvard MS.
'I see you have made the order to Scott for £225 per Quarter therefore don't present my Draft tomorrow for the £100 till we meet. Let me see you *early in the morning*.'

10. To Sir Robert Barclay. *Wm.*: 1804. ½ past 9 Harvard MS.
'I have stay'd to the last moment I am obliged to attend a meeting of importance at Gen. Fitzpatricks in Arlington St. where you will find me for an hour. Home here again at one and again at 5.'

11. To Sir Robert Barclay. *Wm.*: 1805 Monday Harvard MS.
'Come to me at nine o'clock at *Holland-House* don't send up your name, but that Mr. *Peake* wants to speak to me—it is of great importance.'

12. To Sir Robert Barclay. Thursday Harvard MS.
'I enclose you a Letter from Graham to yourself. He is very kind about you in his to me which I will shew you—but I must try to give Moncriefs a lift as he desires. We have a committee tomorrow at three precisely at P Moores. I conjure you not to fail it is of vital consequence—'

13. To Sir Robert Barclay. *Dock.*: 26 octo 1811. Southill Thursday Harvard MS.
'Pray if our friend P. Moore can give us dinner on sunday don't fail to meet me.'

14. To Bell. 17 Mar. 1801. McAdam MS. *Dock.*: Mr. Sheridan to Bell Wine Merchant.
'Please send Claret Port and Sherry two Dozen of each. I have directed Mr. Peake to settle your account next week.'

15. To Messrs. Brandon. [*After 6 Oct. 1814*] *Pub.*: Maggs Catalogue 804 (1951), item 1088.
Requesting a good place for his son Charles 'to see Miss O'Neil'.

16. To Wm. [Mr. ?] Burgess. Somerford, Wednesday Evening, July 8, 1802. *Pub.*: Myers Catalogue 348 (1947), item 377.
'I am sadly disappointed for want of the £100.'

17. To Henry Burgess. Monday 25 [*Sept. or Dec.*] 1809. *Pub.*: S.C., 22 May 1897, lot 86.
Asking him to give money for a cheque, to procure the means of preventing a disgraceful seizure at S.'s country place.

18. To C. Carpenter, Fludyer St. 25 May, Sunday. Pierpont Morgan Library MS.
'I return to Town on tuesday—were you and I to meet for half an hour the next Day at Mr. Fauxblanques I cannot think that any ground for misunderstanding would remain.'

19. To James Cobb. n.d. Harvard MS.
'If you can do anything in the India-warehouse way for the Bearer Robt. Dashwood I shall be very much obliged to you. He is the Son of an old Servant of mine and a very deserving young man who has served with credit at Sea.'

20. 8 Nov. 1799. Hertford-St. To the Lord Mayor Elect [H. C. Combe]. Amy A. C. Montague and Gilbert H. Montague MS., New York Public Library.
Presents his respects to the Lord Mayor Elect and the Sheriffs and 'will certainly do himself the Honor of waiting on them'.

21. To Mrs. Coutts. n.d. *Pub.*: Maggs Catalogue 433 (1922), item 3695.
'. . . however inattentive I may have appeared, the delay has been unavoidable, in my view of your compleating the security according to Mr. Coutts and Mr. Adams's wishes, every difficulty is now got over and I shall not be afraid of coming to make your peace.'

22. To Mr. Davies, Attorney, Lothbury. Thursday, Jan. 24 [*1798*]. *Pub.*: Myers Catalogue 354 (1948/9), item 196.
'Hoping he and Mr. Sadler can meet him.'

23. To Mr. Davis. 25 January [*1798*] *Pub.*: S.C., 18 May 1874, lot 3697.
[Wishing to have an interview with him and Mr. Sadler together on some special occasion.]

24. To W. Downes. [*1805?*], Monday Evg. The late Richard Border MS. *Dock.*: 'Received Tuesday 2nd July 1808' [? 1805]. 'Everything is safe 'till I see Mr. Hudson on Thursday.'

25. To William Dowton. n.d. *Pub.*: Kelly, ii. 113. Tries to persuade him to return to D.L.Th.

26. To Mr. Dunn. Friday June 12 [*1799?*]. Osborn MS. 'Pay Mr. Dale from to Nights receipt five guineas advanced to me.'

27. To Lady Duncannon. [*c. 20 Mar. 1789.*] *Pub.*: *Lady Bessborough and her Family Circle* (1940), p. 45. The Prince had seen the Queen on Friday and they had reached agreement. S. was going to the Prince, who had sent for him.

28. To R. W. Elliston. July 1799. *Pub.*: G. Raymond, *Memoirs of R. W. Elliston, Comedian* (1844), i. 123. Encloses a note from the Duchess of Devonshire to Mrs. Elliston, and will himself write to Elliston in a day or two. [The original manuscript was at one time in the Pierpont Morgan Library, and was there dated '5 July 1795'.]

29. To Thomas Fosbrook. April 7th, 1793. *Pub.*: Newark Galleries Sale Catalogue, New Jersey, 10 Dec. 1931, lot 159. Asking him to lend him £500 as he had to pay Mr. Cocker immediately.

30. To Mr. Fosbrook. Decr. 19th. Gilmore MS. 'Take Mr. Holland's Directions for making the best private Passage to the Private Boxes and which is in future to be the only access to them without Payment.'

31. To Lady Elizabeth Foster. [*July 1791.*] *Pub.*: D. M. Stuart, *Dearest Bess* (1955), p. 57. Wished to insure himself but could not do so until after the 14th.

32. To Mr. Fozard. Wednesday Evening Egerton MS. 1975, ff. 121–2. *Pub.*: P. Fitzgerald, *The Sheridans* (1886), ii. 238. Is vexed that Peake has not sent Fozard the payment promised. 'I am sure you would not press me so, if you were not press'd yourself.' Hopes to hear that night that Fozard will be satisfied with £40 next day and £20 in each succeeding week.

33. To T. [F.?] Freeling. June 21, 1812. *Pub.*: S.C., 25 June
1884, lot 64.
Introducing his friend and relation, Mr. Homan.

34. To Sir W. Geary. [*After 1797*.] Thursday 7 o'clock. Add. MS.
33964, f. 376. *Dock.*: Sir W. Geary.
'I have been kept all the morning at Carlton-House or I should
myself have brought the 300 it is safe in Mr. Peake's hands and
will be sent to you early in the morning or to Night if you please.
I think by your Note you may wish to see me upon something
else if so I will come to you in Wimpole St.'

35. To 'Gentlemen'. 22 Sept. 1795. Osborn MS. *Dock.*: 'This was
intended as a gift but I never got the Money R P'.
'Pay Mr. Peake fifty Pounds on account of the Proprietors of
Drury-Lane Theatre.'

36. To 'Gentlemen'. [*1796?*] Harvard MS.
Pay Hammersley and Co. £2,000 from money due to 'me on our
Partnership'. S. authorizes them to receive this from the first
payment to be made to him. This is to pay 'Grubb's acceptances
for £2,000 dated   and to be applied to no other purpose'.

37. To 'Gentlemen'. 25 Aug. 1797. Harvard MS.
'We hereby authorize you from the Receipts of the ensuing
season in addition to the hundred Pounds per Night to take and
set apart the further sum of twenty Pounds per Night for the
express and sole Purpose of paying the two thousand Pounds
acceptances of Mr. Grubb endorsed *Polesden* by Messrs Hammersley's and Co. These Bills, being four of five hundred Pounds each
to be delivered to Mr. Grubb as the above nightly sums shall have
discharged them.'

38. To Aaron Graham. 9 Feb. 1807. *Pub.*: *Election Reports and
Papers, 1806–7*, iii. 474.
Asking him to come, as a magistrate, to Somerset Place, to
examine a person.

39. To John Graham. *Wm.*: 1794. Sunday. Osborn MS.
S. has agreed with Tycho 'who touches £200 tomorrow—and
gets a Fortnights time for the remainder.' All is going well. 'You
have the Gout I suppose owing to the intemperate Life you lead!'

40. To J. Graham. Saville-Row Novr. 17 [*1812–15*]. N.L.S. MS. 582, f. 35.

Fairbrother will explain the confusion of names and writing which caused S. to neglect Graham's application. S. will be glad to make an early appointment.

41. To John Graham. Thursday Evening Harvard MS.

S. wishes to meet Graham at Wright's next day at four. He thought everything settled and cannot understand reason for new apprehension. 'As to the manner of making the sale which *has* taken place I have exactly follow'd the advice of you and Mr. Wright—and as to the Payments for the Sale if there is *Delay* it only requires exertion to make it impossible there should be any ultimate *disappointment.*'

42. To John Graham. Wednesday Night John Rylands Library MS., Manchester.

'I wish to see you with the most friendly anxiety—tomorrow it is impossible, but on Friday at two I will come to you.'

43. To John Graham ('My Fidus'). n.d. Sunday. Osborn MS.

'You must not interrupt me and my Publicans tomorrow, and on *tuesday* at 3 *o'clock* you shall find every thing to your satisfaction pray apprize Hindle.'

44. To J. [R. ?] Gray, Duchy of Cornwall Office. 9 March, 1806. *Pub*: Maggs Catalogue 210 (1905), lot 828.

Making an appointment.

45. To Mrs. Gubbins. 28 Apr. [*1795–1801*], Hertford-St. Egerton MS. 1975, ff. 47–48.

Gubbins's 'relation to the Theatre by the Duke of Bedford entitles him to any interest of Mr. Sheridan's in the Theatre'. S. begs Mrs. Gubbins to accept the enclosed card.

46. To Messrs Hammersley and Co., Pall-Mall. 20 Nov. [*1795 ?*]. Harvard MS.

'Please to shew Mr. Grubb the accounts of Drury-Lane-Theatre The Trust account etc. the same as the Proprietors.'

47. To Miss Hicks. *Wm.*: 1798. Saturday morn. Egerton MS. 1975, ff. 43–44.

S. spoke to Peake and is surprised she has not received her arrears. She may receive her salary by her father or Stidder. 'Lanza may be assured He shall be paid in five Days—but if He discontinues his Lessons again the Proprietors will employ another Master.'

48. To Prince Hoare. n.d. *Pub.*: S.C., 11 May 1905, lot 128.
No text given.

49. To B. Hobhouse. n.d. Friday morning. *Pub.*: P. & S.C., 12 Aug. 1863, lot 322.
Excusing himself for not keeping an engagement. 'I have just received the Prince's command to attend him at Carlton House.'

50. To Henry Holland. Sunday Night *Dock.*: Novr. 18th 1792. Gilmore MS.
'We have a meeting at Hammersley's tomorrow at two which I hope will remove all difficulties—pray come.'

51. To Henry Holland. Monday Evening *Dock.*: 10th Dec. 1792. Gilmore MS.
'I am exceedingly sorry I was kept at Isleworth to Day—and could not get to Pall-Mall 'till just as you were gone. Pray if possible be at Hammersley's tomorrow at half past two—I will come without fail.'

52. To Henry Holland. Tuesday *Dock.*: March 19 1793. Gilmore MS.
'Are you returned. Where can I see you tomorrow morning? I have a house in Lower Grosvenor St: where I shall be at three o'clock.'

53. To Henry Holland. Thursday *Dock.*: Oct. 4 1793. Gilmore MS.
'There is a fatality attending my appointments with you that brings them to peculiar Disgrace—I return on monday and then will give every hour to your business.'

54. To Henry Holland. Sunday morning *Dock.*: 30 March 1794. Gilmore MS.
'It really was *impossible* for me to get to you last night—but I want excessively to have your opinion. I am peremptory for monday next. I shall be at home till two tomorrow and then at the Theatre.'

55. To Henry Holland. Sunday Night *Dock.*: Decr. 29 1794. Gilmore MS.
'It is of enormous consequence to me to have the enclosed sign'd by you if you approve of it by *ten tomorrow morning*. If you chuse you may scratch out the projecting and widening the Boxes.'
[P.S.] 'I send a fair copy—and fit for signing—could you call in Burlington-St. before 12? it must be dated and *address'd* to the Three Trustees by name. date yesterday.'

56. To Henry Holland. Friday June 12th: [*1795*]. Gilmore MS.
'It is for many reasons necessary that Mr. Hanson should have his Certificate for the whole of his Demand immediately and the Trustees have agreed to pay it.'

57. To Henry Holland. 8th December 1796. Gilmore MS.
'Messrs. Sleigh and Jones wait on you to have Assignments of six £50 Annuities and Three Private Boxes executed, and which I'll thank you to do.'

58. To Henry Holland. Saturday 3 o'clock. Gilmore MS.
'I find it impossible to get to Hammersley's as I hoped, shall you happen to look in at the Opera in the evening?'

59. To Henry Holland. Wednesday Evening. Gilmore MS.
Asks him to meet S. at three next day at Hammersley's.
[P.S. Friday] 'After writing this I forgot to send it. Where can I see you tomorrow?

60. To Messrs Jennings, Shire Lane. *Wm.*: 1798. Friday N.L.I. MS. 3901, ff. 19–20.
'I am vex'd to my Heart at not being able to send you the Trust-Deed with Hammersleys Name but Drewe comes back I understand to Day and nothing shall prevent its being with you by one tomorrow will you be so good as to appoint Those who have been promised at two when I will also call.'

61. To Mr. Jewell or Mr. Shenderdine, King's Theatre. n.d. Osterreichische National-Bibliotek MS., Vienna.
'Pray let Mrs. Worthington have the best Box you can'

62. To John Johnston, Esq., Piazza, Convent Garden. 29 Mar. Facsimile in *Isographie des Hommes Célèbres* (1828–30), iii.
'I was in hopes that Mr. Westley would have been so in cash that it would not have been necessary to have ask'd you to get the enclosed renew'd but so it is—only I can assure you that this will be the last time, and the bill be punctually and finally discharged. We have added interest as before—'

63. To James Jones. n.d. *Pub.*: P. & S.C., 23 Mar. 1876, lot 334.
No text given.

64. To Mr. Jones, Scotland-Yard. 11 Feb. 1798. Brinsley Ford
MS. *Dock.*: Recd. 12 Febry. 1798 Of Mr. Jones a Proprietors
Share No 3 being one of Ten Shares granted on Drury Lane
Theatre for a Security.
'Deliver Mr. Graham one three thousand Pound-Share I have
written the Requisitions to the Trustees.'

65. To Michael Kelly. n.d. *Pub.*: Kelly, ii. 255.
'In my way of viewing the profession, and treating its professors,
I never considered it fit that the proprietors should, every year,
weigh and gauge the decrease of theatrical power which time or
accident may have occasioned; and, overlooking past services,
hunt after every change and substitute which may, for the
moment, be advantageous.'

66. To Mrs. Lacy. Wednesday Evening. Shuttleworth MS.
Graham, Peake, and Fosbrook are with him and have agreed to
send their accounts to Lacy and to pay him the balance. 'I indemnify them from the Risks of the Renters claim which I am
sure will never be made. I hope to see Lacy soon.'

67. To Mrs. Lacy. Friday [*1803–8.*] Facsimile in *The Autographic
Mirror* (n.d.), ii. 235.
'Being confined by illness I beg you will do me the Favor to call
in G. St: at one tomorrow.'

68. To Lady Caroline Lamb. [*1812–16.*] Saville Row. *Pub.*: S.C.
15 Dec. 1920, lot 585.
Thanking her for enquiries as to the health of some member of
his family.

69. To the Lord Mayor Elect of London. Hertford St., November 8,
1799. *Pub.*: Myers Catalogue 343 (1945), item 407.
Accepting an invitation by the Lord Mayor Elect.

70. To the Lord Mayor Elect. [*1808–11*], 5 Queen-St: Mayfair.
Fitzwilliam Museum MS., Cambridge.
Presents his respects to the Lord Mayor Elect and Sheriffs and
will wait on them on Wednesday next.

71. To Gertrude Mara. Thursday Evening. Robert H. Taylor MS.
'Pray excuse my sending you the enclosed so late which Mr. Westley begs you will exchange for the other Note due tomorrow —and which was given in confidence that the Theatre would be open'd. The interest is added to this and you may depend on its being punctually paid—and this arrangement will much oblige.'

72. To Charles Mathews. Saturday morning. *Pub.*: Mrs. Mathews, *Memoirs of Charles Mathews, Comedian* (1838), ii. 62.
'You will oblige me exceedingly by favouring me with your company.'

73. To T. [C.?] Mathews. [*1806–7*], Saturday Night. Hyde MS.
'Will you meet some Stafford Friends of Tom in Somerset Place tomorrow to Dinner at six?'

74. To Mr. Mitchell. Osborn MS.
'I will positively fix a Day on tuesday—I am vex'd you should expose yourself so to the servants.'

75. To Mr. P. Moore, Sydmouth. December 23rd 1808. Osborn MS.
'Please to transmit to Mr. Peake a Draft as before for my 35 for the month of December.'

76. To J. W. Payne. [*1786–94.*] Windsor MS. 41703.
'The Prince told me he had spoken to Lord Southampton to apply to the Chancellor in Favor of Almon the Bearer of this—The Time presses so much that you will do the poor man a great Favour to see him, and remind the Prince or Lord Southampton of his situation.'

77. To James Perry. *January 1811*. *Pub.*: S.C., 25 May 1954, lot 265.
Regarding his political character.

78. To Pigott. Friday. Harvard MS.
'Our young Friend must be on the *extra-establishment* for one *week* or ten Days at most previous to my placing him in the situation I have fix'd for him and then he may rely on no further delay. I return to Town Monday.'

79. To T. Pittman Esq., Newman-St., Oxford-Road. Friday Evening Nov. 24th 1797. Widener MS.
Has received his note with cancelled draft enclosed and is much obliged.

80. To Joseph Richardson, Essex St., Strand. 19 May 1796. Pierpont Morgan Library MS.
'Seven days after Date pay to Mr. Smith or order one hundred Pounds value received.'

81. To James Ridgeway. 6 May 1800, Saville Row, Monday [? Tuesday, or 1816]. From Mr. F. W. Bateson's transcript of an unlocated manuscript in the U.S.A.
'Pray give me a call in the course of the evening or tomorrow between three and six.'

82. To Samuel Rogers. *Pub.*: Clayden, i. 141.
'When will you come and choose a spot in our Arcadia? I have a commission from T. Moore to find him a cottage.'

83. To Richard Sharp. Thursday, Feb. 19 [*1807*]. *Pub.*: Myers Catalogue 356 (1949), item 369.
Asking for his attendance 'on the subject of the Westminster Election'.

84. To Shaw. (*1807*.) Pierpont Morgan Library MS. *Dock.*: 1807 Augt 7
'Send me down a £1 note by the bearer—*in a Note.*'

85. To Thomas Shaw. [*c. 1807?*], Chancery Lane Mr. Holloways Wednesday —. Yale MS. *Dock.*: Sheridan He did not attend at either Place herein mentioned. Mem.:—Sent me to Mr. Moore who, he said had some money for me from him I sent to Mr. Moore—and mentioned this—His ans[we]r was, that he had none.
'I wish extremely you could call on me at Albany Tavern before ten this evening—if not I will meet you here tomorrow at twelve punctually.'

86. To T. Shaw. 9 Oct. 1811. *Pub.*: P. & S.C., 18 Aug. 1865, lot 438.
No text given.

87. To Mr. Solomon. [1812–5], Saville Row Dec 26. *Pub.*: S.C., 15 Dec. 1930, lot 145.
Concerning a debt of £400.

88. To a Stafford supporter n.d. Osborn MS.
'I cannot frank this Letter without requesting *you* to accept my kindest remembrance; which I entreat you also to communicate to Drakeford, Dr. Ward W. Horton and the other old Friends of mine whom I shall never cease to remember but with the utmost Gratitude.'

89. To Thomas Stepney. n.d. *Pub.*: S.C., 4 July 1892, lot 524.
No text given.

90. To Richard Troward. [*c. 1801.*] *Pub.*: *Monthly Mirror*, xii (1801), 350.
S. agrees to the whole of the pit money being taken by Ford and Hammersley until the arrears due to them were paid. After that, they should take £45 per night for the payment of the renters' shares.

91. To A. Wallis. [*1795–6?*] *Pub.*: Maggs Catalogue 203 (1904), item 744.
Relating to a play written by Ireland.

92. To H. Walters, Esq., Secretary of the St. Patrick Society. n.d. *Pub.*: J. M. L. Tregaskis Catalogue 627 (*c.* 1892), item 627.
Mentions Dillon.

93. To W (?) Warren of Stafford. [*9 Mar. 1790.*] Add. MS. 35118, f. 50.
S. will send him the heads of a petition 'on the Tobacco Business'.

94. To Charles Ward. Saville Row, Wednesday June 27th [*June 29th 1814?*]. *Pub.*: S.C., 27 Feb. 1893, lot 122.
Respecting some shares which are for disposal.

95. To C. W. Ward. Saville Row, Friday, 7 April [*1815.*] *Pub.*: Anderson Auction Co., New York, Cat. 17 May 1915, lot 349.
Showing Sheridan to have been in financial troubles, as was so often the case.

96. To Mr. Ward | Mr. Warren | or | Mr. Dibdin. Wednesday Oct 18 [*1815*]. Harvard MS. *Wm.*: 1811.
'Pray put the Bearer and Friend into the House for me.'

97. To 'W.' [C. Ward?]. Monday morning *Pub.*: *The Marlay Letters, 1778–1820* (ed. R. W. Bond, 1937), p. 123.
Send S. £50 by bearer. S. will wait for him until Wednesday. Ward is to make the committee as early as he can.

98. To Thomas Westley. 24 Dec. 1776. *Pub.*: Sichel, i. 525.
'. . . Although securities to the amount of £21,000 are lodged in the hands of Messrs. Hammersley and Co., with a power of sale at the end of four months from the 4th of this present December to indemnify them against the engagement for £16,000 for the payment of Mr. Wallis, yet as they declare they understood that

they were to have the counter-acceptances of the Proprietors of Drury Lane, we hereby authorise you to accept the same . . .'

99. To Thomas Westley. *Dock.*: 4 Febry. 1793. *Pub.*: Rhodes, p. 268.

'Mad. Mara must positively be paid [and] have her weekly salary from the beginning of season immediately or the Opera will be finished up—I will see this money returned from the Opera account. Her engagement is £1000.'

100. To Thomas Westley. 16th January, 1793. *Pub.*: *New M. Mag.* (1838), Pt. iii. 227.

'Pay Madame Mara the whole sum mentioned in her engagement with Mr. Kemble last season, without deduction; and for the present season let her salary of one thousand guineas for forty nights, be paid weekly, on the Drury Lane account, and pay all arrears for the same.'

101. To George White? [*Before June 1803*], Friday 7 o'clock. Harvard MS.

'At a Late Dinner—incog—at the Shakespear—happy to see Mr. White. Burgess here.' (Also signed by J Richardson.)

102. To Richard Wilson. Thursday Night. Yale MS.

'Remember our appointment at three tomorrow—I have fixed McMahon.

103. To Richard Wilson. Sunday Evening. *Wm.*: 1807. Edinburgh University Library MS., La. ii. 367.

'I could not get to you yesterday—but what are you for tomorrow? Now let me give you a cutlet at the St. Alban's Coffee-House—at six.—it is central—and I will forage on you another Day. R.S.V.P.'

104. To [H. S. Woodfall] the Editor of the *Public Advertiser*. *Pub.*: S.C., 1 Mar. 1955, lot 433.

'As a real Friend and Wellwisher to your paper, my friend Sampson. . . .'[1]

---

[1] Left unfinished by S. It is headed 'The Detector No. 1'. Letters with this signature are to be found in the *Pub.Adv.*, 30 Mar., 22 Aug., 6, 22 Sept. 1769; 21 Mar. 1770; 28 Jan., 4 Feb. 12 Feb., 1773; 21 Sept. 1779. A series of letters under this pseudonym was written by Scott for Warren Hastings in the *Morning Herald*, from 7 Oct. 1782. I think Sichel, i. 467, is wrong.

105. To John Wright. [*c. 1795*]. *Pub.*: C. Baron-Wilson, *Memoirs of Harriot, Duchess of St. Albans* (1839), i. 187.
It was scarcely worth while for a lady of Miss Mellon's talents to appear towards the close of a season which the manager intended should be a short one; but when they were about to reopen he trusted to hear from her again.

106. To – Wyatt, Esq. *Pub.*: S.C., 11 June 1888, lot 349.
No text given.

To Unidentified Correspondents

107. Weymouth, Aug. 17, 1777. *Pub.*: Charles F. Libbie Sale Catalogue, New York, 1 May 1912, lot 707.
No text given.

108. *Dock.*: Octr. 13th. 1795. Harvard MS.
'Notice in writing must be sent to the Treasury every Saturday Morning of all articles wanted for the ensuing week.'

109. Saturday March 26th: [*1796*]. Osborn MS.
'I entreat you to move Heaven and Earth Night and Day to bring out Mr. Whaleys Play with all possible expedition.'

110. *1796–7*. Players Club MS., New York.
'T.R.D.L. Admit Mr. W. Dunn to any Part of the Theatre return this Card.'

111. [*c. 1797*]. *Pub.*: S.C., 10 Mar. 1908, lot 100.
Instructions regarding the addition of a private box at D.L.Th.

112. [*c. 21 Mar. 1798*]. Grubbe MS.
S.'s £100 is to be drawn out of a dividend of £140 due to Grubb.

113. [*1799?*]. 2 o'clock in the morning. *Pub.*: P. and S.C., 27 Apr. 1847, lot 529.
About *Pizarro*.

114. *Dock.*: Sept. 30. 1800. Boston Public Library MS., Mass.
'Admit Mr. Becket to the Theatre whenever he calls, and behind the Scenes.'

115. 29 Dec. [*1800?*], Monday. Shuttleworth MS.
'You will *particularly oblige* me by accommodating Mr. Lacy and I will positively return it within a fortnight.'

116. 31 Jan. 1804. *Pub.*: P. & S.C., 3 Apr. 1860, lot 235.
No text given.

117. *Pm.*: 9 FE 1804. Price MS. *Pub.*: A. M. Broadley, *Chats on Autographs* (1910), p. 265.
'Allow me to ask you a favour—it is not to present the Draft to Hammersley before 4 tomorrow—in the mean time I am authoris'd by Sir M. Bloxam [?] to say that he will pay the money.'

118. May 13 1806. *Pub.*: Anderson Auction Co. Sale Catalogue, New York, 26 May 1913, lot 166.
No text given.

119. 27 Sept. [*after 1806*]. *Pub.*: *A.P.C.* v (1920–1), 182.
Asking for the release from imprisonment for debt of Homan.

120. [1806–7], Saturday Night. Harvard MS.
'For the Honor of Stafford and Tom I beg you to forego other engagements and meet som[e] Stafford Friends in Somerset Place tomorrow to Dinner at Six—'

121. [*1808*]. *Pub.*: S.C., 22 Mar. 1855, lot 275.
Regarding the acting of T. Hook's *Siege of St. Quintin*. 'Tom knows better how to manage it than I do.'

122. Febry. 17, 1808. *Pub.*: F. G. Netherclift, *The Handbook of Autographs* [1862,] Pt. iii. 116.
'in future I will discharge my account every month.'

123. Saville Row June 10 [*1812–1816*]. *Pub.*: Anderson Auction Co. Sale Catalogue, New York, 26 May 1913, lot 167.
No text given.

124. Savile Row, Thursday, May 19 [*1814*]. *Pub.*: City Book Auction, New York, Sale Catalogue, 20 November 1943, lot 166.
No text given.

125. June 1 1814. *Pub.*: Libbie Sale Catalogue, New York, 2 May 1901, lot 1155.
No text given.

126. London May 4. *Pub.*: Anderson Auction Co. Sale Catalogue, New York, 20 Feb. 1905, lot 7846.
Regarding the conduct and apparent ingratitude of one of the performers of D.L.Th.

127. n.d. *Pub.*: Christie, Manson & Woods Sale Catalogue, 25 April 1906, lot 203. Cf. *Documents and Autographs*, 2 (1965), item 91. 'Now the dissolution appears certain.'

128. Monday Evening. Egerton MS. 2137, f. 175.
'The Bearer will bring to Mr. Sheridan the No. of the 5 Boxes sold by Mr. Novoscielski etc. to Messrs. Hammersley—as Mr. Hammersley desired.'

129. n.d. *Pub.*: R. H. Evans Sale Catalogue, 10 March 1841, lot 1537.
An affecting letter on his 'Desperate Situation'. 'I must render myself to night.'

130. n.d. *Pub.*: R. H. Evans Sale Catalogue, 10 March 1841, lot 1537.
On the Speaker's interrupting him. 'I will take an opportunity to make the Speaker remember this.'

131. Saturday. Harvard MS.
'It is not in my Power to see you to Day—but on tuesday at eleven I will *effectually* and pray bring the Drawings with you.'

132. Saturday. Harvard MS.
'I am extremely sorry but I really am not well enough to have the Pleasure of joining your Party to Day.'

133. n.d. Drury-Lane-Theatre Sunday Evening Harvard MS.
'The Proprietors wish to see you tomorrow at the Theatre if not inconvenient to you at one o'Clock.'

134. n.d. Hyde MS.
'I will see Aikin this Evening. you may rely on anything I can do. tho I should be glad to see you tomorrow on the Subject.'

135. Leatherhead, Wednesday. N.L.I. MS. 3901, f. 21.
'Your Ladies express'd a wish to see Polesden—will they allow me to give them a Gypsey Lu[n]ch there between two and three? when we can also have some talk as I go to Town on Friday to meet Mr. Metcalfe—'

136. Tuesday. *Pub.*: Newark Galleries Sale Catalogue, New Jersey, 10 Dec. 1931, lot 159.
Asking him not to go out of town till Sunday and asking for another ten pounds, to be repaid on Friday.

137. Friday morning near 9. *Pub.*: Newark Galleries Sale Catalogue, New Jersey, 10 Dec. 1931, lot 159.
Regarding some money at Coutts's that he wished to draw on. 'I send Peter in a coach for expedition sake.'

138. To 'My dear Sir'. n.d. New York Public Library MS., Lee Kohns Memorial Collection.
'I have seen Peake too having call'd to prepare him for tomorrow, but I find He is going on a water party—so I shall be happy [to] see you here at half past six.'

139. n.d. Osborn MS.
'. . . catalogue before the Parcells are moved. If you send me the account I will send the money to your order.'

140. Thursday Evening Osborn MS.
'It is indispensable that you should meet us tomorrow at Hammersleys at two o'clock.' [Also signed by J. Richardson.]

141. n.d. *Newport* Private. *Pub.*: P. & S.C., 16 Dec. 1853, lot 414. No text given.

142. To 'My dear Sir'. Monday. Princeton University Library MS.
'Pray send the enclosed immediately. I have forgotten his address. I am taking measures so that the Bankers can be in no advance on Saturday.'

143. Farnham, Thursday Night. *Pub.*: Quaritch Catalogue 457 (1932), item 124.
Announcing safe arrival at Farnham and asking for some money to be sent to him and to 'Mrs. I.' [Mrs. S.?].

144. n.d. *Pub.*: S.C., 30 July 1930, lot 577.
About a play, the subject of which is unsuitable for the stage, however humorously handled.

145. n.d. *Pub.*: S.C., 1 May 1888, lot 112.
'Locking up a Quaker Farmer in Prison is a curious way of admitting a Dissenter into a place of Trust and Power.'

146. n.d. *Pub.*: Winifred A. Myers Catalogue 4 (1962), item 35.
'I insist on the arrears to the Carpenters being paid immediately.'

147. n.d. Bath. Leeds University, Brotherton Collection MS.
'Truly [?]'

F. *Departmental Letters*

Written in 1783 when S. was Secretary to the Treasury

1. To Mr. Steuart. Treasury Chambers, 24 April 1783. N.L.S. MS. 5033, f. 53. Only the signature is in S.'s hand.
   The Lords Commissioners of the Treasury require Steuart's opinion on James Bruce's memorial, praying payment of his salary up to 10 Oct. 1782 as collector of customs at Pensacola.

2. To Charles Steuart Esq. Treasury Chambers, 8th August 1783. N.L.S. MS. 5033, f. 98. Only the signature is in S.'s hand.
   The Lords Commissioners have considered Steuart's letter of 25 Apr. 1783, and direct him to pay Bruce his salary to 5 Apr. 1783 once Bruce has paid in the balance due from him to the Crown.

3. To Lord ——. Treasury Chambers, Oct. 31st 1783. Harvard MS. Only the signature is in S.'s hand.
   Only the subscription is available. The text of the letter has been torn away.

4. To – Call, Esq. 10 Nov. 1783. *Pub.*: Myers Catalogue 360 (1949), item 272.
   Written from Treasury Chambers, regarding the Duchy of Lancaster.

5. To various correspondents. *MSS.*: *Out Letter Book, North Britain* (P.R.O., T. 17/22).
   The volume contains copies of twenty-nine letters by S., written between 2 May and 13 Dec. 1783. They are to be found on pp. 22–24, 353–4, 356, 362–3, 365–6, 387, 399, 401, 427, 445, 463–5, 472.

G. *Letters in Sheridan's Hand drafted for a Copyist*

1. To George III. [After May 1787.] *Pub.*: Maggs Catalogue 825 (1954), item 552.
   '. . . The Prince laments the great inaccuracy of the short estimate delivered to Mr. Pitt by Mr. Holland previous to the application to Parliament in May 87 and humbly entreats that his Majesty will be graciously pleased to direct such investigation as His Majesty shall see proper of the whole of the . . . accounts relating to Carlton House, which by his Majesty's bounty and kindness was intended

to have been made a proper residence for the Prince of Wales, but which in consequence of some unfortunate misapprehensions remains imperfect and unfinish'd at the same time that a heavy debt is incurr'd to artists and workmen employ'd in the business. . . .'

2. [To Lord Thurlow, Dec. 1788?] Windsor MS. 38295.[1] *Pub.*: Rae, ii. 97. Cf. S.C., 1 Mar. 1955, lot 434: endorsed by S., 'Copy of Paper sent to the Chancellor—words added by the Prince.'

'The Prince conceives the pressing a *Decision* on the *Question of Right* to be personally injurious and insulting to him—and any opportunity taken of discountenancing that Proceeding will be considered as a decisive act of Friendship to the Prince.

'The Prince most readily acquiesces in every measure that is necessary to secure the Kings repossession of the Government on the return of his health as he conceives that as absolutely necessary but hopes that no measures not necessary to that object, but which may tend to weaken or distract his Government at a crisis when every support is necessary, will be pursued by anyone who professes not to have a personal *distrust* of him or at least no limitations or restrictions whatever will be exacted as the *condition* of Parliament's consenting to his being placed in the Regency.

'The Custody of the King's Person, and the Power of making the most liberal and respectful appointments for attendance on his Majesty is an object which the Prince expressly wishes to be in the Hands of others.'

3. To Robert Graham of Gartmore, Brighton, 12 Aug. 1789. Windsor MS. 38499. For a draft, see S.C., 25 May 1954, lot 273. *Pub.*: *Caledonian Mercury*, 14 Sept. 1789, over J. W. Payne's signature.

The Prince of Wales thanks the delegates of the Burghs meeting in convention for their kind addresses during his Majesty's late lamented illness.

4. To Queen Charlotte, 1789. Yale MS. *Pub.*: Moore, ii. 63–66. The Prince of Wales outlines his attitude towards Pitt's proposal that the direction and appointment of the King's household should be placed under the Queen's separate authority.

5. To George III, 1789. Yale MS. *Pub.*: Moore, ii. 67–69. The Prince of Wales proposes to submit to the King a memorial vindicating his own conduct and that of the Duke of York during the King's illness.

[1] A recent hand has docketed this as to Lord Lonsdale.

6. [To the Linleys.] *Wm.*: 1795. Harvard MS.

'The salvation of the theatre depends on abolishing written orders. Mr. Sheridan has never written *one*—nor scarcely given an ivory since the commencement of the season.' Mrs. Linley and W. Linley shall have the same number of ivories as Grubb and Richardson. By S.'s direction £3 a week will be paid in future to Miss Linley, and Mrs. Linley's and Mr. W. Linley's salaries will be punctually paid every Saturday. Their arrears are enclosed.

7. To Wright and Graham, 20 Nov. 1797. Add. MS. 35118, f. 74.

S. has given directions for repayment to them of £200 (rent of Lord Spencer's box) at £25 a night, and has made over his Fruit office rent.

8. [To J. Burchell.] [*1798?*] Egerton MS. 1975, f. 103.

S. had given directions for the payment of £8 a week on Mrs. Storace's account. Encloses the amount due last week, and will be punctual in future. Also sends £27. 10s. 0d. for poundage.

9. [To holders of D.L.Th. debentures], Crown and Anchor Tavern, 4 Nov. 1800. Egerton MS. 1975, f. 11. *Dock.*: Mr. Sheridan's Advertisements of Meeting at C. and Anchor.

Charles Butler was elected a trustee of D.L.Th., in the room of Albany Wallis, at the meeting held that day.

10. To ——. *Wm.*: 1801. Theatre Royal Drury Lane, Monday. Egerton MS. 1975, ff. 45–46.

Sends the enclosed tickets which recipient will sign and fill up for use in the same manner as the proprietors exercise their privilege. 'I beg leave also to trouble you to inform me to what other Persons connected with your Publication you wish similar admissions to be sent.' They shall be forwarded with 'a proposition for permanently placing the mode substituted in lieu of the Free List on the most satisfactory footing.'

11. To Wright. *Wm.*: 1797. [*1802?*] Widener MS.

'Mr: S. will have explained to you the necessity we are in of making up a sum of money in the course of next week—He has inclosed you my acceptance for the Firm, for which I trust and rely on receiving your Draught by return of Post. We are doing famously well and Mr. S. is making a Theatrical arrangement which will enable him to fill the Stafford Boys to the Brim.'

12. To the D.L.Th. renters, Treasury-Office, August 15th: 1805. Harvard MS. Over Richard Peake's signature.

'By order of the Principal Proprietor I am to request your

attention to the enclosed Note a copy of which He has directed
me to enclose to every Renter.'

13. To ——. *Wm.*: 1808. Harvard MS. Over Richard Peake's
signature. Confidential.
'Mr. Ward having been suddenly obliged to leave Town on
account of the dangerous illness of his mother He put a Letter of
yours into my hands with a request that I should either see you or
write to assure you that he considered everything as amicably
settled according to your wishes.'

14. [To the D.L.Th. Trustees]. *Wm.*: 1808. Egerton MS. 1975,
f. 26. Confidential.
'In transmitting to you the enclosed confidential proposition which
has been referr'd to and is much approved by Mr. Sheridan I am
to request your observations upon it as a Trustee and I have also
to desire a statement from the Proprietors and Partners and from
the Trustees if agreeable of the extent of their expectations as to
the voluntary contribution with the names of the Persons and the
sums they conceive such contributors are ready to subscribe on
application.'

15. To Raymond. [*c. 1808.*] Egerton MS. 1975, ff. 127–8.
'I am desired by Mr. Sheridan to express his extreme astonishment
at the Letter you have thought proper to write to Mr. Peake.
Your talking of "*lending him* the £100 he *wants*" he considers as
an insult and not proceeding from ignorance real or pretended of
the Proposition he made to you, which was that you should
actually abate £100 from your salary this year and certify it to
the Trustees in consequence of your having taken so enormous a
sum of money last year from the Theatre for doing comparatively
so little, with this addition that even this deduction shall be made
up to you, at the end of the Season out of the profits of the season
should any arise.' Will enquire into the alleged engagement for
five years, and now asks for a copy of the agreement with Graham
and T. Sheridan and the permission they gave him to take over the
management of the Opera House next season. Recommends him
to make a proper and speedy apology to S.

16. [To S. himself?] [*c. 1809–10.*] Harvard MS.
'In answer to your desire for my Opinion I am positively certain
that had you not given up for this season as you have done the
whole of your Theatre income allot[t]ed to you by the Lord
Chancellor's order it would not have been in your Power to have

procured the continuance of the Salary of £500 to Mr. T. Sheridan, nor to have provided for Those whom you considered as having claims on the good Faith of the late Drury Lane Property.

'Upon your second Question I can not but say that your having settled with Mr. Carpenter and taken up the Bond and interest in his hands to the amount of about £1600, in which I was equally implicated as well as Mr. T. Sheridan was not only the greatest relief to his mind on his return from abroad—but also to mine, on whom the Burthen must have fell should anything happen to Mr. T. Sheridan or whenever Mr. Carpenter chose to put the Bond in Force.

'On the 3 Question I am ready to make oath if necessary that the whole sum of five thousand six hundred Pounds paid to the Renters in the year came from the Theatre or Trustees as is well known to Mr. Graham Mr. Hammersley and every Person concerned.'

17. To Spencer Perceval. [4 Feb. 1811] Osborn MS. and Harvard MS. *Pub.: The Times*, 18 Feb. 1811.

'The Prince of Wales considers the moment to be arrived which calls for his Decision with respect to the Persons to be employ'd by him in the administration of the executive Government of the Country, according to the Powers vested in him by the Bill passed by the two Houses of Parliament and now on the Point of receiving the sanction of the Great Seal.

'The Prince feels it incumbent on him at this precise juncture to communicate to Mr. Percivals his intention not to remove from their Stations Those whom He finds there as his Majesty's official servants. At the same Time the Prince owes it to the Truth and sincerity of Character which He[1] trusts will appear in every action of his Life in whatever situation placed and[2] explicitly to declare that the irresistible impulse of filial Duty and affection to his beloved and affected[3] Father leads him to dread [that] any act of The Regent might in the smallest act[4] have the effect of interfering with the Progress of his Sovereign's recovery. This consideration alone dictated[5] the Decision now communicated to Mr. Percival.

'Having thus performed an act of indispensable Duty from a just sense of what is due to his own consistency and Honor The Prince has only to add that among the many Blessings to be derived from his Majesty's restoration to Health and to the personal exercise of

---

[1] The Harvard portion begins here and runs to the end of the paragraph.

[2] Colchester, ii. 316, publishes the version received by Perceval from the Prince of Wales. Here he omits 'and'.

[3] Colchester reads 'afflicted'.

[4] Colchester reads 'degree'.

[5] Colchester reads 'dictates'.

his Royal Functions, it will not in the Prince's estimation be the least that that most fortunate event will at once rescue him from a situation of unexampled embarrassment, and put an end to the state of affairs ill calculated He fears to sustain the interests of the united Kingdoms[1] [in] this awful and momentous[2] perilous Crisis and most difficult to be reconciled to the genuine[3] Principles of the British Constitution.'[4]

H. *References in other Correspondence to Lost Sheridan Letters*

1. C. J. Fox to the Duke of Portland, 29 Jan. 1784. *Pub.*: *Fox Corr.* iv. 276.
   'I have just received a note from Sheridan, who tells me that Pitt has given an answer, and that you must give one at eleven o'clock, and wish to see me first.'

2. Mary Tickell to Elizabeth Sheridan, [*24 Aug. 1785*]. Folger MS.
   'S.'s letter came to T[ickell] about Parr and Tom. . . .'

3. Mary Tickell to Elizabeth Sheridan, [*Oct.–Nov. 1785*]. Folger MS.
   Thomas Linley had a letter from S. about Cobb's opera which S. admitted he had never read.

4. Mary Tickell to Elizabeth Sheridan, [*c. Jan. 1786*]. Folger MS.
   Thomas Linley has answered a letter from S.

5. Mary Tickell to Elizabeth Sheridan, 11th [*Jan. 1786*]. Folger MS.
   Burgoyne received a letter from S. and expected an epilogue with it, but no epilogue was enclosed.

6. Mary Tickell to Elizabeth Sheridan, 23 Oct. 1786. Folger MS.
   Thomas Linley has received a good-natured letter of excuse from S. at Chatsworth, 'which consoles him for any neglect'.

7. Elizabeth Sheridan to Mehitabel Canning, Crewe Hall, 8 Dec. [*1787*]. Canning MS.
   'S. writes me word today, that Mrs. Leigh is safely deliver'd. . . . S. likewise tells me your Bess is more improv'd in every respect than any creature he ever saw.'

8. Richard Tickell to Joseph Richardson, [*c. 1789*]. *Pub.*: Watkins, ii. 227.
   Received a letter from S. on Tuesday.

---

[1] Colchester reads 'Kingdom'.
[2] Colchester omits 'momentous'.
[3] Colchester reads 'general'.
[4] For other letters written by S. on behalf of the Prince, see Moore, ii. 384; R. Huish, *Memoirs of George the Fourth*, i. 270–1, ii. 95–97.

9. The Duke of Richmond to T. Westley [*Oct. 1791*]. Winston MS., 1788–93.

So far from being likely to send immediate directions to Westley to return the subscription money paid for the Duke's box, S. will allow the Duke every convenience consistent with the interests of the theatre.

10. Dr. James Ford to Richard Ford, Rouen, 18 Jan. 1792. Brinsley Ford MS.

S. had said that Ford's stay in France was now 'a meer matter of unnecessary caution'.

11. Lady Bessborough to Lord Granville Leveson Gower, Roehampton, [Apr. 1797]. *Pub.*: *Leveson Gower Corr.* i. 146.

'Sheridan very good-naturedly wrote twice also.'

12. Joseph Richardson to John Bannister, 1798. *Pub.*: J. Adolphus, *Memoirs of John Bannister, Comedian* (1839), ii. 29.

Franklin will show Bannister S.'s letter.

13. Richard Nowell to Hammersley and Co., 11 June 1800. Grubbe MS.

S. had written to Nowell and Butler to secure the postponement of the sale of Grubb's house for a fortnight. The letters were sent before 20 Dec. 1799, and on that date Nowell went to see Butler about the proposal.

14. Dr. Samuel Goodenough to Richard Ford, [*1800–1*]. Brinsley Ford MS.

After the interview between S. and Goodenough last Friday, S. wrote to Goodenough to say that the most 'rigorous proceedings possible' would be executed against Westley.

15. Fox to S., [early May 1805]. *Pub.*: Moore, ii. 333.

'I did not receive your letter [about Roman Catholic claims] till last night.'

16. Grey to Fox, 5 July 1805. Grey MS.

A note from S. 'by last night's Post informs me of the Doctor's [Sidmouth's] resignation.'

I. *Letters doubtfully ascribed to Sheridan*

1. To the Editor of the *General Evening Post*, 25–27 Aug. 1772. *Pub.*: *General Evening Post* of that date.

A letter of some sixty lines on the '*precipitancy* with which the Dissenters . . . run into the very measures into which the opponents of the petitioning clergy wished to draw them'. The writer,

'R. B. S.', goes on to deal with aspects of the Subscription controversy, and to quote from and attack the views of a supporter of Dean Tucker's defence of clerical subscription to the thirty-nine articles.

The manner of argument is like that of S., but he was not normally interested in religious controversy.

2. To the Rev. Dr. Tucker, Dean of Gloucester. *Pub.*: *London Chronicle*, 16–18 Mar. 1773.

'In your two Letters to the Rev. Dr. Kippis, you have taken great pains to recommend yourself to the good opinion of the Gentleman and his brethren the dissenting Clergy in general. Whether you have succeeded to the *utmost* of your wish I much doubt, and heartily wish you may not succeed *so far*. For then they must entertain a bad opinion of many good men, and of one of the worthiest causes that ever engaged the attention of the English nation. . . .'

The writer, 'R. B. S.', goes on in this strain for a further fifty lines.

3. To Mehitabel Canning, [*Aug. 1786*]. W.T. *Pub.*: Rae, ii. 287. W.T. notes that it is signed 'E. and B. S.' Rae states that the letter is by S., but I question this: tone and style are nearer Mrs. S.'s than S.'s.

4. To Georgiana, Duchess of Devonshire, Crewe, 29 Oct. 1786. *Pub.*: Vere Foster, *The Two Duchesses* (1898), pp. 111–13. This is customarily ascribed to S., but it is worth noting that the signature at the foot of the letter appears in Vere Foster's work as 'Sheridan', and that the tone and style again suggest that the author was Mrs. S.

5. To Captains and Commanders of His Majesty's Ships of War, London, 3 Nov. 1806. *Pub.*: *Election Reports and Papers, 1806–7*, iii. 477.

This is the letter that S. was alleged to have signed (as Treasurer of the Navy) to authorize one Emmanuel Harris to serve different ships with slops, in return for votes which Harris could obtain for S. in the Westminster election of Nov. 1806. There is no suggestion that the letter itself was composed by S.

6. To the Editor of *The Satirist*, Southill, 15 Jan. [1814]. *Pub.*: *The Satirist*, New Ser., no. 18 (1814), 136–42, under the title of 'Southill Theatricals; or, Whitbread the Manager's Play'. Though it is signed 'R. B. Sheridan', the letter seems to me to be written as

a pastiche of S.'s style. Some passages are worth quoting for their general interest:

'. . . the game of opposition being for the present pretty well up, my friend Sam, who must be plotting about something or other, set to work to write a play—a real comedy, by the Lord! I would as soon have suspected a Greenland bear of inditing love elegies! Well, while I, who have had some credit for dramatic compositions (though, I lament to say, my credit otherwise has been but indifferent, and my creditors never approved of any composition I had to offer) while even I was living by my shifts rather than by my wits, what does my brewing crony but usurp my proper occupation; and, between original genius, and managerial pilferings, absolutely (by G—d, I'm not jesting) bring forth a laughable comedy, which he gravely said he had made himself!!. . . .

'Well, my honest Sat., the things having been composed, and dresses and decorations brought hither from the Theatre, in three drays, all amply loaded, a large company was invited to a jollification. There were a few of our opposition neighbours, who having, like Sam, nothing to do at present, thought it as well to come and amuse themselves with this new whim. Brand, forgetful of reform; Bennett, that silly young man, whom you may have heard trying to make speeches once or twice in the House of Commons; Tavistock, imbued with all the sense and good qualities of his family; Ongley and his train of descendants;[1] poor Lady Asgill; Mrs. Wilmot and her fantastic daughter; my Rib and myself; with an immense mob of stupid old Dowagers, giggling Misses, dull country Gentlemen, and booby Beaux, filled up this crowded medley of nearly two hundred spectators, who came to witness the farce of Dramatic Entertainments, by the Brewer-Statesman-Manager-Author, at Southill. . . .

'You may have seen, from a Paragraph in the Paper to which I have already alluded, and which I need scarcely assure you did not, any more than the pieces in question, (all connexion [with] which I solemnly disavow) proceed from my "elegant pen", that "the dining-room was converted into a Theatre, with all the appropriate appendages and dresses from Drury-lane. Two *inimitable* pieces were performed, produced by the elegant pen of Mr. Sheridan; the one presenting a village scene, called *The Happy Return*; the other a deep tragedy, founded on real facts, called *Fatal Duplicity*.

---

[1] Robert Henley-Ongley, 2nd Lord Ongley (1771–1814), lived at Old Warden, near Southill. He had five sons, and the oldest of them was (in 1814) eleven.

The characters were represented in an exquisite style and manner,[1] and chiefly by the able and distinguished *ability* of the *Manager* and family."

'As *The Happy Return* went off quietly on the part of the able Manager, who, being a good deal employed in personating one of the characters, suffered me to enjoy a very comfortable nap undisturbed, I shall not trespass upon you, like many critics I know, with a description of what I neither saw nor heard. . . .

'After a rapturous encore [of a song called 'The Publican tapping the mellow Beer-Cask'], came the deep tragedy of *Fatal Duplicity*; a tragedy truly described as being "inimitable". Nay, I am free to confess that it is still more, it is indescribable. The deepest distress pervades every scene, but, alas, my personal sufferings far exceeded those of the mimic actors and actresses. . . .'

7. To the Countess of Blessington. Decr. 16th. [1815]. *Pub.*: Hodgson Sale Catalogue, 12–14 Dec. 1917, item 39.

No text is printed. Charles James Gardiner (1782–1829) was created Earl of Blessington on 12 Jan. 1816. His first wife died in Oct. 1814; he did not marry his second until 1818.

---

[1] Playbills giving details are to be found in Thomas Dibdin, *Reminiscences* (1827), ii. 383–4.

APPENDIX OF FURTHER LETTERS

1. To the Printer of the *Morning Chronicle*

Pub.: *Morn. Chron.*, 2 Feb. 1775.

[*29 Jan.–1 Feb. 1775*]

Sir,

I was one among many who attended both[1] representations of The Rivals: and I cannot help congratulating the lovers of Comedy on the present success of a piece, which, from some levities, and want of experience, was near being crushed the first night—but now on the strength of its own merit, and an acquiescence to the taste of the public, will certainly stand foremost in the list of modern comedies.

There was a candour, and at the same time a spirit, in the alterations in the *Prologue*,[2] which had a happy effect—I need not say that the Serjeant was inimitably supported by Woodward.[3] Mr. Clinch[4] makes the genteelest Irishman we have on the stage, and there are some true Hibernian touches (which passed unnoticed before) but which now appeared admirably characteristic. All the most laboured portraits of Hibernian assurance, do not perhaps amount to so humourous an instance as Sir Lucious O'Trigger's forgetting the very name of modesty. Lucy tells him, her Mistress won't like him if he's so impudent. 'Faith she will, Lucy' (says the Baronet) 'that same—pho!—what's the name

---

[1] First performed on 17 Jan. 1775 at C.G.Th. The revised text was acted on 28 Jan. For their reception, see W. F. Rae, *Sheridan's Plays Now Printed As He Wrote Them* (1902), pp. xvi–xxxiii.

[2] The prologue for 17 Jan. is now lost, but a quotation from it appeared in *Lloyd's Evening Post*, 18 Jan., and is reprinted in *The Rivals . . . As it was first Acted* (ed. R. L. Purdy, Oxford, 1935), p. xii. See also pp. xiii–xxi.

[3] The Serjeant-at-Law was acted by John Lee on 17 Jan., but by Henry Woodward (1714–77) on 28 Jan. He was a fine comic performer, especially

in Bobadil and Touchstone.

[4] John Lee had played Sir Lucius on 17 Jan. and had been severely criticized for his poor brogue and bad memory, though it was said that he had taken the part 'at the instance of the author himself' (*Morn. Post*, 20 Jan. 1775). For the way in which S. remodelled the character, see *The Rivals . . .* (ed. Purdy), pp. xxvi–xxviii. He changed Sir Lucius from a stupid fortune-hunter to a fire-eating man of honour, and the part was triumphantly represented on 28 Jan. by Laurence Clinch.

of it?—*Modesty*—etc.'[1] The contrast between him and Acres in the duel-scene, is finely pursued, and is particularly excellent, when he finds his *valour oozing away*[2] at the approach of his antagonist; Shuter in Sir Antony seemed piqued to exert himself, threw the house absolutely into a convulsion of laughter.[3] It may be said that Woodward is too old for his character,[4] but I will venture to assert, that there is no man in England could *now* play it better, and that there never was one of his age could play half so well. The character of Faulkland[5] will improve on the audience the more it is understood; and Mrs. Bulkeley[6] never appeared to more advantage than in the amiable and elegant Julia. | I am, Sir, your's, etc. | *Aristarchus*.[7]

2. [To Thomas Linley]

Harvard MS. [Ph].

[*1775*][8]

Dear Sir,

Before I attempt to offer my sincere Sentiments on the subject of your last, I must premise that you must not take ill my giving them with the greatest Freedom, on an Affair

[1] II. i. Identical in both versions.

[2] 'I feel it oozing out as it were' (V. iii). Identical in both.

[3] Edward Shuter (1728–76), comedian. He was the original Hardcastle in *She Stoops to Conquer*. Of his Sir Anthony on 17 Jan., 'Impartialist' wrote, 'Shuter [was] shamefully imperfect in his part, though he occasionally exerted his usual drollery' (*Morn. Post*, 20 Jan. 1775).

[4] Jack Absolute.

[5] 'Faulkland, in most respects, [is] a new, and a very good character, but badly sustained by Mr. [W. T.] Lewis' (*Morn. Post*, 20 Jan. 1775)

[6] Mary Bulkley (born Wilford) had been a dancer at C.G.Th. and was married to a member of its band. She was the original Miss Richland in *The Good-Natured Man*, and Miss Hardcastle in *She Stoops to Conquer*. Her playing of Julia and her elegant speaking of

the epilogue were generally commended.

[7] On 4 Sept. 1817 [?] Thomas Wilkie replied to a request by Lord Holland for S.'s 'Letters of "Aristarchus"', saying, 'I am not aware that Mr. S. ever wrote any Letters under the signature of "Aristarchus"' (Holland House MS.). He then assumed Holland meant *The Love Epistles of Aristaenetus*. He may have been correct, but it is clear that Holland had heard S.'s name connected with the pseudonym 'Aristarchus'. Writing in the *Morn. Post*, 21 Jan. 1775, 'A Briton' described some newspaper criticisms of *The Rivals* as 'the wretched puffs of an author's friends'. It is likely that the man who was to create Mr. Puff had a hand in at least one of them.

[8] From internal evidence, I judge that it belongs to the period between 3 May and 21 June.

which must certainly either establish or undo your Comfort and Welfare for the rest of your Life, and which also involves the entire Prosperity of so large a Part of your Family.— I shall venture to speak more freely because I am convinced that I am better acquainted with the Scene of Life into which you propose to enter, than you are yourself: A Scene which I had always an Instinctive Abhorrence of, and which I am now more than ever convinced is, for its extent, the greatest Nursery of Vice[1] and Misery on the Face of the Earth.— I am aware that you are prepared for my *Prejudices* on this Subject; and that you will probably misconceive part of my *motives* in wishing you to cherish the same. However, tho' I still think myself bound to urge my Opinion with Frankness, I request no other Effect from it to arise in your mind than that you will but for a little while *suspend* your Resolution—it is a subject which you cannot weigh too minutely— nor consider too often—and this too should be done when a little cool'd from the first Effects which a sanguine Imagination may have received from an apparently flattering Prospect, and above all it should be done when free from the immediate Influence of one of the most artful and selfish Men that ever imposed on Merit or Honesty.—Mr. G. I should suppose cannot at present have trepann'd you into any absolute Promise[2]—(or it would have been useless to have mentioned a word of the matter to me—for as to the Question of *what* you should ask, I am entirely unfit to decide—because upon my Honour and Soul I look on your Children as surely and utterly ruined by the scheme—to which no *Price* can be

[1] 'What are the Playhouses but the Nurseries of Vice, the Sink of Debauchery, the Destruction of all Religion?' (George Whitefield, *A Sermon Preach'd at Blackheath* (1740), p. 6).

[2] In Oct. 1770, George Colman had approached Thomas Linley about Mary Linley's joining the Haymarket company. Linley replied that he would not allow his daughter to become an actress 'unless it were to ensure to myself and family a solid settlement by being admitted to purchase a share of the patent on reasonable terms . . . (R. B. Peake, *Memoirs of the Colman Family* (1841),

pp. 242–4). Garrick approached him on the subject in Oct. 1772, but made no progress: see *Garrick Corr.* i. 488. In 1775 he tried again, and on 20 Apr. wrote to Colman from Bath to say, 'I believe I may engage the blood of the Lindleys!' (*The Letters of David Garrick* (ed. D. M. Little and G. M. Kahrl, Cambridge, Mass., 1963), p. 1003. Linley's ambitions were satisfied in the following January when, with Ford and S., he bought a moiety of the patent of D.L.Th. Mary Linley never became an actress.

adequate)—Or if He has—as you have not yet even *proposed* your Terms—nothing binding can have pass'd—so that surely a Fortnight's or a Month's Reflection on the matter cannot injure either Party, or materially affect your Plan if it shall then appear to you in the same Light as at Present.—If Mr. G. pretends that his Engagements are such as make a speedy Answer from you necessary, that He cannot keep the Proposal open, that He must immediately look elsewhere if He does not close with you—if, I say, He should urge this—He will utter what He knows to be insidious and false:—There is no period of his Season in which He would not eagerly catch at such an Engagement. He is conscious that it has long been an Object with him—He has look'd with the longing of a Baud on the Promise of Genius in your Family, and finds his Theatre never more in want of it than at Present—and He is at present particularly stimulated by the Reputation of what Maria[1] promises to be, in whom He hopes to forestall at least another Mrs. S.—It may be said that this may be his Idea, and yet the Proposal turn out no less advantageous to you.—Now putting every other consideration out of the Question—I would stake my Life on it that even in point of *Pecuniary* Advantage you and your Family, will be Losers by[2] changing the Turn of your Profession.—But as I cannot think this the most important Consideration, it may be waived for the present—and give me leave to endeavour to Justify those apprehensions I have express'd with regard to the *Happiness*, and what *ought* to be esteem'd the *Wellfare* of your Chi[l]dren, particularly your Daughters. I know that it is a Thread-bare Topick to declaim against the Hazard of the Scenes to Won[der at?] the Indecency of the Profession, the Contagion of Example etc. etc. but you say that you believe it to be the general Opinion that there is no difference between a public Singer and an Actress.—Here I own I have very different Sentiments. In the Judgement of every one of Sense and Delicacy there is a material Difference made between the two Situations. The Daughter of a Musician, having Talents to benefit her Father in the same Profession, treads only in the Path in

---

[1] Maria Linley (1763–84) took Mrs. S.'s place at her father's concerts. Cf. Kelly, ii. 115.   [2] Manuscript 'be'.

which she was born. Her appe[a]rance in Public is natural and not unexpected, it argues no *Choice*, no Passion for becoming a Spectacle, no low Vanity of being the unblushing Object of a Licentious gaping Croud—if she be in herself good, modest, and well bred—*there* is her Character—and the Part she may always appear in: in her Performance there is nothing address'd to the grosser Passions, nor anything to inflame or corrupt her own Feelings.—In the other Situation every thing is reversed: it is her evident Inclination and Passion to obtrude herself into a conspicuous Scene of all that's *indelicate, immodest, immoral*: In her former Sphere she is accountable to no one, She is evidently the Pupil of, and under the Wings of her Parent; in the Latter She is the Creature of a mercenary Manager, The Servant of the Town, and a licens'd Mark for Libertinism:—She leaves a situation comparatively *private*, where her abilities only distinguish her, to become a Topick for illiberal News-Paper Criticism and Scandal, and to enter the list of envious Contention with a set of practised Harlots on one side, and profligate Scoundrels on the other.—Whatever the Promise of her Abilities may be—the event is precarious—it is a Profession of all others without any standard of true Taste—The Theatre is at present deserted by all the Higher Ranks of People—The Mob are the Rulers in it, and as to *eminence* and *Fame*—Miss *Catley*[1] is greater than Mrs. *Barry*,[2] and a good Columbine equal to either.—As to the *real* modesty of an Actress every Body looks on it as a Farce—and the Reputation of it is rather an Injury, and I think very justly, for it certainly does not belong to the Profession.[3] There is a strong connexion between the Countenance of every Virtue and the Reality—if the Resolution to face an Audience is an *assumed* Character, does not at once deprive a woman of all the out-works of Virtue—*Bashfulness* and *Reserve*, it is certain that a very little Practice does radically relieve her from two Qu[a]lities so evidently calculated to embarrass her Per-

[1] Ann Catley (1745–89), soprano. She sang at C.G.Th. from 1763.

[2] Anne Barry (1734–1801), celebrated for her acting in pathetic roles and high comedy.

[3] 'In no situation of life is the conduct of females less reproached than on the Stage, and particularly in Country companies, where the Ladies are often as free in conferring favours as the Gentlemen are eager to solicit them' (*The Secret History of the Green Room* (1795), i. 318).

formance.—What is the *modesty* of any Women whose trade it is eternally to represent all the different modifications of Love before a mix'd Assembly of Rakes, Whores, Lords and Blackguards in Succession!—to play the Coquet, the Wanton, to retail loose innuendos in Comedy, or glow with warm Descriptions in Tragedy; and in both to be haul'd about, squeez'd and kiss'd by beastly pimping Actors!—what is to be the Fate of a Girl of seventeen in such a situation?—what of a Girl of Polly's[1] particular Attractions?—The Protection, the Advice of Parents may preserve their Child while she is *their's*—but *Clarinda*,[2] *Monimia*[3] *Calista*[4] are not subject to such vulgar Rules—everything round them is unchaste—their Studies are Lessons of Vice and Passion.—Like Wretches who work in unwhol[e]some Mines, Their senses are corrupted in the opperation of their Trade.—it would be endless to enumerate all that suggests itself on this subject—it would be needless to add the circumstance of a Girl's making a Shew of herself in Breeches (—and I suppose Mr. G. would bring out Polly in the Country-Girl—)[5] however even this is little worse than the rest—the Point is that the event has always justified what Reas[o]n must foresee—under such circumstances—all Actresses whose eminence has made their Characters worth being enquired into, from Mrs. Oldfield[6] down to Mrs. Barry, have been uniformly found to be Ladies of easy Virtue, to say no worse, it is true that now and then we hear of some unwieldy Heroine, who having no other way to *distinguish* herself, has affected the singula[ri]ty of Chastity—however even their Virtue—except in cases of eminent Ugliness—has been usually reported as very problematical:—At present there are not three at both Theatres who labour under the least suspicion of such a Quality. The only one at Covent-Garden in that predicament is a Miss *Brown*[7]—and even here we must not credit the

---

[1] Mary Linley.
[2] Heroine of *The Orphan* (1680), by Thomas Otway (1652–85).
[3] Heroine of *The Suspicious Husband* (1747), by Benjamin Hoadly (1706–57).
[4] Heroine of *The Fair Penitent* (1703), by Nicholas Rowe (1674–1718). All three plays were stock pieces.

[5] Garrick's free adaptation (1766) of Wycherley's *The Country Wife* (1675).
[6] Ann Oldfield (1683–1730), queen of the stage from 1707 to 1727.
[7] See i. 95, n. 2. The *Morn. Chron.*, 6 June 1775, printed a note by 'Cosmopolitus' saying, '. . . . I felt for her, on account of the many inticements which

News-Papers—however without being very unusually pretty she has the satisfaction of knowing that she has a constant Retinue of humble-Servants ogling her from the Boxes—who, if they fail in their Designs on her Person, have already nearly secured the consolation of having destroy'd her Character.

The Cause of this Stigma on the Profession is obvious—No Gentleman of Character and Fortune ever yet took a Wife from behind the Scenes of a Theatre—if in the Annals of the Stage there were but ten instances of Female eminence, meeting the reward of a *virtuous* Union with some independent Man of Honour, it would be some excuse for the Infatuation which has plunged so many well-disposed Girls into this Abyss of profligate misery. But their situation precludes every Hope of such a thing—they soon become conscious of it, and while their occupation is a daily alarm to all the Passions and romantic Folly which lead Women into Error, they are by that occupation shut out from any chance of inspiring a Virtuous Attachment in Others.—You will say that Polly is to be in a different Light—is to have a Particular Countenance, Protection etc. This is what Mr. G. has promised to hundreds—and as for any Restriction that may be made before her Appearanc[e] against her being forced into any particular Line of acting—They are all mere words, and nothing more. The Reputation and Progress of a young Actress once engaged is entirely in the Power of a Manager—and if she refuses to comply with his Choice or re[c]ommendation in her Business She may as well throw up the Profession at once.—and G. has damn'd and sunk numbers whom he had first cajoled, and fo[u]nd afterwards not servilely manageable. As to the delusive Nonsense that captivates Girls Imaginations, and begets a *Passion for the Stage*—no Deception wears sooner off. Nine out of Ten of the Profession that I have conversed with (and those too of

from her situation in life, her youth and inexperience, presented themselves to draw her from the paths of innocence and virtue. She must be sensible, that the only road to Fame is to pursue the track of virtue; Why does she adopt any other system ? if she is so enchanted with the manners of a C[atle]y as strictly to copy her gestures and her impudence, she loses all the merit she possesseth; and instead of gaining admiration, is pitied, nay renders herself contemptible. . . .'

some eminence) have bitterly regretted the Hour they first thought of the Stage—they have all in their turns felt the wretched servility of their State: and those who do not acknowledge this are actuated by no other Principle, than the envy of Prostitutes who delight in seducing others to the Level of their own Infamy.—When I imagine to myself your Daughter Polly familiarized to what I *know* she must be in such a course of Life—I declare solemnly that the most immediate consequence that I can foresee (and probably by no means the worst) will be her being wrought to a marriage with some such Fellow as Brereton[1] (who will be her Jaffier and Castalio thro' the winter) and then—not to speak of her own Positive Ruin—the visionary Idea of her assisting her Family is at an end at once. Her Sister *Maria*— (so young brought to what she will think the grandest Scene in Life!) will doubtless at a proper age find equal Charms in some artful *Damon*—and your only acquisition will be such Relations as it will be a disgrace to be connected with.— I must repeat it again that it is above a Million to one that this will be the event—in proportion to their Abilities the Temptation encreases. They are shut from your Inspection or Intuition[2]—every hour of their Business teems with Opportunities to favour the views of any artful Fellow-Labourer of that artful Crew.—Mrs. Linley[3] may constantly attend their musical Rehearsals, their Play-Rehearsals, Farce-Rehearsal, Dancing-Rehearsal—their Dressing Room— Green-Room—Scene—Stage—yet all the Precaution or Penetration on Earth is feeble in superin[ten]ding those whose Trade—Practise and Duty is—mask'd Levity— Simulation—and confidence. Sensibility and modesty are so unal[l]ied to this infernal Trade that those who possess them are only so much the less a match for the native Deceit and immorality of its abandoned Professors.—Sure the slightest Deductions of one's own Reason (tho' inexperienced) must convince us that the Life of an Actress is in no material

---

[1] William Brereton played Jaffier (the hero of Otway's *Venice Preserved*) for the first time at D.L.Th. on 3 May 1775. He had earlier acted the part of Chamont in Otway's *The Orphan*, but did not take Castalio there.

[2] Manuscript 'Intuation'.

[3] 'A shrewd worldly woman, and clever enough in her particular way' (Smyth, p. 63).

respect similar to that of a Singer in your Daughters Situation—They are just as Opposite as the Public Rooms at Bath[1] to the Public Stews in London—both I grant are *public*—but the one for decent and elegant Entertainment— the other for Riot and immodest Craft.—And this applies to both cases—yet can you say in the eye of the world there is no Difference. To disprove this I will confidently urge the instance of your Daughter *Betsey*. She—being in the Profession[2] her Sister is in now—married a Man from whom she could derive no consequence either thro' Birth, Fortune or Connections, yet I will venture to assert that she now stands in the Estimation and Respect of the World, far above what any Man of fifty Times my advantages could have raised her to—had He taken her from behind the Scenes of Drury-Lane Playhouse—let her merit *there* have been ever so great.—Nor will Polly—once she has set foot on those Boards,—ever see again the Respect which she may command at Present.—But the Estimation of the World is a secondary consideration—I lay not the smallest stress on it in this Case—It is the impending—the more than probable Ruin and Shame that I dread may imbitter those Days of your Life which should be Peace, that makes me impatient at the Idea of this Step, and warm in my wishes to prevent it.—You must not take ill any expressions I make use of in delivering my Opinion on this Subject. Sincerely interested for the welfare of all your Children, I have the same Feelings for the *Honour* of your Daughters as of my own Sisters— their present situation—or any public situation—is not *without* Hazard—but I look on that Hazard to be so infinitely encreased in the other Line—that Honour is scarcely probable—and at all events Insult is licens'd against Resent-

---

[1] See i. 23, nn. 1 and 2.

[2] There is an unnoticed and ambiguous paragraph concerning Walter Long's proposal to Elizabeth, in the *London Chronicle*, 30 July–1 Aug. 1775: 'It is confidently asserted that Mr.L——g never made proposals of a dishonourable nature to Miss L——y. The fact is said to be this:—that he was for stipulating within a day or two of the intended marriage, that the young Lady should retire to his Seat, and promise not to be seen at Bath or in London for the space of two years: on this unexpected overture the Lady desired leave to Consult her friends; her friends seemed to demur, and the Gentleman went off.' This suggests that Long was anxious to make a complete break between her appearances in public as a singer and as his wife.

ment.—And so rooted are my apprehensions—and so hurt
I am sure I should be if verified—that I most solemnly
Protest that if I had at this Instant an independent Fortune,
and *Polly's* necessity for going on the Stage was *want* of
Fortune, I would gladly give her any Portion of it whatever
to prevent Her—and if she was my own Sister—upon my
soul and honour I had rather see her dead.

If you imagine that my earnest Prejudice on this Point is
in the least assisted by any selfish Pride that so near Relations
should not be in a Profession which I think so ill of—you
will do me the greatest Injustice—I own that in my Opinion
the Change—even in Point of Credit, as in every other
particular,—will be for the worse—but this is a paltry consideration—and to one circumstanced as I am it would be
the grossest absurdity to waste a Thought on it—if any
motive of Pride or Vanity operated on me in resolving that
Betsy should sing no more[1] They were founded on very
different Principles than merely objecting to the thing itself
—for if she were my sister I would give her the same advice
that has been given to me. But when I speak of a *Stage* Life
as utterly different, I put the Dignity of either Profession
entirely out of the Question—and you will believe that my
keen repugnance to the Idea of your engaging with G——
can proceed from no nonsensical Pride—when I inform you
that my *Father* is *certainly* to be on Convent-Garden Stage
next-winter[2]—and I am glad that He is to be—but God
forbid his *Daughters* should be there!

What I have hitherto said is against your scheme in
general—but I own I am more astonish'd at your represent-
ing it in the light you do even on the Point of Interest and

[1] Johnson's opinion is well known:
'He resolved wisely and nobly to be sure.
He is a brave man. Would not any gentle-
man be disgraced by having his wife
singing publicly for hire? . . .' (*Boswell's
Life of Johnson* (ed. G. B. Hill; rev. L. F.
Powell, Oxford, 1934), ii. 396). Cf.
Charles Davies's letter to S. from the
Music Room, Oxford, on 26 May 1773:
'. . . the [Musical] Society wish that Mr.
Sheridan's resolution had not put it out
of their power to offer his Lady a Gra-

tuity in some degree proportion'd to the
pleasure and Assistance they receive.
At present they only beg leave to secure
Mr. and Mrs. Sheridan Lodgin[g]s in
whatever part of the city they think
most agreeable' (Yale MS.). The matter
was of sufficient public interest for the
Virginia Gazette, 14 Oct. 1773, to report:
'We are informed that Mrs. Sheridan
has been offered £1500 to sing next
winter at the Pantheon.'
[2] See i. 91.

worldly Benefit to your Family.—But the same insinuating, artful Trickster, who has won you from those just Prejudices which I know you once entertained against the Stage-Life for your children, has also, as may be proved, blinded you as to your Profit in the Change.—To talk of Mr. G——['s] *selfishness*—*Cunning*—*Avarice*—and *Insincerity* is literally to advance a Position which no one that has ever had any Dealings with him will attempt to controvert.[1] It is proverbial that no one ever yet made a treaty with him that they had not the worst of, and that they did not soon repent of.— His Wealth and unrivall'd merit in his Profession have placed him in a Point of Respect, which his Art and Finesse have supported him in notwithstanding the most notorious ill-Qualities—and in other Respects very moderate Parts.— His Professions to me and his [Con]duct in his interposition relative to our marriage[2] was a scene of interested overstrain'd Craft—that could not have imposed on a Child. Why He should on a sudden become the Quintessence of Honour and Generosity in a treaty with you (as you intimate He is) who never in his Life shew'd a Particle of either to any other human Creature beside, is in my opinion an instance of miraculous reformation that requires some thing more than Profession to deserve Credit.—But from what I understand of his Proposals I think He may be acquitted of this Inconsistency—as to me there appears plainly in them the same interested overreaching Cunning for which he has so long been eminent.

—*You have told him* (you say) *in confidence what the Income is of your Present Profession—and He thinks it will answer greatly to you in Point of Interest to be with him.*—If you weigh

---

[1] But cf. *The Letters of David Garrick* (ed. cit.), I. xxxiii–xxxiv, l–lv.

[2] His only recorded connexion with the marriage is found in a note (in *Boswell's Life of Johnson* (ed. cit.), ii. 521), drawn from a document signed by Garrick and dated 17 Mar. 1773: 'Mr. Sheridan has desir'd me to remember that he will marry Miss Lindley without any other Conditions than giving up 2,000 pounds of her Fortune to her Father for the Loss he may sustain by not having the use of her Talents for two years and a half to come, the remaining time of Apprenticeship to him—but he desires me to take Notice That if Mr. Lindley should prove that he and his Wife are sinking into distress by her not Singing with her Father as usual, That he will then agree to make a publick use of her talents as formerly to satisfy the Father That he means not to distress him but make him as happy as will be in Mr. Sheridan's Power.'

your present Profits at Bath—with what He would give you and your Family to be with him—I doubt not but the latter would be greatly superiour.—But what is to be the Sacrifice?—you alter the whole Tenour of your Life—you embark in a scene altogether new—partly precarious—you become the Servants of a manager—and Servants by Custom to the Public, you fix your Family in a Line from which there is no retreating, and your Daughters—the Servants of *another*—are exposed in the Vortex of Temptation and contagious Vice.—The Balance here in point of Advantage should certainly be considerable—yet I will not hesitate to affirm that it would not exceed what you might make in your own Profession, without half the risk, provided, as in this Case, you resolve to change your Scene and give up Bath at Once. If you had conducted oratorios last spring in Town *on your own account*—you might have clear'd £1000 or £1200.—Maria's Reputation is spreading amazingly— whatever you *did* get by Betsy—and what more you *might* have got had you come sooner to Town or had I not robb'd you of her—you *may* get and if you rely only on yourself, certainly *will* get by Maria.—You have yourself deserved Reputation—it is no little credit to have bred and taught the acknow[ledg]'d best English Singer that has been—you have a right to the Attention of the Public in introducing another —and surely if such a Man as Arnold[1] was encouraged in attempting oratorios on his own account, no one can expect that you will again share with others the fruits of any other excellent Singer you may Produce—especially when you have so little obligation to any of them. Polly is certainly at present considered *here* as the best *Oratorio* Singer there now is, and tho' her Sister Maria may come to surpass her in some things —She will always be respectable and in the first Line.— From this Prospect I will not allow that it admits of Doubt but that you may, if you will Quit Bath, establish the Best, and most probably the only Oratorio in London.—Bach[2]

[1] Samuel Arnold (1740–1802), organist and composer. His oratorios, *Abimelech* (1768) and *The Prodigal Son* (1773) were given at the Haymarket, and *The Resurrection* (1770) was performed at

C.G.Th.
[2] Johann Christian Bach (1735–82), composer. With C. F. Abel he had been responsible for the Lent oratorios at the King's Theatre in Mar. 1775.

will undertake it no more—and I think it would be madness for you to join Stanley.[1]—This would be respectable, independent, and highly beneficial.—You would be no Man's Servant—your Family would still be your own—and No Change, Jealousies, or Caprice could distress you. In the other Case—You succeed Mr. *Dibdin*[2]—in a Post of no *great* Eminence, however dignified by Restrictions—which would not signify a Pin if once you were on ill Terms with the Manager. The Labour and Servility of the Employment of such sort as would be most irksome to you—new Proposals would be made you—which you must consent to— (Dibdin leaves G—— for having broke every promise to him)—Polly would be an Actress—*probably* successful— *possibly* not—Maria Actress, Singer, etc. and poor Tam[3] hedg'd in to answer the temporary Purpose of a singing Boy—or Chorus in a Sphere which He would soon grow out of, and be fit for nothing else there, nor anywhere else.— Here every advantage of their Abilities to you in their present Profession is cut off.—By the Time Polly or Maria have warbled Ballads a couple of winters on Drury-Lane no Person would give sixpence to hear them in Particular, in Oratorios.—Stage Singers necessarily and speedily grow out of Estimation with the Politer Ranks—tho' they may for a while continue the Miss *Brents*[4] of the Galleries—therefore once on the Stage look for no Particular attraction or advantage in them for Oratorios. On the subject of Oratorios—you say that Mr. G. *has engaged to join you in them with Stanley*[5] *or if S. refuses—that He will himself be concerned*

[1] See i. 85–86. He had conducted the Lent oratorios at D. L.Th. in Mar. 1775.

[2] Charles Dibdin the elder (1745–1814), actor, playwright, and author of nautical songs. He was house-composer at D.L.Th., but quarrelled with Garrick in 1775, and left. His new comic opera, *The Quaker*, was given at D.L.Th. on 3 May 1775, after S. had praised it.

[3] Tom Linley: see i. 87.

[4] Charlotte Brent (?–1802), soprano. Arne wrote the part of Madane in *Artaxerxes* (1762) for her. She married

Thomas Pinto, violinist, in 1766.

[5] The *Morn. Chron.*, 22 June 1775, reported: 'It is said that Mr. Stanley and Mr. Linley of Bath are jointly engaged to carry on Oratorios at Drury-lane Theatre next Lent; if so, no women singers will be wanted more than they have in their family; better is not to be had; though the Italians may not be well pleased at our so bluntly asserting it.' Mary and Maria Linley duly performed at the Lent oratorios at D.L.Th., 1776, under the leadership of their father and Stanley.

in them with you. This Bounty in my opinion amounts just to this.—That if you are willing to ford this musical Pactolus[1] *He* (Mr. G.) will undertake to hang a Mill-Stone round your Neck, or if the Mill-Stone won't hang you shall dive for the Golden Sand yourself and He will share it with you.— What Attraction Mr. G's Name would have to bring People to an oratorio I can't conceive—and Stanley can never be anything but a dead weight on such a scheme. G.'s Generosity to the Latter this Winter—was no greater than that of the Musicians. The Latter gave up their Pay first and G's munificence limp'd after. Polly's Talents for the Stage you say are undoubted—I grant it—yet is her Success precarious—Her constitution may not be Robust enough to carry her thro' the Practice of tragedy Parts—and I should hope she would never acquire assurance enough to be perfectly easy in Comedy—but still Mr. G. *promises* that you shall always be at Liberty to withdraw—*provided you do not engage in any other Theatre.*[2] This I think the most insidious and iniquitous Clause that He could shackle his Generosity with. When once you have exposed and made cheap your Daughters on the Stage He very well knows that *there* must lie their[3] future Profession—Unsuccessful *there* or retiring from thence upon whatever discontent—they never could regain the Respect or eminence of their former Situation when the Town had already heard them down to the one shilling Mob—in Operas and Farces—what Price would ever after be set upon their Performance in Con[c]erts or Oratorios!—yet the Restriction is that they sha'n't be received on any *other Theatre* and consequently they are upon his own Terms to continue fix'd on his!—This is Honour and Generosity with a Vengeance!—You say—you are convinced that *Mr. G. studies your advantage and will act honourably in the Affair.* This conviction I own is unaccountable to me—you did not once think so highly of him—as to his Countenance, Protection etc. to *Polly*—that is all of course and I dare say might be the case. However that would be but of a short Date.—G. has to *my certain knowledge,* this Winter endeavour'd to dispose of his share of the Patent.—

---

[1] The river Midas bathed in, leaving golden sands behind him.

[2] Manuscript 'Thearte'.

[3] Manuscript 'there'.

He waits but for his Price—and would certainly be glad to put it up to sale as well supported as He could—this would be help'd by an Engagement with you including Polly and Maria—(bound to leave it for no other Theatre!—an obligation *unprecedented*!)—I am much mistaken if *Coleman*[1] will not then be your Manager—or be it who it may—all Mr. G.'s services end of course, and the new Manager may have other Favourites, and as for the clause of your *right* to continue *seven* or *fourteen* years—that I again repeat, were not the Manager entirely content, would be impossible with Credit or Comfort.

In short it is my sincere opinion that Mr. G. went to Bath[2] on Purpose to draw you into some agreement with him—that He thinks Maria principally will be a Treasure to him—and that his whole Plan is insidious, and selfish, and his Professions insincere.—If you determine to leave Bath—I think you may in point of Profit only succeed infinitely better by having no connection with the Stage— and in Point of Credit and Happiness that you would soon find the latter your bane: and above all I hold in my own mind the most ominous Conviction that you will see the Day which, for your Daughter's sake, will make you curse the Deceiver who first drew you into that Scene of Life.—In what I have said here relative to G—— I protest solemnly I am not influenc'd by the least Personal Enmity—He has on the contrary lately spoke rather well of me and I make no doubt would have no objection to be on any Terms with me —Connection with Theatres are always fluctuating and I think it just as probable that I may bring out a Piece, at Drury-Lane some time Hence as at Convent-Garden. And in that Case it might certainly be serviceable to me—to have so strong a Party at the House as you might prove.—But so far from my being Witness, or in the least concern'd in any agreement of that kind you may make with him, or so far from acquiring any interest myself by it with him—that I declare to God I should ever after regard him with the

---

[1] See i. 93–94.
[2] His letters from Bath are dated between 1 Apr. and 4 May 1775: see *The Letters of David Garrick* (ed. cit.),

pp. 1000–5. The *Morn. Chron.*, 14 May 1775, noted, 'Yesterday arrived from Bath in perfect health, David Garrick, Esq.'

utmost Detestation—nor ever view him or think of him but with the most rooted and veng[e]ful Enmity—as a Man who had by Craft and mercenary Deceit deprived me of the Satisfaction of seeing Relations whom I loved in the probable Road to Comfort and happiness, and had instead made their Welfare and Peace subservient to his own Vanity and insatiable Avarice.—

There is only one argument more which I shall make use of—tho'[1]

3. To John Bromley

Osborn MS. *Address*: Mr. J. Bromley[2] | Painter | Little-Queen-Street *Dock.*: Janry. 4th—78

4 Jan. 1778

Sir,

I have received a very rude Note sign'd John Bromley, which alludes to some Letter which I do not recollect to have seen, and relates to some Demand of Mrs. French's[3] on the Theatre. As the adjusting the Bills of the Theatre is a matter I do not interfere in, I could give you no satisfaction on the subject if I understood the Purport of your application.[4]—I should conceive that all the Salary or Demands of the Late Mr. French must have been discharged long since —however if you will apply to Mr. Evans at the Treasury He will inform you—and if there is any further Demand, the explanation will come to me from him.—It is very probable that I have been applied to on this Business before—but I cannot call to mind the circumstances; if Mrs. French is under the unfortunate circumstances you mention, I shall

[1] The manuscript breaks off at this point.
[2] For Bromley (later employed as a scene-painter at C.G.Th.) and his father William Bromley (a scene-painter at D.L.Th), see S. Rosenfeld and E. Croft-Murray, 'A Checklist of Scene Painters Working in Great Britain and Ireland in the 18th Century', *Theatre Notebook*, xix (1964), 12. One John Bromley wrote to S. on 14 May 1773, enclosed an account, and hoped 'that every article gives a general satisfaction': see Add. MS. 35118, f. 11.
[3] Elizabeth widow of John French (d. Oct. 1776), who had been house scene-painter at D.L.Th. under Garrick. See S. Rosenfeld and E. Croft-Murray, op. cit., p. 55.
[4] The first two sentences are quoted in S.C., 9 Nov. 1964, lot 441.

very readily do any thing in my Power to serve her, but I do not comprehend on what ground you inform me of your resolutions or her Creditors Threats to distress her. I conceive it would be better to recommend her writing a few lines herself, stating her situation—and what she requires | Yours | Obediently etc. | R B Sheridan.
Sunday evening
    Great-Queen-Street.

4. 'To the Freeholders of England'

Pub.: *The Englishman*, 13 Mar. 1779.[1]

Mar. 1779

Before I attempt to explain the plan of this publication, which it is intended to continue during the sitting of parliament (and after, if it appears to have gained the attention of the public) I think it necessary to repeat, that this introductory paper is addressed to, and solely calculated for, such of you plain Freeholders as have just sense enough to comprehend facts, when they are stated in plain language, and just spirit enough to form an opinion of your own from them, if you believe them to be true. Now if ever there was a crisis

---

[1] *The Englishman* was published in seventeen numbers between 13 Mar. and 2 June 1779, and consistently attacked North's administration for its incapacity and 'miserable attachment to place and pension'. For some discussion of the authorship of the seventeen issues, see Sichel, i. 593. S.'s part in writing them is still open to question. The *Staff. Adv.*, 20 July 1816, stated that he was active 'in the conduct of *The Englishman*—the whole of which passed through his hands to the bookseller, Mr. Wilkie'. John Wilkie's son, Thomas, wrote to Lord Holland to say, 'I think all the Letters marked with the signature D. were Mr. Sheridan's' (Holland House MS.; *Wm.*: 1817). This would make S. the author of nos. 1, 2, 4, 8, 13. A pencil note in the copy of *The Englishman* in the Bodleian Library (Hope fol. 16) suggests that all the papers under the signatures D, F, and H, were by S.: this would add nos. 10, 14, 15, 16, 17, to his total. Against these larger claims may be placed more modest estimates. O'Beirne declared to Moore that S. '*edited* it, but did not write', but Moore noted that this was 'all wrong'. John Townshend told him that S. wrote 'at least two . . . that on Lord George Germaine [no. 4] and the first' (Moore, *Journal*, ii. 295, 312). J. C. Hobhouse (Broughton, *Recollections of a Long Life* (1909), i. 204) quoted S. himself as saying (in his old age), 'I wrote the first two numbers'. Wilkie may well have been correct, but the only common factor in this conflict of evidence (and ignoring O'Beirne's strongly questioned statement) is that S. wrote the first number, given above.

when *you*, who are neither Scholars nor Gentlemen, might claim a right to judge, or even to act a little for yourselves, it is the present. When I say that you are not *scholars*, I do not mean to insinuate you are so entirely ignorant and incapable of forming right judgments, as some of your worthy representatives describe you to be; and when I say you are not *gentlemen*, I only mean to distinguish you as that class of the community, who are commonly called the *honest* and *industrious*. However, be your dispositions what they may, it is certain that any foreigner who had ever read the English history, and who, by residing here during the last seven years only, had been a witness to the wonderful speed with which the country has been reduced to its present distressed and contemptible situation by one sett of ministers, and those still continuing in trust and power:—I say, it is certain that such a one could form but these two conjectures on the subject—either that the constitution had been so changed, that the body of the people was now excluded from all possible right of judging or meddling *in any case whatever*, as much as the basest peasants of the most arbitrary government in Europe, or that the whole race of you must have become so thoroughly degenerate, that no injuries or calamities could provoke you even to reason on your situation.

Every well-wisher to the liberties and prosperity of this country, will wish to account for your strange insensibility by any other cause than this last: because if this really were the case, the whole affair is desperate. Rather than adopt this opinion, such a person will find out a hundred excuses for you; and luckily one of the first that presents itself is nearly sufficient to justify you: which is, that no Party has ever thought it worth while to give you *plain and authentic information* of facts and events from time to time, with little insight into characters and future expectations. This is absolutely your own excuse: and, be the event what it may, it will be no bad caution in you to begin pleading it to your children, to account for your leaving them (as they probably will be left, if you do not die so yourselves) beggars and slaves. For if it were supposed that from the first of this American *Rebellion* (as it used to be called, before his

Majesty, God bless him! altered his tone) there had been a simple detail of facts put into your hands, *containing* the direct assertions of his Majesty's ministers from the beginning; and on the other hand, the assertions of those who opposed them, with the events uniformly proving those ministers in the wrong—*containing* the hopes and promises of one side constantly failing, and the predictions of the other as regularly fulfilled, so that the blind infatuation or obstinate wickedness of one party, should seem not more wonderful, than the spirit of prophecy which appeared in the other—*containing* in short a list (and necessarily a very abridged one) of all the deceptions, falsehoods, and corrupt acts, by which these ministers have induced your complaisant representatives to trust them with near forty millions of your money, and near forty thousand of your fellow-subjects' lives for this strange war, with a brief account of the miserable blunders and impracticable plans, through which we have purchased only shame and present danger, at this moderate expence of treasure and blood.—Surely if such accounts *had* been punctually and faithfully laid before you, and you were now tamely enduring the situation these men have brought you into, it would not be too much to say, that you must be the most corrupt and abject pretenders to the privileges of *Englishmen*, or the title of *Freemen*, that ever assisted in betraying their country, without even the common policy of getting something by it; and, indeed, the only comfortable reflection to any one of a different Feeling would be, that there is no possible slavery or misery that could fall on you, which you would not *deserve*.

However, this is not to be dwelt on as a probable case. A late event has furnished ground for two conclusions of a different sort. The one is, that the spirit of *Englishmen* is *not* exhausted, nor even abated; the other, that this spirit is certainly to be reached by the plainest narrative of facts, where the relation carries with it the stamp of truth. It must be evident to you that the circumstance I refer to, is the manner in which the whole Country testified its sentiments on the acquittal of Admiral Keppel.[1] On this occasion there

---

[1] Keppel had been court-martialled for not pursuing battle. His acquittal was greeted with jubilation and anti-government riots.

certainly *did* appear many marks of that true indignation and resentment which, as a free people, you were ever accustomed to express against treachery and oppression. If the spirit shewn on this occasion had been seen in London only, it might have been said, however falsely, that it was industriously raised by the *friends* of the honourable admiral, or the *enemies* of Lord Sandwich: but the former have scarcely emissaries in every town and village of the kingdom; and the latter, however numerous they may be (as his lordship is pretty well known) were certainly not equal to the effects I speak of. The plain cause, then, of your appearing so suddenly roused on a particular question is, that it was a question of which you were made masters by distinct and regular information. The proceedings of the court-martial, published accurately enough as to facts in all the news-papers, came to you with sufficient authority, being uncontradicted, to justify your forming a judgment of your own; and that not a hasty one, as the intervals in the publication gave you time to reflect and communicate on what you had been reading, or had heard read.

That you are capable of judging also with some degree of discernment, is evident from the conclusions you formed on this business. You do not consider Mr. Keppel's acquittal as a matter of triumph merely because an innocent man had escaped from a malicious persecution; but you very properly thought the defeat of a treacherous and unprincipled minister (who appears, indeed, to have been created for the destruction and disgrace of your great constitutional defence, your navy)[1] a ground for the highest exultation to every honest Englishman; a better, it may be asserted, than any victory over your avowed enemies would be. The injuries which may fall on you from your armies or navies being defeated, is a matter you cannot have much notion of from experience; but there is not one of you but must have a pretty clear idea of what it is in the power of bad ministers to inflict on this country. A race of men who, if you were to measure enmity by the injuries proceeding from it, ought to be looked on as your only *natural enemies*.

[1] Sandwich was First Lord of the Admiralty, 1771–82. His name had become synonymous with corruption.

If it should be said to you, and you chuse to believe it, that it is mere presumption to suppose that the first lord of the admiralty, or any other of the ministry, were concerned in the notable scheme of ruining your gallant Whig Admiral, and that no *proof* of such a conduct has appeared, I can only say, that it is truly unfortunate for the noble lord that his character is of that stamp and notoriety, that the mere apparent baseness of any proceeding in his department, is sufficient to make all the good people of England believe he must be at the bottom of it. Nor does it immediately strike us, that other ministers must have been equally clear of the matter, because it was an *unlucky business, wretchedly conceived, and miserably ill calculated to obtain its object*; language, which, since its *failure*, their friends have very candidly bestowed on the whole of the prosecution.

This affair has been dwelt on the longer, because, in fact, the present address to you owes its birth to the evidence which it has afforded, that there is *still* a spirit left in the nation, equal to any constitutional exertion; and that this spirit, as before proved, is certainly to be raised and directed by a regular and unornamented appeal to the understandings of the middling class of people: who, notwithstanding the contempt which Gentlemen of certain principles affect to hold them in, have ever had, and ever will have, in times of actual peril, a deciding voice for the removal, and exemplary punishment of incapable or unprincipled ministers.

The reason why this mode of addressing you is preferred to that of a newpaper, is, that the channels of those motley publications, have of late fallen into particular disrepute on the chapter of politics.[1] For where the Paper takes a side, the virulence of gross partizans too readily finds a quick and convenient vent, in petulant paragraphs and bold assertions, wherein a strict adherence to *truth* is seldom considered as a necessary ingredient; and when the Paper affects impartiality (that dullest absurdity in political morality) the excessive ridicule of a string of opposing facts staring each

[1] Largely because of the use of the *Morning Post* by the administration for propaganda purposes, and of other newspapers by John Wilkes and his associates: see L. Werkmeister, *The London Daily Press, 1772–1792* (Lincoln, Nebraska, 1963), pp. 7–8.

other in the face, with columns of jarring paragraphs, giving and receiving the lie alternately; and contending correspondents, whose praise and abuse is carefully disposed to keep their patrons' characters in exact equilibrium, has on the whole just this effect, that plain Readers like *you*, unable to sum up so intricate a controversy, take the balance for granted, with the ready conclusion, that all parties are rogues alike.

Upon the whole, from these and other causes, the ill name which newspapers have got, does certainly counteract any effect which might otherwise be expected from many well written essays and shrewd observations: even our belief being never immediately granted to any assertions contained in them, unless to such points as extracts from the Gazette (when ministers are not concerned) or to accounts of matters of such notoriety as Admiral Keppel's trial.

The first object then of this publication will be, to merit that credit and confidence, which can only be obtained by a strict and uniform adherence to *truth* in all *assertions*, *charges*, and *relations of events*, and a direct and ingenuous method of arguing and drawing conclusions from them.

On this principle, the whole pretensions of this publication will be rested; and if in any single instance it shall ever be made appear to your unbiassed judgments, that the writer has advanced a direct Falsehood (in the manner of Lord S. in the House of Lords) or with pitiful equivocations evaded the Truth (in the manner of Lord N. in the House of Commons) let the undertaking meet with that contempt and opposition which is due to such a conduct, though supported by such high authorities.

The chief objects for your consideration, which it is proposed to lay before you will be,

1st, A Brief recapitulation of the conduct of the administration in the principal facts relating to the American war, and its *consequences*—without any other comment than simply contrasting the *opinions* and *predictions* of the ministry with those of their opposers, and stating the events which have decided between them.

2dly, Early intelligence of the councils actually adopted

by government, and preparing to be carried into execution, whether relating to war or peace, and the outlines of the plans depending on them.

3dly, Faithful and ungarbled narrations of the success of all enterprizes, and the events of all expeditions naval and military, for which the ministers have obtained so ample and unprecedented a provision of men and money!

4thly, A Regular detail of every principal business agitated by your representatives—with the sum of the arguments on both sides—and on important questions a list of the voters—which perhaps may be thought worthy of your attention, at a period certainly not very distant from a general election.

In the course of this it is probable, that some papers may be addressed to particular persons in power; but you will pardon the interruption, if it serves to give you insights into the characters and views of those, to whose *abilities* and *principles* this country is at present content to trust, not her welfare merely, but her actual existence as a nation.

In the mean time, it is only required of you not blindly to credit the monstrous assertions of those, who would persuade you, that although we have been *unfortunate*, although we have been *misinformed*, although we have been *ill-treated*; in short, although the nation is reduced from the first station of glory and prosperity, to a situation of general contempt in the eyes of Europe, and daily increasing misery at home, yet *ministers have not been to blame.*

If there is any one among you who has entered into the detail of these ministers' justification, or has any single charge which has been brought against them done away to his satisfaction, I will allow him to support this opinion: otherwise, the single great fact of the present situation of your country, ought to be argument sufficient to convince you that you must have been wronged.

For whatever information may be laid before you of the misconduct of your ministers, or whatever palliation of it may be attempted, one powerful rule for the mass of the people to form their judgment on will for ever remain, which is—that *wise men produce wise measures; and wise measures are generally successful measures.*

This may be excepted against as an unfair argument, and instances may be brought of the wisest statesmen being uniformly foiled in their plans; while some may assert that our affairs *would* have been prosperous, that our cause *would* have prevailed, and all our plans and expeditions *would* have succeeded, *but* for mere ill-luck—to be sure in a very extraordinary number of circumstances: such as winds, waves, spies, fire, friends, foes, factions, and, above all, in a continual *unlucky* choice of Generals, Admirals, Allies, and Ambassadors! all this any ministerial advocate may affect to believe, but it is impossible that any of you can either comprehend or credit a single syllable of it.

However, waving all argument from the mass of ill success, and without proceeding to accuse any person as the cause, your assent for the present is only required to this one assertion, a fact left for you to reflect on, and which you will find no person whatever attempt to dispute, viz.

THAT THERE DOES NOT EXIST, NOR EVER DID EXIST A NATION WHICH HAS EXPERIENCED LOSSES AND DISGRACES OF THAT MAGNITUDE, WHICH THE KINGDOM OF GREAT-BRITAIN HAS UNDER THE PRESENT ADMINISTRATION.

D.   THE ENGLISHMAN.

5. To ——

Widener MS. *Dock.* [by S]: Renters not to be renew'd.

$[1789–91]$[1]

Proposals for paying off The several Mortgages on Drury Lane Theatre and exonerating Dr. Ford from remaining in the security for the same and for rebuilding the said Theatre and Houses thereto Belonging according to the following Plan.

—It is proposed to assign the whole Property to four Trustees.

---

[1] S. purchased Ford's quarter for £18,000 on 16 Sept. 1788, and assigned it to Greenwood and Sleigh on 18 Oct. 1788, to secure the payment of £8,500 to Morland and Hammersley. This sum was due on a bond from S. and Westley: see 'Drury Lane Theatre General Abstract' (Garrick Club MS.), f. 20.

The above incumbrances which are proposed to be so paid off are as follows—

Upon the Moiety purchased of W. Lacy Esqr. by R. B. S. there are two mortgages one of 22,000, to D. G., the other of £5,000 to Franco and 2,000 these incumbrances.

Upon the Quarter purchased by Mr. S of Dr. Ford there is a mortgage of £8500 to Messrs Hammersley.

Upon the Quarter belonging to Mr. Linley a sum of 6,000 due to G. and 6,000 due to Ford.

These several sums make
$$\begin{cases} 22,000 \\ 5,000 \\ 2,000 \\ 6,000 \\ 6,000 \\ 8,500 \end{cases}$$

49,500

6. [To Prospective Subscribers to the Rebuilding of Drury Lane Theatre]

Gilmore MS. Copy. *Dock.*: [by Henry Holland] Proposal for rebuilding the Theatre Royal in Drury Lane Nov. 5 1791 Copy from Mr. Sheridans MS.

5 Nov. 1791

Proposal for Rebuilding the Theatre Royal in Drury Lane upon an insulated Plan to be surrounded by four Rows of Houses.

Whereas His Grace the Duke of Bedford by a deed bearing date ——[1] has covenanted to grant to the Proprietors of the Theatre Royal in Drury Lane a Lease of all the said Theatre Ground and Premises now in their Possession for the further term of 99 years to commence on the expiration of their present Lease in the year[2]

And whereas his Grace for the further accommodation of

---

[1] 30 July 1791. The draft proposals were amended and enlarged in a document of the same name and dated 25 Nov. 1791 (Widener MS.).

[2] The Widener MS. reads: 'for the Term of 99 years from Christmas 1795 (which with the present leases makes a term of 104 years from Christmas last feast). . . .'

316

the said Proprietors and in order that a perfect and magnificent Theatre may be erected to be surrounded with proper[1] Taverns, Coffee houses, Public Houses, and Shops, with Houses, Chambers, and Apartments proper to be rented by[2] the numerous Persons connected with the Theatre has purchased the estates of ———[3] so as compleatly to insulate the Theatre with its own appropriate Buildings. The whole of which Purchases His Grace has also covenanted to lease to the Proprietors of Drury Lane Theatre for the Term of one hundred and four years from the present Time[4] at the rate of 4 per cent per annum[5] on the purchase money

And Whereas The Proprietors of Drury Lane Theatre have agreed with Thomas Harris Esq for purchase of the Dormant Patent belonging to Covent Garden Theatre which with the consent of His Majesty's Lord Chamberlain and the Duke of Bedford as expressed in the Agreement lodged with Messrs Moreland and Hammersley, is to be perpetually and inseparably annex'd to the new Theatre Royal to be built in Drury Lane[6]

And Whereas the said proprietors of Drury Lane Theatre have in the said deed and lease bound themselves within the space of two years[7] to erect and compleat a new theatre with buildings surrounding upon the annexed extensive and magnificent scale.

It is proposed in order to effect the same in a manner not liable to disappointment or future embarrassment to raise a Fund sufficient to pay off all the present Incumbrances in the said Property as well as to afford a Surplus adequate to

[1] The Widener MS. reads: 'commodious'.

[2] Mention of rent is omitted in the Widener MS. which reads: 'fit for the accommodation of'.

[3] Premises in Drury Lane and Little Russell Street bought by the Duke of Bedford from Trevor Cuckow and others: see 'Drury Lane Theatre General Abstract' (Garrick Club MS.), ff. 23–28.

[4] The Widener MS. reads: '103 years from the 25th day of December next'.

[5] No percentage is mentioned in the Widener MS., but the Garrick Club MS. mentions a charge of 4 per cent. 'on

such Premises as the Duke should purchase'.

[6] S.'s belief in its value is to be seen, in 1801, in the 'Outline of the Terms on which it is proposed that Mr. Kemble shall purchase a Quarter in the Property of Drury Lane Theatre' (Harvard MS.): see Moore, ii. 305, for 'the value . . . is out of all comparison'.

[7] The Widener MS. reads: 'the Trust Deeds shall contain a clause to compel the said proprietors to complete the Building according to the annexed plan on or before the 31st day of December 1793'.

ensure the accomplishment of the whole of the Plan by granting Two Hundred and Forty Mortgages Renters Shares of £500[1] each upon a proper Trust and upon the following terms

The shares shall be for the whole of the Term of the Leases and the price £500

Each share will entitle the Holder to a rent of 2s. 6d. upon every Night of Performance and with a Right of Free Admission to all Entertainments whatever—[2]

The shares to be numbered and countersigned by the Trustees and to be placed in every respect on the same footing as the £300 renters—Shares granted by the late David Garrick Esqr. in the Year ——[3] with this Material difference in favor of the present Share viz: the Rents granted by Mr. Garrick were a charge on the Profits of the Theatre after the many prior Mortgages and Incumbrances

And in the present case the whole Theatre, Patents, Property and Houses are to be assigned in the Security of these Shares extinguishing all other Mortgages.

Each Mortgage-Renter to have a Separate assignable Deed and Title to his Share

The whole of the Property, The Theatre Patents, Leases, Scenes, Wardrobe Furniture as well as all the Houses in the annexed Plan to be assigned by way of Mortgage to Four Trustees[4] in whom shall be invested all powers which Council shall judge necessary for the security of the said Shares. And for the further securing of the Punctual Payments of the Dividends on the said Shares The Treasurer of the Theatre shall give good and sufficient Security to the satisfaction of the Trustees that he will on each and every night

---

[1] The Widener MS. adds to the number, stating 'That 300 Rent Charges shall be granted at the price of £500 each'.

[2] The Widener MS. reads: 'That the Rent charges shall be made transferable and the Grantees or assignees shall have the privilege of annually nominating or appointing the person to be intitled to the admission in respect of every such rent charge provided notice . . . be given . . . in writing.'

[3] Cf. i. 166, n. 2. Note, also, the 'Renters Book' (Folger MS.), that names the 'Renters [£ ?] 400 Shares Granted Septr. 1775 for 21 years and paid 192 Nights for Season 1794–5' a sum of £19. 4s. each. The Widener MS. omits the paragraph referring to the shares granted by Garrick.

[4] The Widener MS. reads: 'the Trustees to be immediately named shall be Albany Wallis Esq. Richard Ford Esq., and Thomas Hammersley Esq.'

of Performance set apart and reserve the Sum of Thirty Pounds[1] or 2s. 6d. for each Share, and once in every week pay over the same into the Hands of such Banker as shall be agreed upon between the Proprietors of the said Theatre by the Trustees and to the account of the said Trustees.

Provided always that whatever may be the number of Performances in one Season the Dividends to the Holders of the Shares are never to exceed five and half Per Cent and if by any accident or Public Calamity the number of performances should at any time be diminished so as to reduce the Dividends to less than four and a half Per Cent in any Season then the Treasurer shall be bound to encrease the Dividend on the ensueing Season to five and half Per Cent whatever may be the number of nights of performance[2]

No new or additional incumbrance of any sort is ever to be charged upon this Property, and the present existing Renters Shares and Free Admissions shall never be renewed but be extinguished as they fall in unless upon any unforeseen accident happening to the Theatre The Trustees shall deem it expedient to make use of such resource for the Benefit of the Property

The Proprietors of Drury Lane Theatre have agreed with the Duke of Bedford in the Deed before mentioned, that His Grace shall insure the Theatre to its full value and add the expence of the same to the rent of the Theatre,[3] But in case of any neglect of such insurance on the whole value of the Property not being fully insured the Trustees shall be at Liberty to insure the whole of the Property, and to draw on the Treasurer for the usual amount.

Upon the Death of any of the Trustees a meeting of the Mortgage Renters shall be called by Publick advertisement and their nomination is always to supply the vacancy.[4]

[1] The Widener MS. reads: '£37. 10. 0.'
[2] This paragraph is omitted in the Widener MS.
[3] The Widener MS. reads: 'That the whole of the premises Scenery Machinery Wardrobe and Furniture shall be insured and kept insured against Fire for the full value of the same.' 'Drury Lane Theatre General Abstract' (Garrick Club MS.), f. 29, noted, that the Duke 'might insure the theatre etc. in £20,000 and pay the Duty', and that S. and Linley should recoup him by paying an additional rent of eighty pounds. See also Ian Donaldson, 'New Papers of Henry Holland and R. B. Sheridan', *Theatre Notebook*, xvi (1962), 94–96.
[4] 'Each person having as many Votes as he possesses Rent charges' (Widener MS.).

Each Subscriber to deposit One Hundred Pounds upon a proper Deed of Trust being executed and the Patents and other securities being lodged with the Trustees. A further Payment of two hundred Pounds to be made on Midsummer Day next and the further and last payment of two Hundred Pounds upon the opening of the New Theatre[1]

These several sums to be paid to the Trustees and proper receipts to be given by them to the Subscribers

Interest of Five Per Cent to be paid on the several advances, and each Subscriber to be entitled to the Freedom of the King's Theatre until that of Drury Lane is rebuilt.

This engagement not to be binding on the Subscribers, nor any deposit to be call'd for until *the whole of the said Sum of One Hundred and Twenty Thousand Pounds*[2] *shall be subscribed.*

As the whole of the Sum is to be payable to the Trustees only, it is to be issuable only by their order, and applicable to the following purposes alone.

Viz. First to the Paying off and extinguishing all the present Mortgage, Incumbrances, and then the whole of the surplus to be applied to the expences of pulling down and rebuilding the Theatre Royal in Drury Lane and other charges attending to the same according to the annexed Plan and Estimate and to no other purpose whatsoever

All further expence attending the New Theatre of internal decoration, New Stock of Scenery or Furniture of Houses etc. and not included in the annexed Estimate to be borne from the Profits of the Theatre or the Rents of Private Boxes,[3] but no further subscription to be required or any addition to be made to the present proposed number of subscribers which is finally limited to 240.[4]

John Maddocks and Arthur Piggot Esqrs. or such other

---

[1] The Widener MS. arranges for an immediate payment of £100; a further £150 on delivery of the 'Declarations of Trust'; £100, 'on the Theatre being covered in'; and £100 at the opening.

[2] Not mentioned in the Widener MS. It substitutes 'unless the whole number of Rent charges shall be subscribed for within 6 weeks from the date hereof'.

[3] The proprietors were to be 'at liberty to raise the same [i.e. 'Expences beyond what is provided for by the Estimate hereafter set forth'] by Leases of private boxes not exceeding 15 in a number or for a longer term than 14 years such leases being countersigned by the Trustees' (Widener MS.).

[4] Increased to 300 in the Widener MS.

Counsel as the Trustees with the approbation of the subscribers shall nominate To prepare the proper Deeds for
carrying the above Plan and Trust into Execution in which
Deed are to be inserted all Clauses Provisions, and Declarations as in their Opinion shall be proper or necessary for
effectuating the Trust proposed, and for securing the rights
and Interest of the Subscribers to the proposal[1]

The present incumbrances and Estimate of the New
Buildings are as follow:

Due on Mortgage to Messrs Garrick and Franco made by Wm[2] Lacy previous to the moiety being purchased by Mr. Harrison the present Proprietor	£31,000
Additional Mortgage on the same moiety since to Mr. Weebley[3]	2,000
Mortgage to Mr. Garrick from Mr. Linley on two quarter Shares	8,000
Ditto to Dr. Ford from Ditto	7,000
Mortgage to Messrs Ransom Morland and Hammersley on the Quarter purchased from Dr. Ford by Mr. Sheridan	8,500
Ditto on the same Quarter to Skinner and others	4,500
Total incumbrances	**61,000**

---

[1] The remainder of the material is not in the Widener MS.

[2] Copyist's error for 'Willoughby'. The 'Drury Lane Theatre General Abstract' (Garrick Club MS.), ff. 30–42, lists the following encumbrances: to Wallis, as Garrick's surviving executor and on Lacy's account, £22,000 principal, £5,972. 14s. 8d. interest, and £325 for costs. The Francos were owed £5,000 principal, and £1,660 interest. Linley owed Wallis (for Garrick's estate) £8,900 principal, and £895. 18s. interest. S. owed James Ford £7,700 principal, and £256. 6s. 11d. interest. S. owed Morland and Hammersley £8,500 on the share purchased by S. from Ford, and £209. 0s. 6d. interest. S. owed £2,000 to, jointly, Thomas Skinner, Robert Wilkes, H. C. Combe, John Currie, George Shum, Nathaniel Newnham, and Nathaniel Wright, as well as £193. 17s. 2d. Westley had advanced S. £3,491. 17s. 11d., and was also owed £417. 16s. interest.

[3] Copyist's error for 'Westley'.

7. To Thomas Greenwood

Roe-Byron MS. C. 68 / 326, pp. 1–4, Newstead Abbey (Nottingham Corporation). [Ph.] *Address*: Mr. Greenwood

[*1794–7*]

My Dear Sir,
  Suspend other Operations a little—and look to the Scenery of 'the *Haunted Tower*'[1] which I am wit[t]ling down into an after-Piece and have good hopes of—it will be brought out on Saturday sev'night and tell Johnson from me to look after his Part of it. I think we might use some of our first of June[2] Sea-Scenery in the opening of the first act[3]— or if anything could be done so as to say new Scenery without expence it would be well— | Your's truly | R B Sheridan Wednesday Night

8. [To Members of the Piscatory Party]

Yale MS.[4] *Wm*.: 1794

[*After 1794*][5]

Piscatory Party
in commemoration of Isaac Walton

Rules and Regulations for the same.

1st Each male member of the Party shall forthwith subscribe the sum of five Pounds 5 shillings towards the general expences.

2d That each Subscriber do really pay the same into the Hands of the Treasurer.

---

[1] James Cobb's comic opera was first produced on 24 Nov. 1789 at D.L.Th.

[2] For *The Glorious First of June*, see ii. 12, n. 4. In 1797 it was altered to become *Cape St. Vincent, or British Valour Triumphant*.

[3] It is worth noting that *The Glorious First of June* was presented at D.L.Th. on 18 Oct. 1795, and that on Monday, 20 Oct., *The Haunted Tower* was given, though not as an afterpiece.

[4] It bears the note: 'The accompanying Manuscript of Richard Brinsley Sheridan Esqr. was presented to the Walton and Cotton Club—and the autograph vouched by W. Dunn 22 Charlotte Street Bedford Square 9 May 1814.'

[5] Cf. S.C., 15 July 1929, lot 48, where it is reasonably dated 'c. 1800', and is published in part. See ii. 102–3.

3d Such Payment shall be made on or before the first of May, or the member making Default shall not be admitted but on the payment of ten guineas

Henry Ogle Esqr is appointed Treasurer—He is to keep an accurate [account] of his disbursements to be submitted to the members on the breaking up of the Party—and it would not be amiss if the said Henry Ogle were

4 to take that opportunity of producing his accounts and *vouchers* as Treasurer of the Isle of Wight Party

5 Henry Scott Esqr. Captain of the Light Infantry of the South Hants to be deputy Treasurer and Collector of the said Subscriptions in the Town Department—The said Captain having given a great Proof of ability for that office in as much as He has already collected five guineas from Gigas alias Mathew Lee Esqr. and the Society have the strongest Hopes that He will give an equally unexpected Proof of his integrity by paying over the said sum into the Hands of Henry Ogle—

6 No Person can arrive at the Honor of belonging to this Party but by the Unanimous consent of the existing members—

7 A Journal is to be kept of the occurrences of each Day which among other interesting matters is to contain an account of the number of Fish Caught, their respective weights, by whom caught etc. etc. The said Journal is at a proper time to be printed and publish'd and Altho' the Party are confident that the said Journal will also be a record of wit Humour Pleasantry and possibly even

8 of deep observation from the acknowledged and vario[u]s Talents of the said Party, yet disdaining all personal advantage it is resolved in humble imitation of the example set by the Revd. W. L. Bowles[1] that in case any copies of the said Fresh-water Log book should be sold the Profits shall be solely applied to the Benefit of the Widows[2] and Orphans of deceased Fishermen—

9 No Drawing, Painting, Sketch or Model of any Trout shall be taken at the general Expence unless such Fish shall have exceeded the weight of five Pounds and shall

---

[1] Cf. ii. 222, n. 2.   [2] Manuscript, 'Widoows'.

have been bona fide caught by one of the Party and not privately bought at Stockbridge.

10 Any member describing the strength size and weight of any immense Fish which He had skillfully hook'd, dexterously play'd with, and successfully brought to the Bank safe, by the Clumsiness of the man with the landing Net 'only conceive how provoking!' the said Fish got off—shall forfeit half a guinea—and so toties quoties for every such Narrative—to prevent unnecessary trouble the said Forfeits are to be collected by the said John Ogle.

11 There shall be but one hot meal in the course of the Day and that shall be a Supper at nine o'clock—Cold meat and other refreshments in the Tents or at the waterside at two o'clock.

12 A committee is to be appointed to provide these Repasts —which shall be call'd and entitled the Catering Committee, and their Decision both as to Lunch and supper shall be Final. Captain Scott to prepare the said lunch[?]

13 Any Member willing to send in any Stores for the general Benefit at his own expence shall be permitted so to do, and entitled to be laughed at accordingly.

14 Grace is to be said before supper by the Rev. J. Ogle, and after supper by the Revd. W. L. Bowles.[1]

15 All Fish by whomsoever caught are to be consider'd as general Property—and if there are sufficient to send any as Presents, The choice of the Fish shall be determined by Lot always excepting such as shall be sent to the Deanery,[2] which are to be a Tribute from the Firm.

16 Any Gentleman falsely shabbily and treacherously concealing the number of Fish he had caught, and slily sending off the same as a Present to ladies or others shall forfeit on Detection one guinea for each Fish he purloin'd from the company Stock and be publickly reprimanded at Supper for the —— Mr. T. Sheridan is not to order less than ——

17 Any Person restless and fidgety presuming to insinuate that Sea Fishing is preferable to the tame and tranquil

---

[1] Regulation 14 is cancelled.   [2] Of Winchester.

occupations of this Party, and endeavoring to inveigle from their Duty on board the Phaedria any of the leige and dutiful subjects of Isaac Walton shall on conviction be sentenced to fourteen minutes abstinence from all Beer Porter Wine Brandy Rum Gin Hollands Grogg Shrubb Punch Toddy Turpins Caulkers[1]—Pipe Segar Quid—Shag—Pigtail—Short-cut varinas canaster and Pideto—and if such culprit shall appeal against the severity of the above sentence as a Punishment disproportion'd to the utmost excess of human Delinquency He shall be entitled to have the hearing and Mr. Nathaniel Ogle assign'd to him as counsel.

A copy of these Rules and Regulations fairly and legibly transcribed is to be posted over the chimney of the eating Room of the Society House at Leckford. Provided the Pannell on any side of the said Room is of size to contain such Paper—if not authentic copies thereof shall be delivered to each member. No Way-farer begging Charity is to be relieved from the general Fund—the appeal of all such must be to the detach'd generosity of the Individual.

If any of the Party deserting the Rod shall assume the Gun it is recommended to them, as white-w[h]ales are not likely to be seen, and Black whales are unworthy their Pursuit to direct all their attention to Green Whalles[2] alias Plovers which will afford not merely good Sport to the Shooter but considerable aid to the larder. The Revd. John Ogle is not to chew the Tobacco call'd Pigtail after Sunset— as He will then join the Society of the Ladies nor for the same rea[son] is Joseph Richardson Esqr. M. P.[3] and author of The Fugitives to flick his snuff about during supper even tho' he should have been competing with Nat Ogle. | R B Sheridan

[1] A dram. In the *O.E.D.* its earliest usage is dated 1808.
[2] Possibly 'Wheele[r]s'. The 'wheeler' is the night-jar, but the reference may be to green plovers (lapwings).

[3] For Newport, Cornwall, 1796– 1803. *The Fugitive*, a five-act comedy, was produced at the King's Theatre by the D.L.Th. company, on 20 Apr. 1792.

9. To ——

Add. MS. 35118, f. 64 *Dock.*: R B S Security

August 1st. *1795*

Messrs Westley and Peake the Treasurers of the Theatre Royal in Drury Lane being engaged in several securities for the Proprietors and in advance of monies for liquidating the accounts of the said Theatre the Proprietors hereby make over to them the Debts of their Royal Highnesses the Prince of Wales and the Duke of York the Duke of Portland Lord Coventry Mr. Bamfeild[1] Lady Bath[2] etc. and all other Debts due on account of Boxes to the said Proprietors and the money[s] received on account of the said Debts are to go in Part of Payment of the sums advanced or engaged for by the said Treasurer. | R B Sheridan | For self and Mr. Linley

10. To ——

Harvard MS. *Dock.*: Tu: Octr. 13th, 1795

13 Oct. 1795

Notice in writing must be sent to the Treasury every Saturday morning of all articles wanted for the ensuing week.

11. To 'Mr. Graham'

Osborn MS. *Address*: Mr. Graham | North-Place | Gray's Inn Lane *Dock.*: Sheridan

[1795–1801]

My Dear Sir,

I beg *very particularly* you will let me see you at *eleven* tomorrow morning. | Yrs truly | R B Sheridan
Saturday Evening
Hertford-St.

---

[1] Sir Charles Bampfylde (1753–1823) was on friendly terms with S.: see Kelly, ii. 56. The reference may be to one of his brothers, either Amias or Richard.

[2] Henrietta Pulteney (1766–1808) was a baroness in her own right. She married General Sir James Murray on 24 July 1794.

12. [To a Member of the Lord Chamberlain's Staff]

Pub.: Parke-Bernet Catalogue, New York, 22 Oct. 1963, lot 373.

23 May 1797[1]

[Explaining why he is late delivering a text of the play.]

13. [To George Canning]

The Earl of Harewood MS.: George Canning 66a (Leeds Central Library). [Ph.]

[24 Apr. 1798 ?]

Private

Your Letter was perfectly to the Purpose,[2] and I think the Prince is sincerely convinced that should his application to the King[3] fail it is in no respect to be attributed to Mr. D.[4] or any of the ministers. I certainly think He might be easily gratified but am not the least judge of the objections. I have hitherto been of opinion that He should make his application thro' the Ministers and not by a direct appeal to the King; The circumstances under which They stand on this subject put that out of the Question, and yet it was with

[1] This letter is laid in a copy of *Pizarro*, and may be no. 367: see ii. 118, n. 1.

[2] Canning was Under-Secretary of State for Foreign Affairs, 1796–9. In a letter to S. (Osborn MS.) merely dated 'Thursday', McMahon suggested that Canning's optimism had affected the Prince: 'You cannot avoid, my Good Friend, to detest me as an Eternal Tormentor. I was honor'd with a Letter yesterday, and another this day from The P! I know you love him in your Soul and I would swear that He Loves you! Could you read all that he feels at your neglect of him, at this eventful moment, it would cut you to the heart My Dear Friend. His Royal Highness is more wretched than I can express at not having a single line even from you; and the hopes of Success which you

convey'd to him, as being Canning's sentiment, has led him to be perhaps too sanguine. He relies upon your se[e]ing Mr. D tomorrow and reporting to him the result of what relates to him. For Heaven Sake, press the business quickly, for I know *from the best Authority* that it does not admit of delay. . . .'

[3] On 25 Apr. 1798 the Prince of Wales wrote a long letter to the King asking for a military command in spite of the King's previous objections. He mentioned 'a Crisis like this, unexampled in our History, when every Subject in the Realm is eagerly seeking for, and has his post assign'd him . . .' (Sidmouth MS.; copy). The King again refused the application.

[4] Henry Dundas was Secretary for War, 1794–1801.

difficulty I convinc'd him of the impropriety of his continuing to ask them to disobey the King's Commands. The End is a Letter from him to the King, which He will chuse his own mode of conveying, sending a Copy of it, as a proper attention to the Cabinet.

Thus it was settled this morning and the Letter written—since which I met him at the Opera[1] and He told me He had appointed Mr. Wyndham[2] to call on him tomorrow—on which I could only say that I could not see the use or meaning of it, but if no alteration in his Plan takes place The Letter will go in the morning to the King,[3] I should think by the Chancellor,[4] and a Copy of it to Mr. Dundass. | Yours truly | R B Sheridan
Tuesday Evening.

14. To Lord Holland

Holland House MS. *Address*: Lord Holland | Holland House

[*July 1797–Nov. 1801 ?*]

My Dear Lord
I meant to have deserted a Party long invited to dine here tomorrow and to have had the Pleasure of obeying your's and Lady Hollands commands but I find I must not do it, and am obliged to send this excuse.

Will you dine with me tomorrow sev'night to meet *Harry* Erskine?[5] | Your Lordship's | ever truly | R B Sheridan
Hertford St
Saturday Evening

[1] *Il Matrimonio Segreto* was given at the King's Theatre on 24 Apr. 1798. Windham was present (see *The Diary of . . . Windham* (ed. Baring, 1866), p. 394), but I can find no report of the Prince's attendance.

[2] Windham was Secretary at War, 1794–1801. He dined with the Prince on 1 May (ibid). The *Salopian Journal*, 9 May 1798, reported that he saw the Prince at Carlton House on 'Saturday',

about a rank in the army for the Prince.

[3] *The Times*, 27 Apr. 1798, reported that the Prince and the Duke of York 'had audiences of the King yesterday at Buckingham House'.

[4] Loughborough.

[5] Henry Erskine (1746–1817), brother of Thomas Erskine, and Lord Advocate, 1783 and 1806–7. For his wit and gaiety, see Campbell, vi. 704–8.

15. To Richard Peake or William Dunn

Butler Library MS., Columbia University.

8 Jan. 1800

Give Mr. Burgess £10—on my account— | R B Sheridan
Mr. Peake or Dunn
Jany. 8th 1800

16. [To George Canning]

The Earl of Harewood MS.: George Canning 66a (Leeds Central Library). [Ph.] *Wm.*: 1796

[19 July 1800 ?][1]
Saturday

I was certainly misunderstood if it was supposed that I intended to take any step or make any motion on monday—and I am perfectly sensible that every effort to do any real good must stand the better for being previously communicated to Those who have the best means of information both as to the Peril and the Resources of the Country. As you say you are going out of Town tomorrow and I must go to Woburn on Tuesday I think we had better meet at the Theatre this evening— | your's truly | R B S.

[1] The letter seems to belong to the period (Jan. 1796–Feb. 1801), when Canning was in office, first as Under-Secretary of State, and, afterwards, as Joint Paymaster-General. He became a member of the Privy Council on 28 May 1800, and spoke at length in the debate on subsidies to the Emperor of Germany on 18 July. S.'s concern over foreign affairs at this period is shown in his motion (27 June) for 'a call of the House on the present awful conjuncture', and his support (9 July) of Western's motion for a committee on the state of the nation. Possibly a rumour was current that S. intended to speak on foreign affairs on 21 July, when all he really intended to do was to support Burdett. See ii. 134–5.

17. To Lord or Lady Holland

Holland House MS. *Address*: Lord or Lady Holland | Holland-House

[*22 Dec. 1800?*]

Monday

I have cross-examined The Sorcerors, Imps Furies, and Devils in the New Pantomime[1] and there certainly is neither Cannon Gun Pistol or cracker in the Piece—an innocent Bengal-Light in a Lighthouse and a little muf[f]led Thunder are the only things in the Fire or noise way

However I advise Lady Holland not to go—for should this turn out not a good [one] a Pantomime is never worth seeing till after the second or third [performance]—and ours I learn is very imperfect— | R B S

18. To William Godwin

Lord Abinger MS. [Ph.] *Address*: W. Godwin Esqr.[2] | Polygon[3] | Somers Town *Fr.*: R B Sheridan *Dock.*: 1802

6 Jan. 1802 [*?*]

Dear Sir

I assure you I have done everything in my Power to disengage myself from every particular business which at this moment I am compelled to attend to in order to have the Pleasure of waiting on you and meeting the company you

[1] Possibly *Harlequin-Amulet, or, The Magic of Mona*, given at D.L.Th. on Monday, 22 Dec. 1800.

[2] The political philosopher, novelist, and publisher (1756–1836). His tragedies, *Antonio* and *Faulkner*, were performed at D.L.Th. on 13 Dec. 1800 and 16 Dec. 1807, with no success. He admired S., attended his funeral, and 'visited his grave many times'. He recalled with particular pleasure a party at Kemble's that was attended by S.,

Curran, and Mrs. Inchbald. 'The conversation took a most animated turn and the subject was of Love' (F. K. Brown, *The Life of William Godwin* (1926), pp. 310, and (quoting Hazlitt) 370). J. P. Kemble's diary (Add. MS. 31973, f. 272) gives particulars to suggest that this was a dinner party on 27 Oct. 1799.

[3] Godwin lived there between 6 Apr. 1797 and Aug. 1807. See *Shelley and his Circle, 1773–1822* (ed. K. N. Cameron, 1961), i. 185, 211, 215, 236–42.

mention tomorrow—but I absolutely cannot do it which I very much regret— | I am Dear Sir | yours very truly | R B Sheridan
Wednesday
Jan 6th [?]

19. To Charles Ward

Pub.: S.C., 15 Dec. 1964, lot 525.

[3 Jan. 1806]
Pavilion, Thursday

. . . I was suddenly sent for by the Prince on a matter of the greatest importance and meant to have returned to Town to Day—I share in your affliction[1] most sincerely—you ought to have received £20 by yesterday's Post. I swear to you most solemnly that the enclosed draft shall also be punctually answer'd. I enclose also the order on Mrs. Linley[2] she ought not to hesitate a moment—In the melancholy state matters are I almost fear to hear from you. . . .[3]

20. To Arthur Morris, High Bailiff of Westminster

Pub.: *The Times*, 10 Nov. 1806.

Somerset Place, Nov. 1806

Sir,
    I have this moment been honoured with your Letter; I am confident I need not assure you, that, from the commence-

---

[1] Jane Ward's last illness. On 22 Dec. 1805, Ward had written to S. (Osborn MS.) to say that he had hurried to Iver and found her 'as ill as my worst fears had apprehended'. He added, 'it is now six years since I confided in your promises to do justice to her claims by an equivalent for that property of hers, you have held in your hands . . . for that period I have struggled against want and the importunity of Creditors, you have done nothing, but the time is now arrived when I am pledged to payment and must stand the consequence of failure—Remember my being separated from a wife in the last gaspings of life by your neglect is an event, no future compunction, no activity of exertion can recall, there is still time to avert it. It is due to poor Jane, it is due to justice, it is due to your own Character.'

[2] She wrote to Ward on 3 Jan. 1806 (Osborn MS.), to say that she was too unwell to come to Iver, but that she would be (as Ward noted) 'a Mother to the poor deprived Babes'.

[3] Lot 525 at this sale also included a letter by S. to the Rev. Edward Ward, promising to attend Jane's funeral. Cf. ii. 256–7.

ment of the Election, I have felt and expressed the greatest anxiety to oppose and suppress every thing tending to tumult and disturbance, and even to dissuade from unruly and illiberal personalities, either by words or prints; and I pledge my word to you, that no provocation shall induce me to depart from this line of conduct. I have transmitted your Letter to the Committee who, I doubt not, will immediately adopt your suggestion,[1] which is an extremely proper one, and such as the Candidates ought to be obliged to you for proposing. | I have the honour to be | Your obedient servant, | Richard Brinsley Sheridan
A Morris, Esq.

21. To [C. ?] James[2]

Pub.: N. E. Enkvist, 'British and American Literary Letters in Scandinavian Public Collections', *Acta Academiae Aboensis*, Humaniora, xxvii. 3 (Åbo, 1964), 104, from the Palsbo MS., Royal Library, Copenhagen.

Richmond-hill
Wednesday, Oct. 7 [*1807*]

My Dear Sir,
    Are you in Town? and when will it be most convenient to yourself for me to see you respecting what remains unsettled with Sir W. Geary which has been unaccountably neglected? | Yours truly | R. B. Sheridan
—James Esqre:

[1] A copy of Morris's letter to S. is printed in the same issue: candidates had asked him to exercise his authority to prevent confusion at the election, but he suggested that order would be best attained by 'a deputation from each Committee, to be stationed at the end of the Hustings which leads to the Pollbooks'. Peter Moore then advertised that the High Bailiff's suggestion would be adopted.

[2] I assume that this (like No. 495) is written to Charles James, because he was the partner of Abel Jenkins, Geary's solicitor; but the possibility remains (in spite of S.'s unreliability in the matter of initials) that both letters were (like No. 704) to W. James. *Clarke's New Law List* (1812), p. 68, includes William James, 39 Lucas Street, and William Robert James, 3 Earle Street, among the London attorneys.

22. To Richard Peake

Pub.: S. C., 15 Dec. 1964, lot 250.

[*1808 ?*]

One Tun. Thursday past seven[1]

You must come to me here instantly. . . .

23. To Thomas Harris

Folger MS.: 'Covent Garden Theatre Scrapbooks', ix. Copy in the hand of James Winston, who dates the letter 1808.

1808

Dear Harris

Among all our Theatrical Matter there is nothing of equal importance to any attempt to invade our Monopoly. I am well informed that very vigorous and special endeavours are making to obtain a Licence for the Lyceum.[2] Holloway will give you further information on the subject and believe me we ought to lose no time in exerting ourselves | Yours ever | R B Sheridan

[1] The only other document dated from this address is signed by Frederick Jones and S. at the '1 Tun St. James's Market' on 1 Feb. 1808: 'Mr. Jones bets Mr. Sheridan a Hogshead of Claret, that the Theatre of Drury Lane will be indebted on this day two years Ten thousand pounds more, than it is at present. | It is agreed that no compromise is to take place, in the decision of the above debt.' Cf. Moore, ii. 354–6.

[2] Presumably by S. J. Arnold, who approached the Lord Chamberlain (Dartmouth) in 1808 with a plan to establish an English Opera and build a theatre. This was modified, and on 15 Feb. 1809 Arnold asked (P.R.O., L.C. 7/4, f. 475) for a licence to cover 'Musical Dramatic Entertainments and Ballets of Action' at the Lyceum Theatre. The licence was granted on 26 Feb. 1809. In a letter to Mash of 14 Mar. 1809 (loc. cit., f. 482), Arnold wrote, 'I must also remind you, should his Lordship again mention the Lyceum, that altho' Mr. Sheridan, in moments of hostility, may have threatened to involve that property in a Chancery suit (which hostility he has since acknowledged personally and by letter to me, was founded on misunderstanding) I am advised by counsel that nothing can impeach my title to the premises or prevent my possession of them.' In May 1816 he claimed that he possessed a deed executed by S., in which 'on the part of himself and the other Proprietors [of D.L.Th.], he formally recognises the Licence so granted . . .' (P.R.O., L.C. 7/4).

24. To ——

Pub.: Parke-Bernet Catalogue, New York, 22 Oct. 1963, lot 183.
Cf. *A.P.C.* v (1922), 182.

27 Sept. [*1808–12*]

It is impossible for me to say how greatly you will oblige
me by procuring my friend's liberation. I will engage my
Life and find any security that Mr. Homan[1] will more
honourably return to your custody, at a moments notice if
he does not pay the debt within a fortnight. . . .

25. To S. J. Arnold

Liverpool City Library MS.: Boaden, *Memoirs of Kemble*, ii. 557
(HL 18/4). [Ph.]

[*1809 ?*]
Wednesday Evening

Dear Arnold

I meant to have call'd on you with the enclosed notifica-
tion from our amiable Partner[2]—or you should have had it
sooner—

The Project of the new private subscription Theatre is
given up and I must say in a most handsome communication
sent from their committee this day to ours—

your Letter to me will be answer'd by our committee on

---

[1] On the verso of the letter is a note by
Homan reading: 'Tho I have not the
pleasure of knowing you personally
your character is familiar to me. I pledge
my honor to attend you if the money is
not paid in the time mentioned. . . .'
Cf. iii. 48.

[2] Usage of the period suggests that a
woman is meant here: for Mrs. Richardson, see ii. 65. But it is possible S. intended a reference to Greville. For
Mash's assertion that S. intimidated
Greville into joining him, see H.M.C.,
MSS. of Rye and Hereford . . . (1892), p.
505. He added that S. slept at Kelly's
one night with the idea of accompanying

the Prince to Windsor next day and of
presenting a memorial to the King.
'Unfortunately having made too free
with Kelly's wine, he could not rise till
near two, and thereby lost a fine opportunity of carrying his threats into execution.' Greville himself wrote that S.
knew 'that Lord Dartmouth had given
me authority to convert the Pantheon
into an English Opera House for the
winter, and he knew I had united with
Mr. Arnold, who was licenced for the
summer; he dreaded an opposition
though only by Operas, and he made a
union of interest' (*Morn. Chron.*, 23 Jan.
1812).

monday next and I hope to your satisfaction. | Your's truly |
R B Sheridan

26. To Sir Arthur Pigott

Liverpool City Library MS.: Picton Autograph letters, iii. 163. [Ph.]
Address.: [Le]atherhead December twen[ty-five?] | Sir Arthur Pigott |
Brunswick-Square | Russell-Squar[e] | Londo[n] *Fr.*: R B Sheridan
FREE DE 1809

Randalls
Monday Decr. 25th *1809*

My Dear Pigott,
  I wish you could make a few idle Holidays—you will
find a good bed here, if Mr. North could accompany you
I should be very happy and we will find him some shooting—
Sharp[1] and some Friends would meet you on thursday. |
yours ever sincerely | R B Sheridan

27. 'To Performers'

Add. MS. 35118, ff. 110–11. Copy, with corrections and insertions
by S. *Dock*.: 1810 | Mr. Sheridan's | Original Letter | to Performers.

1810 [*?*][2]
Treasury Office Drury Lane

  We are directed by the Patentees of the late Drury Lane
Theatre to inform you that the Lyceum Theatre under their
direction will be open'd at the usual time, the middle of
September next ensuing.
  The Proprietors propose no abatement or compromise of
Salary but will pay their Company according to the Lord
Chancellors arrangement in the same manner as before the
Calamity of the Fire.

---

[1] Richard ('Conversation') Sharp
(*c*. 1759–1835), M.P. for Castle Rising,
1806–12. Byron described him as 'a man
of elegant mind'.

[2] This may be one of the circular
letters mentioned in iii. 67. S.'s corrections are significant: l. 1, 'Proprietors'
becomes 'Patentees'; l. 2, 'under the
direction of Mr. Thos. Sheridan' becomes 'under their direction'; ll. 6–7,
'Engagements and Ratio previous to'
becomes 'Lord Chancellors arrangement in the same manner as before'.

Due Notice will be given of the day of opening when the punctual attendance of every Member of the Company is particularly required | yrs etc.

An immediate answer notifying the receipt of this Letter is expected in confirmation of your proposed Engagement, of course no Performer but those to whom this Letter is address'd and from whom answers are received will be considered as Members of the Company those only excepted whose former Engagements are not expired

N.B. This Paragraph is not to constitute a Part of the circular Letter to those actually engaged —but only to be address'd to those whose engagements are profess'd to be renew'd

28. 'To the Kings most excellent Majesty'

P.R.O. MS., L.C.,7/4. Copy. *Dock.*: *Copy 1810 6 Sept* | To the Kings most excellent Majesty | The humble Petition of the | Proprietors of the late Theatre | Royal Drury Lane *Wm.*: 1807

6 Sept. 1810

The humble Petition of the Proprietors of the late Theatre Royal Drury Lane in behalf of themselves and others greatly interested in the re-establishment of the destroyed Property, and the rebuilding of the said Theatre.

Sheweth.

That the late Theatre Royal Drury Lane was erected in the year 1793, by means of Subscription Shares, amounting to £150,000.

That owing to the unfortunate miscalculation in the estimated expence of building the said Theatre, and to other unforeseen circumstances it became necessary to raise an additional Sum nearly equal to the original Subscription and to make the Property responsible for the same.

That the whole of this Property was embarked on the faith that the purchase at a considerable price of Killigrew's

Patent then belonging to Convent[1] Garden Theatre had been made under the sanction and honor of your Majesty's Approbation.

That under these circumstances, and while the Property was in the progress of clearing itself from the unavoidable embarrassments attending such excess of expenditure beyond the original estimate, the whole was destroyed by fire in the Month of February 1809, having been insured by the Trustees, owing to the high terms demanded by the Insurance Offices, only to the amount of £35,600.

That after the destruction attending the said Fire while the Proprietors were employed in making arrangements for satisfying all the just claims on the Property, and for re-establishing the same, they encountered great difficulties in meeting the numerous Attempts made to take advantage of the Calamity which had befallen their Property by the various Plans proposed for erecting a new Theatre for the advantage of new Speculators,[2] but to the irreparable ruin of your Petitioners. The Justice and equity of your Majesty's most honorable Privy Council however decided against the Petitions[3] and applications for their object, and by so doing gave confidence and an impression of Security to all interested in the Drury Lane Property.

Encouraged by such protection, your Majesty's Petitioners obtained an Act in the last Session of Parliament enabling them to dispose of the Property in the only way calculated in their Judgment to produce a Fund equal to satisfy the reasonable expectations of the just Claims on the late destroyed Property and to restore the same, to which Act your Majesty's most gracious Assent was given.[4]

That while your Majesty's Petitioners were proceeding to carry into effect the purposes of the said Act, their progress was suddenly stayed by the following notice[5] by authority of the Lord Chamberlain and addressed to the principal Patentee dated 28th June last.

---

[1] This suggests that S.'s own manuscript was in front of the copyist.
[2] Cf. H.M.C., *MSS of Rye and Hereford* . . . (1892), p. 503.
[3] See iii. 74–75.

[4] A printed copy of it (dated 21 June 1810) is in Add. MS. 42721, ff. 42–49.
[5] For another copy, see P.R.O., L.C. 1/40, f. 192ᵛ.

'Lord Chamberlain's Office June 28th 1810

'Sir—I have it in command from the Lord Chamberlain to acquaint you that it has been intimated to him that you purpose employing the Dormant Patent for a new Theatre and his Lordship, having no doubt of the illegality of that Instrument,[1] thinks it necessary to apprize you that it is certainly his intention to oppose any Theatre being opened within the Liberties of Westminster under such Authority. I have the honor to be Sir your obedient Servant. T. B. Mash.'

That the subsequent illness of Mr. Mash and his prolonged Absence from Town for the recovery of his health, considerably delayed the means of explanation or discussion with the Lord Chamberlain respecting the important subject of the said Notice; Your Majesty's Petitioners, however, sincerely confiding in the justice and equity of his Lordships intentions, notwithstanding they might differ in Opinion, deemed it a deference due to his Lordship's official Situation under your Majesty, not to proceed in the course authorized by the Act, nor to appear as contending against his Lordship's Notice although the loss attending every days delay in the execution of their Plan can hardly be estimated which together with the continued floating reports respecting a third Theatre, however destitute of Fact, encrease the difficulty of your Majesty's Petitioners proceeding to carry into effect the purposes of the said Act, and must assuredly in a short time render every effort ineffectual to rescue the Property from utter destruction.

In these circumstances of grievous and ruinous embarrassment your Majesty's Petitioners respectfully wa[i]ving all discussion respecting the validity of Killigrew's Patent, confine this their humble Petition to your Majesty, solely to pray, that their Property may be placed in the Situation in which it stood before the Fire, by your Majesty being graciously pleased to grant to them the accustomed renewal of the 21 years Patent purchased from Mr. Garrick, under the Authority of which they hope to be able to arrange and

---

[1] See i. 118–19, n. 1.

carry into execution a Plan for rebuilding the Theatre and satisfying the just Claimants thereon. At the same time humbly, but confidently relying, that your Majesty will not during that interval allow their just endeavours to be frustrated and their means of restoring their Theatre intercepted, by the Grant of any third Patent or Licence to any of the numerous Applicants who, in the humble judgment of your Majesty's Petitioners have applied for the same, without any reasonable plea or fair pretence to the preference they solicit.

Your Majesty's Petitioners have only further to add that in their present Application, thus limited, to your Majesty, they have already received the concurrence of the Lord Chamberlain's approbation. | And your Majesty's Petitioners shall ever pray. | R. B. Sheridan | Sarah Richardson | Thos. Sheridan
London the 6th September
1810.

29. [To the Editor of the *British Press*]

Whitbread MS. 4397. *Pub.*: The *British Press*, 19 Sept. 1810.[1]
Dock.: Mr. Sheridan | Poem written in his hand. *Wm.*: 1805.

[*1809–10*]

Had Shakespeare when first he took charge of the Stage
Lived in half so judicious or moral an age
He'd have spared all his pains and instead of his wit
Would have treated the town with O P in the pit[2]
    O P in the pit
    O P in the pit

[1] Anonymously, and under the title of 'O.P.—A New Song.' The printed version is normally punctuated. It omits the last stanza. Other variations occur in line 2, where 'judicious' becomes 'enlightened'; line 9, his' becomes 'our'; line 23, 'Oh no freedom's' becomes 'There's no freedom'; line 26, 'mean' becomes 'keen'; line 28, 'whores' becomes w—r—s'; line 32, 'Shall stifle all fashion and banish' becomes 'Shall rail down all fashion and stifle'. Italics are used for 'to be heard' in line 18, and

'one' in line 24.
[2] After the fire C.G.Th. was rebuilt on an expensive scale, and Kemble found it necessary to increase the charges of admission at the reopening. From the first night (18 Sept. 1809) onwards, the audiences were most turbulent, insistently calling for 'Old Prices'. After sixty-one nights, the management gave in to the clamour. A satirical account of the 'Grand Reconciliation Dinner' is given in the *Morn. Chron.*, 3 Jan. 1810.

Oh there's nothing like it
For it nerves us for Freedom for morals and wit

What need of his dramas constructed with art
Of thought or of language that go to the heart
We depend not on Genius, our Publick is Free
And the lowest of blockheads can bawl out O P
    O P in the Pit
    O P in the Pit
    It eclipses all wit
All Garrick performed and all Sheridan writ.

A right to hear Plays would be very absurd
He who pays at the door, has a right to be heard
And his right is so precious that if 'tis his whim
The rest have a right to hear nothing but him
    O P in the pit
    O P in the pit
    Oh no freedom's like it
Where to one score of blackguards whole crowds must
  submit.

Then what drama so moral what preacher so nice
What fanatick so mean a suppressor of vice
Its he, who in zeal to the Manager roars
To turn out the Ladies and let in the whores
    O P in the pit
    O P in the pit
    With such modesty smit
Shall stifle all fashion and banish all wit.

And Lo Io triumphs, the Managers beat
Wit Beauty and fashion must sound a retreat
Pure Morality reigns as before in the boxes
Surrounded by prostitutes bullies and Poxes
    O P in the pit
    O P in the pit
    What Censor so fit
To judge of our morals our freedom and wit?

30. To ——

Pub.: American Art Association Catalogue, New York, 3 Apr. 1928, lot 558.

June 1811

[S. asks his correspondent to answer by bearer so that he may show the agreement to his bankers and complete his business of payment of tax arrears on the morrow.]

31. To the Committee for Rebuilding Drury Lane Theatre

Garrick Club MS. Copy: only the signature is Sheridan's.

14 Feb. 1812

Gentlemen

Please to pay John Ellis Esq.[1] One hundred and Eight Pounds out of the first monies which you will have to pay me on account of the sale of my Property to the Drury Lane Corporation under the late Act of Parliament when the money for such sale shall be payable to me[2] | R B Sheridan February 14th
1812

32. To Samuel Rogers

Price MS. *Address*: S Rogers Esq | St. James's Place *Fr.*: R B S

[1813–16]
Saville-Row
Wednesday morning

Dear Rogers

Pray send me one of those little Lists or a copy by the Bearer | Yours truly | R B S
Is it true that Lord B[3] is returned and in Town?

[1] An attorney of 14 Gray's Inn Square: see *Clarke's New Law List* (1812), p. 58.
[2] Cf. Moore, ii. 434.
[3] Byron and S. were on particularly friendly terms in 1814–15, but S.'s question may refer to some rumour current after Byron left London for the Continent on 23 Apr. 1816.

33. [To Thomas Dibdin?]

Osborn MS. *Dock.*: 1816 | Mr. Sheridan | Feby.

Saville-Row
Thursday Feby 1st *1816*

My Dear Sir
There is an old deaf Theatrical Friend of mine who having formerly done me and the Theatre some service[1] I always continued his single name on the Free List, and he now conceives that I have some revived interest in the Theatre and that I might procure him to be re-instated—He is very old and will not be troublesome. I should be obliged if it can be done.[2] | yours truly R B S.

34. To Charles Ward

Pub.: *The Reminiscences of Thomas Dibdin* (1827), ii. 387.

1816
Monday.

My dear Friend,
Believe me, that nothing, but its being absolutely out of my power, should prevent my being of your party to-day, which I wished particularly to join, but I cannot without serious risk of adding to my present ill health. I beg you will make my particular apologies to Mr. Rae and Mr. Dibdin. I have kept my carriage at the door above this hour, which I am now obliged to send with this excuse, most reluctantly. | Ever yours, | R.B.S.

Mr. Ward.

35. To George Canning

The Earl of Harewood MS.: George Canning 66a (Leeds Central Library). [Ph.] *Dock.*: Received in the House of Commons and | Answered June 19th that I would send the answer next day | June

---

[1] S. crossed out 'for nearly'.
[2] Dibdin remarks (*Reminiscences* (1827), ii. 103) 'it had always been usual for the acting manager to have the privilege of distributing . . . nightly orders (or temporary free admissions). . .' He was joint acting manager of D.L.Th. with Alexander Rae (1782–1820).

20th Sent a Draft on Drummonds[1] for £100. | July 1. Returned the Note of hand cancelled.[2]

Saville-Row
Wednesday June 19th.—[1816]

My Dear Canning

You will be as much surprised at receiving this Letter as I feel myself in writing it. Perhaps No Person, not un-a[c]quainted with difficulties, ever more perseveringly abstain'd from incurring pecuniary obligation from private Friendship than I have done,—but in one brief word, a sudden exigency has fallen on me which (having just now your name before me) occasions this application—you will very much oblige me by accommodating me by the Bearer with the amount of the enc[l]osed which you may positively *rely* on being answer'd at its date.—I waive at present wishing you personally joy for many late events—I think I shall come among you by next Sessions. Ever yours | R B Sheridan[3]

[1] Bankers at 49 Charing Cross.

[2] In Canning's letter to S. of 1 July 1816 (Harewood MS.), he offered S.'s son Charles a junior clerkship (worth £100 a year) at the Board of Control. In a postscript to the same letter he wrote about the note of hand: 'I was going to destroy the inclosed in the view of re-moving from your mind any anxiety about it when it occurred to me that, to answer this purpose effectually, I had best restore it into your hands. God bless you.'

[3] For other letters by S., see the following catalogues: S.C., 22 May 1897, lot 86 ('March 22 1809'); Maggs Catalogue 166 (1899), item 1184 ('a letter of introduction in favour of Mr. Buxton, Sept. 10, *c.* 1800'); S.C., 4 Dec. 1922, lot 84 ('Leatherhead, Feby. 1815, to T. Metcalfe'); Anderson Galleries Sale Catalogue, New York, 27 Apr. 1925, lot 254 ('To Charles Wood [Ward?], North Court, Monday, on financial trouble and the threatened sale of his house'); S.C., 7 July 1931, lot 68 ('I find several people were at my door and nobody to let them in'); S.C., 4 Dec. 1944, lot 603 ('To the poet [pawnbroker?] Charles King'); Swann Galleries Sale Catalogue, New York, 25 May 1961, lot 53 ('To White and Townes [Fownes?], 1 June 1814'); Parke-Bernet Sale Catalogue, New York, 8 Oct. 1963, lot 203 ('To Ward, empowering him to act as S.'s attorney in the sale of some Drury Lane theatre shares', 8 Mar. 1814): cf. iii. 276, no. 94. Several covers not containing letters, are extant. They are to 'Mr. Hickey | St. Albans-Street' (Huntington MS.); to 'Wm. Priestley Esqr./Bath' (Widener MS.); and to 'Mr. Samuel Wardon | 32 Frith Street | Soho | London' (Widener MS.). The last two are marked 'Free | R. B. Sheridan', so must belong to the period (1780–1812) when S. was a Member of Parliament. P.R.O., H.O. 42/110, does not contain a copy of the letter to Richard Ryder, Home Secretary, that S. said he wrote on 13 Jan. 1811 about the execution of a con-vict 'when all access was closed to the fountain of mercy' (Hansard, 1st Ser., xviii. 830–1).

INDEX

Persons and places mentioned in the letters and notes are listed in alphabetical order. Married women are shown under their married names. The main entries for noblemen appear under their family names. Foreign persons, even when of noble birth, are given under the names by which they are usually recognized in England. Plays are to be found under their authors' names, when known. Theatres, streets, and buildings of Sheridan's day are entered under 'London'. Twentieth-century references to London buildings are given separately. Manuscripts are listed by their locations at the time when I read them. Since the Prince of Wales is usually called 'the Prince' in the text, he is entered under that name here. For abbreviations, see i. lvii–lxi.

Handel, George Frederick (1685–1759), ii. 169. *Acis and Galatea*, i. 23*n*. *Messiah*, i. 23*n*.; ii. 169. *Judas Maccabeus*, i. 23*n*., 77*n*.

Hankey, Mrs. [said to be the daughter of the Duke of Chandos, but *Kearsley's Peerage* (1804), p. 634, gives Elizabeth de Blaquiere (b. 1785) as second daughter of John, Lord Blaquiere], iii. 215.

Hanrott, Francis, ii. 83*n*.

Hanrott, Philip Augustus, attorney, iii. 32*n*.

Hansard, 1st Ser., ii. 133*n*., 135*n*., 240*n*., 269*n*., 273*n*.; iii. 1*n*., 3*n*., 5*n*., 16*n*., 26*n*., 37*n*., 38*n*., 52*n*., 75*n*., 77*n*., 96*n*., 99*n*., 100*n*., 119*n*., 122*n*., 146*n*., 147*n*., 153*n*., 154*n*., 155*n*., 158*n*., 160*n*.

Hanson, Joseph, ii. 57; iii. 4*n*., 14, 272.

'Hardcastle, Miss' (Goldsmith's *She Stoops to Conquer*), iii. 293*n*. 'Mr. Hardcastle', iii. 293*n*.

Harden, James, i. 36*n*.

Hardy, Joseph, iii. 250.

Hare, iii. 50, 124.

Hare, Mr. Arnold, iii. 69*n*.

Hare, James, ii. 73, 136, 150*n*.

Harewood MSS., the Earl of, i. 236; iii. 327, 329, 342, 343*n*.

Hargrave, Francis, i. 213; ii. 108. *Letter to*, i. no. 146. *Brief Deductions*, i. 214*n*.

Harlequin Amulet (? by William Powell), iii. 330*n*.

Harlequin's Frolics, i. 103*n*.

Harlequin's Invasion, see David Garrick.

Harley, ii. 131–2.

Harley, Thomas, i. 6, 154.

Harper, John, ii. 127–8.

Harrington, Henry, i. 91.

Harrington, John, i. 221. *Letter to*, i. no. 150.

Harris, Emmanuel, iii. 289.

Harris, Henry, son of Thomas Harris, ii. 274, 282.

Harris, James, 1st Earl of Malmesbury (1746–1820), ii. 77; iii. 49*n*. *Letters of*, i. 20*n*.

Harris, Thomas, chief proprietor of C.G.Th., *The Rivals* written at his request, i. 85; sanguine about the success of *The Duenna*, but wants Linley to supervise the music, i. 87–

88; purchases King's Theatre, but withdraws later, i. 116*n*.; signs proposals for a third theatre, i. 121; S. arranges with him for the payment of Pacchierotti, i. 151–2; optimistic about a third theatre, i. 168; S. could have joined him in management, i. 169; his personal friendship with S. prevents the dormant patent being used against D.L.Th., i. 171; with S. seeks to maintain their monopoly, i. 215*n*.; ii. 274*n*.; iii. 333; negotiations over the use of the dormant patent, i. 229–32, 245*n*., 247*n*., 248, 256, 266, 268; iii. 317; wishes to borrow D.L.Th. recitatives, ii. 32–33; claims Mrs. Billington's services, ii. 158–9; engages Betty, ii. 220*n*., 221*n*., 232. *Other references*, i. 123; iii. 26*n*., 29*n*. *Letters to*, i. no. 84; iii. Appendix, no. 23.

Harrison, [? John, who had renters' shares in D.L.Th. in 1775], iii. 321.

Harrison, William, i. 215*n*.

Harrow MSS., i. 2, 161*n*.; ii. 37*n*., 292; iii. 13, 19, 24, 45, 74–75, 91, 119, 136, 207.

Harrow School, i. 1, 2*n*., 21*n*., 24*n*., 36*n*.

Hart (of 3 Stafford Place, Pimlico), ii. 63.

Hartfordbridge, ii. 223.

Hartley, ii. 86*n*.

Hartley, W. [probably James], iii. 221–2. *Letter to*, iii. no. 904.

Hartsink, ii. 27*n*.

Harvard MSS., i. 71*n*., 79*n*., 81*n*., 93*n*., 116, 132*n*., 134*n*., 142, 162*n*., 166, 183, 221, 242*n*., 257, 266; ii. 2, 19–20, 24–29, 32–35, 37, 41, 43, 47, 51, 54, 57–62, 64, 69–70, 72–73, 75, 77–88, 90–92, 96, 97*n*., 101–2, 104, 106, 107*n*., 108*n*., 110, 112–16, 122, 124*n*., 133, 157*n*., 158, 162, 166*n*., 170, 187, 195, 198–9, 206, 208–10, 217, 246*n*., 267, 291–2, 300, 307–9; iii. 2, 14*n*., 18*n*., 20, 23, 39, 42, 48, 50, 53, 61–64, 66, 68, 73, 74, 88, 90, 113, 116, 117*n*., 124–6, 127*n*., 129*n*., 130, 141, 163*n*., 166, 168, 180, 183, 196, 199*n*., 205, 225, 249, 256–8, 262, 265–7, 269–70, 274, 276–80, 282, 284–6, 293, 317*n*., 326. Amy Lowell Collection, iii. 168.

Harvey, Charles, ii. 128–9.

Link, Richard, attorney, ii. 209.

Linley, Elizabeth Ann, *see* Elizabeth Sheridan.

Linley family, i. 23, 79*n*., 132*n*., 249*n*., ii. 16; iii. 253, 284, 294*n*., 302, 303, 307.

Linley, Jane Nash, *see* Jane Ward.

Linley, Maria, third daughter of Thomas and Mary, iii. 295, 299, 303–4, 306.

Linley, Mrs. Mary (Johnson), wife of Thomas Linley, sen., i. 68*n*., 82, 95, 114; ii. 66, 210; iii. 284, 299, 302*n*., 331.

Linley, Mary, second daughter of Thomas and Mary, *see* Mary Tickell.

Linley, Ozias, sixth son of Thomas and Mary, i. 249*n*., 250.

Linley, Thomas, the elder, music master at Bath, sings in a natural style, i. 20–21; sings with family at New Assembly Rooms, i. 23; persuades his daughter to return home from France, i. 27*n*.; wants her to break off her relationship with S., i. 35*n*.; promises to give S. the letters of Clarges, ii. 68*n*.; friendly with Storace, i. 79*n*.; arranged that his daughter Elizabeth should sing at Worcester, but S. wishes to withdraw her from the engagement, i. 79–81; warns S. about Elizabeth's 'seminal weakness', i. 84*n*.; Garrick approaches him with the offer of London engagements for himself and his daughters, but S. tries to dissuade him from accepting, iii. 293–307; writes 'Letters upon Music', i. 86*n*.; S. seeks his help in composing *The Duenna*, i. 86–93; joins S. and Ford in buying Garrick's moiety of D.L.Th., i. 93–101; Lacy promises to write to him, i. 102; his security to Garrick, i. 167; death, ii. 20*n*. *Other references*, i. 83*n*., 85*n*., 108*n*., 169, 213*n*., 216, 219, 233*n*., 242*n*., 260; ii. 56*n*., 64*n*., 108*n*., 256*n*.; iii. 129, 266, 287, 316, 319*n*., 321, 326. *Letters to*, i. nos. 30, 33–39, 42–43; iii. Appendix, no. 2.

Linley, Thomas, the younger, i. 23*n*., 82, 87, 89, 95, 103; iii. 304.

Linley, William, i. 87*n*.; iii. 200, 284.

Liphook, Hants, iii. 257.

Lisbon, i. 182*n*.

Liskeard, Cornwall, iii. 80*n*.

Little Testwood, Hants, ii. 231.

Liverpool, ii. 14*n*., 15, 41*n*., 221. City Library MSS., iii. 247, 334–5.

Liverpool, Lord, *see* Jenkinson.

Llandaff Court, near Cardiff, i. 24*n*., 30*n*.

Llangollen, 'the Ladies of', *see* Sarah Ponsonby and Lady Eleanor Butler.

Lloyd, Gamaliel, ii. 93*n*.

Lloyd, James Martin, ii. 261, 262.

Lloyd's, iii. 70.

Lloyd's Evening Post, iii. 292*n*.

Lockhart, J. G. (1794–1854), iii. 188*n*.

'Lodovico' (Shakespeare's *Othello*), i. 127.

Loggerheads, ii. 188.

LONDON: *general references*, i. 3*n*., 6*n*., 20, 23, 26*n*., 27–28, 30, 36, 56, 65–66, 70, 77–79, 86, 100–1, 118*n*., 121, 131, 135–6, 141, 143, 148*n*., 154–5, 161, 165, 177*n*., 178–80, 182*n*., 183, 185–6, 189, 192, 194, 199–200, 209*n*., 214, 216, 223, 228, 234, 241–3, 246, 248–51, 255–6, 262, 264, 269, 271; ii. 2*n*., 22, 74–78, 92*n*., 93–96, 100, 110–12, 130–5, 137–9, 141, 143, 146, 149, 158, 177*n*., 179–81, 186, 190, 191, 194, 198, 202, 207, 215, 216*n*., 218, 221, 223, 229–31, 235, 238, 243, 248, 249, 251, 257, 261*n*., 276*n*., 283*n*., 287*n*., 292 5, 301*n*., 308; iii. 2, 5*n*., 19, 41, 43–44, 47–48, 52–53, 62, 66, 69, 83, 91, 93–94, 98, 102, 108, 115*n*., 116, 120, 126, 130, 134, 142, 143*n*., 156, 163–5, 168, 169, 171, 175*n*., 176–8, 182, 185, 187, 190–1, 196, 199–200, 203, 208–9, 213, 216, 219–20, 223, 225, 227–30, 234, 237, 239, 245, 247, 254–5, 263–5, 267, 274, 280, 285, 289, 300*n*., 303, 311, 329, 331–2, 338, 341.

— *specific references*, Albany, The, iii. 9, 275; Albemarle St., i. 155; iii. 163*n*.; Apsley House, iii. 158; Arlington St., iii. 266; Arundel St., i. 126, 129; Austin-Friars, ii. 83; Barlett's Buildings, Holborn, ii. 6*n*., 80; Battersea, i. 103; Beaufort Buildings, Strand, i. 1; Bedford Coffee House, Covent Garden, i. 29, 31, 65, 69; Bedford House, i. 245, 257*n*.; Bed-

PRINTED IN GREAT BRITAIN
AT THE UNIVERSITY PRESS, OXFORD
BY VIVIAN RIDLER
PRINTER TO THE UNIVERSITY